Computing in Science and Technology (CST 2018)

ITM Web of Conferences Volume 21 (2018)

Rzeszow-Muczne, Poland
11 – 14 June 2018

Editors:

T. Kwater
B. Twarog
Z. Gomolka
J. Bartman

ISBN: 978-1-5108-7314-8

Printed from e-media with permission by:

Curran Associates, Inc.
57 Morehouse Lane
Red Hook, NY 12571

Some format issues inherent in the e-media version may also appear in this print version.

Printed by Curran Associates, Inc. (2018)

For additional information, please contact EDP Sciences – Web of Conferences at the address below.

EDP Sciences – Web of Conferences
17, Avenue du Hoggar
Parc d'Activité de Courtabœuf
BP 112
F-91944 Les Ulis Cedex A
France

Phone: +33 (0) 1 69 18 75 75
Fax: +33 (0) 1 69 28 84 91

contact-edps@webofconferences.org

Additional copies of this publication are available from:

Curran Associates, Inc.
57 Morehouse Lane
Red Hook, NY 12571 USA
Phone: 845-758-0400
Fax: 845-758-2633
Email: curran@proceedings.com
Web: www.proceedings.com

TABLE OF CONTENTS

Preface

The scientific conference 'Computing in Science and Technology', which took place from 11-14 June 2018 in Muczne (Bieszczady Mountains), is the continuation of a series of conferences organized alternately by the Department of Computer Engineering at the University of Rzeszow and the Department of Applied Informatics at the SGGW in Warsaw since 2010. This year the conference was held under the patronage of the Ministry of Science and Higher Education and the Marshal of the Subcarpathian Voivodship. The meeting strategy was focused on the interdisciplinary integration not only of different scientific environments, but also industrial production centers. The innovative nature of the subject matter allowed for the inclusion in the research processes of representatives of industrial company teams, thanks to whom it will be possible to implement the technological assumptions in correlation with academic research at universities.

The main topics of the conference were: IT, artificial intelligence, discrete production processes, electrical engineering, data mining, automation of industrial processes, digital image processing, and applied computer science. The meeting was attended by dozens of participants, including representatives of various universities from Poland and abroad, and companies from Subcarpathia (the University of Rzeszow, Warsaw University of Life Sciences, AGH University of Science and Technology, Rzeszow University of Technology, University of Information Technology and Management in Rzeszow, West Pomeranian University of Technology in Szczecin, Mugla Sitki Kocman University of Turkey, State Higher School of Technology and Economics in Jaroslaw, University of Applied Sciences in Nysa). The dedicated discussion panel "Symbiosis of Science and Industry", taking place during the conference, was devoted to the exchange of ideas between the scientific team and representatives of companies with whom research topics for the implementation of grants implemented by the National Center for Research and Development and the Subcarpathian Innovation Center may be undertaken. The current edition was attended by such companies and organizations as: Elektromontaż S.A. Rzeszów (various types of electrical installations), FANUM Skorupski-Wójcik Sp. J. (multi-axis CNC machining centers), Asseco Poland S.A. (modern IT solutions), Telecommunications Cooperative OST Tyczyn (ICT services), Elektronika journal, the Office of Technical Inspection, the Polish Information Processing Society, the Association of Polish Electrical Engineers

The scientific deliberations were carried out in a number of thematically organised plenary sessions, in which participants of many scientific centers delivered their presentations. The conference achieved a measurable effect in the form of in-depth discussions on such research topics as intelligent ALMM system - implementation assumptions for the knowledge base, automatic identification of drill status during drilling using LSTM neural networks, adaptive selection of the amplification factor in state estimation, forecasting one day ahead of energy generation in photovoltaic systems, synchronization of robot control in distributed control systems, backward fractional propagation algorithm, modeling and analysis of priority queuing systems, optimization of G-codes, improving the dynamics of CNC machines, power problem in electric circuits with deformed waveforms, load balancing in networks with link-state routing protocols, virtual machine migration strategies in cluster systems. One should mention the accompanying interest of both students and the media as well as the post-conference publications provided by the organizers in the materials of the Elektronika journal and the materials indexed in the Web of Science.

Thanking all participants of the conference for their active participation, we hope that the next edition will allow the further expression of scientific values in the relationship between science and industry, and all speakers will return to their universities with unforgettable artistic and creative impressions.

We would like to thank all authors, reviewers, and participants of the conference for their excellent contributions to the success of the conference.

The website of the conference is http://sti.ur.edu.pl/ .

Editors

Tadeusz Kwater, Boguslaw Twarog,

Zbigniew Gomolka, Jacek Bartman

Scientific Committee

Statement of Peer review

In submitting conference proceedings to *Web of Conferences*, the editors of the proceedings certify to the Publisher that

1. They adhere to its **Policy on Publishing Integrity** in order to safeguard good scientific practice in publishing.
2. All articles have been subjected to peer review administered by the proceedings editors.
3. Reviews have been conducted by expert referees, who have been requested to provide unbiased and constructive comments aimed, whenever possible, at improving the work.
4. Proceedings editors have taken all reasonable steps to ensure the quality of the materials they publish and their decision to accept or reject a paper for publication has been based only on the merits of the work and the relevance to the journal.

Title, date and place of the conference

Computing in Science and Technology (Symbioza Techniki i Informatyki) 2018
11 - 14 June 2018, Rzeszow, Muczne 2018

Proceedings editor(s):

prof. UR dr hab. inż. Tadeusz Kwater

dr inż. Boguslaw Twarog

dr Zbigniew Gomolka

dr inż. Jacek Bartman

Date and editor's signature

19.09.2018r

ITM Web of Conferences **21**, 00002 (2018) https://doi.org/10.1051/itmconf/20182100002
CST 2018

Intelligent ALMM System - implementation assumptions for its Knowledge Base

Ewa Dudek-Dyduch[1], *Zbigniew* Gomolka[2*], *Boguslaw* Twarog[2] and *Ewa* Zeslawska[3]

[1]AGH University of Science and Technology Cracow, Department of Biomedical Engineering and Automation, Krakow, Poland
[2]University of Rzeszow, Faculty of Mathematics and Natural Sciences Department of Computer Engineering, ul. Pigonia 1, 35-959 Rzeszow, Poland
[3]University of Information Technology and Management in Rzeszow, Faculty of Applied Informatics, Department of Applied Information, ul. Sucharskiego 2, 35-225 Rzeszow, Poland

Abstract. The paper introduces the concept of implementation assumptions about the Knowledge Base (KB) system cooperating with intelligent information system for the discrete optimization of problem solving, named Intelligent ALMM System. This system utilizes a modeling paradigm named Algebraic Logical Meta Model of Multistage Decision Processes (ALMM) and its theory, both developed by Dudek-Dyduch E. The system solves combinatorial and discrete optimization problems including NP-hard problems with possible user assistance. The models of problems are stored in a Problem Model Library. In this paper the idea of KB for the storage of the properties of problems is presented. The concept of the KB on problems presented in previous works has been extended by introducing an additional module pertaining to the properties of a problems library. A discussion was presented in the context of the selection of tools that enable the construction of such a library as well as its architecture. In the adopted strategy of storing the properties of problems, the interface for exchanging information is compatible with the library of problems using polymorphic and component properties of object-oriented programming. Considerations are explained by means of a sample UML diagram and interface prototypes.

1 Introduction

The article concerns the Intelligent System ALMM designed for solving combinatorial problems and problems of discreet optimization. This system is based on the paradigm of the Algebraic Logic Meta Model (ALMM) presented in chapter 2. The concept of the Intelligent ALMM system was proposed by Dudek-Dyduch E. in [1]. The main purpose of the ALMM System is not only to solve the problems of discrete optimization, but also to help the user in choosing the right method and algorithm for solving them. This intelligent approach is based on the use of specific properties of solved problems and through the links they have with appropriate methods or algorithms. This is accomplished via the knowledge

* Corresponding author: zgomolka@ur.edu.pl

base consisting of two parts: Library of Problem Models and Module of Problem Properties. The investigations on the system takes place simultaneously in two areas: theoretical and conceptual concerning the way the system works, its structure and the assumptions of the implementation project. Assumptions and fundamentals concerning the Library of Problem Models were presented in [2 - 3]. This article concerns the basic assumptions about the implementation of the project Module of Problem Properties and presents the development of links between the Library of Problem Model and the Module of Problem Properties.

2 ALMM modelling paradigm

At this point the paradigm of creating formal models of problems of discrete optimization based on the Algebraic Logical Meta-Model of multi-stage decision-making processes (ALMM) will be presented. [3] The idea of ALMM paradigm was proposed and developed by Dudek-Dyduch E. [4, 5], [6 - 7] and mentioned in many papers among others [8]. It has a wide variety of applications. ALMM includes formal models of two types of multistage decision processes: dynamic and common. The model of multistage dynamic decision process (MDDP) takes into account the fact that all restrictions may be time-dependent, while for common process (cMDP) these constraints are static. Let us recall the main concept of the Algebraic Logical Meta Model of the multistage dynamic decision process. The concept of the so-called 'generalized state' is used here, defined as a pair: a state and a time instant.

Definition. "Multistage dynamic decision process is a process that is specified by the sextuple $MDDP=(U,S,s_0,f,S_N,S_G)$ where U is a set of decisions, $S=X\times T$ is a set named a set of generalized states, X is a set of proper states, $T\subset\Re^+\cup\{0\}$ is a subset of non-negative real numbers representing the time instants, $f:U\times S\to S$ is a partial function called a transition function, (it does not have to be determined for all elements of the set $U\times S$), $s_0=(x_0,t_0)$, $S_N\subset S$, $S_G\subset S$, are respectively: an initial generalized state, a set of not admissible generalized states, and a set of goal generalized states, i.e. the states in which we want the process to take place at the end. Subsets S_G and S_N are disjoint i.e. $S_G\cap S_N=\varnothing$.

The transition function is defined by means of two functions, $f=(f_x,f_t)$ where $f_x=U\times X\times T\to X$ determines the next state, $f_t:U\times X\times T\to T$ determines the next time instant. It is assumed that the difference $\Delta t=f_t(u,x,t)-t$ has a value that is both finite and positive.

The transition function f is defined as partial. This allows various restrictions on "reasonable" decisions in different states too be taken into account by means of the so-called sets of possible decisions $U_p(s)$ defined as: $U_p(s)=\{u\in U:(u,s)\in Domf\}$. An important feature of this modeling paradigm is that decisions can be generally complex decisions. Therefore in the most general case, sets U and X may be presented as a Cartesian product $U=U^1\times U^2\times\ldots\times U^m$, $X=X^1\times X^2\times\ldots X^n$, i.e. $u=(u^1,u^2,...,u^m)$, $x=(x^1,x^2,...,x^n)$. In particular, u^i, $i=1,2,\ldots,m$ represent separate decisions that must or may be taken at the same time or at the same stage (for cMDP) and relate to particular objects. There are no limitations imposed on types of the sets; in particular they do not have to be numerical. Thus values of particular co-ordinates of a state or a decision may be names of elements (symbols) as well as some objects (e.g. finite set, sequence etc.).

We obtain the definition of the common multistage decision process (cMDP) from the definition of MDDP by reducing the set S to the set X and the transfer function f to the function f_x Because all the elements specifying MDDP, i.e. $U,S,s_0,f,S_N,S_G,U_p(s)$ can be defined using both algebraic and logic relations, hence the name "algebraic logic". Based on the ALMM, the formal models of problems, the so-called AL models, can be created for an extensive class of optimization problems (and their instances), for which the solution can be presented as a sequence (or set) of decisions. All limitations of a given problem regarding the admissible solution are represented by elements of the appropriate multistage decision process marked as **P**. The optimization problem is defined as a pair **(P, Q)** where **Q** is a criterion. An optimal (or at least admissible only) sequence of decisions and the corresponding trajectory is sought. In the articles [4 -6, 9 - 12] that lay the groundwork for the basic ALMM theory, Dudek-Dyduch E. has presented AL models for discrete manufacturing process control, for logistics problems, knapsack problem, and a model for a complex real-life problem encompassing both manufacturing and logistics. Other models, including the disturbances in production processes, are presented in [13]. In addition, the ALMM paradigm allows for the definition of a number of properties of problems relevant to their final solution. Based on the ALMM paradigm, new methods for solving discrete optimization problems have been created too and described in [3, 14 - 17]. An overview of the new methods is given in [6].

ALMM provides a structured way of recording knowledge of the goal and all relevant constraints that exist within the problems modeled. In line with this idea, all information is split into pre-defined basic components (elements) with appropriate links, defined both through algebraic and logical formulae.

3 Concept of ALMM Intelligent System

The concept of an intelligent system based on ALMM technology comes from Dudek-Dyduch E. and was firstly presented in [1]. The basic goals of this system are as follows:

- determining admissible or optimal (possibly good enough) solutions for combinatorial and discrete optimization problems,
- support the user with an appropriate choose of the method or algorithm which gives a solution.

Basic knowledge about the problem is passed on with the help of the AL problem model. Solving problem instance relies on the appropriate generation and/or modification of one trajectory or appropriate subsets of the trajectories. In work [18] the concept of ALMM Solver being a software tool aimed at solving discrete optimization problems using constructive algorithms has been presented. As part of the further development of ALMM Solver, Dudek-Dyduch E. and Korzonek S. presented in [2 - 3] a way of creating software representations of AL models and the component construction of a new crucial module, namely the Library of Problem Models significantly expanding the original concept of the ALMM Solver. The next step was a completely revolutionized concept of the Intelligent ALMM System [1]. Fig. 1. shows a schematic structure of its main modules.

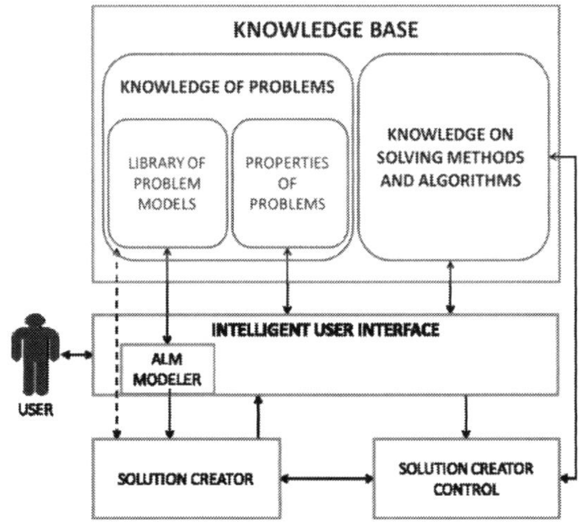

Fig. 1. The structure of Intelligent ALMM System [1]

The basis of the system is the information about the problem being solved in the form of an AL problem model and its instance as well as its software representation model. Both can be entered directly by the user, downloaded from the Library of Problem Models (PML) or created from the components of this library. Thus knowledge about the problem and its instance is forwarded from PML or ALM Modeler to the main module, named the Solution Creator, that carries out the computations.

The Knowledge Base consists of two main mutually joined components: "Knowledge on Solving Methods and Algorithms" and "Knowledge of Problems". The first part contains basic methods and algorithms written for the system using ALMM technology. The method (an algorithm) chosen by the user controls the calculation of the module Solution Creator via the Solution Creator Control.

The second part of the Knowledge Base consists of two further parts: Library of Problem Models and Properties of Problems. The idea of the component construction of the Library of Problems results from the structure of AL, models of problems and their mutual dependencies, which have been already described in [1], [3].

The intelligence presented in the [1] ALMM System consists in the implementation of two functions: helping a user create new AL models from components found in PML as well as support a user in determining the appropriate method and algorithm for problem solving. For both these functions, it is necessary to define a number of problem properties and link them with methods and algorithms. In works [8, 10, 19] a series of definitions of the properties of discrete optimization problems expressed using ALMM terminology have been given. In particular, they refer to the elements defining the process P and the most frequently used criteria. A number of trajectory properties were also given. In [1] it was shown how relevant properties are exploited to select methods such as branch & bound, (or pruning) dynamic programming, A* algorithms, and learning methods based on ALMM technology [20 - 25].

4 Assumptions for implementing the Problem Properties Knowledge Base

Knowledge Base is responsible for collecting data about solved problems and their properties. Due to the programming environment assumed at the initial stage of the project and programming language to be used for implementation of the IT model, three different models of databases were considered that could be used to construct the Knowledge Base (KB) module:

- databases working in the object oriented technology,
- databases operating in the mixed relational-object technology,
- knowledge bases using the properties of individual objects and semantic relationships between them.

4.1 Accessible tools and programming strategies

In accordance with the adopted Microsoft C# programming environment for the System under design, the solution to the task of organizing the Problem Library and their properties will be possible using a MS SQL Server and the Language INtergrated Query (LINQ) module. LINQ is part of the .NET Framework technology that allows us to manage object collections in a similar way to the SQL query language (see Fig. 2). Thanks to this, full control of data types and their conversions in individual mechanisms mediating the downloading of data is maintained. Data can come from the database (LINQ to SQL) and ordinary objects (LINQ to Objects). The knowledge representation is the basic concept for the various types of decision-making based processes and becomes the fundamental problem that has not been fully resolved. In knowledge engineering, the representation of knowledge is treated as a way of presenting in formal language the whole range of knowledge which is usually required for intelligent system behavior. The main aspects of knowledge representation includes the syntax, as the structure of representation (language), semantics, or by the meaning of represented knowledge (interpretation) and inference, i.e. the process by which knowledge is used to derive conclusions [26 - 28].

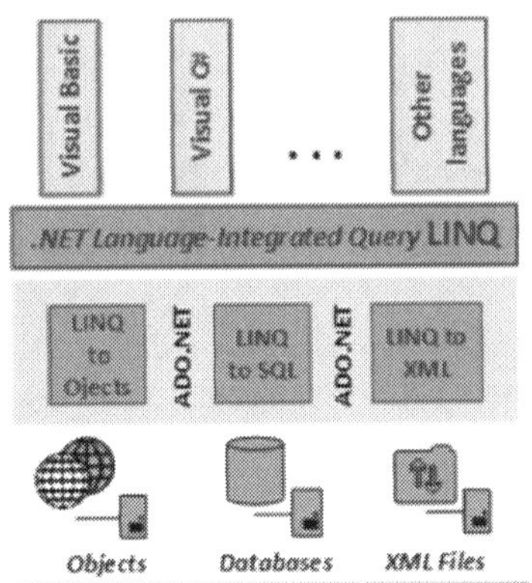

Fig. 2. Architecture of Language INtegrated Query proposed by authors

4.2 Knowledge base about problems in the ALMM concept

The intelligent system interface is currently prepared for well-known users who know the names of most problems and have the knowledge of ALMM terminology. There are three classes of users:

- oriented - who know the names of the classic problems of discrete optimization well and the algorithms to solve them,
- semi-oriented possessing partial knowledge,
- un-oriented who do not have knowledge about problems, but they want to use an intelligent system to solve their own problems, e.g. searching for the shortest path, the existence of mutual connections in the set of objects.

The knowledge base is constructed in such a way that all three groups can use the Intelligent ALMM System. The Knowledge of Problems consists of the Library of Problem Models and Properties of Problems. Due to the fact that the problem library will be implemented using the C# language, it was decided that the MS SQL Server data-base and LINQ database as well as the Object Relational Database will be used.

Knowledge Base about problems will store knowledge about:

- different properties of individual problems with the separation of this knowledge into process properties and criteria ones,
- rules combining properties of problems with the possibilities of using selected methods and algorithms to solve problems.

A characteristic feature of the created knowledge base is the fact that, once saved, properties will not be modified. However, it is expected that new properties might be added, which will be modified with relative infrequency. The Intelligent ALMM System created will be a multi-access system and work in a client-server standard. The organization of the knowledge base will depend significantly on the type of queries generated by system users and the recording range of additional properties. The organization of properties storing from the point of view of problems property implementation is divided into the following properties (Fig. 3):

- universal (suitable for many problems, whether or not encountered by them),
- private (closely related to the problem under consideration).

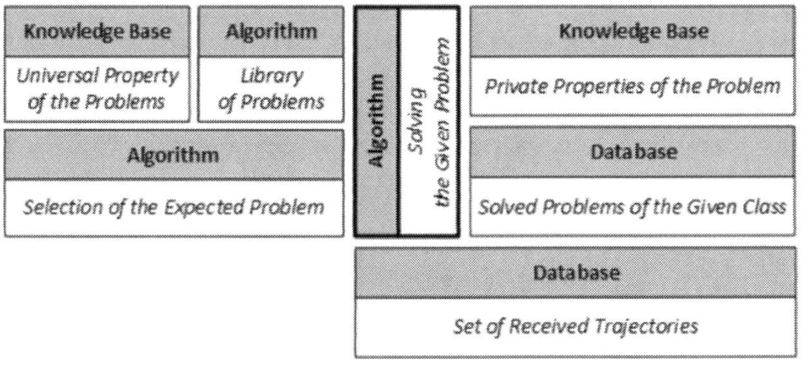

Fig. 3. The organization of Properties of Problems in Knowledge Base

Therefore, its universal properties will be stored in the knowledge base about proper-ties: Knowledge Properties of Problems.

4.3 Software representation of properties knowledge base AL Model's

The implemented Problem Properties Library is a set of functions and data structures with a set of rules for combining elements of a given set into a single functional module. The C# object platform used allows for the organization of data and methods that correlate their processing in a communicative way in management. The proposed library is characterized by high flexibility and many possibilities of adapting to a diverse class of problems. It will be possible to expand the properties library of problems using the step-by-step method, including simple rules for adding new com-ponents. The proposed library provides a set of component properties for various problems solved in the Intelligent ALMM System. Any application or module cooperating with the Library will cooperate in the client server technology.

In the article [2, 3] the IT project was proposed for AL problem model designated as an IT model problem. Therefore, the methodology of the module's implementation must easily link properties to individual problems and to the relevant elements of their AL model. The problem property model is implemented as a class named cProblemProperties.

In order to present the structure of the problems in the reality which are described by data, processes, data structures and programs that construct the system structure, a logical diagram of classes in UML was proposed. Fig. 4 presents a diagram of the classes and dependencies between the property interfaces of individual AL model elements that will be responsible for communication between the modules of the Library of Problem Models and Properties of Problems: iProperStateSet, iControlDecisionSet, iNonAdmissibleStateSet, iGoalStateStatement, iPossibleDecisionSet, iInitialState, iTransferFunctionALConditions.

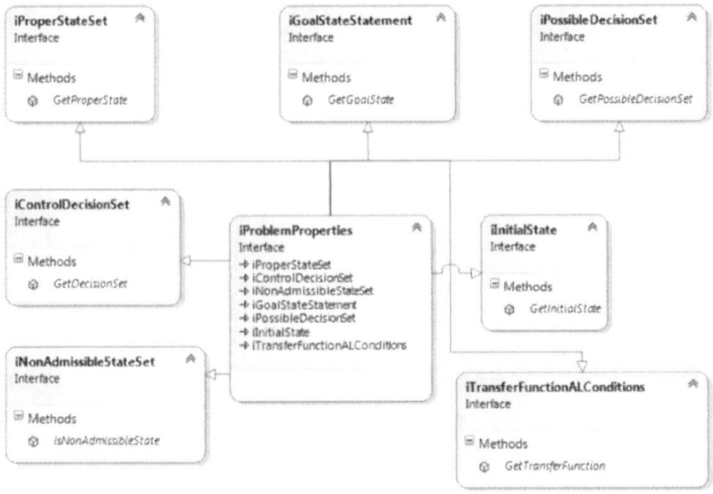

Fig. 4. Class diagram of Problem Properties

The Algebraic Logical Meta Model defines the individual elements of AL problem models and allows to define their detailed properties. The following property types should be defined in the *cProblemProperties* class: properties related to decision structure, state structure, initial state, transition function, set of decisions possible in given states, set of not admissible states, set of goal states and properties of problem data structures. The class interface modeling the problem property should provide methods related to the above elements:

- *cStateSet GetProperState(cProblem ProcessProperties)* – representation of the properties of a set of proper states;
- *cStateSet GetDecisionSet(cProblem ProcessProperties)* – representation of the properties of a set of control decisions or control signals;
- *cStateSet IsNonAdmissibleState(cProblem ProcessProperties)* – representation of the property of a set of generalized nonadmissible states;
- *cGoalState GetGoalState(cProblem ProcessProperties)* – representation of the properties of the set of generalized target states;
- *cStateSet GetPossibleDecisionSet(cProblem ProcessProperties)* – representation of the properties of a set of proper states;
- *cStateSet GetInitialState(cProblem ProcessProperties)* – representation of the properties of a generalized initial state;
- *cFunctionAL GetTransferFunction(cProblem ProcessProperties)* – representation of properties of the transition function;

5 Conslusion

The paper refers to a specialised IT System applied to solve discreet optimization problems; specifically an intelligent ALMM System. The system uses the special paradigm of problem modelling, namely algebraic-logical general model of multistage decision processes, both common and dynamic. The intelligent ALARM system not only has to solve discrete optimization problems, but also advises the user to apply the appropriate method/algorithm, based on the problem's properties. The system has a knowledge base containing the properties of the Library of Problem Models and Properties of Problem. The model of each problem is defined by means of elements: state structure, decision structure, initial state, transition function, sets of possible decisions and a set of admissible and non-admissible states. The main contribution of this article is to present the concept of assumptions regarding the implementation of the knowledge base of problems, in particular the relationship model problems with their properties. Three basic types of knowledge base construction were considered, and appropriate programming tools were proposed in the context of the data architecture modelling. The initial implementation of the project modules for managing the flow of information about the properties of the problem is presented using the UML scheme and class declarations in C #.

References

1. E. Dudek-Dyduch, Intelligent ALMM System for Discrete Optimization Problems – the Idea of Knowledge Base Application, ISAT, vol. 657, (2017)
2. E. Dudek-Dyduch, S. Korzonek: ALMM Solver for combinatorial and discrete optimization problems - Idea of Problem Model Library, ACIIDS Part I. LNAI, vol. 9621, (2016)
3. S. Korzonek, E. Dudek-Dyduch, Component Library of Problem Models for ALMM Solver, Journal of Information and Telecommunication, 1:3, pp. 224-240, (2017)
4. E. Dudek-Dyduch,: Modeling Manufacturing Processes with Disturbances - a New Method Based on Algebraic-Logical Meta-Model. ICAISC, Part II. LNCS, vol. 9120, (2015)
5. E. Dudek-Dyduch, E. Kucharska, L. Dutkiewicz, K. Rączka: ALMM Solver-A Tool for Optimization Problems. ICAISC 2014, pp. 328-338 (2014)
6. E. Dudek-Dyduch, E. Kucharska: Learning method for co-operation. ICCCI 2011 Part II. LNCS, vol. 6923, pp. 290-300. Springer, Heidelberg, (2011)
7. E. Dudek-Dyduch, L. Dutkiewicz: Substitution tasks method for discrete optimization. ICAISC 2013, Part II. LNCS, vol. 7895, pp. 419-430, (2013)
8. E. Dudek-Dyduch, E. Kucharska: Optimization Learning Method for Discrete Process Control. In: ICINCO 2011, vol. 1, pp. 24-33, (2011)
9. E. Dudek-Dyduch, E. Kucharska, L. Dutkiewicz, K. Rączka: ALMM Solver-A Tool for Optimization Problems. ICAISC 2014, pp. 328-338, (2014)
10. L. Dutkiewicz, E. Dudek-Dyduch: Substitution Tasks Method for Co-operation. In: Recent Developments in Computational Collective Intelligence, pp. 103-113, (2014)
11. E. Dudek-Dyduch: Learning based algorithm in scheduling. Journal of Intelligent Manufacturing (JIM), vol. 11, no 2, pp. 135-143., (2000)
12. E. Dudek-Dyduch,: Problems of knowledge representation in expert system aided control of DPP (in Polish), part I, pp. 147-154, Wrocław, (1993)

13. E. Dudek-Dyduch,: Algebraic Logical Meta-Model of Decision Processes - New Metaheuristics. ICAISC, Part 1. LNCS, vol. 9119, pp. 541-554, (2015)
14. E. Dudek-Dyduch,: Modeling Manufacturing Processes with Disturbances – Two-Stage AL Model Transformation Method, MMAR, pp. 782-787 (2015)
15. E. Dudek-Dyduch: Discrete determinable processes - compact knowledge-based model, Notas de Matematica No 137, Universidad de Los Andes Venezuela, (1993)
16. E. Dudek-Dyduch: Formalization and analysis of problems of discrete manufacturing processes. Scientific bulletin of AGH University, Automatics vol.54, (in Polish), (1990)
17. K. Rączka, E. Dudek-Dyduch, E. Kucharska, L. Dutkiewicz: ALMM Solver: the Idea and the Architecture. In: Rutkowski at al. (eds.) ICAISC 2015, Part II. LNCS, vol. 9120, pp. 504-514, Springer International Publishing, (2015)
18. P. Jędrzejowicz, E. Ratajczak-Ropel: Reinforcement Learning Strategy for Solving the MRCPSP by a Team of Agents, Intelligent Decision Technologies, Smart Innovation, Systems and Technologies, vol. 39, Springer, pp. 537-548, (2015)
19. E. Dudek-Dyduch: Information systems for production management (in Polish) Wyd. Poldex, Kraków ISBN 83-88979-12-4,(2002)
20. L Anselma,. L. Piovesan, A. Sattar, B. Stantic, A. Paolo Terenzian, Comprehensive Approach to 'Now' in Temporal Relational Databases: Semantics and Representation, IEEE Transactions On Knowledge And Data Engineering, Vol.: 28, Issue: 10, pp: 2538-2551
21. E. Dudek-Dyduch, T. Dyduch: Formal approach to optimization of discrete manufacturing processes. in: Hamza, M.H. Proc. of the Twelfth IASTED, Acta Press, Zurich, (1993)
22. F. Rossi, P. Van Beek, T. Walsh,: Handbook of Constraint Programming, Elsevier, (2006)
23. P. Terenziani, Nearly Periodic Facts in Temporal Relational Databases, IEEE Transactions on Knowledge and Data Engineering, Volume: 28, Issue: 10 , Pages: 2822-2826, (2016)
24. E. Kucharska, E. Dudek-Dyduch: Extended Learning Method for Designation of Cooperation. In: Transactions on Computational Collective Intelligence XIV, pp. 136-157, (2014)
25. J. M. Medina, C. D. Barranco, O. Pons, Evaluation of Indexing Strategies for Possibilistic Queries Based on Indexing Techniques Available in Traditional RDBMS, (2016)
26. F. Abdelhedi, A.A. Brahim, F. Atigui, G. Zurfluh, Big Data and Knowledge Management: How to Implement Conceptual Models in NoSQL Systems?, Knowledge Engineering And Knowledge Management, vol. 3 (KMIS), pp: 235-240, (2016)
27. J Błażewicz., K. Ecker, E. Pesch, G. Schmidt, J. Węglarz: Handbook on Scheduling. Springer Berlin Heidelberg New York, ISBN 978-3-540-28046-0, (2007)
28. R.E. Smith, N. Taylor: A Framework for Evolutionary Computation in Agent-Based Systems, Proc. of Int. Conf. on Intelligent Systems, pp. 221-224. ISCA Press, (1998)

ITM Web of Conferences **21**, 00003 (2018) https://doi.org/10.1051/itmconf/20182100003
CST 2018

Application of CLP for technical objects construction with an exemplary bucket elevation

Grzegorz Bartnik[1]*, *Andrzej* Marciniak[2], and *Krzysztof* Gołacki[1]

[1]University of Life Sciences Lublin, ul. Głęboka 28, 20-612 Lublin, Poland
[2]University of Economics and Innovation in Lublin, ul. Projektowa 4, 20-209 Lublin, Poland

Abstract. The paper presents the application of the Constraint Logic Programming (CLP) language for designing technical objects. The method was described and illustrated based with the help of on the bucket elevator design. The hierarchical structure of the object, way of system configuration and exemplary sets of fitted components are presented.

1 Introduction

The aim of designing process is a symbol, formal and workable specification of a technical object satisfying specified functional, structural, material, durable resistant, reliable etc. requirements. They can be recorded in the form a finite set of constrains imposed on the quantities characterizing a projected object and depending on the designer`s decision. The quantities, which depend on the designer's decision, are called decision variables. They can be of different character e.g. numerical, categorical and logical variables as well as elements of specified sets. From the point of view as elements of imposed on the variables, for which the designer imparts values, have the form of predicates or otherwise n-arguments relations.

The complete recording of the construction through specification of constraints imposed on decision variables and recorded in the predicates logic languages becomes a computer program whose execution results in assignment to the decision variables, such values which fulfil a given set of constrains as far as these values exist in the domains corresponding to the variables. The program indicating the construction problem solution recorded in the language e.g. Prolog (Programing Logic) in which the predicates represent construction – exploitation requirements and constrains imposed on the designed object is its sufficiently declarative specification. The development of Prolog Language, adjusting it syntactically and semantically to the description of the problems fulfilling constrains, initiated a new

*Corresponding author: grzegorz.bartnik@up.lublin.pl

category of programming languages called Constraint Logic Programming (CLP). The solution satisfying the constrains can be zero or more. In the case there are no such solutions, possibility of constrains attenuation should be taken into consideration. When there are many solutions, one can consider the problem of construction optimization that is searching for the best possible solution after defining one or more criterion functions. The method in which the consideration of requirements imposed on the object and recorded in the CLP language becomes automatically a declarative program determining the variable values being the object of designer's decision. The paper presents the general methodology and gives a specific example of a technical object an with its application in the CLP methodology.

2 Problem with Formulation in the CLP Language

The quantities which acquire values from the designer`s decision are decision variables xi, i = 1 … n denoted by Di, i = 1 … n corresponding to the domain of these decision variables. The domains D1 can be of any type consistent with the semantics of corresponding variables. The constraints imposed on the decision variable values have the form of m – argument predicates where m = 0 or more. The complex two – argument predicates representing the constraining relations between two construction components of the designed object are most frequently applied.

$$r(X,Y):\text{-}C_1(X),\ C_2(Y),\ C_3(X,Y) \tag{1}$$

where: r, C_1, C_2, C_3 – are the symbols of predicates
X, Y – the variables representing pairs of construction parts
, - the symbol of construction (logical "i"),
: - - the symbol corresponding to logical implication.

The above expression is a typical syntax structure of the Prolog language. The right side is a conjunction of the conditions which must be satisfied in order to fulfill the constraint presented by the left side. Generally, the expression r(X, Y) is interpreted as the statement that the construction element X "fits" the element "Y" or element "X" is compatible with the element "Y". The predicates C1, C_2, C_3 can be also conjunctions of the lower order constraint predicates. The relation "fits" can be also more than the two – argument one. The program declaring the problem under consideration is a set of tasks recorded in accordance with the Prolog language syntax. The program declares the specific solutions of the problem as a set of sentences written with the Prolog language syntax. In order to separate individual constraints, the hierarchical decomposition of the object used as an example in the applied method was made. The constraints can be divided into external and internal ones. The external constraints qualify the requirements for the object as the whole (e.g. output, elevation height etc.) but the internal ones define compatibility between the object components an individual planes of its decomposition. Searching for combination of values of individual variables which satisfy given constraints is a combinatorial problem of exponential calculation complexity. This requires very effective search algorithms including heuristic ones. In the considered case the search method with constraints propagation was applied due to a small complexity of the object used as the designing example. Each constraint was illustrated by means of a suitable search tree. The bipartite graphs are an expressive form of constraints presentation.

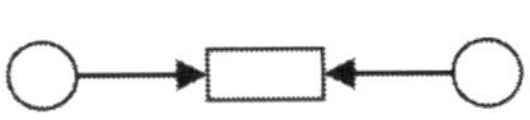

where: ○ corresponds to the decision variables and □ represents the constraints which are most often Boolean expressions in the considered case. Constraint Logic

Programming was elaborated in the late eighties of the last century by J. Jaffar and J.L. Lassez. Generally, this programming can be perceived as combination of logic programming, constraints solution and optimization [1, 2 ,3 ,4].

3 Solution of constraints

CLP is a tool which can be used to form constraint solution problems (CSP). Calculation problems accompanying various investigation fields can be modeled and solved as constraint variables solution ones. CSP describes the assumptions of a finite variables number and a finite values number for each variable. The constraint solution problems can be defined as follows:

- The finite set of S variables $X_1, X_2, \ldots, X_n$, is given,
- For each variable – the final set of domains $D_1, D_2, \ldots, D_n$,
- The set of constrains $C_i(X_{i1}, X_{i2}, \ldots, X_{ik})$ being the subset of the Cartesian product D_{i1} x D_{i2} x … x D_{ik}, which determines the variable values fitting each other in the way defined by the problem in question.

The PSO solution is such on assignment of the values to all variables from their domains that all constraints are met. Additionally, such a solution can satisfy the condition of maximization of and minimization of a given quality index. This is the optimal constraint fulfillment problem (POSO) [5, 6, 7, 8]. In the case of real decision problems the decision space which should be tested by the algorithm proves to be too large. This is the time needed for testing all combinations which can be formed by the algorithm is too long. Therefore, to increase the effectiveness of decision space inspection the constraint logic programming can be applied. It is based on the standard method of recurrences and their modifications combined with constraints propagation. This enables significant constraint of search set and at the same time allows to determine all admissible solutions consistent with the constraints fulfillment problem. Logic programming during problems solving is based on so called active constraints which can include not only materialized variables but also those deprived of value that is immaterialized. There the following domains of CLP can be distinguished:

- logical - the constraints assume only the values: true/false,
- total and real - the constraints are integers and real number,
- linear - all constraints are presented in the form of linear functions,
- finite - where constraints are defined as sets of finite power,
- mixed domains - combination of two or more above mentioned domains.

The finite domain has been the most extensively applied. Some problems in the operation research range are identified with the CLP just in this domain [7, 9, 10, 11, 12].

4 Constraints propagation

Most decision problems in the combinatorial optimization range are practically insolvable for a large number of variables. The search for decision problems solution space by means of complete inspection is ineffective so additional methods of constraint of this set are used. The constraints propagation application is one of the method of decision space constraint in constraint logic programming.

The main assumption of constraints propagation is the application of constraints for reduction of variable domains. Propagation consist in removal from the domain all the variables which do not satisfy the assumed constraints. Each constraint declared in the model is propagated separately whereby every time each constraint propagation brings the values of all other domains up to date. The constraint programming languages can express variables from the range of natural number domains (most often applied) intervals of real numbers, sets and others. However, the constraint propagation itself very rarely gives solution. Therefore it is always combined with distribution and search [1]. In some cases propagation is not a sufficient operation for solving Constraint Satisfaction Problem (CSP), however it increases the process effectiveness (significant acceleration) in order to find an admissible solution. One of the optimization mechanisms used in the CLP is the Branch and Bound (BaB) mechanism. Its aim is to find an optimal solution based on the value of quality index and rejection of all the branches of solution tree which produce the values worse than the current minimum constraint and then to date the minimum constraint bringing up when a better solution than the current one is found [7, 9]. To this end there can be applied one of two methods of decision tree inspection: search deeper or across the decision tree.

5 Exemplary bucket elevator construction

Bucket elevators are used for transport of materials in bulk from one level to another one (higher)) [13]. Their main job of transportation of loose materials to the places of their storage as far as granulation remains at a proper ratio to the sizes of bucket inlet. The transported material does not form a continuous stream but it is placed in suitable containers which makes it different form tape, link, plate or driver conveyors [14, 15, 16, 17, 18]. Figure 1 presents the hierarchical structure of such elevator.

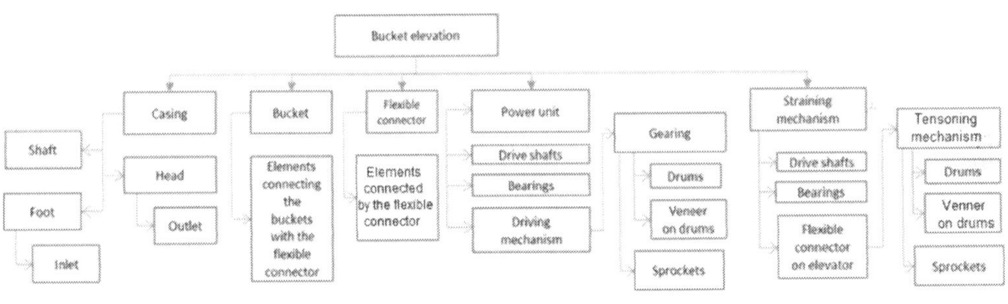

Fig. 1. Hierarchical structure of the object

In order to simplify the choice of individual parts of the bucket elevator dependent on the height of elevation, efficiency and kind of transported material, their review division was made (Tab. 1). The bipartite graph presenting constraints of the elevator kind choice.

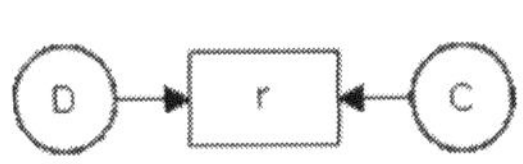

$D \in \{D1, D2\}$ $C \in \{C1, C2\}$

r – is interpreted as "fits for" or "is compatible with"

Table 1. List of conditions for the selection of elevator parts and components elevator [15].

<table>
<tr><td colspan="4">Input parameters</td></tr>
<tr><td colspan="2">A – elevation height</td><td>B – output</td><td>C – kind of elevated material</td></tr>
<tr><td colspan="4">Components</td></tr>
<tr><td>No.</td><td>Name of subassembly/parts</td><td>Symbol of subassembly/parts</td><td>Selection dependence</td></tr>
<tr><td>1</td><td>Kind of elevator</td><td>D</td><td>C</td></tr>
<tr><td>2</td><td>Load-bearing flexible connector</td><td>E</td><td>A, B, C</td></tr>
</table>

3	Bucket	F	B, C, D
4	Power unit	G	A, B
5	Flexible connector drive	H	A, B
6	Flexible connector links	I	A, E
7	Buckets linking	J	E
8	Ratchet	K	B
9	Driving mechanism	L	C, E
10	Straining mechanism	M	C, E
11	Bearings	N	B, C
12	Inlet	O	B, D
13	Outlet	P	B, D
14	Veneer on drums	R	C
15	Casing	S	A, D
A1 – height up to about 25m, A2 – height up to about 80m, B1 – output up about 80t/h, B2 – output up about 300t/h, C1 – nonabrasive material, C2 – abrasive material, **Kind of elevator:** D1 – high-speed (centrifugal), D2 – slow-speed (gravitation) **Load-bearing flexible connector:** E1 – rubber tapes, E2 – plate link chain, E3 – coil chain, E4 – forget chain …			

Table 2. Relation between the kind of bucket elevator and transported material [15].

	D1	D2
C1	1	1
C2	0	1

The relation between the kind of bucked elevator and transported material (Tab. 2) can be presented in the form of search tree (Fig. 2).

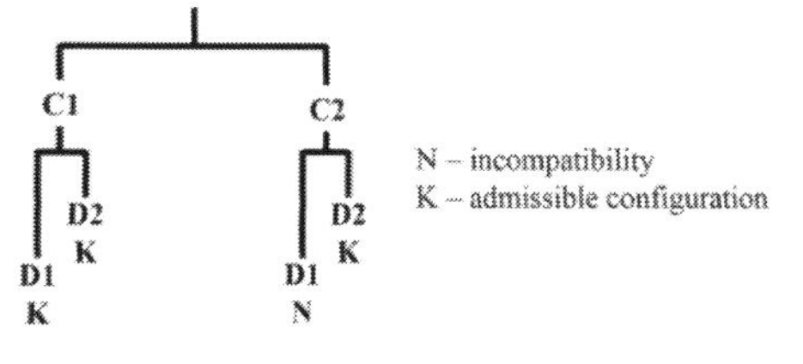

Fig. 2. The search tree using the complete inspection method for the choice of a kind of bucket elevator [15].

Optimal solution of bucket elevator choice depending on the transported material takes construction strength into consideration. Figure 4 presents the search for the best solution based on the complete inspection method.

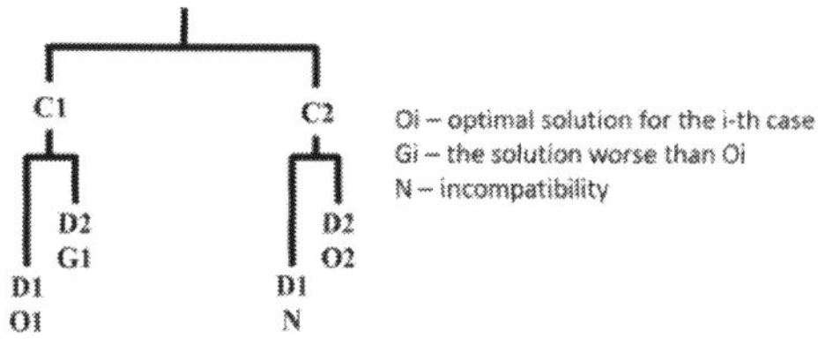

Fig. 3. The search tree for the optimal choice of the bucket elevator based on the strength criterion [15].

As follows from Fig. 3 in the case of nonabrasive materials transport the best solution is the use height–speed elevator but for abrasive materials transport the slow–speed elevator proves to have better strength.

The bipartite graphs presenting constrains in the choice of the kinds of carrying connector de-pending on the height of transported material (A), output (B) and the kind of transported material (C).

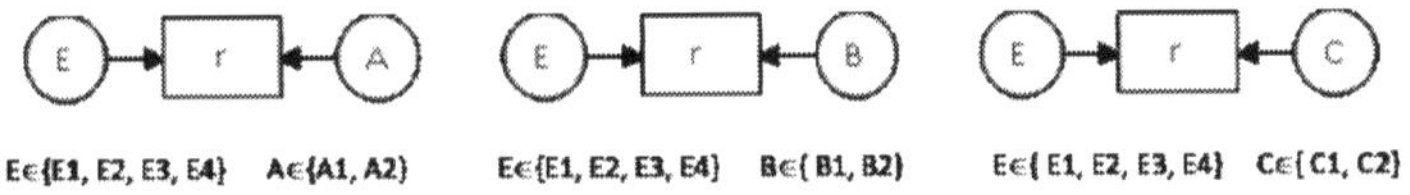

Table 3. Dependence of flexible connector choice [15].

	E1	E2	E3	E4		E1	E2	E3	E4		E1	E2	E3	E4
A1	1	1	1	1	B1	1	1	1	0	C1	1	1	0	0
A2	1	0	1	0	B2	1	1	1	1	C2	1	0	1	1

Table 3 presents the specification of kinds of flexible connectors used in bucket elevators. However, its graphic image is Figure 4 showing the tree of complete search for flexible connector depending on the height of elevator lifting, output and kind of transported material. The search is often made for optimal solution whose price is the lowest. This solution can be obtained by means of the Branch and Bound (BaB) method [14]. Table 4 presents the result of search for optimal solutions.

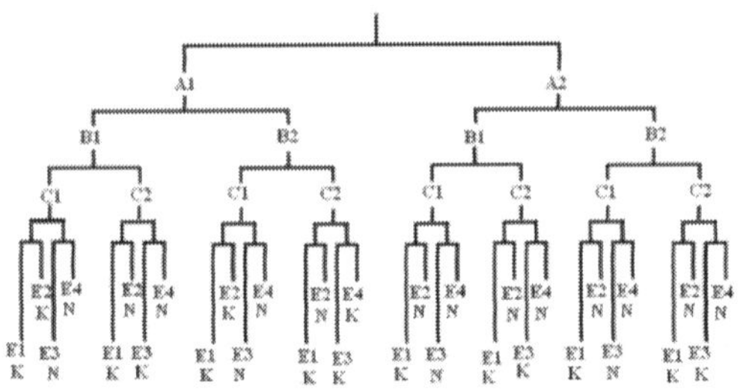

Fig. 4. The search tree using the complete inspection method for the choice of flexible connector [10].

The BaB method can be used for the choice of a suitable connector depending on the kind of bucket elevator (Fig. 5).

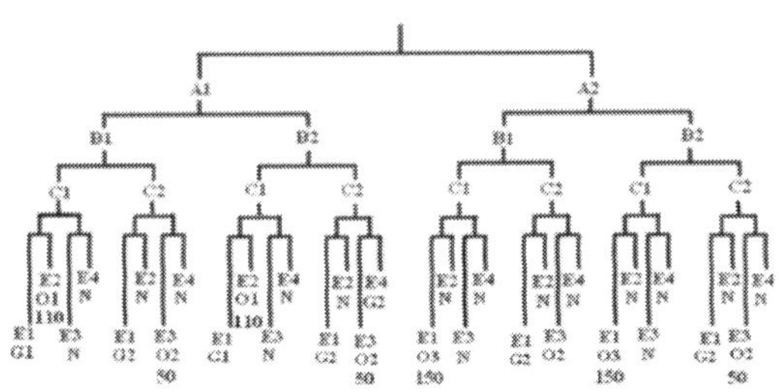

Fig. 5. The search tree using the BaB method for the optimal choice of flexible connector [15].

Table 4. The sets of fitted components [15].

Number of set	**Conditions of elevator work**	**Optimal set (WEH – with elevation height control, OEH – without elevation height control)**
I.	A1, B1, C1	Z1 = {D1, E2, F9, G1, H1, I9 (ZRP), I8 (BRP), J3, K2, L3, M3, N1, O1, O4, P1, P3, S1, S4, S5}

II.	A2, B1, B1	Z2 = {D1, E1, F9, G1, H1, I6 (ZRP), I2 (BRP), J1, K2, L1, M1, N1, O1, O4, P1, P3, R1, S1, S3, S5}
III.	A1, B2, C1	Z3 = {D1, E2, F9, G1, H1, I9 (ZRP), I8 (BRP), J3, K2, L3, M3, N2, O2, O4, P2, P3, S1, S4, S5}
IV.	A1, B1, C2	Z4 = {D2, E3, F9, G1, H1, I12 (ZRP), I12 (BRP), J5, K2, L6, M3, N2, O1, O3, P1, P4, S2, S4, S6}
V.	A2, B2, C1	Z5 = {D1, E1, F9, G1, H1, I6 (ZRP), I2 (BRP), J1, K2, L1, M1, N2, O2, O4, P2, P3, R1, S1, S3, S5}
VI.	A2, B1, C2	Z6 = {D2, E3, F9, G1, H1, I12 (ZRP), I12 (BRP), J5, K2, L6, M3, N2, O1, O3, P1, P4, S2, S3, S6}
VII.	A1, B2, C2	Z7 = {D2, E3, F9, G1, H1, I12 (ZRP), I12 (BRP), J5, K2, L6, M2, N3, O2, O3, P2, P4, S2, S4, S6}
VIII.	A2, B2, C2	Z7 = {D2, E3, F9, G1, H1, I12 (ZRP), I12 (BRP), J5, K2, L6, M2, N3, O2, O3, S2, S3, S6}

The process knowledge in the informal form can be transformed to the form of codes by means of such conceptual schemes as bipartite graphs (Fig. 6). From the point of view of logics, a language of bipartite graphs passes expressiveness of predicates logic of the first order which seems to be sufficient for formal description of the structures of technical objects.

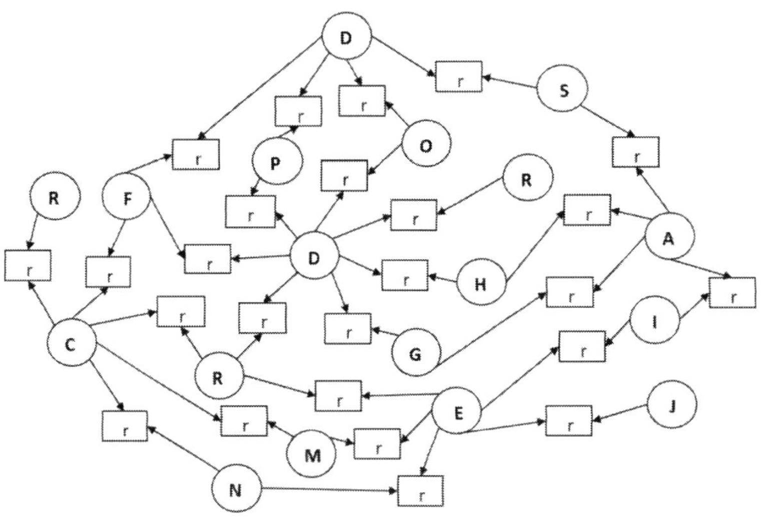

Fig. 6. The object structure presented by means of bipartite graphs comparison [15].

6 Conclusions

The paper presents the application of programming methods in the constraint logic programming (CLP) language for designing technical objects. It describes the designing method illustrated by the example of the bucket elevator projection. The hierarchical structure of the object, way of system configuration as well as the sets of fitted components one included. The presented way of projection is exemplary and simplified. In fact the number of constraints imposed on the projected technical objects is much higher (e.g. concerning safety, environmental protection etc.). Due to the calculation complexity domains of individual decision variables should have a finite and not very large number of values. This indicates that the described projection method is suitable for the approach used for the configuration of projected object from the standardized and earlier projected ready components of known characteristics taken into consideration in specification and control of compatibility constraints. This way of projection object conceptualization is of universal character. It can refer to projection of technical objects, construction materials, bio- and nano - technological products as well as food produce. Formalization of the above presented conceptualization is presented and exemplary illustrated.

7 References

1. http://www-users.mat.umk.pl/~fly/materialy/pl/referaty/CLP_rosi.pdf (2018)
2. J. Jaffar, M. J. Maher, *Constraint Logic Programming: A Survey*, Journal ofLogic Programming, **19-20**, 503-581 (1994)
3. T. Tatoń, Wybrane problemy aukcji i przetargów kombinatorycznych. http://docpl ayer.pl /37987537-Wybrane-problemy-aukcji-i-przetargow-kombinatorycznych.html (2017)
4. H.P. Williams, *Logic and Integer Programming*, Springer (2009)
5. K. Apt, M. Wallace, *Constraint Logic Programming using Eclipse*, Cambridge University Press, (2006)
6. R. Bart'ak, *On-Line Guide to Prolog Programming*, http://kti.mff.cuni.cz/ bartak/prolog/, (2010)
7. J. Hansen, *Constraint Programming versus Mathematical Programming*, Orbit, 3 (2003)
8. A. Niederliński, *Programowanie w logice z ograniczeniami*, Wydawnictwo Pracowni Komputerowej Jacka Skalmierskiego, (2010)
9. http://www.hakank.org/ECLiPSe/, (2018)
10. Janczura K., Gabiga T. *Wprowadzenie do Programowania Logicznego z Ograniczeniami z wykorzystaniem ECLiPSe*. PWSZ Tarnów (2009)
11. Ł. Mazur, *Paradygmat programowania CLP. Metody rozwiązywania trudnych problemów kombinatorycznych*. http://software.com.pl (2012)
12. T. Żurek, *Metody sztucznej inteligencji*, Wydawnictwo UMCS, (2011)
13. Goździecki M., Świątkiewicz H. *Przenośniki*, Wydawnictwo Naukowo – Techniczne, Warszawa 1979.
14. L. W, Kurmaz, O. L. Kurmaz, *Projektowanie węzłów i części maszyn podręcznik* (2007)
15. A. Lipczak, *Koncepcja konstrukcji segmentowego przenośnika kubełkowego*, AR Lublin (2012)
16. M. Markowski, *Przenośniki*, Wydawnictwo Politechniki Łódzkiej, I, edition III (1995)
17. M. Markowski, *Przenośniki*, Wydawnictwo Politechniki Łódzkiej, II, edition II (1986)
18. R. Raczyk, *Środki transportu bliskiego i magazynowania*, Wydawnictwo Politechniki Poznańskiej, (2009)

Backpropagation algorithm with fractional derivatives

Zbigniew Gomolka[*]

University of Rzeszow, Faculty of Mathematics and Natural Sciences Department of Computer Engineering, ul. Pigonia 1, 35-959 Rzeszow, Poland

Abstract. The paper presents a model of a neural network with a novel backpropagation rule, which uses a fractional order derivative mechanism. Using the Grunwald Letnikow definition of the discrete approximation of the fractional derivative, the author proposed the smooth modeling of the transition functions of a single neuron. On this basis, a new concept of a modified backpropagation algorithm was proposed that uses the fractional derivative mechanism both for modeling the dynamics of individual neurons and for minimizing the error function. The description of the signal flow through the neural network and the mechanism of smooth shape control of the activation functions of individual neurons are given. The model of minimization of the error function is presented, which takes into account the possibility of changes in the characteristics of individual neurons. For the proposed network model, example courses of the learning processes are presented, which prove the convergence of the learning process for different shapes of the transition function. The proposed algorithm allows the learning process to be conducted with a smooth modification of the shape of the transition function without the need for modifying the IT model of the designed neural network. The proposed network model is a new tool that can be used in signal classification tasks.

1 Introduction

Here we briefly recall some approaches to neural networks connected with gradient methods of error minimalization. The algorithm of backpropagation was firstly pro-posed by the Finnish student Seppo Linnainmaa in 1970, but without any indication of its possible relationship with neural networks [1, 2]. In the history of the development of neural networks, this was the period directly after the 1969 publication of Minsky and Papert titled *Perceptrons*, in which they presented proof of the limitations of the network of linear perceptrons for solving linearly non-separable tasks, eg XOR [1, 3]. Paradoxically, this fact initiated a period of stagnation, in which the idea of neural networks development was frozen for several years, becoming an un-fulfilled dream of artificial intelligence applications. Fortunately at the beginning of the 1980s a novel approach was presented (in some aspects earlier by Grossberg in 1973 [3]) by Werbos in 1982, Parker 1985, and LeCun in 1985, which overcame the non-linear XOR problem by using the mechanism of errors

[*] Corresponding author: zgomolka@ur.edu.pl

minimization via gradient descent, specifically using complex derivative of error function [1,3 - 9]. The classical backpropagation algorithm that uses this mechanism of minimizing the error function assumes that the expression within the error function is differentiable. Because in such notation, the error function is a complex function, there is a need among other things to differentiate the transfer function of a single neuron, hence the key limitation of the possible applications of transient functions that must satisfy the condition of differentiability. In practice, more or less accurate approximations of transition functions are presumed, which in consequence leads to a simplification of the general model of the network. In addition, the assumed network structure forces the use of the same IT model, which includes the numerical implementation of the derivative of the transfer function of a single neuron, eg *sigmoid*, *tanh*, Gauss, log. In the author's opinion, this is a limitation which is a significant simplification of both the dynamics of individual neurons and the strategy of conducting their learning processes. Taking into account the above and assuming that biological neural cells can adopt any transitional character, the idea arose to design a mechanism that would allow for a smooth modeling of their dynamics. The concept of the smoothly changed transfer functions was already presented in works [10] and [11]. The main assumption is that the mathematical model of a neuron that uses base functions derived from a number of sigmoidal functions that assumes a dynamic change depends on the order of the used derivative, which in the general case may have a non-integer value.

2 Model of the Fractional Back-Prop network

Let us assume the following model of the L layered neural network, for which the model with fractional order derivative mechanism [13-15] will be given (see Fig.1.). Excluding transfer functions this model resembles the classic model of the feedforward network in which the input signal is presented by the matrix of input vectors: $P=[\vec{p}, \dots, \vec{p}, \dots, \vec{p}]$ where $q \in \langle 1, Q \rangle$, Q denotes the number of vectors in the training set, whereas $A_L = [\vec{a}_L, \dots, \vec{a}_L, \dots, \vec{a}_L]$ is the matrix of the network response vectors for the excitation $\vec{p}$ in the input layer. The input signal of the network is defined as: $\vec{p} \quad [p \; 1), \dots, p^Q(R)]^T$ while the output signal in the l layer is: $\vec{a}_L \quad [a_L \; 1), \dots, a_L^q(N)]^T$ where R denotes the number of receptors, N stands for the number of network outputs. The form of the expected value vector matrix was similarly defined as $T([\vec{t}, \dots, \vec{t}, \dots, \vec{t}])$ where consecutive vectors $\vec{t}$ are of the form: $\vec{t} \quad [t \;), \dots, t^q(N)]^T$. For the sake of notation simplicity, it was assumed that in a given learning step the q index can be omitted.

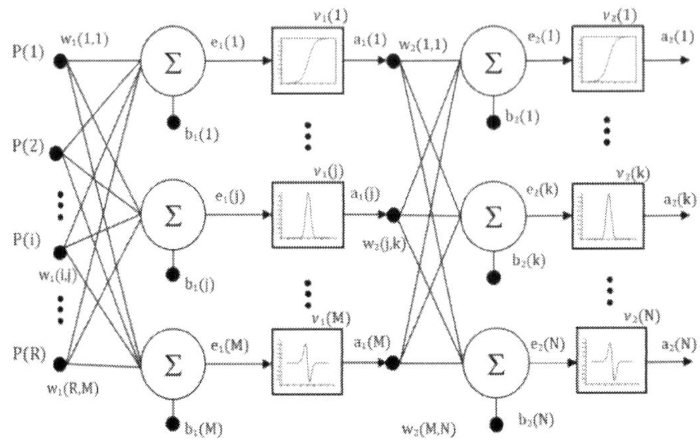

Fig. 1. Presumed model of the network

The flow of the signal within the network can be described as following. The input signal to the $j-th$ neuron in the first layer equals:

$$e_1(j)=\sum_{i=1}^{R} w_1(i,j)P(i)+b_1(j) \tag{1}$$

where: $w_1(i,j)$ - element of the matrix of weights connecting the receptor layer with the first layer of neurons, i - the number of the receptor on the input layer, j - the number of the neuron in the input layer, $p(i)$ - denotes $i-th$ element of the input vector, $b_1(j)$ - $j-th$ vector element of bias values in the first layer. Activation of neurons $a_1(j)$ in the first layer is expressed as follows:

$$a_1(j)=f(e_1(j)) \tag{2}$$

where: $f_B(e_1(j))$ - is the neurons transfer function in the first layer. Similarly, the input signal for $k-th$ neuron in the second layer is equal to:

$$e_2(k)=\sum_{j=1}^{M} w_2(i,j)a_1(j)+b_2(k) \tag{3}$$

where: $w_2(j,k)$ - element of the matrix of weights connecting the first layer with the second layer, $b_2(k)$ - $k-th$ vector element of threshold values in the second layer. Similarly, neuron activation in the output layer is:

$$a_2(k)=f(e_2(k)) \tag{4}$$

Typically, the bias vector might be placed in the weight matrix, then the beginning of the i and j index notation changes respectively.

$$a_2(k)=f\left(\sum_{j=0}^{M} w_2(j,k)f\left(\sum_{i=0}^{R} w_1(i,j)p(i)\right)\right) \tag{5}$$

In the presented model (differently than in the classic approach), the transition function of a single neuron is taken as a Grünwald- Letnikov fractional derivative (GL) [16- 20] of log base function. Based on the definition of the integer derivative and the fractional derivative, the GL derivative is described by the formula:

$$_{e_0}D_e^{v} f(e)=\lim_{h\to 0}\frac{1}{h^{v}}\sum_{n=0}^{[(e-e_0)/h]}(-)^{n}\binom{v}{n}f_B(e-nh) \tag{6}$$

where $\binom{v}{n}$ denotes the Newton binomial, v – order of fractional derivative of basis function $f_B(x)$, e_0 – the interval range, h - step of discretization. For the given discrete function $f(e)$ of real variable e defined on the interval $\langle e_0, e\rangle$, where $0 \le e_0 \le e$, we assume the backward difference of fractional order v $_{e_0}\Delta_e^{(v)}$ where $v \in R^+$:

$$_{e_0}\Delta_e^{(v)} f(e) = \sum_{n=0}^{(e-e_0)/h} a_n^{(v)} f_B(e-nh) \tag{7}$$

where consecutive coefficients $a_n^{(v)}$ are defined as follow:

$$a_n^{(v)} = \begin{cases} 1 & dla \quad n=0 \\ (-1)^n \dfrac{v(v-1)(v-2)\dots(v-n+1)}{n!} & dla \quad n=1,2,3,\dots,N \end{cases} \tag{8}$$

N stands for the number of discrete measurements and $f_B(e)$, which might be defined as:

$$f_B(e) = \left(\log\left(1+\exp(\beta e)\right)\right) \tag{9}$$

where $\beta = 1$ denotes the inclination coefficient. The set of the possible basis functions as well as their retrieval has been shown in [11]. When $h \to 0$ and $v = 1$ this GL derivative of $f_B(e)$ becomes:

$$_{e_0}D_e^1 f_B(e) = \frac{1}{1+\exp(-e)} \tag{10}$$

The BP learning method is based on the minimization of the error function, which takes the form for the presented architecture as follow:

$$E = \frac{1}{2}\sum_{kq}\left[t^q(k) - {}_{e_0}D_e^1 f_B\left(\sum_{j=0}^{M} w_2^q(j,k)\, {}_{e_0}D_e^1 f_B\left(\sum_{i=0}^{R} w_1^q(i,j)\, p^q(i)\right)\right)\right]^2 \tag{11}$$

where q - means the number of the input vector, for which the appropriate vector is desired at the output of the network t^q. This is the normal equation of the least squares method (LSM). The expected change in the weight values, which minimize the error, is expressed:

$$w^{(q+1)} - w^{(q)} = \Delta w^{(q)} = -\eta \frac{\partial E^{(q)}}{\partial w} \tag{12}$$

where: η – the speed of learning. Thus, starting from the output layer, respectively, we can rewrite:

$$\Delta w_2^q(j,k) = -\eta \frac{\partial E}{\partial w_2^q(j,k)} = -\eta \frac{\partial E}{\partial a_2^q}\frac{\partial a_2^q}{\partial e_2^q}\frac{\partial e_2^q}{\partial w_2^q(j,k)} \tag{13}$$

$$\frac{\partial E}{\partial a_2^q} = -\left[t^q(k) - a_2^q(k)\right] \tag{14}$$

$$\frac{\partial a_2^q}{\partial e_2^q} = {}_{e_0}D_e^{v+1} f_B(e) \tag{15}$$

$$\frac{\partial e_2^q}{\partial w_2^q(j,k)} = a_1^q(j) \tag{16}$$

By introducing additional notations $\delta_2^q(k)$

$$\delta_2^q(k)=\left[t^q(k)-a_2^q(k)\right]\frac{\partial a_2^q}{\partial e_2^q} \tag{17}$$

We can write the final equation of weight correction in the output layer as:

$$\Delta w_2^q(j,k)=-\eta\frac{\partial E}{\partial w_2^q(j,k)}=\eta a_1^q(j)\delta_2^q(k) \tag{18}$$

For $v=1$ and $h\to 1$, regarding (10) and additivity property of derivatives [21 - 26] we have:

$${}_{e_0}D_e^{v+1}f_B(e)={}_{e_0}D_e^{v}\left({}_{e_0}D_e^{1}f_B(e)\right)={}_{e_0}D_e^{1}f_B(e)\left(1-{}_{e_0}D_e^{1}f_B(e)\right) \tag{19}$$

or directly:

$${}_{e_0}D_e^{v+1}f_B(e)={}_{e_0}D_e^{2}f_B(e) \tag{20}$$

For the first layer, the considerations are analogous

$$\Delta w_1^q(i,j)=-\eta\frac{\partial E}{\partial a_1^q}\frac{\partial a_1^q}{\partial e_1^q}\frac{\partial e_1^q}{\partial w_1^q(i,j)} \tag{21}$$

with the exception of the following component described by the measure of the next layer error:

$$\frac{\partial E}{\partial a_1^q}=\sum_k w_2^q(j,k)\left(\left[t^q(k)-a_2^q(k)\right]\frac{\partial a_2^q}{\partial e_2^q}\right) \tag{22}$$

$$\frac{\partial a_1^q}{\partial e_1^q}={}_{e_0}D_e^{v+1}f_B(e) \tag{23}$$

$$\frac{\partial e_1^q}{\partial w_1^q(i,j)}=p^q(i) \tag{24}$$

$$\begin{aligned}\Delta w_1^q(i,j)&=\eta p^q(i)\left\{\sum_k w_2^q(j,k)\left(\left[t^q(k)-a_2^q(k)\right]\frac{\partial a_2^q}{\partial e_2^q}\right)\frac{\partial a_1^q}{\partial e_1^q}\right\}=\\ &\eta p^q(i)\left(\sum_k w_2^q(j,k)\delta_2^q(k)\frac{\partial a_1^q}{\partial e_1^q}\right)\end{aligned} \tag{25}$$

Introducing additional similar designation $\delta_1^q(j)$ we have:

$$\delta_1^q(j)=\sum_k w_2^q(j,k)\frac{\partial a_1^q}{\partial e_1^q}\delta_2^q(k) \tag{26}$$

Inserting into the expression defining ${}_\Delta w_1^q(i,j)$ we get finally:

$${}_\Delta w_1^q(i,j)=-\eta\frac{\partial E}{\partial w_1^q(i,j)}=\eta p^q(i)\delta_1^q(j) \tag{27}$$

Based on the presented considerations, the general formula for weight modification for L layered neural network with modified transition function can be given:

$$w_1^q(i,j)=w_1^{q-1}(i,j)+\eta\delta_j^l a_i^l \tag{28}$$

where the value δ_j^l, while presenting the $q-th$ pattern, will be written as:

$$\delta_j^l=\begin{cases}\left(t_j-a_j^l\right){}_{e_0}D_e^{v+1}f_B(e) & for\quad l=L \\ {}_{e_0}D_e^{v+1}f_B(e)\sum_{k=0}^{N^{l+1}}\delta_k^{l+1}w_{l+1}(j,k) & for\quad l<L\end{cases}\quad then\quad j\equiv k \tag{29}$$

where: l - means the number of the considered layer, j - the number of the neuron in layer l, k - is the number of neurons in the layer $l+1$, N - is the number of neurons in layer l. In the above considerations, it was assumed that in the presented network architecture the parameter v is the same in each layer and for individual neurons because of the first stage of the presented investigations.

2.1 FBP net under the XOR problem

For the accepted network model with fractional backpropagation (FBP) mechanism, experiments were carried out to examine the convergence of the proposed learning algorithm. The XOR problem was assumed as the input task for the neural network.

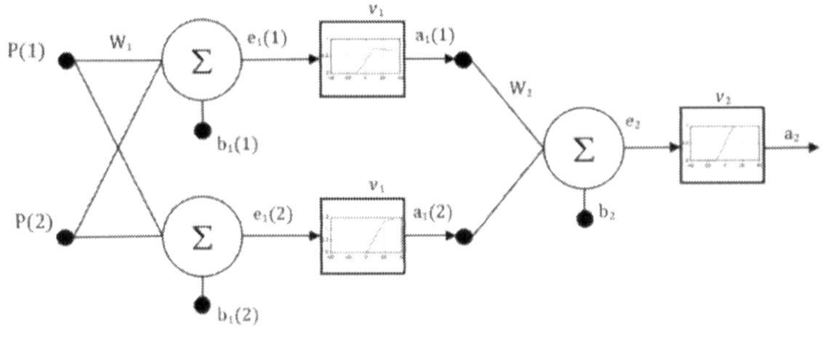

Fig. 2. FBP network architecture for the XOR problem.

The diagram of the network designed for this purpose is shown in Fig. 2. It has been assumed that for a randomly selected set of weights and bias $S\{w_1, b_1, w_2, b_2\}$ a learning process will be performed for successive smoothly changing values of parameter v in the presumed range $0 \le v \le 1.1$ for comparisons in series of tests. The network uses a discrete approximation of the fractional GL derivative of the log base (9) function f_B in case of shape and derivative acquiring respectively:

$$ {}_{e_0}D_e^{(v)} f_B(e) = \lim_{\substack{h\to 0 \\ e-e_0=kh}} \frac{1}{h^{v}} \left[a_0^{(v)} \cdots a_N^{(v)} \right] \begin{bmatrix} f_B(e) \\ f_B(e-h) \\ \vdots \\ f_B(e-kh) \end{bmatrix} \tag{30} $$

$$ {}_{e_0}D_e^{(v+1)} f_B(e) = \lim_{\substack{h\to 0 \\ e-e_0=kh}} \frac{1}{h^{v+1}} \left[a_0^{(v+1)} \cdots \right] \begin{bmatrix} f_B(e) \\ f_B(e-h) \\ \vdots \\ f_B(e-kh) \end{bmatrix} \tag{31} $$

The initial values of $S\{w_1, b_1, w_2, b_2\}$ have been shown in Table 1 and these values are common to each subsequent learning process. Those values have been obtained with standard randomizing procedure within the Matlab environment.

Table 1. Initial values of weights and biases.

w_1	b_1	w_2	b_2
$\begin{bmatrix} -0.6437 & 0.3816 \\ 0.2959 & -0.5189 \end{bmatrix}$	$\begin{bmatrix} 0.3594 \\ 0.9453 \end{bmatrix}$	$\begin{bmatrix} 0.4676 \\ 0.8049 \end{bmatrix}$	$\begin{bmatrix} -0.3847 \end{bmatrix}$

3 Results

In the experimental part of the work, it was assumed that the proposed FBP model will be tested in the task of solving the XOR problem. This is a task in which both the ability of the network to solve non-linearly separable tasks can be demonstrated as well as the convergence of its learning process can be tested. Using the initial values of the weights and biases, a number of learning processes were carried out and the obtained weights with biases are presented in Table 2.

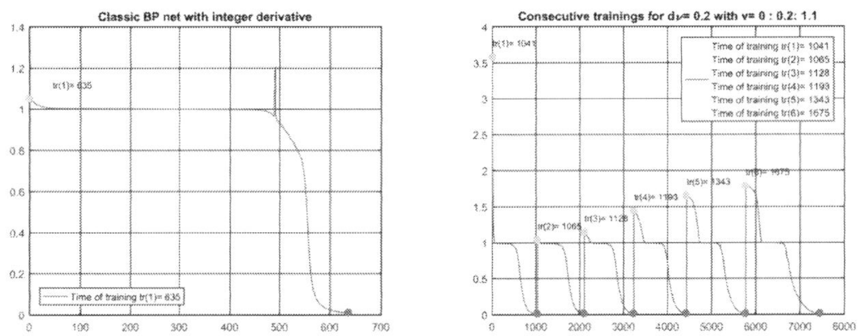

Fig. 3. The process of learning in classic BP network and FBP network.

In the initial phase of the experiments, we checked in general whether or not it is possible to obtain the convergence of the FBP algorithm for non-integer values of base function derivatives. The left part of Figure 3 shows the course of the learning process for the classical BP algorithm performed with the set of initial weights and biases set from Table 1. At the right part the course of the learning process in the FBP network for different values of the factor ν is shown. The BP network used for com-parisons uses the momentum mechanism and adaptive change of the learning rate coefficient.

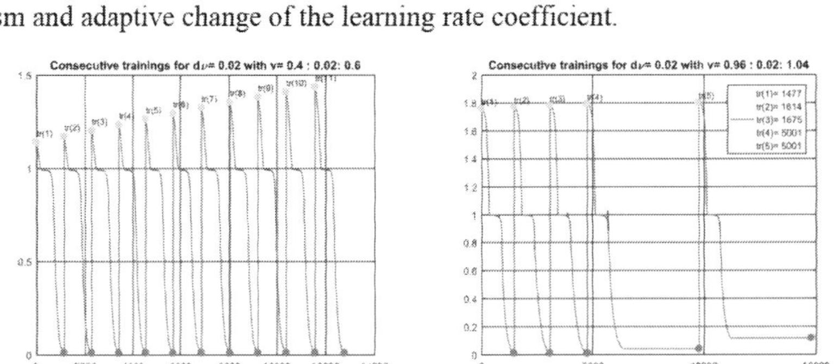

Fig. 4. The process of learning in FBP network with changing values of ν

The green circle marks denotes the beginning of the learning process, while the red circles indicates the end of the learning process. Figure Fig. 4 presents a juxtaposition of the learning processes of the designed network while changing values of the order of the fractional derivative.

Table 2. Exemplary set of output weights and biases

v	w_1	b_1	w_2	b_2
0	$\begin{bmatrix} -1.7680 & 1.9924 \\ 1.7593 & -2.0166 \end{bmatrix}$	$\begin{bmatrix} 0.2737 \\ 0.7265 \end{bmatrix}$	$\begin{bmatrix} 4.8772 \\ 3.7517 \end{bmatrix}$	$[-10.9198]$
0.4	$\begin{bmatrix} -2.4017 & 2.5566 \\ 2.4331 & -2.6003 \end{bmatrix}$	$\begin{bmatrix} 0.5253 \\ 0.9094 \end{bmatrix}$	$\begin{bmatrix} 24.6784 \\ 21.2607 \end{bmatrix}$	$[-11.6261]$
0.8	$\begin{bmatrix} -6.4156 & 6.7210 \\ 6.4970 & -6.8104 \end{bmatrix}$	$\begin{bmatrix} 1.6580 \\ 1.8947 \end{bmatrix}$	$\begin{bmatrix} 109.1401 \\ 103.2894 \end{bmatrix}$	$[-16.6733]$
0.95	$\begin{bmatrix} -9.2876 & 9.6286 \\ 9.3702 & -9.7175 \end{bmatrix}$	$\begin{bmatrix} 2.4140 \\ 2.6122 \end{bmatrix}$	$\begin{bmatrix} 178.4342 \\ 171.7803 \end{bmatrix}$	$[-19.5039]$
1.00	$\begin{bmatrix} -10.9679 & 11.3125 \\ 11.0490 & -11.4003 \end{bmatrix}$	$\begin{bmatrix} 2.6919 \\ 2.8678 \end{bmatrix}$	$\begin{bmatrix} 216.6709 \\ 209.9594 \end{bmatrix}$	$[-21.0725]$
1.05	$\begin{bmatrix} -13.0336 & 13.3789 \\ 13.1125 & -13.4647 \end{bmatrix}$	$\begin{bmatrix} 2.9994 \\ 3.1545 \end{bmatrix}$	$\begin{bmatrix} 262.5784 \\ 255.8864 \end{bmatrix}$	$[-22.7550]$

In the initial phase of the experiments, two exemplary variation ranges of v were adopted. In the first case for $v \in \langle 0.4, dv, ..., 0.6 \rangle$, where $dv = 0.02$. In the second case the network convergence process for $v \in \langle 0.96, dv, ..., 1.04 \rangle$ is shown. The process of BP and FBP networks training was carried out by assuming the following general learning parameters: $ME = 5000$, $EG = 0.01$, $\eta = 0.01$, where ME is the maximum epochs number, EG network SSE error, η the learining rate coefficient.

The modification of weights was performed with the use of the *Quickprop* mechanism, i.e. adaptive change of the learning rate coefficient combined with the momentum mechanism. Table 2 presents a sample result sets of weights and biases respectively, which were obtained as a consequence of successive learning processes.

4 Conclusion

The presented paper presents the FBP network model using a fractional order derivative mechanism. The network uses a GL derivative to obtain a base function and to calculate a discrete approximation of its derivative in individual layers. The proposed network learning model is a new approach that overcomes the limitations associated with properties of the single neuron transfer function known in the current subject literature. For the proposed FBP network model, simulations of network convergence under the XOR task were performed. The courses of the learning process illustrated in Fig. 3 and Fig. 4 allow the conclusion to be drawn that it is possible to carry out the learning process using a derivative of fractional order. The resulting weight sets presented in Table 2 indicate that it is possible to achieve the same minimum error function for different values of the derivative order and the assumed shapes of the base function. The accuracy of the fractional derivative approximation has a key influence on the accuracy of the determination of the weights and biases sets. The new algorithm of the error function minimization can be used for various base functions without the need to modify the IT model of the NNet. As a continuation of the ongoing research, experiments should be undertaken to determine the optimal selection of derivative approximation parameters for individual base functions. It is also necessary to examine the possibility of selecting specific base functions according to the class of the input signal being analyzed.

References

1. J.L. McClelland, Explorations in Parallel Distributed processing: A Handbook of Models, Programs, and Exercises, (2015)
2. J.Schmidhuber, Who Invented Backpropagation?, 2014 (updated 2015) http://people.idsia.ch/~juergen/who-invented-backpropagation.html
3. M Minsky, S Papert., Perceptrons: An Introduction to Computational Geometry, Expanded Edition Paperback, December 28, The MIT Press, Cambridge MA, ISBN 0-262-63022-2, (1987)
4. G. Dralus: Global models of dynamic complex systems – modelling using the multilayer neural networks, Annales UMCS Sectio AI Informatica Vol. 7, No 1 pp. 61-71, (2007)
5. E. Dudek-Dyduch: Algebraic Logical Meta-Model of Decision Processes - New Metaheuristics, Artificial Intelligence and Soft Computing Volume, ICAISC, pp 541-554, (2015)
6. Z. Gomolka, Neural networks in the analysis of fringe images (in Polish), PhD thesis, (2000)
7. Y. Kondratenko, V. Kondratenko: Soft Computing Algorithm for Arithmetic Multiplication of Fuzzy Sets Based on Universal Analytic Models, Information and Communication Technologies in Education, Research, and Industrial Application. Communications in Computer and Information Science, Springer International Publishing Switzerland, pp. 49-77, (2014)
8. T. Kwater, J. Bartman: Application of artificial neural networks in non-invasive identification of electric energy receivers, Progress in Applied Electrical Engineering (PAEE), Koscielisko, pp. 1-6, (2017)
9. B. Twaróg, Z. Gomółka, E Żesławska.: Time Analysis of Data Exchange in Distributed Control Systems Based on Wireless Network Model, Analysis and Simulation of Electrical and Computer Systems, Vol. 452, pp. 333-342,(2018)
10. Z. Gomolka, E. Dudek-Dyduch, Y.P Kondratenko.: From Homogeneous Network to Neural Nets with Fractional Derivative Mechanism, In: Artificial Intelligence and Soft Computing. ICAISC 2017. Lecture Notes in Computer Science, vol 10245, (2017)
11. Z. Gomolka, Neurons' Transfer Function Modeling with the Use of Fractional Derivative. In: Zamojski W., Mazurkiewicz J., Sugier J., Walkowiak T., Kacprzyk J. (eds) Contemporary Complex Systems and Their Dependability. DepCoS-RELCOMEX 2018. Advances in Intelligent Systems and Computing, vol 761. Springer, Cham, (2019)
12. U. Ghosh, S Sarkar., S. Das: Solution of system of linear fractional differential equations with modified derivative of Jumarie type, American Journal of Mathematical Analysis 3, No 3, pp. 72–84, (2015)
13. I. Moret: Shift-and-Invert Krylov Methods for Time-Fractional Wave Equations, Numerical Functional Analysis and Optimization, Vol. 36, Issue 1, pp. 86-103,(2015)
14. M. D. Ortigueira: Riesz potential operators and inverses via fractional centered derivatives, Int. J. Math. Math. Sci, Article ID 48391, pp. 1–12, (2006)

15. A. Oustaloup, F. Levron, B. Mathieu, F. M. Nanot: Frequency-band complex noninteger differentiator: characterization and synthesis, IEEE Trans. on Circuits and Systems I: Fundamental Theory and Applications I, Vol. 47, pp. 25–39,(2000)
16. D., Cao Labora, R. Rodriguez-Lopez From fractional order equations to integer order equations, Fractional Calculus and Applied Analysis, Vol. 20, No 6, pp. 1405-1423,(2017)
17. Y. Q. Chen, K. L. Moore: Discretization Schemes for Fractional-Order Differentiators and Integrators, IEEE Trans. On Circuits and Systems - I: Fundamental Theory and Applications, Vol. 49, No. 3, pp. 363–367, (2002)
18. H., Li, C. Ding: High-order algorithms for Riesz derivative and their applications, Numerical Methods for Partial Differential Equations, Vol. 33, Issue 5, (2017)
19. W.-H. Luo, C. Li, T.-Z Huang., Gu X.-M., Wu G.-C.: A High-Order Accurate Numerical Scheme for the Caputo Derivative with Applications to Fractional Diffusion Problems, Numerical Functional Analysis and Optimization, Vol. 39, Issue 5, pp. 600-622, (2018)
20. D. Xue: Computational Aspect of Fractional-Order Control Problems, Tutorial Workshop on Fractional Order Dynamic Systems and Controls, Proceedings of the WCICA'2010, China, (mechatronics.ece.usu.edu/foc/cdc10tw/code-matlab-simulink /xdy_foccode.rar), (2010)
21. D. Hengfei, L. Changpin, Ch. YangQuan: High-Order Algorithms for Riesz Derivative and Their Applications, Journal of Computational Physics, Vol. 293, 15, 2015, pp. 218-237
22. M. D. Ortigueira, J.A. T. Machado: What is a fractional derivative?, Journal of Computational Physics, Volume 293, 15 July 2015, pp. 4-13, (2015)
23. I. Petraš: Fractional Derivatives, Fractional Integrals, and Fractional Differential Equations in Matlab, Computer and Information Science – Engineering Education and Research Using MATLAB, ISBN 978-953-307-656-0, pp. 239-264, 2011
24. I. Podlubny: Matrix approach to discrete fractional calculus, Fractional Calculus and Applied Analysis, Vol. 3, pp. 359–386, (2000)
25. H. Sheng, Y. Li, Y. Q. Chen: Application of numerical inverse Laplace transform algorithms in fractional calculus, J. Franklin Inst., Vol. 348, pp. 315–330, (2011)
26. B. M. Vinagre, I Podlubny., Hernández A., Feliu, V.: Some approximations of fractional order operators used in control theory and applications, Fractional Calculus and Applied Analysis, Vol. 3, pp. 231–248, (2000)

ITM Web of Conferences **21**, 00005 (2018) https://doi.org/10.1051/itmconf/20182100005
CST 2018

Adaptive concept of state estimation with incomplete state vector measurement

Tadeusz Kwater[1*], *Paweł Krutys*[1], *Robert Pękala*[2], *Bogdan Kwiatkowski*[1]

[1] University of Rzeszow, Faculty of Mathematics and Natural Sciences, Department of Computer Engineering

[2] The State Higher School of Technology and Economics in Jaroslaw

Abstract. The paper presents the design and simulation experiments of the adaptive approach in the estimation of the object state realized by filter whose gain is calculated on-line. The adopted concept of determining the gain uses a defined for this purpose signal called an error and on the basis of its waveform features introduces an incremental correction of the amplification factor of the estimation filter. The obtained results of state estimation are characterized by stability and strong correctness even for cases of non-stationary disturbances

1 Introduction

Presently in engineering due to the contemporary requirements formulated to increase research and development of methods available makes it dominate the so-called "soft tasks", the essence of which are: probabilistic methods, approximate sets, uncertain variables, fuzzy logic, neural networks and adaptive algorithms. They provide a highly differentiated formal apparatus, especially as these methods can be combined. It seeks to apply first of all specialized computer techniques, thanks to which processes of automation of measurement and globalization of information systems are more effective [1]. Approaches associated to adaptation strategies can lead to sequential Monte Carlo algorithms also called molecular filter methods [1, 2, 3]. This is connected to additional requirements in terms of computing power. Many issues related to object recognition are solved using ANN-learning. In such cases there is a need for a learning process usually associated with data preprocessing [4, 5, 6]. The article proposes the construction of an algorithm with an adaptive approach to state estimation by a filter (similar to the Kalman filter), in which the gain coefficient is modified depending on the some characteristic features of the error signal defined for this purpose. Simulation studies were conducted for a biochemically contaminated river described by partial differential equations. When interpreting the description of these phenomena along the so-called characteristics, a set of ordinary differential equations was obtained [7]. This approach ensures unchanged accuracy of the description of biochemical phenomena in the river. For a thorough assessment of estimation process is employed the Root Mean Square Error (RMSE) similar as were used in [8, 9].

2 Mathematical model of the polluted river

Two indicators, ie biochemical oxygen demand (BOD) and demend oxygen (DO), were used to describe river water quality. Model equations were obtained by considering the

* Corresponding author: tkwater@ur.edu.pl

mass balance of oxygen. For a better interpretation of large lateral tributaries, the river was divided into sections between these tributaries.

The mathematical model BOD-DO for the part of the river considered by the i-th section of the river takes on the form [7, 10 - 11]:

$$\frac{d}{dt}x_i + \frac{d}{dz}Vx_i = Ax_i + Bw \tag{1a}$$

with boundary conditions:

$$x(0,t),\ x(z,t_0) \tag{1b}$$

where: $x(x,t) = col[x_1, x_2]$ - vector representing respectively BOD and DO, $w_r(z,t)$ - vector representing the noise of a distributed, $V = \begin{bmatrix} v & 0 \\ 0 & v \end{bmatrix}$ - diagonal matrix with flow velocities v, $A = \begin{bmatrix} -k_1 & 0 \\ -k_2 & -k_3 \end{bmatrix}$ - a state matrix in which the coefficients k_i of the self-purification rate of water, $B = \begin{bmatrix} 1 & 0 \\ 0 & 1 \end{bmatrix}$ - matrix influence of the disturbances, $w = col[w_1 \ \ w_2]$ - Vector of influenced of the local sources of oxygen from photosynthesis, oxygen consumption by bottom sediments or BOD and DO small inflows [10, 11].

The boundary conditions included in the model are described by initial and boundary conditions.

Initial condition – refers to the whole length of the segment at the moment $t = t_0$

$$x_i(z,t_0) = x_{i0}(z) \tag{2}$$

Boundary condition - refers to the beginning of the section under consideration in the time domain:

$$x_i(0,t) = M_i x_{i-1}(1,t) + w_{bi}(t) + R_{bi}u_{bi}(t) \tag{3}$$

Another way of interpreting the process of river purification is to convert partial differential equations into many ordinary differential equations along the so-called characteristics. It is based on the interpretation of the description of water pollution in the case when BOD and RT index values are observed for a freely moving volume of water. Then the quality indicators depend only on time. For the *i-th* section of the river the characteristics are defined by the dependence:

$$\frac{d}{dt}z_i(t) = v_i(z_i(t)) \tag{4}$$

whose boundary points satisfy the condition:

$$\int_{t_{0,i}}^{t_{0,i+1}} v_i(z_i(t))dt + z_{oi} = 1 \tag{5}$$

where $z_{0i} \in [0,1]$ It is the coordinate of the initial point t_{01}.

It was assumed that the measurement is carried out only one coordinate state. Selection is based on ease of implementation measurements and concerns the x_2 (DO). The resignation of x_1 (BOD) measurements results from the need for long-term laboratory service, which makes them useless, for exemple in the control process. So the measurement equation is as follows:

$$y(t) = Cx_2(t) + v_p(t) \tag{6}$$

where: $C = [0,1]$ – this is a measurement matrix, $v_p(t)$ – This is a measurement distortion with Gaussian distribution.
The state of polluted river on the characteristics described by ordinary differential equations receiving form:

$$\frac{d}{dt}x(z_i(t),t) = A(z_i(t))x(z_i(t),t) + Bw_r(x_i(t),t) \tag{7}$$

where the initial condition takes the form: $x(z_i(t_0),t_0) = x_0(z_{i0})$, $i = 1,2,3,...$
B - matrix influence of the disturbances, and w_r is the signal noise of disturbance. For the object described by equations (7) and measurements (6), we formulate the problem of estimation [11 - 13].

3 The process estimation of state by the filter

Approximation of actual description of phenomena by means of mathematical modeling is not an easy task. Among the many solutions to, the following: a mathematical model of the stochastic signals are added to the appropriate distribution. They represent the variability of external factors. The main task of estimation in such cases is to obtain the best possible information about the system based on measurements. A good solution is to use the Kalman filter. In this class of linear estimators, it provides a minimum mean square error of estimation. In practice, it may happen that the measurement does not include all coordinates of the state vector. This means that not all elements of the state vector are used to reproduce the full state vector [11, 14 -16]. This effect is especially useful in control systems where missing system information can be obtained from disturbed and indirect measurements. In general, the Kalman filter is a recursive algorithm for estimating the state vector model of a dynamic system using measurements of this system.
The Kalman filter equation is given by the following differential equation:

$$\dot{\hat{x}}(t) = A\hat{x}(t) + K_F(t)(y(t) - C\hat{x}(t)), \hat{x}(t_0) \tag{8}$$

where: y – measurements, and K_F – the gain coefiction of Kalman filter:

$$K_F(t) = \tilde{P}(t)C^T R^{-1} \tag{9}$$

in which $\tilde{P}(t)$, C, R are, respectively, the estimation error covariance matrix, the measurement matrix and the covariance of measurement disturbances from equation (6).
In order to determine $K_F(t)$ the matrix $\tilde{P}(t)$ representing the covariance of the estimation error should be known we need to know this matrix. It fulfills the following Riccati's differential equation:

$$\frac{d\tilde{P}}{dt} = A\tilde{P}(t) + \tilde{P}(t)A^T - \tilde{P}(t)C^T R^{-1} C\tilde{P}(t) + LQL^T, t \geq t_0, \tag{10}$$

with initial condition,

$$\tilde{O}(s_/) < O's_/(\tag{11}$$

Finally, to determine the state estimate is necessary to solve two equations, ie. A filter equation and Riccati equation. The quality of the estimate obtained from equation (11) depends to a large extent on the filter gain $K_F(t)$. Its value depends on the characteristics of the stochastic signals affecting the given data object in the form of covariance of system and measurement disturbances. Determining the covariance of disturbance signals is sometimes a difficult task. Therefore, other solutions to eliminate these obstacles are being sought. One of the proposals is an approach in which the filter gain coefficient adaptively adjusts.

5 Adaptive modification of the filter gain

In the proposed filter based on measurements recursively determines the estimate of the state vector of the object and modification gain filter. It should be noted that both the object and the measurements are subjected to disturbaced signals. This approach avoids the inconvenience of having to estimate the characteristics of the signals affecting the object under consideration. They can be much differentiated. At Kalman's approach, nonlinear differential equations are solved to determine the filter gain coefficient. The essence of the proposed approach is the application of the difference between the measurement and the corresponding co-ordinate state estimate. This defined signal will be used to correct the value of the gain coefficient. This correction is made for each measurement moment with a suitable precaution coefficient. With these assumptions, the constructed filter determines the estimation values based on the measurements and the actual gain KF . The value of the filter gain correction it comes from the minimization error of the estimation, which results in the "adaptation" to the current conditions of the object's functioning. The algorithmic diagram of the algorithm is presented in Fig. 1.
The definition of an adaptive error is defined by the following relationship:

$$\varepsilon(t) = y(t) - \hat{x}_2(t) \tag{12}$$

where: $y(t)$ – the measurement at time t, and $\hat{x}_2(t)$ – estimate indicator of DO.

An error derivative is also used for the gain correction calculation, which assumes the following form:

$$\frac{d\varepsilon(t_2)}{dt} = \left(\varepsilon(t_2) - \varepsilon(t_1)\right) / dt, t_2 > t_1 \tag{13}$$

The change in gain coefficients was assumed to be incremental, as did the change in weights in neuronal networks, according to the following formula:

$$K_{F_N} = K_{F_S} + \eta \cdot dK_F \tag{14}$$

where: K_{F_N} - value of the filter gain factor after adjustment, dK_F – correction of filter gain increase, K_{F_S} – Initial value of the filter gain coefficient, η =(0….1) – Coefficient of change precaution .

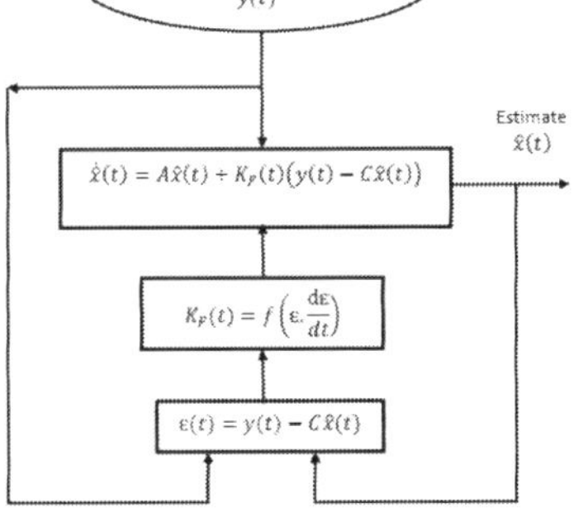

Fig. 1. Block diagram of adaptive estimation of state.

Calculation of the increase of gain filter dK_F taken as a proportional function or in the form of tabulated and made dependent on the threshold value of the error ε, and the operation of addition or subtraction of the gain is carried out depending on the sign of the derivative of error. The implementation of this task is shown in the block diagram in Figure 2. In the case of large errors of the ε, the value of precaution ηis smaller, which affects the stability of the algorithm. The values of η in the algorithm were chosen using the experimental method. Stabilization and improvement of the quality of the adaptive algorithm was also obtained by taking into account several previous measurements relative to the current one. The change in the error value from the previous step significantly affected the change in the filter gain coefficient. Stabilization and improvement of the quality of the adaptive algorithm was also obtained by taking into account several previous measurements relative to the current one. The change in the error value from the previous step significantly affected the change in the filter gain coefficient.

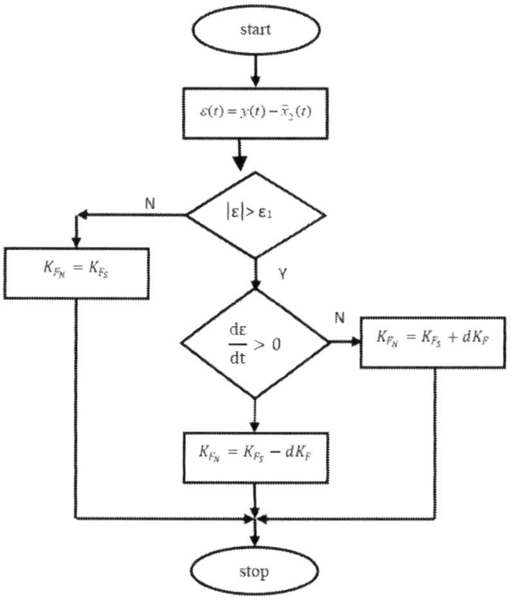

Fig. 2. Block diagram for calculating increment of filter gain coefficient changes.

The global block diagram of the adaptive algorithm is shown in Figure 3. It is worth noting that Block A is a schematic in which the conditions for changes in the gain factor of a filter are determined based on the value of errors and their derivatives in the so-called observation window.

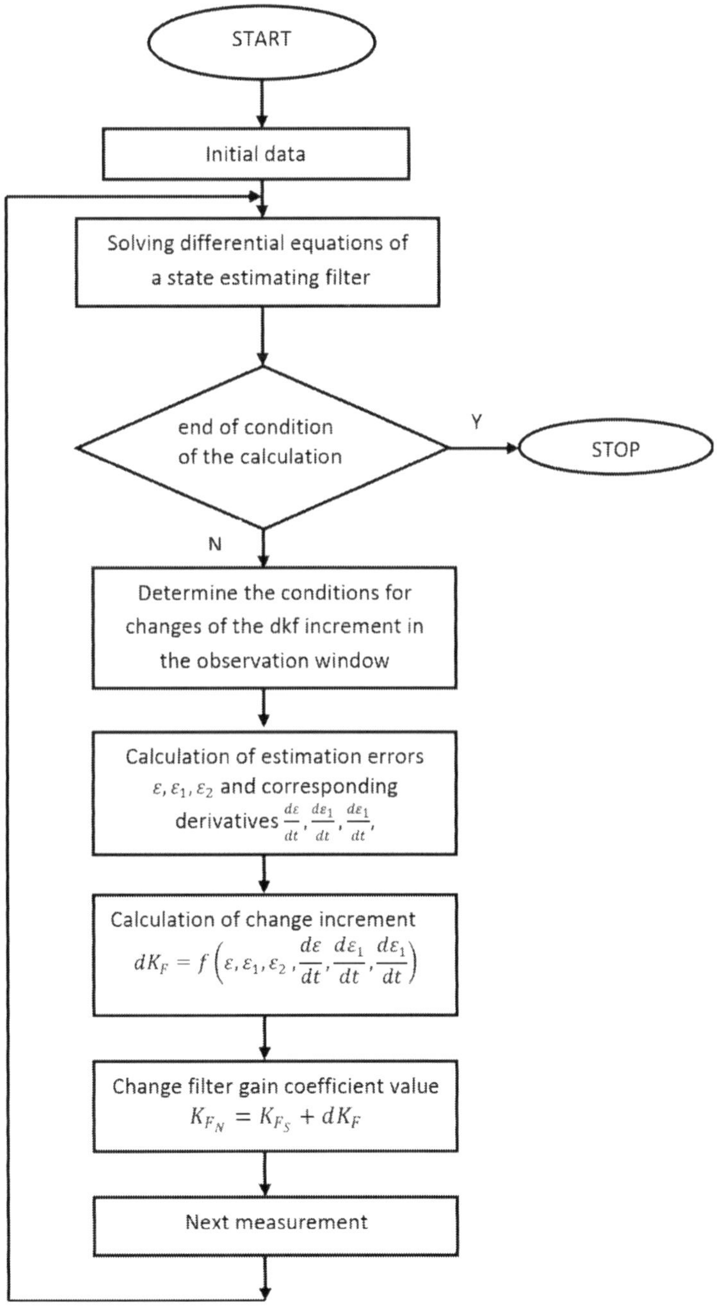

Fig. 3. Schematic flow diagram of an adaptive state estimation

The conducted simulation experiments were made for different values of configuration parameters occurring in the algorithm. As a measure of the quality of estimation accepted the square root of the integral squared estimation error, respectively for BOD and RT expressed formulas:

$$WSB = \sqrt{\frac{1}{T}\int_0^T \varepsilon_1^2 dt} \tag{15a}$$

$$WSB = \sqrt{\frac{1}{T}\int_0^T \varepsilon_2^2 dt} \tag{15b}$$

In which $\varepsilon_1(t) = x_1(t) - \hat{x}_1(t)$, $\varepsilon_2(t) = x_2(t) - \hat{x}_2(t)$ and x_1 , $\hat{x}_1$ is the coordinate of the BOD state and its estimate, while x_2 , $\hat{x}_2$- is the DO coordinate and its estimate.

6 The simulation results

In simulation studies, many algorithms were changed. In each case, stable solutions were obtained, ie estimations followed the changes in the state vector.

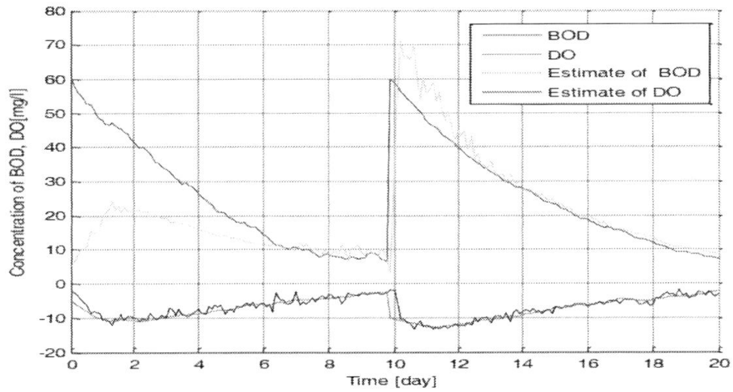

Fig. 4. BOD and DO changes and their estimation.

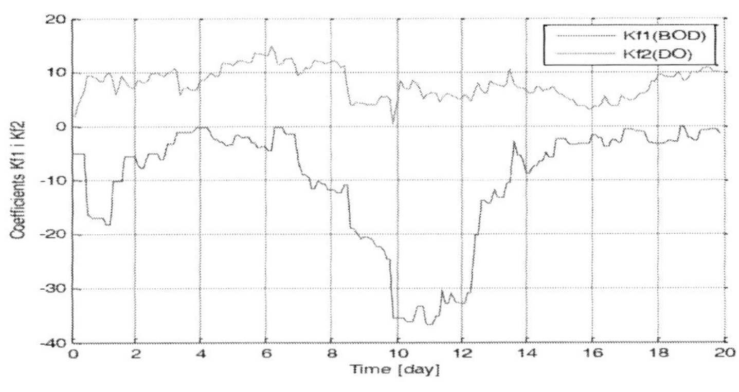

Fig. 5. Filter gain coefficients.

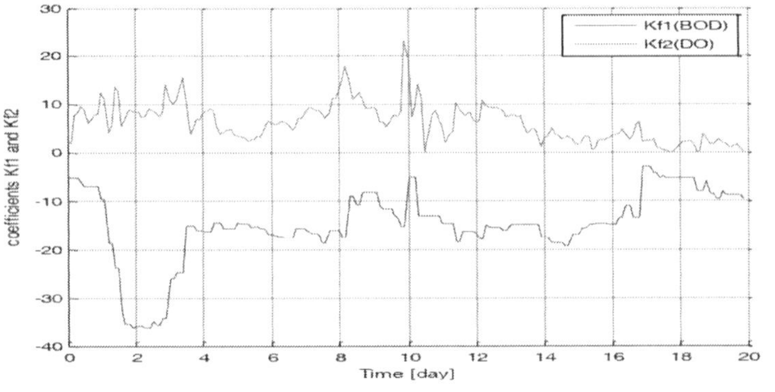

Fig. 6. Filter gain coefficients.

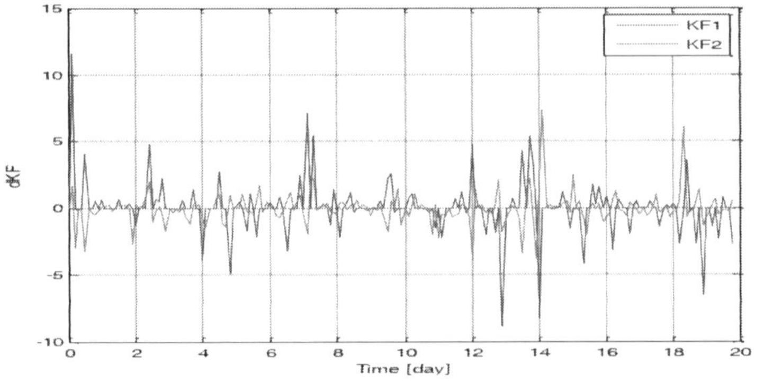

Fig. 7. Changes in gain coefficients.

In numerous simulation experiments, the intensity of measurement and system disturbances was changed. The sample results of the estimation quality tests are presented in Table 1. In all cases, the correctness was obtained, which consisted in the fact that the BOD (15.a) rates always took much higher values than the ratios for RT (15.b).

Table 1. Values of estimation quality indicators.

Nr.	Standard deviation for the BOD ratio	Standard deviation for the DO ratio	Standard deviation of the measurement	Estimation quality indicator for BOD	Estimation quality indicator for DO
1	5.0	2.0	1.0	13.5	1.5
2	3.0	4.0	2.0	13.5	1.75
3	10.0	5.0	2.0	17.5	1.3
4	5.5	2.5	1.0	14.5	1.0
5	5.0	2.0	1.0	12.5	1.2

This is due to the nature of the process being carried out, for which only the coordinate RT is measured. This means that information from the measurement of the BOD are small hence the great value of the index for the estimation of the BOD. The slight differences between positions 1 and 5 for the estimation indices (columns 5 and 6) result from a different implementation of the generated disturbances.

Summary

The article proposes an algorithm to estimate the state in the form of a filter similar to the Kalman filter with adaptive selection of its gain. Its operation was realized using a defined error as the difference between the measurement and the corresponding indicator. It should be emphasized that the assumptions do not include all the coordinates of the state vector. In order to increase its flexibility and precision of operation, measurement window taking into account several previous measurements. The conducted simulation experiments for a hypothetical river with a length of 400 kilometers of polluted tributary in the middle of its length. The solution of differential equations was implemented by the Runge-Kutta algorithm, fourth order. For all cases, satisfactory results have been obtained, ie, the time course of the estimate and the coordinates of the state have always been consistent. The research involved changing the various parameters of the adaptive algorithm. Sudden large changes in BOD can be regarded as polluted large side inlets or as a non-stationary processes. For such cases, satisfactory results have been obtained. It turned out that the different initial values of the gain factor (if they are from the same range) did not have a significant effect on the results of the estimation of the state. The characteristic of the obtained estimation is the better quality for the estimation for which the measurements are made. The filter, despite the lack of BOD information (no measurements) generated its estimate of the correct trend of change. The implementation of the algorithm does not require high computing Power.

References

1. Kacprzyk J., Hryniewicz O., Kulczycki P. Techniki informacyjne w badaniach systemowych. WNT, Warszawa 2007.
2. Cornebise J., E Moulines, J Olsson, Adaptive refueling in particle filter algorithms, Workshop New directions in Monte Carlo Methods (2007), Fleurance, 25-29
3. Cornebise J., Moulines É., Olsson J., Adaptive methods for sequential importance sampling with application to state space models, 2008.
4. Farhang-Boroujeny B., „Adaptive Filters. Theory and Applicationsl, Wiley, 1998.
5. Kasprzak W., Adaptive computation methods in digital image sequence analysis. Warsaw University of Technology, Warszawa, No. 127, 2000
6. E. Dudek-Dyduch, Z. Gomolka, Neural network design without learning, Neural Networks and Soft Computing Book Series: Advances in Soft Computing, pp: 179-187, (2003)
7. Chapra Steven C., Surface water-quality modeling, Waveland Press Inc., 2008
8. Z. Gomolka, B. Twarog, J. Bartman, Improvement of image processing by using homogeneous neural networks with fractional derivatives theorem, Discrete and Continuous Dynamical Systems- Series AI, ssue SUPPL., Pages 505-514, (2011)
9. Z. Gomolka, Neurons' Transfer Function Modeling with the Use of Fractional Derivative. DepCoS-RELCOMEX 2018., vol 761. (2019)
10. Kwater T., Krutys P.: Estimation of pollution of the river by artificial neural networks, Symbiosis of Engineering and Computer Science Wydawnictwo Uniwersytetu Rzeszowskiego, Rzeszów 2010, ISBN 978-83-7338-620-4, pp.37-66
11. Z.Gomolka, B.Twarog, E. Zeslawska, A. Lewicki, T. Kwater, Using Artificial Neural Networks to Solve the Problem Represented by BOD and DO Indicators, Water 2018, 10(1), 4; https://doi.org/10.3390/w10010004

12. Pooran Singh Mahar, Bithin Datta, Optimal Identification of Ground-Water Pollution Sources and Parameter Estimation, Journal of Water Resources Planning and Management, Vol. 127, Issue 1 (February 2001)
13. Fox D., Adapting the sample size in particle filters through KLD-sampling Res. 22(11), 2008.
14. Haykin S.: Adaptive Filter Theory. Englewood Cliffs, New York: Prentice-Hall, 1991.
15. Singh M. G., Dynamical hierarchical control. North-Holland, Amsterdam 1977.
16. Z. Gomolka, B. Twarog, E. Zeslawska, Cognitive Investigation on Pilot Attention During Take-Offs and Landings Using Flight Simulator. Artificial Intelligence and Soft Computing., vol 10246., (2017)

The monitoring system based on lookup algorithm for objects described by ordinary differential equations

Przemysław Hawro[1*], *Tadeusz* Kwater[2] and *Dariusz* Strzęciwilk[3]

[1] The State Higher School of Technology and Economics in Jaroslaw, Institute of Technical Engineering, 37-500 Jaroslaw, Poland
[2] University of Rzeszow, Faculty of Mathematics and Natural Sciences, Department of Computer Engineering, 35-959 Rzeszow, Poland
[3] Warsaw University of Life Sciences - SGGW, Faculty of Applied Informatics and Mathematics, Department of Applied Informatics, 02-787 Warsaw, Poland

Abstract. The article presents a new approach to monitoring systems of a certain class using the lookup algorithm. The main task is to generate object signals based on measured but only some selected signals. This idea is based on the Kalman filter approach, but the calculation method of the gain coefficients is different. Its values are determined in a similar way as weights in neural networks during learning (incremental method). The proposed lookup algorithm uses expert knowledge a priori for determining gain corrections, and its functioning is presented for the case of two monitoring error zones. The presented results clearly indicate the advantage of the lookup algorithm over the Kalman filter. Two RMSE and MPE indicators were used for the quality of monitoring..

1 Introduction

In the present conditions of society development to ensure required the quality and speed action of diagnostic for dynamic systems monitoring, the latest solutions based on adaptive approaches and more are used. Studies related to this concern most of the linear dynamical systems in a discrete version, and the analysis uses different types of recursive algorithms resulting from the methodology of solving differential equations [1].

The matter of monitoring technological processes or the state of the environment is of key importance for the operational management of this process. Information obtained as a result of monitoring, after their proper analysis, enables a more complete and efficient production process, as well as a more complete picture of environments in which may be signals warning against threats such situations as high concentrations of pollutants [2].

One solution is to use an approach that uses the Kalman filter algorithm and its variations characterized by certain limitations [1, 3-8]. These constraints may concern requirements such as linearity of objects and knowledge of covariance of disturbances signals [9, 10], which in practice is sometimes difficult to determine.

* Corresponding author: przemyslaw.hawro@pwste.edu.pl

The use of the extended Kalman filter algorithm or the Luenberger observer may improve the quality of observed signals and give a greater generalization in relation to the basic Kalman filter, but there are still requirements in the form of the need to know the covariance of disturbances signals [11, 12].

In other approaches, statistical methods are proposed that use certain sets of data collected over a longer period of time, which is inconvenient by the need to collect these data and these calculation are not able to determine dynamic changes in current monitoring signals [6].

Very often for support the process monitoring systems use the capabilities of artificial intelligence to [13, 14]. Signal waveforms with dynamic changes are obtained there, but it is necessary to knowlege the mathematical model of the object and to collect and storage of data sets necessary in the process of teaching artificial intelligence.

2. Kalman filter

The Kalman filter is used for dynamic systems described by linear differential equations. It determines the estimate of the state vector, using the knowledge of input and measurement signals. It should also be assumed that the disturbances affecting system signals and measuring noise have a normal distribution with known covariances [1, 9]. The Kalman filter algorithm uses the following relationships:

$$\dot{\hat{x}} = A\hat{x} + K_F[y - C\hat{x}], \hat{x}(0) \tag{1}$$

$$K_F = PC^T V^{-1}, \tag{2}$$

in which K_F is the filter gain coefficient to determine which one needs to know the estimation error covariance matrix P. This matrix is determined by solving the Riccati non-linear differential equation::

$$\frac{d}{dt}P = AP + PA^T - PC^T V^{-1} CP + DWD^T \tag{3}$$

where: V – measurement error covariance matrix, W – system disturbances covariance matrix, A – matrix of system dynamics, C – measurement matrix, D – disturbances interaction matrix.

The optimum of the Kalman filter depends mainly on the determine the statistics accuracy of the disturbances interacting on system and measuring which are characterized by their covariances W and V. However, if the covariance of these signals is insufficiently defined, the accuracy of the estimation will deteriorate, leading to the lack of optimality of the solution. Accurate specification of disturbance characteristics is a difficult task, especially when these signals result from changing environmental conditions.

This article proposes a solution using an adaptive approach that does not require knowledge of disturbance signals and high accuracy of the mathematical model of the monitored system.

3 The monitoring system using lookup algorithm

In the article, the studies are aimed at determining on-line the desired object signals. An interesting situation is when no signal measurements are made, and it is expected monitoring these signals is required. One of such solutions may be the use of the certain idea Kalman filter algorithm in which the final results are obtained from calculations carried out in a different way.

The monitoring system consists in generating signals when their an immediate measurement is not possible. It uses only easy and quick to implement measurements. The system, which monitoring only measurable signals, gives an incomplete picture of the object (see Fig. 1). The estimators or state observers are often used to determine the immeasurable signals of object's [11].

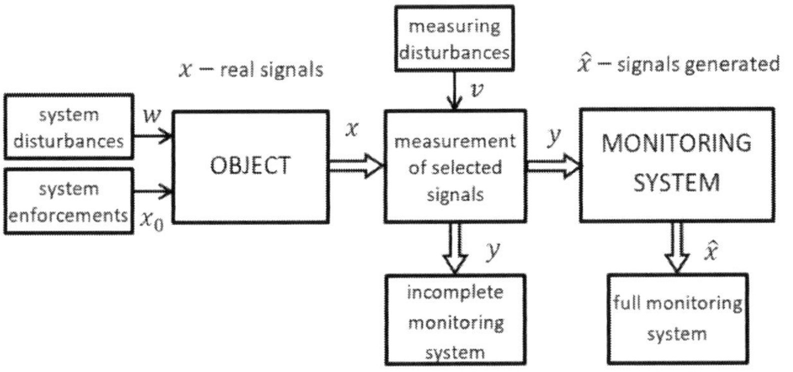

Fig. 1. Block diagram of the idea of the monitoring system.

Fig. 1 presents the idea of an monitoring system that generates all the interesting signals even without knowing the characteristics of measurement or system disturbances affecting the object. The idea of this monitoring system is based on clever lookup algorithm of gain coefficient value.

The proposed algorithm consists in determining the current gain values in equation (1) for each measurement step. Determination of this gain does not depend on the knowledge of the parameters of the extortion signals statistics, which we assume as an undefined disturbances. The authors assumed gain will be incrementally modified by determined gain corrections ΔK. The values of these corrections depend on the value measurable signal $\varepsilon(t)$ defined for the needs of the algorithm, called in future considerations as current measurement monitoring error. Its value was defined as the difference between the current measurement $y(t)$ and the corresponding coordinate of the monitored signal vector $\hat{x}$ defined by the dependence:

$$\varepsilon(t) = y(t) - C\hat{x}(t) \tag{4}$$

where $\varepsilon(t)$– current measurement monitoring error in a given step, C – measurement matrix.

The current value of the gain coefficient K_{S_i} is determined in accordance with the following expression:

$$K_{S_i} = K_{S_{i-1}} + \Delta K_{Z2} \tag{5}$$

in which: K_{S_i} – the gain coefficient in a given time step, $K_{S_{i-1}}$ – the gain coefficient in the previous step, ΔK_{Z2} – correction of the gain coefficient resulting from the accepted assignments $\varepsilon(t)$ to the zone.

The general block diagram of the proposed algorithm for object monitoring is shown in Fig. 2.

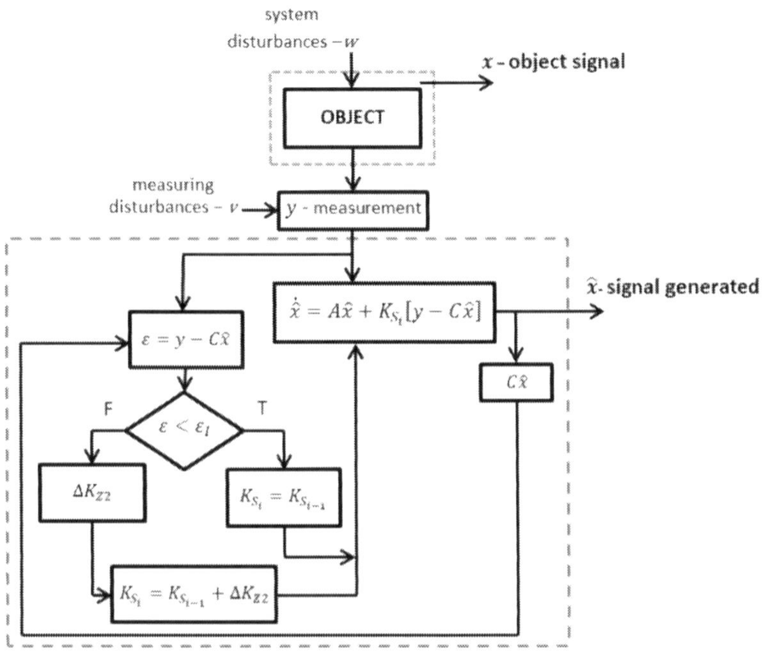

Fig. 2. Block diagram of an clever lookup algorithm

The presented algorithm selects the appropriate correction of the gain coefficient ΔK_{Zi} depending on the current value of the current measurement monitoring error ε. In the case when the value of the error ε is lower than the assumed error limit ε_I (first zone) then the correction of the gain coefficient is zero (see Fig. 3). This means that an actual monitoring error is at most equal acceptable error ε_I. If the current measurement monitoring error is greater than restriction of error , the correction of the gain coefficient is different to zero and taken from table (see Fig. 3 again). The general pattern of gain coefficient modification is carried out in accordance with the rule (5). It is worth emphasizing that the gain is updated for each measurement step.

In the proposed solution, only two values of gain corrections are determined. This means that the ranges of current measurement monitoring error values obtained during the process of approximating the monitored signals have been divided into only 2 zones. For each zone a fixed value of the correction of the gain coefficient ΔK_{Zi} (i = 1,2) was adopted.

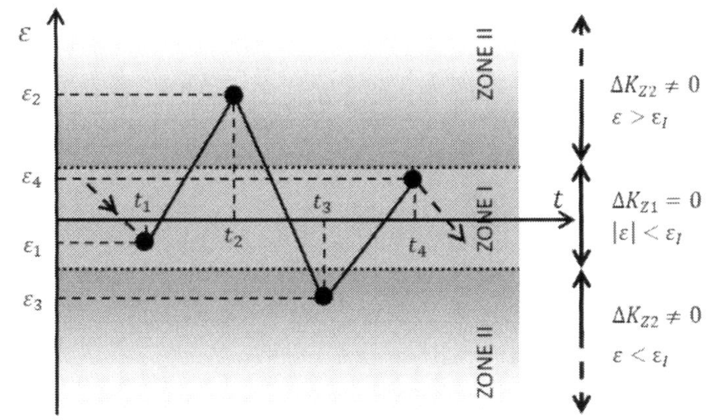

Fig. 3. Current measurement monitoring error and gain corrections of the monitoring system

The value of the correction ΔK_{Zi} in the proposed algorithm depends on the specificity of the given object and is selected experimentally on the basis of expert knowledge. This correction may take different values depending on the adopted assumptions.

The gain update is incremental in a similar way as is the case with weights in the neural network learning process [15]. The algorithm is able to correctly execute the process for unknown initial conditions and even for the initial K_{S_i}gain coefficient of zero.

4 Object - biochemically polluted river

The mathematical model of the biochemically polluted river usually describes partial differential equations of the hyperbolic type [16]. To simplify the model, without losing the accuracy of description of phenomena, considerations along the so-called characteristics, which results in a set of ordinary differential equations. This interpretation concerns changes in time of water quality indicators, i.e. biochemical oxygen demand (BOD) and dissolved oxygen (DO) deficiency in a free flowing volume of water moving at a certain speed [17].

The values of these indicators is determined by the differential equations presenting the kinetics of the physico-chemical properties of the form:

$$\frac{d}{dt}x_1(t) = -k_1x_1(t) + w_1 \tag{6}$$

$$\frac{d}{dt}x_2(t) = -k_2x_1(t) - k_3x_2(t) + w_2 \tag{7}$$

in which: x_1 [mg/l] – concentration of organic pollutants (BOD), x_2 [mg/l] – deficiency DO, t [day] – time, k_1, k_2, k_3 [day^{-1}] – coefficients speed of indicators (BOD, DO) reaction, w_1 [mg/l·day] – intensity of pollutants BOD, w_2 [mg/l·day] – oxygen production intensity (eg bottom sediments, sedimentation).

The equations (6, 7) can be written in a vector form:

$$\frac{d}{dt}\mathbf{x}(t) = A\mathbf{x}(t) + D\mathbf{w}(t) \tag{8}$$

with initial conditions $\mathbf{x}(0)$,
where: $\mathbf{x} = \begin{bmatrix} x_1 \\ x_2 \end{bmatrix}$ – vector representing concentrations from (6, 7) as water quality indicators, $\mathbf{w} = \begin{bmatrix} w_1 \\ w_2 \end{bmatrix}$ – vector of system disturbances, $A = \begin{bmatrix} k_1 & 0 \\ k_2 & k_3 \end{bmatrix}$ – a matrix defining the state vector coordinates change dynamics $\mathbf{x}$, $D = \begin{bmatrix} 1 & 0 \\ 0 & 1 \end{bmatrix}$ – disturbances interactions matrix.

The measurement equation for our considerations takes the form:

$$y(t) = C\mathbf{x}(t) + v(t) \tag{9}$$

where: $C = [0\ 1]$ – measurement matrix, v – measuring disturbance.

The main disadvantage in the commonly measurement BOD methods is that we get the results with some delay (5–20 days), because they require laboratory service. Other features have DO measurements, they can be easily carried up to date. Therefore, for the purpose of water quality monitoring, an algorithm using only the DO measurement will be used.

The inaccuracy of the model parameters

A very important issue in estimating the state using the Kalman filter is knowing the characteristics of disturbances affecting the object and the exact determination of the mathematical model of the object.

In the case of the river model, the coefficients contained in the matrix A depend in general on the temperature. The research shows that these coefficients can take values from the range: $k_1 = -0.2204 \div -0.3347$ [mg/l], $k_2 = -0.1636 \div -0.2049$ [mg/l], $k_3 = -0.71 \div -0.81$ [mg/l] [18].

Fig. 4 presents the signal waveforms of the mathematical model (8) obtained for extreme values of k_i (i = 1,2,3) during the experiments.

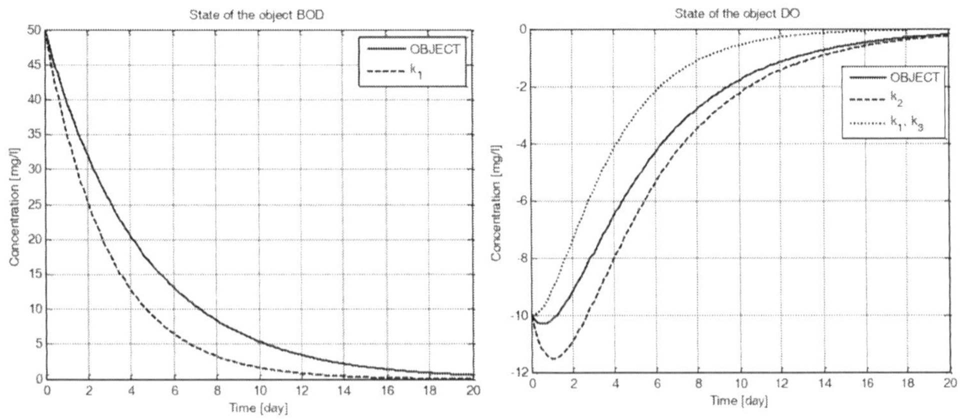

Fig. 4. BOD and DO with changes in the coefficients of the state matrix A.

For the BOD signal, only the change in the coefficient k_1 affects its waveforms, and the maximum difference is around 7 ÷ 8 [mg/l] on the 4th day(see Fig 4 left). The coefficients k_1, k_2, k_3 influence the course of DO, where the maximum difference is around 4 [mg/l] on the 4th day (see Fig 4 right).

Fig. 5 presents simulations of signal waveforms for the Kalman filter and our lookup algorithm with variable values of coefficients k_i.

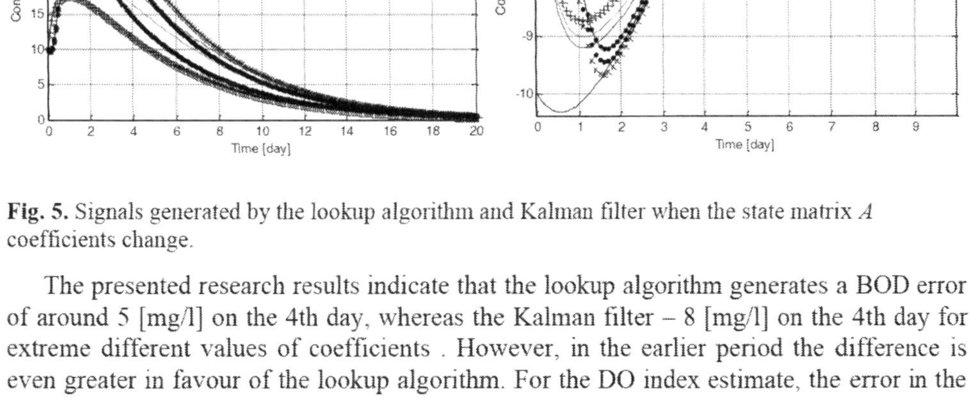

Fig. 5. Signals generated by the lookup algorithm and Kalman filter when the state matrix A coefficients change.

The presented research results indicate that the lookup algorithm generates a BOD error of around 5 [mg/l] on the 4th day, whereas the Kalman filter – 8 [mg/l] on the 4th day for extreme different values of coefficients . However, in the earlier period the difference is even greater in favour of the lookup algorithm. For the DO index estimate, the error in the lookup algorithm is comparable with the Kalman filter in the first day, and in the following days, the predominance of the lookup algorithm is visible.

It should be noted that the DO indicator is measured, therefore it contains current system information and hence its monitoring errors should be lower in relation to BOD.

5 Monitoring quality indicators

The quality of monitoring implemented by the proposed algorithm was compared with the Kalman filter. Two indicators were used to assess the quality of the proposed solution. The calculations these indicators were carried out separately for BOD and DO deficit.

The first indicator of monitoring quality is the Root Mean Squared Error (RMSE):

$$RMSE_i = \sqrt{\frac{1}{n}\sum_{j=1}^{n} e_{ij}^2} \tag{10}$$

where $e_{ij}(t) = x_{ij}(t) - \hat{x}_{ij}(t)$, $i = 1,2$ these are errors of generated signals, i – the number of the state variable, j – step number of the simulation, n – number of simulation steps,

The second indicator is the Mean Percentage Error (MPE):

$$MPE_i = \frac{1}{n}\sum_{j=1}^{n}\left(\left|\frac{x_{ij}-\hat{x}_{ij}}{x_{ij}}\right|\right) \cdot 100\% \tag{11}$$

The RMSE indicator represents the absolute error, while the MPE indicator represents the relative error.

6 Simulation of the monitoring system

Simulation experiments were carried out for a hypothetical three-section river with side tributaries, where each section of the river has tributary and is described by the equation (8).

Fig. 6 shows the waveforms of signals for one section of the river for 20 and 8 days of observation. It turns out that after a period of 8 days, the BOD water quality indicator from the initial value of 60 [mg/l] drops to about 8 [mg/l]. These are average values of BOD pollutants indicator that occur in rivers. Longer observations of impurities they lead to better water quality so way are hypothetical considerations.

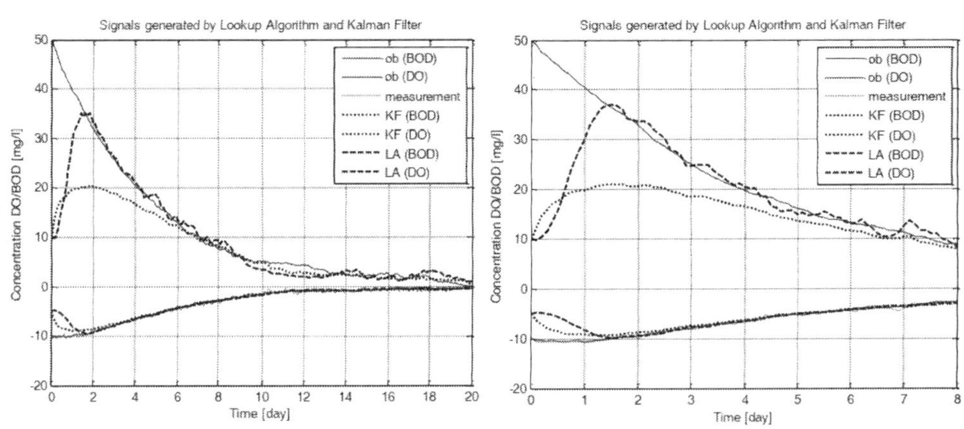

Fig. 6. Signals generated by the lookup algorithm and Kalman filter (20 days, 8 days).

The obtained research results show that better monitoring quality in both 20 days and 8 day observations is obtained using the lookup algorithm. The values of quality indicators (10, 11) are presented in Fig. 7. Left side Fig. 7 presented RMSE indicator and the right side of Fig. 7 show the MPE indicator.

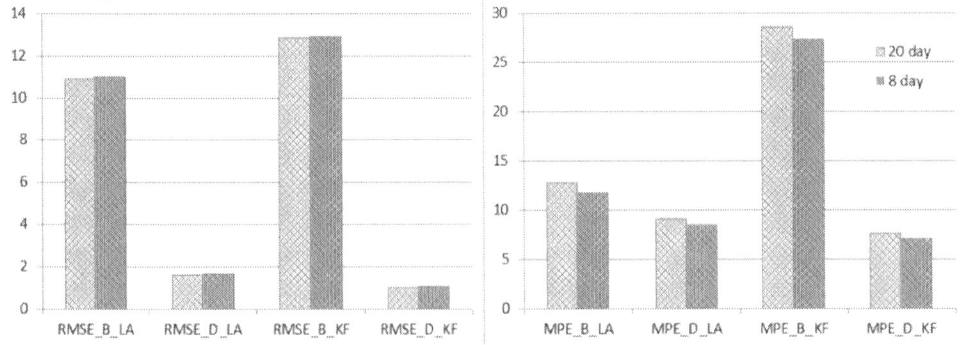

Fig. 7. Graph of monitoring system quality indicators RMSE and MPE for the lookup algorithm (LA) and Kalman filter (KF), BOD (B), DO (D).

From conducted observations carried out it follows, that for DO deficit the indicators (10, 11) always received lower values. This is due to the lack of measurements for BOD. In the case of the MPE indicator for 20 days of observation, we obtain slightly worse results in relation to the 8 observation days. This is due to the small values of variables x_i and as measurements y_i and if there are small values in the denominator of the indicator(11), its value of MPE will significantly increase (Fig.7 on the right).

Figure 8 shows the waveforms of the generated signals of compared solutions for monitoring and the changes in the gain coefficient of the lookup algorithm for the three-section river.

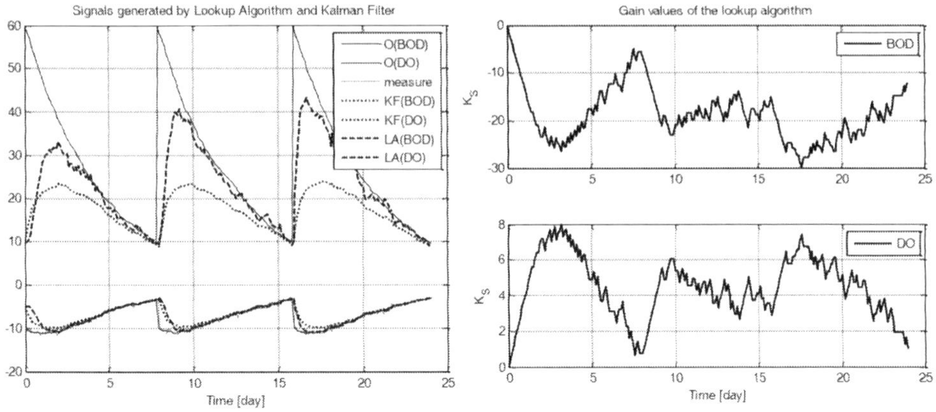

Fig. 8. Monitored signals for lookup algorithm and Kalman filter and also the gain coefficients form the lookup algorithm.

The lookup algorithm gives always much better results, especially for the immeasured signal of BOD, as indicated by both waveforms of generated signals and monitoring quality indicators (Fig. 9). It can also be seen that the values of the gain coefficients change significantly over time. In addition, when the estimation errors decrease, the value of the gain coefficients decreases. This indicates a greater dynamics of signal changes for the lookup algorithm compared to the Kalman filter.

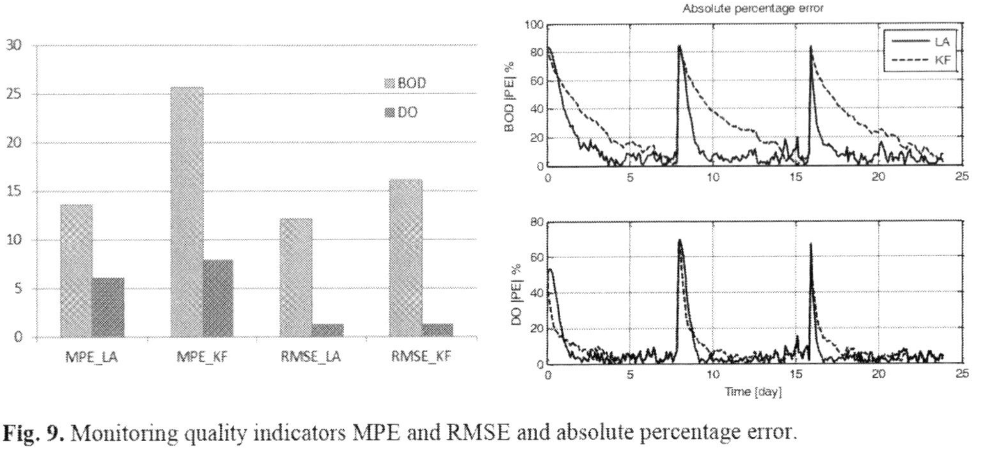

Fig. 9. Monitoring quality indicators MPE and RMSE and absolute percentage error.

The conducted observations indicate that for the BOD signal, the MPE index takes almost twice smaller values (better quality) for the lookup algorithm in relation to the Kalman filter. However, for the RMSE indicator, the differences are smaller. For the DO signal, differences between the quality indicators are much smaller, as the examined signal is measured (contains current information about the object).

In Fig. 9 (right side) showing the absolute percentage error, there are sudden changes in errors waveforms due to the inflow of lateral impurities. For these situations better results are generated by the lookup algorithm (continuous line), cause the errors waveforms reaches small values much faster than in case Kalman filter.

Simulation experiments were also carried out for various intensity of system and measurement disturbances (see Fig. 10).

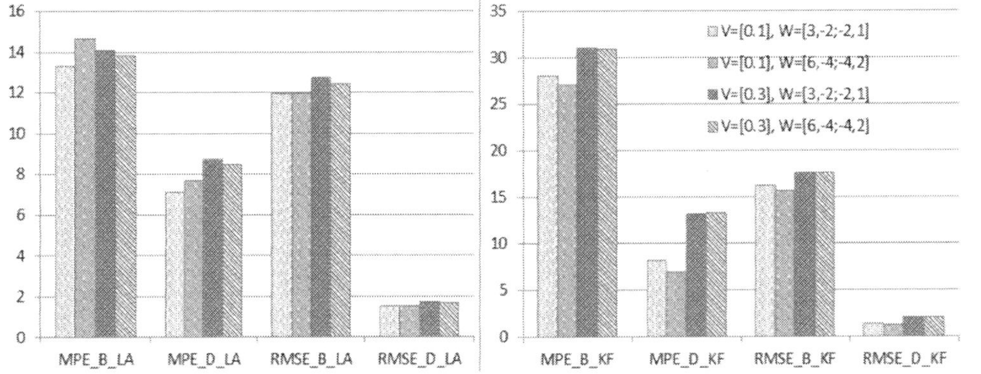

Fig. 10. Indicators of monitoring quality at various system and measurement disturbances covariances.

The intensity of generated disturbances of signals for BOD and DO was determined on the basis of covariances accepted in the research. It turned out that the intensity of disturbances is not important for the quality of monitoring in the case of the lookup algorithm. This is a very important superiority of proposed algorithm over the Kalman filter.

The value of the MPE monitoring quality indicator for BOD at various system and measurement disturbances covariances varies between 27-30% for the Kalman filter, while for the lookup algorithm the values are much lower and amount to 13-15%. For DO deficit, this indicator is 7-13% for the Kalman filter and for the lookup algorithm 7-8.5%. In all data cases tested, a better quality of monitoring was always obtained, measured by indicators (10,11) for the lookup algorithm for both BOD and DO.

7 Summary

In the paper the concept of monitoring system is presented, the idea of which uses the Kalman filter certain idea in which the gain coefficients is updated using the clever lookup algorithm. Was proposed two-zone division of errors (4) which was defined for the needs of the algorithm, which allows gain coefficients on-line update . Usually, the zone values are determined based on expert knowledge. The algorithm works stably and is not sensitive to a change in the intensity of disturbances acting on the object, as well as various initial constraints and initial gains coefficient (various disturbances do not destabilize its functioning). Through a universal and clever approach, it can be used for a certain class of objects representing various technological processes in the industrial fields and ecology. The proposed monitoring system can be included in non-invasive diagnostic systems. It can also be used as an estimators in optimal control process.

It is anticipated that further work will concern applications of this application for chemical facilities in which easy measurements will be used to determine immeasurable signals, e.g. concentrations and also in the field of environmental protection where it seems to be natural to apply this approach, e.g. for water treatment plants, sewage treatment plants or for continuous monitoring of water quality in rivers.

References

1. J. Michalski, P. Kozierski, J. Zienkiewicz, Porównanie metod estymacji stanu systemów dynamicznych, PAR, **4**, 41–47, (2017)
2. Z. Gomolka, B. Twarog, J. Bartman, Improvement of image processing by using homogeneous neural networks with fractional derivatives theorem, Discrete and Continuous Dynamical Systems- Series AI, ssue SUPPL., 505-514, (2011)
3. J. Cheng, D. Chen, R. Landry, L. Zhao, D. Guan, An Adaptive Unscented Kalman Filtering Algorithm for MEMS/GPS Integrated Navigation Systems, J. of App. Math., **2014,** (2014).
4. Z. Gomolka, B. Twarog, E. Zeslawska, Cognitive Investigation on Pilot Attention During Take-Offs and Landings Using Flight Simulator. Artificial Intelligence and Soft Computing. ICAISC 2017. **vol 10246.** (2017)
5. S. Akhlaghi, N. Zhou, Z. Huang, Exploring adaptive interpolation to mitigate nonlinear impact on estimating dynamic states, *IEEE PES General Meeting* (Denver, CO, USA, 2015)
6. S. Bordignon, M. Scagliarini, Monitoring algorithms for detecting changes in the ozone concentrations, Environmetrics, **11**, **2,** 125-137, (2000)
7. P. Marantos, Y. Koveos, K.J. Kyriakopoulos, UAV State Estimation using Adaptive Complementary Filters, IEEE Trans. Control Syst. Technol., **24**, **4**, 1214–1226, (2016)
8. S. Akhlaghi, N. Zhou, Z. Huang: Adaptive Adjustment of Noise Covariance in Kalman Filter for Dynamic State Estimation, *IEEE Power and Energy Conference (PES) General Meeting* (Chicago, IL, 1-5, 2017)
9. R.E. Kalman, A New Approach to Linear Filtering and Prediction Problems, Transaction of the ASME – J. of Basic Eng., 35-45, (1960)
10. G. Welch , G. Bishop, *An Introduction to the Kalman Filter*, University of North Carolina at Chapel Hill, Chapel Hill, NC, (2006)

11. M. Tomera, K. Pozorski, Porównanie metod estymacji zmiennych stanu w układzie kaskadowym dwóch zbiorników, Zesz. Nau. Wydz. Elek. i Auto. PG., **31**, 131-138, (2012)
12. E. Blanchard, A. Sandu, , C. Sandu, Parameter Estimation Method Using an Extended Kalman Filter, *Proceedings of the Joint North America* (Asia-Pacific ISTVS Conf. and Ann. Meet. of Jap. Soc. for Terra. , Fairbanks, AK, 2007)
13. Z. Gomółka, B. Twaróg, E. Żesławska, A. Lewicki, T. Kwater, Using Artificial Neural Networks to Solve the Problem Represented by BOD and DO Indicators, Water 2018, **10(1)**, **4**, (2018)
14. E. Dudek-Dyduch, Z. Gomolka, *Neural network design without learning*, (6th International Conference on Neural Networks and Soft Computing, Zakopane, 2003)
15. Z. Gomolka, E. Dudek-Dyduch, Y.P. Kondratenko, From Homogeneous Network to Neural Nets with Fractional Derivative Mechanism. *Artificial Intelligence and Soft Computing*. (ICAISC 2017)
16. P. Holnicki, Z. Nahorski, A. Żochowski, *Modelowanie procesów środowiska naturalnego*, (2000)
17. T. Kwater, R. Pekala, P. Krutys, The mathematical models of water pollution and interpretation of their distribution. Technol. News 2009, **1**, 130–132, (2009)
18. V. Gourishankar, M.A. Lawal, A digital water quality controller for polluted streams, Inter. J. of Syst. Scie., **9**, 899-919, (1978)

Synchronization of distributed robotics control system

Boguslaw Twarog[1,*] and *Ewa* Zeslawska[2]

[1]University of Rzeszow, Faculty of Mathematics and Natural Sciences, Rejtana Str. 16C, 35-959 Rzeszow, Poland
[2]University of Information Technology and Management, Sucharskiego Str.2, 35-225 Rzeszow, Poland

Abstract. The paper presents the novel project that has been proposed and realized together with the implementation of the process of heating thermosetting components based on advanced industrial equipment and software tools. In the fundamental task of optimization, the phenomenon of process synchronization based on a centralized algorithm adapted to the specific requirements of production was taken into account. The proposed research station was optimized and located in the laboratory of the Interdisciplinary Computer Modelling of the University of Rzeszow, that specializes in raising the efficiency of industrial processes

1 Introduction

Present industrial development requires more and better solutions in the field of production control and management. Optimizing these processes in terms of quality, speed, reliability, and safety enables to achieve higher quality and profitability. As a result of specialist consultations that have been carried out with employees from different companies, such as Prat&Whitney (aerospace components manufacturer) or Borg Warner (automotive manufacturer), it seems that appropriate design and realization of production control system is not an easy task and is often problematic. A frequent issue is the communication problem between different systems of techno-logical lines, especially the synchronization of processes between them, for multidimensional production in particular. Thus, in order to avoid delays and losses in production various security forms are used, such as redundant systems or manual control over particular parts of lines.

Multiple analyses and comparisons of practical solutions that are presented in specialist literature or scientific papers allow to implement suggested optimum and efficient models of final projects. Authors very often recommend or orient on the use of artificial intelligence methods in various industrial processes that pose a significant part of complex technological solutions. The methods of communication and trans-mission between processes and related algorithms suggest that the solution proposed in the present paper is a current approach to the problem [1,2, 3, 4].

A frequently controlled object requires a comprehensive solution which, next to dispersed control, will ensure full visualization of work and archiving of process data, and will deliver report tools. In general, the synchronization is the overall mechanism with the aim of assuring the access of processes to the shared system resources. The problem with synchronization is also present in designing of production process control system. As far as programming of systems with multiple production processes is concerned, the issue of mutual exclusion with the use of critical section is crucial. When one process enters the critical section, it is sure that another process cannot enter it at the same time. Access to the critical section should be regular for all waiting processes and should support mutual exclusion and support limited waiting (no "hunger" effect) [5, 6]. A coordinated mechanism, that is centralized algorithm, was used in order to provide processes with access to a mutual resource. Among available pro-cesses, one is selected to be a coordinator, to which other processes send queue re-quests. If the entry to the critical section is free, the coordinator sends it information. When it is received, the process can enter the critical section. When it leaves the critical section, it must inform the coordinator, and then the coordinator can give access to another process (Fig.1).

```
Coordinator (C)
      loop
        receive(msg);
            case msg of
              REQUEST: if nobody in CS (Critical Section)
                       then reply OK
                       else insert into the queue;
                             No reply
              RELEASE: if queue not empty then
                       remove 1st on the queue
                       reply OK
            end case
      end loop
```

Fig. 1. Centralized algorithm of mutual exclusion (pseudocode)

As a result of conducted analyses, the algorithms were created, programs and visualisations were prepared and proper hardware architecture was selected. During the design and implementation, great attention was paid to the way of synchronization of the programmed production processes. Taking into account the properties of the synchronization algorithm, after sufficient adaptation the concept was used in the designed control system [7, 8

2 The analysis and project of the heating process of thermosetting components

In order to realize and implement the project with success, the analysis was carried out and after that exact assumptions connected with the technological process were determined:

- heating process of thermosetting components will be a major production task;
- components will be delivered from two lines to two accumulators;
- vacuum furnace will be responsible for the heating process;
- components will be delivered to the furnace with the use of two robots, one per each accumulator;
- thermoset components will be put back on the collection belt by robots;
- synchronization of activities between system nodes will be required.

A driver is the most important element in the production process, as it coordinates the work of devices (robots and furnace) and will be responsible for distribution of tasks to particular devices. Appropriately designed LD management program must reflect the requirements set by the assumptions of centralized algorithm. According to this, the waiting processes will be technological lines number 1 and 2 that deliver components which are collected in accumulators. The main driver will allow them access to the furnace when needed. Robots will be activated interchangeably. When one of the accumulators is empty, only the robot which has components for transportation will operate. A general scheme of the operation of main driver which controls the work of lines is shown in the algorithm scheme, Fig. 2.

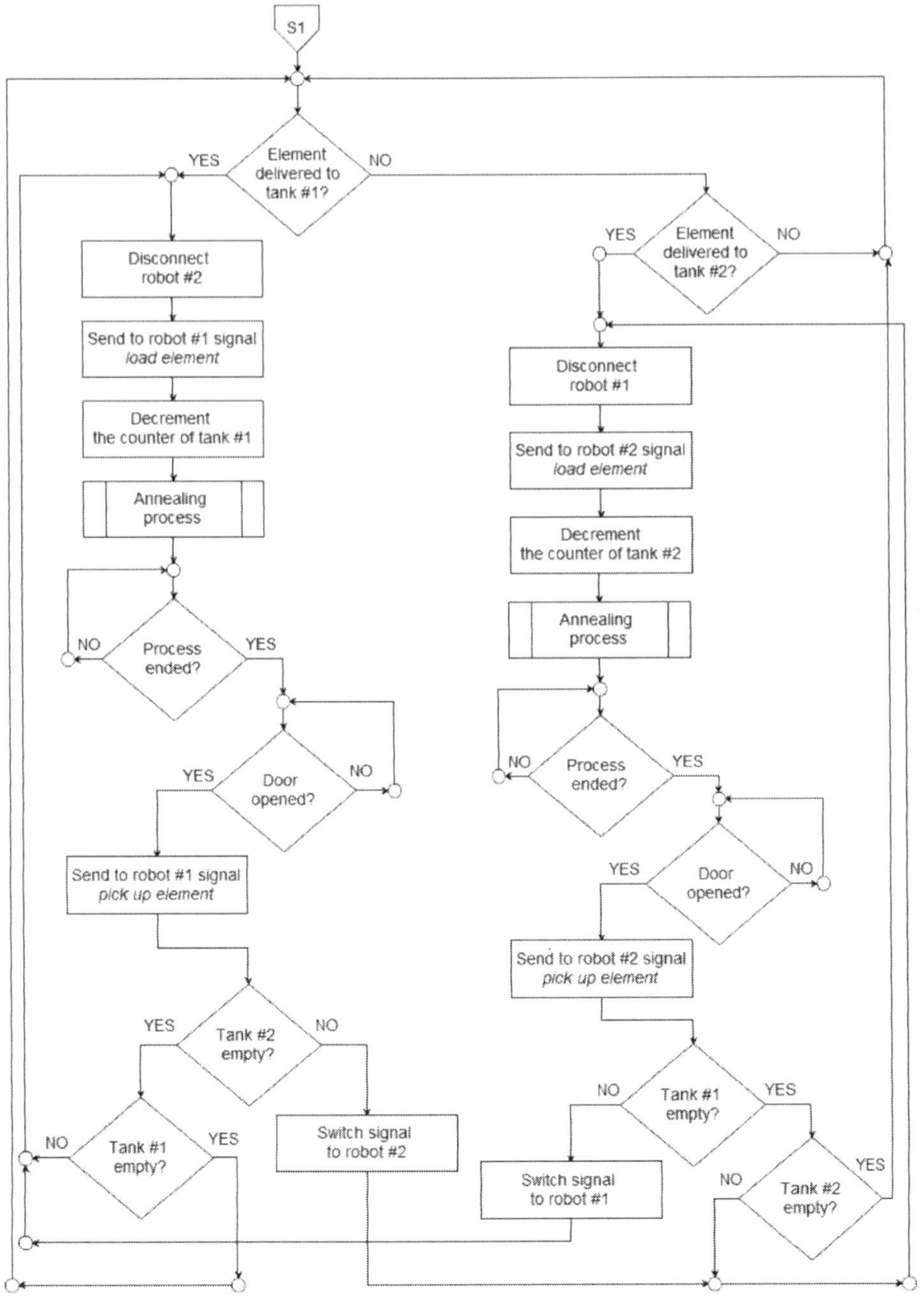

Fig. 2. An essential part of the main algorithm of heating process control.

All the processes were divided into cycles. Robot work cycle starts when a robot receives a signal that a components can be transported from accumulator to furnace. Next, the robot informs that the task is completed and send an informative signal that it is in a safe position, outside the furnace. When the heating cycle is over, the robot receives a signal that the components can be taken out of the furnace. The whole robot work cycle ends when the robot gives information about the completion of the removal task [9 – 14].

3 Equations and mathematics

The evolution of programmable systems that control processes allows the implementation of advanced control algorithms. Their proper deployment and optimization significantly influences the quality of production management. Configuration of proper communication between system elements also plays an important role. In the project of synchronization of the two technological line processes, the following control system devices were used [15 - 18]:

- Astraada PLC (HERCC972) drivers: programmable driver dedicated for small and medium industrial facilities. Equipped with discrete 8/4 inputs/outputs, analogue 8/4 inputs/outputs, 128 KB central processing unit dedicated for control program and the processor realizing the program with the speed of 0.016ms/kB. The program for a driver can be implemented in a few standard languages (LD, ST, IL, FBD, SFC).

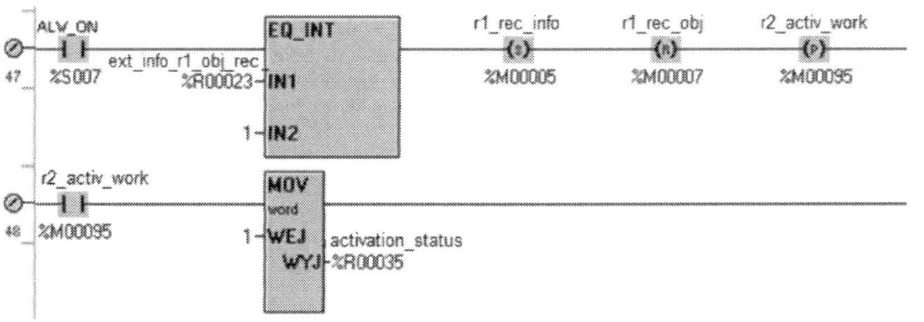

Fig. 3. Part of the code responsible for signal reception informing about the object delivery and about setting proper record marked as the activation status.

The part of control logic, presented above, poses an appropriately adapted implementation of tasks synchronization with the use of selected centralized algorithm. The parts that are in charge of activation and work switch between robots are responsible for giving components from accumulators (process queue) the access to the furnace (critical section). Removing an object from the furnace by a robot is equivalent to the completion of a particular part of the heating process of the component (critical section is over, accumulator is empty) [19 - 21].

- Astraada HMI (AS43TFT0425) touch panels: 4.3” programmable panel for visualization and control over programmed processes. Equipped, among others, with Ethernet communication ports, RS-232, USB, MicroSD.

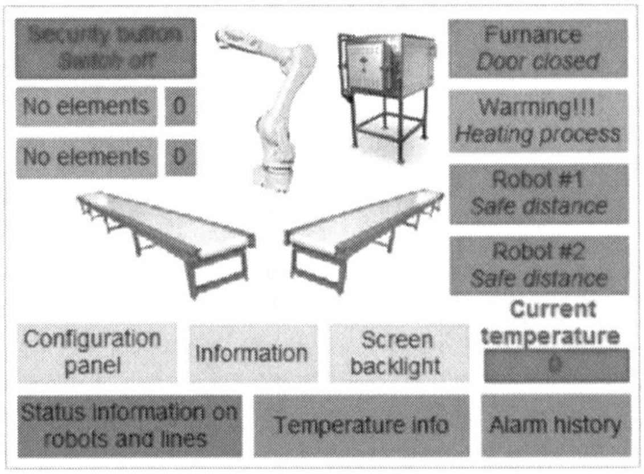

Fig. 4. Main synaptic screen for the lines control driver.

The visualisation or driver support was prepared (fig.4) which enables to collect da-ta from the whole production line. The data were grouped and divided for various screen.

- •Manageable JetNet 4510 Ethernet switches: work well in applications in which high reliability and connection efficiency are required. Equipped with 7 ports 10/100-TX and 3 combo RJ-45/SFP ports.

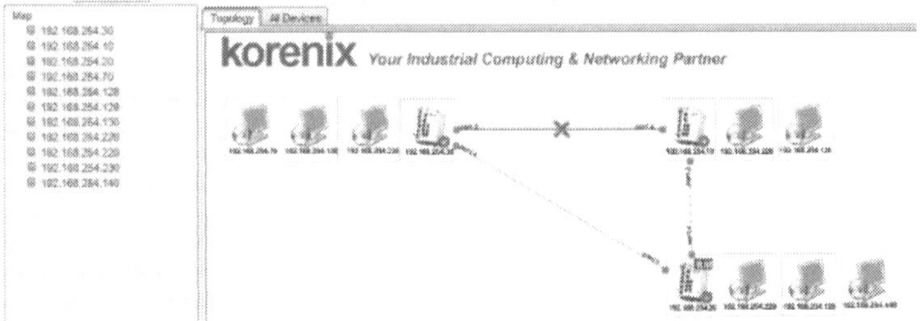

Fig. 5. Checking the operation of *Rapid Super Ring* function after disconnection one of the transmission medium.

Super Ring is an important, implemented function, used for constructing a ring-structured redundant system. In the testing process, disconnecting one of the transmission medium proved that the communication between processes moved to the back-up circuit and data transfer was not interrupted Fig.5 [22].

- •Kawasaki RS003N robots: six-axis device controlled with the controller E70/E7 series. This device is used where high capacity is not required (up to 3 kg), but high speed is required (6000 mm/s), as well as precision and repeatability of operations (±0,05mm). In addition, it is equipped with a pneumatic grab and a SensoPart set for industrial image processing.

Fig. 6. A simulation of the part of line realized in the K-ROSET program

4 Remarks and conclusion

In the presented solution, a real production process that realizes dedicated heating of thermosetting components was designed and implemented. The modelling and configuration process of dispersed industrial automation novel systems based on PLC drivers and robots with multiple degrees of freedom was presented. The methods and original algorithms of synchronization of various processes were also discussed in order to achieve an optimum control over production lines. The project and its practical implementation using available components and devices underwent a verification process and advanced testing plans. All assumptions that were set have been realized, and the project component parts in verification stages have undergone optimization and adjustment to the project requirements. In a complex phenomenon of dispersed control, known from computer systems centralized algorithm was applied, that is used for process synchronization. Its implementation in ladder language (LD) was not easy and it had to be adapted to the designed situation. Centralization of processes is not the right solution, as the failure of the main driver may stop the work of production line. The appropriate solution would be a possible redundancy of this system that is going to be realized in the nearest future investigations.

References

1. E. Dudek-Dyduch, Modeling manufacturing processes with disturbances – a new method based on algebraic-logical meta-models, 14th International Conference, ICAISC 2015, (2015)
2. E. Jezierski, Dynamics of robots, (WNT, in Polish, Warszawa), (2006)
3. B. Twarog, Z. Gomolka, E. Zeslawska, Time Analysis of Data Exchange in Distributed Control Systems Based on Wireless Network Model, Analysis and Simulation of Electrical and Computer Systems. Lecture Notes in Electrical Engineering, vol 452. pp 333-342, (2018)
4. B. Twaróg, Z. Gomółka ,E. Żesławska, P. Krutys, The system that supervises and controls the course of the technological process, (in Polish, Education-Technique-Informatics, 4 (2), 424-430, University of Rzeszow), (2013)
5. B. Wittenmark, J. Nilsson, M. Torngren, Timing problems in real-time control systems, Proceedings of American Control Conference, (1995)
6. A. Noriaki, S. and other, Distrbiuted Component Middleware for RT (Robot Technology), (IEEE/RSJ International Conference on Intelligent Robots and Systems, 10.1109/ACC.1995.531240), (2005)
7. F. Maturana, W. Shen, D.H. Norrie. MetaMorph, An Adaptive Agent-Based, Architecture for Intelligent Manufacturing, (International J. Production Research, Vol.37, No.10, pp. 2159-2174), (1999)
8. W. Nawrocki, Distributed measurement systems, (WKŁ, Warsaw), (2016)
9. I. Hallmann, B. Siemiątkowska, Artificial landmark navigation system, (9th, Int. Symposium Intelligent Robotic Systems. pp. 219-228), (2001)
10. J. Zając, Distributed control of automated production systems, (Monograph 288, Mechanic Series, in Polish, Krakow University of Technology Publisher), (2003)
11. Z. Gomolka, E. Dudek-Dyduch, Y.P. Kondratenko, From Homogeneous Network to Neural Nets with Fractional Derivative Mechanism, Artificial Intelligence and Soft Computing. vol 10245. Springer, Cham, (2017)

12. G. Dralus, Z. Gomolka, Seasonal models of energy forecasting in photovoltaic systems using artificial neural networks, (International Interdisciplinary PhD Workshop 2017 , Springer, to be published), (2017)
13. Z. Gomolka, Neurons' Transfer Function Modeling with the Use of Fractional Derivative. DepCoS-RELCOMEX 2018. Advances in Intelligent Systems and Computing, vol 761, (2019)
14. E. Dudek-Dyduch, Z. Gomolka, Neural network design without learning, 6th International Conference on Neural Networks and Soft Computing Location: Zakopane, Neural Networks and Soft Computing Book Series: Advances in Soft Computing, pp: 179-187, (2003)
15. M. Pawlak, Z. Żarczyński, The distributed measurement system for the diagnosis of industrial electric drives, (Problem Notebooks – Electric Machines No 1/2013 (98)), (2013)
16. P. Tatjewski, Advanced control of industrial objects: structures and algorithms, (EXIT, Warsaw), (2002)
17. K. Dzierżek, M. Rećko, D.S. Pietrala, Quick prototyping of manipulator control system with PLC controller, (23rd International Conference Engineering Mechanics 2017, pp.294–297), (2017)
18. J. Kofman, X. Wu, T.J. Luu, S. Verma, Teleoperation of a Robot Manipulator Using a Vision-Based Human–Robot Interface, (IEEE Transactions on Industrial Electronics", Vol. 52, Iss. 5, pp.1206–1219), (2005)
19. J. Bartman, Accuracy of reflecting the waveforms of current and voltage through their spectrum determined by the standards regulating measurements, (Revue Roumaine Des Sciences Techniques-Serie Electrotechnique Et Energetique, vol. 61), (2016)
20. J. Bartman, The analysis of output voltage distortion of inverter for frequency lower than the nominal, (Journal of Electrical Engineering, vol 68, No 3, pp.194–199), (2017)
21. T. Binkowski, K. Buczek, D. Sobczynski, Control of BLDC motor working as flying hybrid platform component, (Electrotechnical Review (Przegląd Elektrotechniczny), vol. 87, no 8, pp. 30-33), (2011)
22. V. Cicirello, S. Smith. Ant Colony Control for Autonomous Decentralized Shop Floor, Routing. (Proc. of the 5th Int. Symposium on Autonomous Decentralized Systems., IEEE Computer Society, pp. 383-390), (2001)

Evolutionary algorithms with and without adaptive mutation in AI based cryptography

Mateusz Tybura[1,*]

[1] Rzeszow University of Technology, Faculty of Electrical and Computer Engineering, Rzeszow, Poland

Abstract. The key role of cryptography is to make cipher so hard to reproduce without knowing all the details that no one besides the recipient could decipher the message. Those algorithms which are used nowadays gets its security mostly from highly reliable algorithms and/or complicated cryptographic keys. Unfortunately, those human-made methods aren't invulnerable so sooner or later they compromise. So, it could be really useful to make a cipher which could change. But currently only neural networks are capable of thing known as transfer learning. In this article similar method was proposed in order to make it possible to re-learn already established evolutionary algorithm to do new, similar task.

1 Introduction

Cryptography (gr. *kryptos* – hidden, *graphein* – write) a field of knowledge dedicated to hiding data has no doubly concerned peoples through millennials. Mostly because it possibly started as soon as some of primitive cultures had developed written languages. Over the years it evolved from very primitive textual ciphers to those used on computers. Modern solutions could be easily divided into three categories: highly mathematical, device based, intelligent based.

Those highly mathematical are using more less sophisticated theories like very large prime numbers, elliptic curves, chaotic equations or many others. For instance, RSA and ECC are both using very large prime numbers, with the security highly dependent on problem known as discrete logarithm [1]. But because of need for extensive calculations they are used mostly for establishing connection between peers to then exchange keys for less complex, symmetric ciphers [2].

Another way of doing cryptography is to use dedicated devices instead of running any kind of written program on CPU [3-5]. That kind of cipher chips are built with either programmable circuits such as FPGA [4,5] or specially designed security processors. Such electronic circuits are currently widely used in smartphones. It for sure makes it faster and less vulnerable for some certain types of attacks but more prune to the others. Cause as usual even very promising solutions have their flaws. Electronic devices had to be designed not only for doing was is really needed to do but also to not expose a lot of details of their internal processes. Many times, it was overlooked. For instance, some of devices had given

* Corresponding author: tyburam@hotmail.com

a great opportunity to get some internal details of what they are doing just by registering the heat map [5]. Additionally, it's sometimes impossible to change the way the electronics work if it was not designed for making it possible.

The most modern and promising development direction is to use intelligent based techniques to make cryptography algorithms [6-15]. For many years both neural networks and evolution algorithms were used to make ciphers as well as to break ciphers. For example, in 1995 neural networks were used to recreate DES algorithm. That kind of researches are also done in big IT companies such as Google. In spite of that fact this article will be strictly focusing on the usage of intelligent algorithms in the cryptography.

2 Evolutionary algorithms in cryptography

Application of evolutionary algorithms in cryptography relies on the idea of synchronized learning on two separate machines. Which insist on having the same learning configuration, training data and randomness. Making more or less mistakes in setting the same training environment could make it impossible for usage in any kind of real problem. Using those techniques to generate ciphers seems to be good idea as those generated ones aren't as known as the already known ones. Unfortunately, it could also lead to some hidden defects for the same reason. So, they must be treated as a double-sided blade.

An interesting fact is that in scientific articles and theses there are way more usage of neural networks instead of evolutionary algorithms in cryptography itself. Which could be the outcome of overall higher popularity of for instance deep neural networks or GANs and things like that. Also, it seems that the evolutionary algorithms had been used more frequently in both analysing and breaking ciphers instead of making ones. Many researches had shown that they could be used to decipher a message encoded using algorithms such as Vigenere [7] or DES [9]. For the generation task there are methods such as CIGA (Cryptography Inspired by Genetic Algorithms) or ICIGA (Improved CIGA) [14].

3 Instruction set based evolutionary ciphers

Plain genetic algorithm was chosen for the first experiments. Implemented in a way shown on listing 1. It served as a baseline for further comparison and improvement.

Listing 1. Psuedocode for evolution.

```
function evolution
    pop - generate_initial_population(size)
    foreach individual in pop do
        individual.fit = fitness(individual)
    while not stop(pop) do
        offsprings = select(pop, sel_size)
        offsprings = crossover(offsprings)
        offsprings = mutate(offsprings)
        if size(offspringa) < size then
            offspring = fill(offspring, size)
        pop = offspringa
    return best(pop)
```

Every single individual was represented by an integer number encoded instruction. Those instructions were four arithmetic ones (addition, substitution, multiplication, division). All of them operating only on integer numbers. Also, their deterministic nature as well as elementary nature in sense of being implemented in every single modern CPU guarantied multiplatform usability.

First task taken into consideration was to achieve the best possible accuracy in pseudo Caesar cipher, Caesar cipher and some made up substitution cipher with hardcoded shift.

The evolutionary way was much more successful in both correctness and time for getting answer. For instance, when generating pseudo Caesar cipher the right answer arrived just after generating initial population, when there were 20 individuals, just 4 possible operations (add, sub, mul and div) and fitness function which simple checked for the effect of using generated cipher. Adding more operations made the task harder but not as much as when the operations didn't have the addition inside. But there is an exception for the time when the initial population doesn't have even a single individual with a right gene and the mutation probability is set something smaller than 0,5. In that case there's no way of getting even approximated answer, as there's no way to get the right set of genes even after thousands of generations. Thus, it is absolutely necessary to choose genes representing operations which are performed by the algorithm being mimicked and the fitness function really checking for what is needed to be checked and the right way to interpret the genes of the best individual. If not nothing good have happened.

4 Adaptive mutation

As it was already shown in many researches' method named transfer learning could make it possible to reuse pretrained network for more less similar task. But there were many questions. Is it possible to use it when working with ciphers? Do they have to work really similar? And how to make something like transfer learning using evolutionary algorithms instead of neural network?

In the experiments three distinct methods were proposed. First was to just continue learning with no changes in algorithm at all. Unfortunately, every single time the evolutionary algorithms failed. Secondly it was adjusted just a little bit. The evolution was stopped before getting better than about 70% or 50% or any other arbitrary chosen value of fitness function achieved while learning the first cipher but it couldn't really make it. Hence it was clear that just stopping isn't enough to make a genetic adaptation of transfer learning.

It was assumed that changes in parameter such as mutation rate could possibly be the best way into getting better results as that's the only way to change genes in population to those that aren't currently represented in it. So, after the initial failure, new possibilities were tested in order to check which will do the best job for this certain task.

For the first time the algorithm was almost the same but first it had to stop right before getting into 70% of accuracy and two the mutation rate was increased to value 0,5 for the rest of the evolution. It didn't work well. When the best individuals were analysed it something interesting had been found. Just changing mutation rate didn't worked because of introducing to more randomness instead of helping (fig. 1). Hence it seemed to be reasonable to make more intelligent mutation rate changing routine.

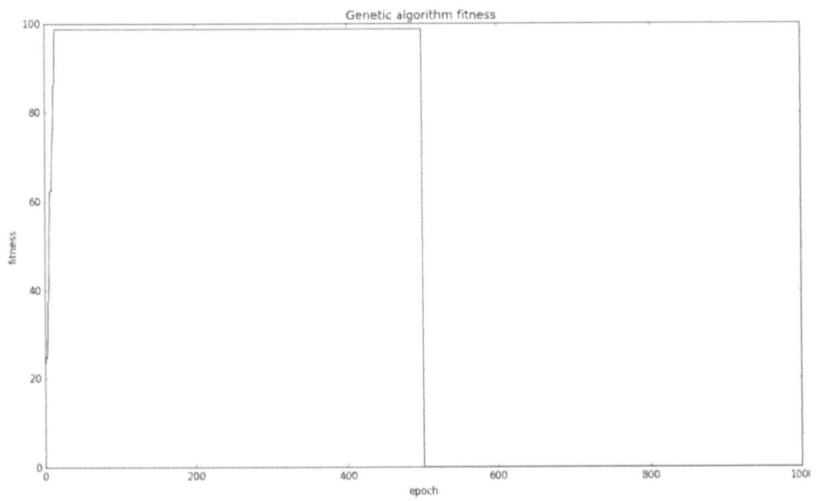

Fig. 1. Evolutionary algorithm fitness function value after switching task and changing mutation rate

In the last attempt special mutation kind was proposed. After a thoughtful process it became clear that this mutation must change a lot of genes in the less fitted ones and at the same time limit the changes made to the best ones. With something like this it These trials had shown that it could work but only when performed well. The most promising one consisted of few main things combined into adaptive mutation method (listing 2).

Listing 2. Pseudocode for adaptive mutation

```
function adaptive_mutate(individuals)
    max_fit = best(individuals).fit
    if max_fit == 0 then
        max_fit = 1
    mutated = <empty_list>
    foreach ind in individuals do
        prob = (max_fit - ind.fit) / max_fit
            if random() >= prob then
                mutated.add(mutate(ind))
     return mutated
```

Proposed method started with checking for the maximum value of fitness function in all individuals available for mutation. If for some reason it is equal to zero, it is adjusted to 1 to avoid errors when dividing by zero. Then for every single individual mutation probability is set to the difference between maximal fitness and fitness of current individual divided by maximal fit. So, the most fitted ones aren't mutated and the less fitted are most likely to be changed. Hence it at the same time tries to avoid losses by not mutating best ones and increases diversity by mutating the worst ones. For experimental set it made way better than plain evolutionary algorithm or that with randomly changed mutation probability (fig. 2).

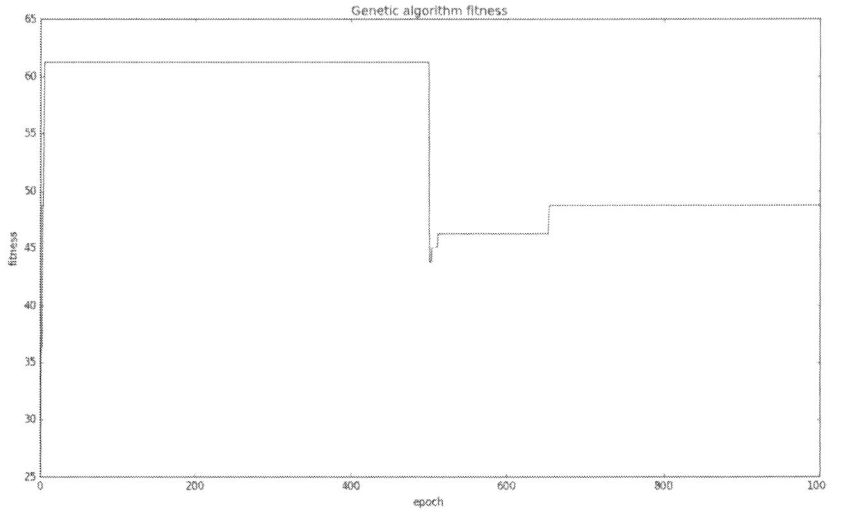

Fig. 2. Evolutionary algorithm fitness function value after switching task and changing mutation rate in adaptive manner

This method had made a huge difference (fig. 2). While still it hadn't made the best possible score, it had changed a lot. Because of removing the randomness and incorporating the adaptiveness the whole population doesn't change so drastically resulting in 0 as a value of the fitness function. Then the fitness even managed to change a little bit in a good way.

Summary

Evolutionary algorithm could be used for making cipher without much of human interventions as in fully human-made solutions. They ability to learn makes quality outcome in just a matter of time. While standard approach makes it difficult to change mind, the adaptive one plays a huge role in making more sophisticated, more adaptive solution.

References

1. Smart N.: Cryptography: An Introduction, McGraw-Hill College, 2004.
2. TLS protocol specification, https://tools.ietf.org/html/rfc5246
3. Ay A. U., Ozturk E., Henriquez F. R., Savas E.: Design and implementation of a constant-time FPGA accelerator for fast elliptic curve cryptography, International Conference on ReCOnFigurable Computing and FPGAs, 2016
4. Bartlik M., Bucek J.: A low-cost multi-purpose experimental FPGA board for cryptography applications, 4th Workshop on Advances in Information, Electronic and Electrical Engineering, 2016
5. Gurkaynak F. K.: GALS System Design: Side Channel Attack Secure Cryptographic Accelerators. PhD thesis, ETH Zurich, 2006

6. Mahmood A., Dony R., Areibi S.: An adaptive encryption based genetic algorithms for medical images, IEEE International Workshop on Machine Learning for Signal Processing, 2013
7. Omran S. S., Al.-Khalid A.S., Al-Saady D. M.: A cryptoanalytic attack on Vigenere cipher using genetic algorithm, IEEE Conference on Open Systems, 2011
8. Feng-Tse L., Cheng-Yan K.: A genetic algorithm for ciphertext-only attack in cryptanalysis, IEEE International Conference on Systems, Man and Cybernetics, 1995
9. Jun S., Huanguo Z., Qingshu M., Zhangyi W.: Cryptanalysis of Four-Round DES Based on Genetic Algorithm, International Conference on Wireless Communications, Networking and Mobile Computing, 2007
10. Zarza L., Pegueroles J., Soriano M.: Evaluation Function for Synthesizing Security Protocols by means of Genetic Algorithms, The Second International Conference on Availability, Reliability and Security, 2007
11. Albassall A. M. B., Wahdan A.-M.A.: Genetic algorithm cryptanalysis of a feistel type block cipher, International Conference on Electrical, Electronic and Computer Engineering, 2004
12. Ribaric T., Houghten S.: Genetic programming for improved cryptanalysis of elliptic curve cryptosystems, IEEE Congress on Evolutionary Computation, 2017
13. Ho Yean L., Samsudin A., Belaton B.: Heuristic cryptanalysis of classical and modern ciphers, 13th International Conference on Networks jointly held with 7th Malaysia International Conference on Communcation, 2005
14. Picek S., Golub M.: On evolutionary computation methods in cryptography, Proceedings of 34th International Convention MIPRO, 2011
15. Clark A. J.: Optimisation Heuristics for Cryptology, PhD thesis, Information Security Research Centre, Faculty of Information Technology, Queensland University of Technology, 1998

Mapping Accuracy of Trajectories of Manipulator Motion

Marek Boryga[1], *Paweł* Kołodziej[1*], *Andrzej* Graboś[2], and *Krzysztof* Gołacki[1]

[1] University of Life Sciences in Lublin, ul. Głęboka 28, 20-612 Lublin, Poland
[2] ARKONA, Nasutów 99C, 21-025 Niemce, Poland

Abstract. The paper presents the algorithm for trajectory planning and the analysis of motion accuracy of an anthropomorphic manipulator whose the end-effector moves over the rectilinear-arc path. The path consists of two rectilinear segments of intersecting directions coupled with the arc of a fixed radius. On these rectilinear segments, the end-effector acceleration is described by a polynomial of 7th-degree. The motion over the arc proceeds at a constant velocity. The dynamic analysis was carried out on the basis of Lagrange`s equations of the second order. Manipulator flexibility and damping were considered according to the Kelvin-Voigt model introducing spring-damping components into the drive system. The simulation test results were presented in the form of spatial courses of the pre-assigned and realized trajectories as well as time courses of trajectory end-effector mapping errors for three paths with different radii of the arc.

1 Introduction

One of the fundamental tasks in trajectory planning operation proves to be the analysis of errors resulting from the manipulator dynamic chain deformability. Manipulator structure, geometry, mass distribution as well as its shape and position in the task space of the desired path have, besides the stiffness and damping, a significant effect on the mappability of the prescribed trajectory. Erkorkmaz et al. [5] proposed a trajectory planning strategy for maintaining the tool positioning accuracy in high speed cornering applications. A 3D contour error estimation algorithm was presented for determining the geometric deviation from the arbitrarily shaped toolpaths. Two spline fitting strategies were developed for smoothening sharp corners. Dong et al. [4] examined the possibility of scheduling or varying the feed-rate by taking into consideration the geometry of the contour that the machine is expected to follow and the physical capabilities of the machine. The paper presents, the constraints on permissible jerk and as a consequence, machine vibrations got reduced, element wear declined and mapping errors in the end-effector path limited. Tseng et al. [8] suggested an algorithm for the jerk-limited acceleration planning. With this algorithm, both the chord error, the maximum acceleration and jerk were within the permissible limits.

Apart from the factors mentioned at the beginning, which influence the accuracy of movement, the way of trajectory parameterization is also very important. Among the

* Corresponding author: pawel.kolodziej@up.lublin.pl

applied methods, parameterization with the use of higher degree polynomials is worthy of mention. Thus way it is possible to obtain smooth trajectories with simultaneous limitation of speed, acceleration or jerk. Boryga and Graboś [1] used polynomials of higher degree for trajectory planning of robot manipulator. The linear acceleration profiles of end-effector were planned as the polynomials of 9, 7 and 5 degree. They also demonstrated the algorithm for Polynomial Cross Method (PCM) to plan the end-effector motion whose path is composed of two rectilinear segments [6]. Boryga et al. [2] applied the Planning Rectilinear-Arc Polynomial Trajectory (PR-APT) method for planning the end-effector motion trajectory during harvesting tomatoes in the greenhouse. The acceleration profile of end-effector was planned as the polynomial of 7th-degree. Milica et al. [7] presented the method for determining the optimal trajectory of a parallel robot. The Hermite polynomial expressions were used as the time function of geometrical parameters. The authors concluded that the use of polynomial functions with the simplest expressions leads to minimization of effort associated with the analysis and mathematical formulation of the optimization problem. Chen et al. [3] proposed the Intermediate Point Obstacle Avoidance (IPOA) algorithm to provide smooth trajectory and efficient movement while avoiding obstacles. Combining the IPOA algorithm in a series, multi-obstacle avoidance by the robotic arm in the complex environment can be accomplished.

The paper is arranged as follows. Chapter II proposes an innovative and very effective algorithm for planning rectilinear-arc trajectories of manipulator end-effector. On the rectilinear segments the acceleration course is described by the polynomial of 7th-degree. Transition from the rectilinear segment to the arc and vice versa proceeds without a change of velocity. Chapter III presents the dynamics model. Flexibility and damping forces in kinematic pairs were taken into consideration introducing spring-damping components into the drive system. Chapter IV depicts the numerical example. For the planned rectilinear-arc trajectory (for three arc radii), prescribed and realized trajectories of end-effector and time courses of position errors were presented.

2 Planning of rectilinear-arc trajectories of end-effector motion

1.1 Assumptions

The first stage in planning a rectilinear-arc trajectory is as follows:

- Coordinates of the initial B, final E and intermediate M points. The points B and E should be located in the workspace of the robot manipulator. The point M is the intersection point of the rectilinear segments and does not lie on the planned path. It can be situated outside the workspace (Fig.1).
- Arc radius R.
- Maximum acceleration on the rectilinear segments a_{max}.

1.2 Algorithm for trajectory planning

Step 1. Determine the scalar equation of the plane π passing through the points B, M, and E.

Step 2. Define the parametric equations of the straight line passing through the points B and M as well as points E and M.

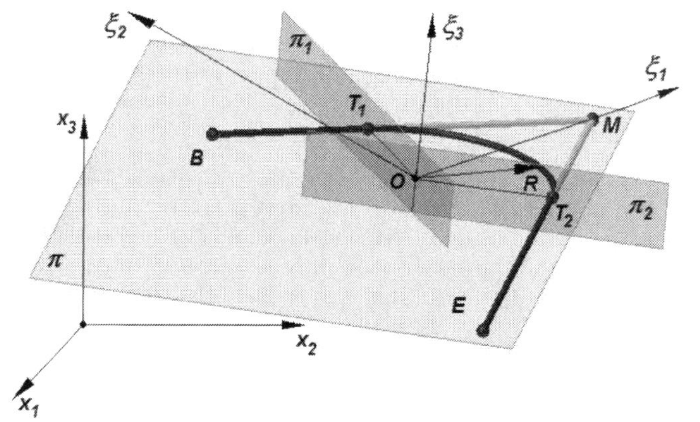

Fig. 1. The rectilinear-arc motion path with the added coordinate systems

Step 3. Establish equations of the π_1 and π_2 planes perpendicular to the straight lines passing through the points B and M (π_1 planes) as well as the points E and M (π_2 planes) and those passing through the center of the arc O.

Step 4. Determine the coordinates of point T_1 as common to the plane π_1 and the straight line running through the points B and M as well as the coordinates of the point T_2 as the common to the plane π_2 and the straight line passing through the points E and M.

Step 5. Define the coordinates of the center of the arc O that lies in the plane π and is tangential to the points T_1 and T_2 to the segments BM and ME.

Step 6. Determine the apex BME and the apex T_1OT_2 angles.

Step 7. Determine matrix transformation A between the local system of coordinates $\xi_1\xi_2\xi_3$ connected with arc and the reference coordinate system $x_1x_2x_3$. The origin of the system $\xi_1\xi_2\xi_3$ is the point O, versor of ξ_1 axis oriented towards the point M and the direction of ξ_2 axis versor intersecting the line passing through the points B and M. The versor of ξ_3 axis is a complement of the right-handed coordinate system.

Step 8. Determine path increments on the rectilinear segments Δs^{BT1} and Δs^{T2E} .

Step 9. Pre-establish motion time for the BT_1 and T_2E segments

$$t = \frac{3\sqrt{210}\sqrt[4]{21}\sqrt{\Delta s \cdot a_{max}}}{49 a_{max}} \tag{1}$$

For the segment BT_1: $t=t^{BT1}$, $\Delta s=\Delta s^{BT1}$. For the segment T_2E: $t=t^{T2E}$, $\Delta s=\Delta s^{T2E}$.

Step 10. Determine velocity in the T_1 and T_2 tangency points

$$v = \frac{105}{64}\frac{\Delta s}{t} \tag{2}$$

For the segment BT_1: $v=v_{T1}$, $\Delta s=\Delta s^{BT1}$ and $t=t^{BT1}$. For the segment T_2E: $v=v_{T2}$, $\Delta s=\Delta s^{T2E}$ and $t=t^{T2E}$.

Step 11. Determine motion time on the BT_1 and T_2E segment.

If $v_{T1} \geq v_{T2}$, then velocity in the tangency points and over the arc should be assumed to be $v^{Arc}=v_{T2}$ and the motion time on the BT_1 segment is derived from the dependency (2) where $t=t^{BT1}$, $\Delta s=\Delta s^{BT1}$ and $v=v_{T2}$ should be substituted. In the case $v_{T1}<v_{T2}$, the velocity at the tangential points and on the arc should be assumed to be $v^{Arc}=v_{T1}$ while the motion time on T_2E segment is derived from the dependency (2) where $t=t^{T2E}$, $\Delta s=\Delta s^{T2E}$ and $v=v_{T1}$ should be substituted.

Step 12. Establish the polynomial coefficient for calculation of acceleration, speed and position for the BT_1 and T_2E segments

$$p = \frac{315}{8}\frac{\Delta s}{t^9} \tag{3}$$

For the segment BT_1: $p=p^{BT1}$, $\Delta s=\Delta s^{BT1}$ and $t=t^{BT1}$. For the segment T_2E: $p=p^{T2E}$, $\Delta s=\Delta s^{T2E}$ and $t=t^{T2E}$.

Step 13. Determine the motion duration time over the arc

$$t^{Arc} = \frac{\beta \cdot R}{v^{Arc}} \tag{4}$$

Step 14. Define the dependence on angular displacement in motion over the arc

$$\beta(t) = \frac{\beta}{2} - \frac{v^{Arc}}{R}(t - t^{BT1}) \text{ for } t^{BT1} \le t \le t^{BT1} + t^{Arc} \tag{5}$$

Step 15. Determine the coordinates of the vectors of position $\boldsymbol{X}^{Arc}$, speed $\boldsymbol{X}'^{Arc}$ and acceleration $\boldsymbol{X}''^{Arc}$ of the motion over the arc in the coordinate system $x_1x_2x_3$

$$\boldsymbol{X}^{Arc} = \boldsymbol{A}\cdot\boldsymbol{\Xi}^{Arc},\ \boldsymbol{X}'^{Arc} = \boldsymbol{A}\cdot\boldsymbol{\Xi}'^{Arc},\ \boldsymbol{X}''^{Arc} = \boldsymbol{A}\cdot\boldsymbol{\Xi}''^{Arc} \tag{6}$$

where: $\boldsymbol{X}^{Arc}=[x_1^{Arc}(t), x_2^{Arc}(t), x_3^{Arc}(t), 1]^T$, $\boldsymbol{\Xi}^{Arc}=[R\cos\beta(t), R\sin\beta(t), 0, 1]^T$

Step 16. Determine translation in time on the T_2E segment

$$t_b = t^{BT1} - t^{T2E} + t^{Arc} \tag{7}$$

Step 17. Perform translation in time of the polynomial depicting the acceleration profile for the T_2E segment by tb value

$$a^{BT1}(t) = -p^{BT1}\cdot(t)^2\cdot(t-t^{BT1})^3\cdot(t-2t^{BT1})^2 \tag{8}$$

$$a^{T2E}(t) = p^{T2E}\cdot(t-t_b)^2\cdot(t-t^{T2E}-t_b)^3\cdot(t-2t^{T2E}-t_b)^2 \tag{9}$$

Step 18. Set the total motion time on the designated trajectory

$$t_{end} = t^{BT1} + t^{Arc} + t^{T2E} \tag{10}$$

3 Dynamics of the open kinematic chain

The motion equations were derived on the basis of the Lagrange equations of the second order. The general form of the equations is written as follows

$$\boldsymbol{B}(\theta)\boldsymbol{\theta}'' + \boldsymbol{O}(\theta)\boldsymbol{\theta}'^2 + \boldsymbol{C}(\theta)\boldsymbol{\theta}'\boldsymbol{\theta}' + \boldsymbol{G}(\theta) = \boldsymbol{\tau} \tag{11}$$

where: $\boldsymbol{B}(\theta)$ - the inertia matrix, $\boldsymbol{O}(\theta)$ - the matrix of centrifugal torques, $\boldsymbol{C}(\theta)$ - the matrix of Coriolis torques, $\boldsymbol{G}(\theta)$ - the vector of gravity torques, $\boldsymbol{\tau}$ - the generalized joint force vector.

The dynamics model takes into account flexibility and damping effects introducing deformable objects (Kelvin-Voigt model) between the drive units and links. The forces generalized in *i*-n[th] kinematic pair were defined by the equation

$$\tau_i = k_{si}(\theta_{gi} - \theta_{ri}) + c_{di}(\theta'_{gi} - \theta'_{ri}) \tag{12}$$

where: k_{si} - the stiffness coefficient [Nm/rad], c_{di} - the viscous damping coefficient [Nms/rad], θ_{gi} - the prescribed link i angular displacement [rad] and θ_{ri} - the accomplished link i angular displacement [rad].

4 Numerical example

The simulation tests were performed for three degrees of freedom anthropomorphic manipulator (Fig.2). Geometrical and mass values are presented in Table 1.

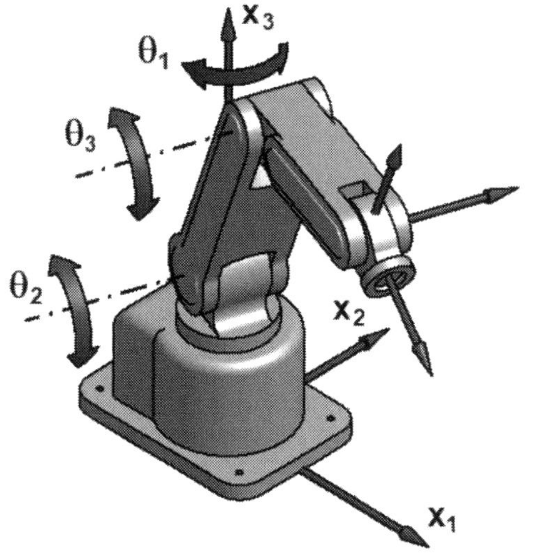

Fig. 2. The anthropomorphic manipulator

Table 1. The geometrical and mass values of manipulator

Link number	Length [m]		Mass [kg]		Mass inertial moment [kgm^2]					
1	λ_1	0.85	m_1	26.2	I_{x1}	–	I_{y1}	0.92	I_{z1}	–
2	l_2	0.95	m_2	10.2	I_{x2}	0	I_{y2}	1.5	I_{z2}	1.5
3	l_3	0.65	m_3	7.2	I_{x3}	0	I_{y3}	0.68	I_{z3}	0.68

The same value for the stiffness coefficient was assumed for all the links, i.e. k_s =2500 Nm/rad and for the viscous damping coefficient c_d =250 Nms/rad. The coordinates of *B*, *E* and *M* points are *B*(0.5,0.5,1), *E*(0.75,0.75,1), *M*(0.5,0.75,1). The assumed maximum acceleration was a_{max} =0.25m/s^2. The simulation tests were conducted for three paths with the arc radii equal to: R_1=0.025m (*Path* 1), R_2=0.01m (*Path* 2) and R_3=0.005m (*Path* 3). The coordinates of the characteristic points of trajectory are presented in Table 2.

Table 2. The coordinates of characteristic points of paths

Path	Tangent point T_1			Tangent point T_2			Arc center O		
	x_1^{T1}	x_2^{T1}	x_3^{T1}	x_1^{T2}	x_2^{T2}	x_3^{T2}	x_1^{O}	x_2^{O}	x_3^{O}
Path 1	0.5	0.725	1	0.525	0.75	1	0.525	0.725	1
Path 2	0.5	0.74	1	0.51	0.75	1	0.51	0.74	1
Path 3	0.5	0.745	1	0.505	0.75	1	0.505	0.745	1

In order to determine the pre-assigned angular displacements at each kinematic pair θ_{g1}, θ_{g2}, θ_{g3} the inverse kinematics problem was solved. There were established the accomplished angular displacements θ_{r1}, θ_{r2}, θ_{r3} as a result of numerical integration of the motion equations (11) and the end-effector positions x_{r1}, x_{r2}, x_{r3} on the basis of the simple problem of kinematics. The end-effector position errors Δx_i were calculated from the dependence $\Delta x_i = x_{gi} - x_{ri}$ for $i = 1, 2, 3$. The simulation experiments provided the courses of the pre-assigned and accomplished trajectory of end-effector motion and the time courses of end-effector position errors (Fig.3).

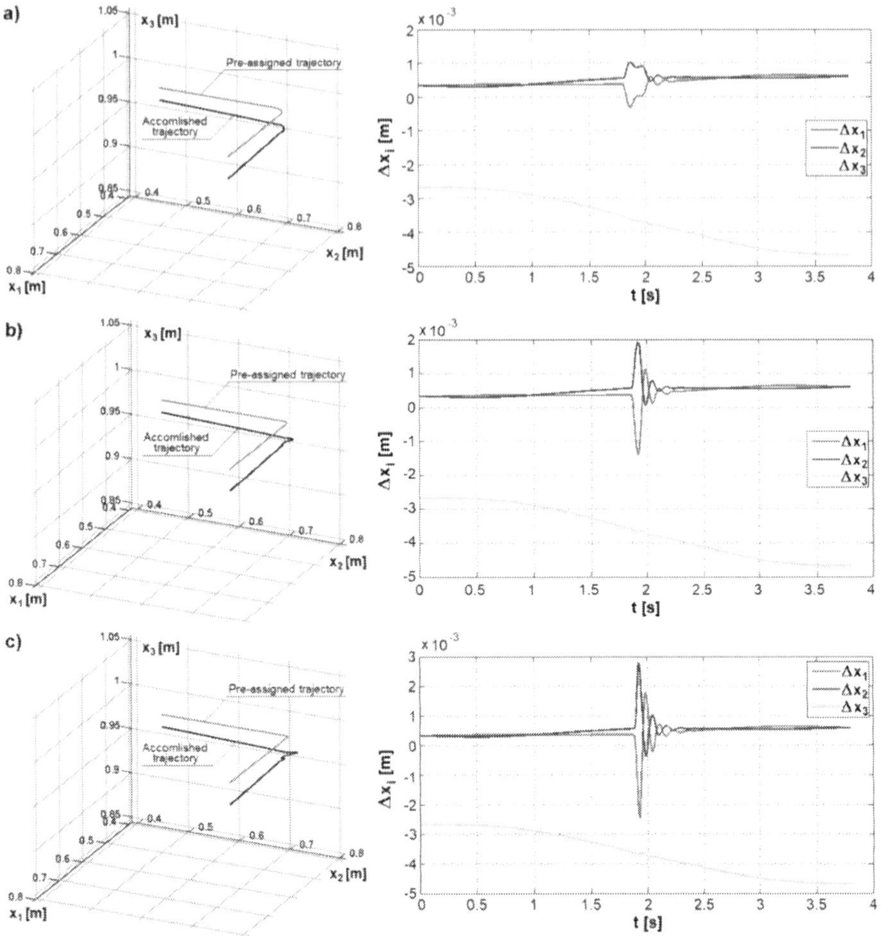

Fig. 3. The pre-assigned and accomplished end-effector trajectory (position error at 5-fold magnification) and the end-effector position errors for: a) *Path* 1, b) *Path* 2, c) *Path* 3

The polynomial coefficients, motion times and motion velocities over the arcs are presented in Table 3.

Table 3. The characteristic values of the planned trajectories

Path	$p^{BT1} = p^{T2E}$ [m/s^9]	$t^{BT1} = t^{T2E}$ [s]	v^{Arc} [m/s]	t^{Arc} [s]	t_{end} [s]
Path 1	0.044401	1.802	0.205	0.192	3.795
Path 2	0.035311	1.861	0.212	0.074	3.796
Path 3	0.032852	1.880	0.214	0.037	3.797

The maximum absolute mapping errors of trajectory are presented in Table 4.

Table 4. The maximum absolute mapping errors of trajectory

Trajectory mapping error	Path denotation		
	Path 1	*Path* 2	*Path* 3
Δx_1 [m]	$6.41 \cdot 10^{-4}$	$1.39 \cdot 10^{-3}$	$2.44 \cdot 10^{-3}$
Δx_2 [m]	$1.02 \cdot 10^{-3}$	$1.92 \cdot 10^{-3}$	$2.79 \cdot 10^{-3}$
Δx_3 [m]	$4.67 \cdot 10^{-3}$	$4.67 \cdot 10^{-3}$	$4.67 \cdot 10^{-3}$

5 Conclusions

Based on the analysis using the proposed algorithm for planning of rectilinear-arc trajectories of the end-effector there can be drawn, the following conclusions:

- The arc radius was found to have a minor effect on the total motion time and at the same time significant influence on position errors. The change of the arc radius from R_1=0.025m (*Path* 1) to R_2=0.01m (*Path* 2) results in the about 2-fold increase in the trajectory mapping errors toward x_1 and x_2 while from R_1=0.025m (*Path* 1) to R_3=0.005m (*Path* 3) – an approximately 4-fold increase. Motion time growth was equal to 0.001s and 0.002s, respectively.
- The errors on the x_1 and x_2 directions result from dynamic loads as the pre-assigned motion proceeded in the x_1x_2 plane. The error toward the x_3 axis is mainly associated with the static load and proved to be almost the same for each arc radius.
- Owing to the assumed small linear acceleration, the dynamic load errors (inertia, centrifugal and Coriolis forces) are smaller than those caused by the static load.
- The errors toward the x_3 axis result from the angular position errors of the second and third links whereas those toward the x_1 and x_2 axes arise chiefly from the angular position error of the first link.

References

1. M. Boryga, A. Graboś, Mech. Mach. Theory **44**, 1400-1419 (2009)
2. M. Boryga, A. Graboś, P. Kołodziej, K. Gołacki, Z. Stropek, Agriculture and Agricultural Science Procedia, **7**, 27-34 (2015)
3. Z. Chen, W.H. Su, B. Li, B.S. Deng, H. Wu, B.Z. Liu, Adv. Mech. Eng. **10**, 1-15 (2018)
4. J. Dong, P.M. Ferreira, J.A. Stori, Int. J. Mach. Tool. Manu. **47**, 1941-1955 (2007)
5. K. Erkorkmaz, C.H. Yeung, Y. Altintas, Int. J. Mach. Tool. Manu. **46**, 1124-1138 (2006)
6. A. Graboś, M. Boryga, Eksploat. Niezawodn. **15**, 182-187 (2013)
7. L. Milica, A. Năstase, G. Andrei, Mech. Mach. Theory **128**, 14-33 (2018)
8. S.J. Tseng, K.Y. Lin, J.Y. Lai, W.D. Ueng, J. Chin. Inst. Eng. **32**, 215-228 (2009)

The modified metric for self-organization wireless MESH networks

Andrzej Paszkiewicz[1,*], and *Przemysław* Zapała[2]

[1]Department of Complex Systems, The Faculty of Electrical and Computer Engineering, Rzeszow University of Technology, al. Powstańców Warszawy 12, 35-959 Rzeszów, Poland

[2] Rzeszów, Poland

Abstract. This paper concerns the modified metrics for MESH wireless networks. This metric is important when a specific data transmission path is being chosen. The parameters regarding the connection quality and overload are introduced in it. Therefore, the proposed metric takes a closer look at changing conditions of the wireless environment and contributes to a better self-organization functioning of this type of network. Its importance increases for networks characterized by the transmission of converged traffic. The paper also presents the results of a simulation showing the dependence of metric values on transmission parameters for selected wireless transmission technologies.

1 Introduction

Self-organization is a known term and increasingly popular in relation to broadly understood computer technologies including computer networks [1-4]. First references to this term were associated with the natural systems, mainly biology [5]. Scientists, observing living organisms, their behavior and reactions to changing conditions (i.e. environmental) create algorithms and self-organizing mechanisms implemented in artificial systems (i.e. telephone networks).

A very good example of network mechanism that adjusts to the dynamic changes of the conditions and transmission parameters are routing algorithms. These mechanisms make decisions to choose the 'best path' for data transmission based on information they have and which is updated. This decision is made individually by each of the nodes. Thus, such a structure resembles a system of independent agents cooperating to achieve a common goal, and their impact on the entire structure (the community) is smaller or larger. It is obvious that computer networks, especially wired ones, to a small extent of their functionality correspond to the definition of multi-agent systems. Whereas wireless networks are very good example of multi-agent systems, especially sensor networks or wireless MESH networks.

MESH networks are a collection of independent nodes, which provide access to the network over a wider area without the need of supplying wired links [6, 7]. This solution

* Corresponding author: andrzejp@prz.edu.pl

allows to cover the large area in which the use of alternative technology is not always possible. To ensure communication in the whole network infrastructure, individual nodes are making independent decisions. They are made within the network without the central unit. Therefore, this structure corresponds to the network consisting of independent agents and fits into a concept of self-organization systems, where individual nodes can connect and disconnect at any time, and the network as a whole system still functions as a coherent environment. The system works according to the determined guidelines and principles to which agents have to adapt, so that actions of all agents are coherent.

Of course, the self-organizing system can be considered from the point of view of different functionalities [8]. In this paper we will focus on the selection of the communication link from the point of view of each node. This choice will be based on the metric that adapts to changing conditions of transmission. This metric directly decides about specific transmission path based on current information. Routing metrics, especially in wired networks, are usually based on simple parameters associated with distance or connection bandwidth. Taking the stability of environment in wired networks into consideration such assumptions may work. However, in wireless networks, especially in the 802.11 technology, there are many transmission interferences and restrictions. Furthermore, the dynamics of these changes is difficult to predict, therefore, the metric should adapt to them.

The fundamental elements responsible for the routes optimization in this protocol are connection metrics, which are also analyzed in this paper. In order to improve the route selection mechanism, the existing metrics were modified.

2 Fundamentals of MESH networks

Nowadays, wireless MESH networks are widely used including provision of communication for fixed and temporary infrastructure [6]. The examples of temporary infrastructure can be big celebrations, sport events, congresses organized in a large area, or providing communication in crisis situations. Excellent examples for permanent infrastructure are parks and university campuses. In these places it is not always possible to bring logical infrastructure (i.e. protection of monuments and wildlife) or the costs are too high in the case of fixed infrastructure.

The MESH network consists of the access points that communicate with each other creating a certain form of self-organizing system Fig.1. In this system, MESH nodes fulfill the role of agents by collecting information from their environment. MESH network is comparable to social model of the multi-agent system.

The role of nodes known as MESH portal is to be a gateway between wired and wireless network. There can be many MESH portals in the given network infrastructure. Thus, reliability is increased and additional load balancing mechanisms can be provided. However, the nodes known as MESH point ensure preservation of the wireless path between MESH nodes. In addition, they can ensure network access for wireless end users. Of course, exactly how this type of network works is described in the 802.11s standard, as well as in numerous publications [7].

Routing protocols have an important role that concerns all types of computer networks. The MESH wireless networks mainly use the Hybrid Wireless Mesh Protocol (HWMP). Other protocols are also possible. The HWMP is a hybrid protocol that is based on a reactive protocol Ad hoc On-demand Distance Vector Routing (AODV) and proactive protocol based on the rule of the tree structure [9]. It works in second layer model ISO-OSI and uses Radio-Aware as a metric for routing.

Thanks to this approach it is possible to create a path structure ready to be used during data transmission, thereby reducing delay associated with creating them. On the other hand, taking into account the variability of parameters in a wireless network environment, there is a chance to select alternative paths with better parameters at the particular time.

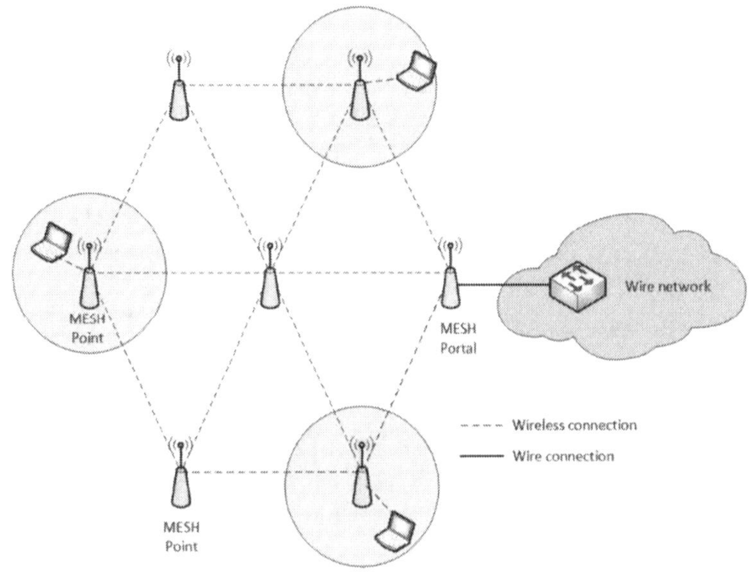

Fig. 1. Example of wireless MESH network infrastructure.

The HWMP allows to create efficient converged networks using WLAN network [10]. The traffic in the converged networks is sensitive to the variability of transmission parameters such as delay, bandwidth, packet retransmission and more. This is why the current update of information about network environment and improvement of the mechanism for choosing "better" transmission paths is the recommended process.

3 Current metric

Various parameters and metrics are used in protocols and routing algorithms for different computer networks. Most popular are: distance (number of hops), bandwidth, links reliability, rate of errors and more [11]. In wireless MESH networks the number of hops and a metric are the most important components in the process of selecting the best route that ensures the connection for this type of network.

The number of hops determines the number of points between a local point and the destination; however, this number is not enough to determine the best route. Sometimes, more beneficial are two fast links to compare with one that is overloaded. The metrics have a data indicator and an error rate indicator. In order to achieve better effectivity, the metrics are used instead of the number of hops. It is important to remember that a given metric can map the current situation from the point of view of a given node, rather than the entire network or transmission path. It is related to high dynamics of possible changes in parameters or interference.

IEEE 802.11s describes standard metrics of connections and determines the use of optional metrics. In order to ensure a possible metric routing, all points are forced to constant actualization of the selection metric. In MESH network 'Airtime Link Metric' is used to calculate the route of each pair. It determines the number of source channels that are used to transmit frames through a specific link. Airtime C_a is described in a category of coefficient modulation r and a bit error expressed by coefficient e_{pt} for the frame size B_t:

$$C_a = \left(O_{ca} + O_p + \frac{B_t}{r}\right)\frac{1}{1-e_{pt}}, \quad (1)$$

where O_{ca} denotes channel access overhead, O_p is a protocol overhead and B_t are constants defined for each type of modulation 802.11 [12].

Table 1. IEEE 802.11s Airtime Link Metric constants.

Parameter	802.11a	802.11b	Description
O_{ca}	75 µs	335 µs	channel access overhead
O_p	110 µs	364 µs	protocol overhead
B_t	8192	8224	number of bits in frame

Nowadays, the used metric is taking into account the channel access overhead, frame heading and protocol overhead, for which parameters O_{ca} and O_p are responsible. Parameter B_t/r determines the time in which the frame will be sent. Parameter $1/(1-e_{pt})$ determines the reliability of the connection. In case of multicast and broadcast traffic, the error rate is not efficient as sent packets are unconfirmed. Thus, the error rate, from the point of view of a given node, will not reflect the real situation. It needs to be remembered that wireless networks are treated as converged networks in which video and audio transmission is as important (and even more important) as traditional data transmission. The MESH networks can be used to stream traffic from monitoring so that link quality and its selection will affect the level of security. Therefore, till now, apart from stable contents in metric, variable values were associated with error rate and the bandwidth of transmission channel.

4 Proposed solution

The proposed modification of the existing metric is based on a single transmission frequency for traffic between nodes, and the traffic between nodes and the end users.

The general principle for selecting a more beneficial metric is as following:

- metric a is better than b, where $a<b$;
- metric a is equal to metric b, where $a=b$;
- metric a is worse than metric b, where $a>b$.

Using this rule, a modification of the existing solution for calculating of metric connection has been proposed. This modification can be presented as follows:

$$C_a = (O_{ca} + O_p + \frac{t}{r} + \frac{d_{fr}}{r})\frac{1}{1-e_{pt}},$$

connection quality | connection overload | connection reliability

O_{ca} is channel access overhead. This value is constant and depends on the IEEE 802.11 standard that is used. The values are defined in Table 1.

O_p is a protocol overhead. This value is constant and it depends on The IEEE 802.11 standard that is used.

t/r determine the quality of the connection. Parameter t defines the delay in connection between a pair of nodes. Parameter r defines the connection bandwidth. The value of the delay parameter should be measured as an average value in specified and constant time intervals.

d_{fr}/r determines the connection overload. Parameter d_{fr} is the sum of packets received and sent. Parameter r is the connection bandwidth. This value precisely determines the load of the channel from the point of view of a given node. We need to remember that during single channel transmission we are dealing with the half-duplex transmission type.
$1/(1-e_{pt})$ determines the reliability of the connection. Parameter e_{pt} is the percentage of the error rate package.
The proposed approach, taking the quality and load of connection into account, adjusts the metric at a given time to conditions in which network operates. This solution makes it possible to predict the overload of connection in the future. This prevents the excessive use of the selected link by individual agents.
The proposed metric is considered in terms of load variability and quality. The metric changes with the change of individual parameters. The chart below Fig. 2 illustrates the relationship between the bandwidth and the total number of packets received and sent. The parameter responsible for the delay in these calculations is constant and its value is 20ms. Reliability of the connection is also constant and its effectiveness is 100%.
By analyzing the charts in Fig. 2 and Fig. 3, metric's declining trend for both IEEE 802.11a and IEEE 802.11b can be observed. This is due to the increase of the capacity for three different values responsible for the connection overload.

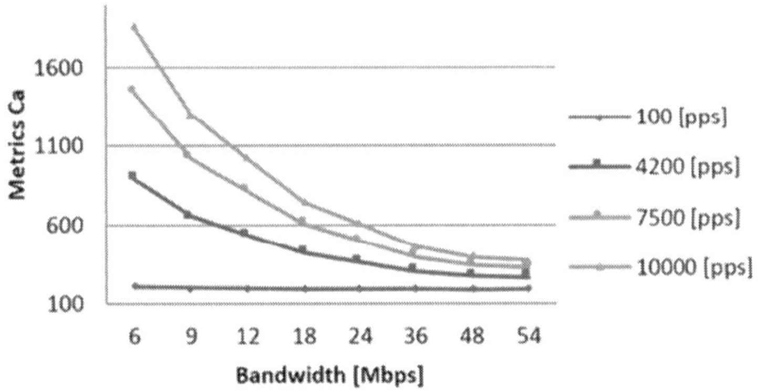

Fig. 2. Airtime link metric – IEEE 802.11a load package.

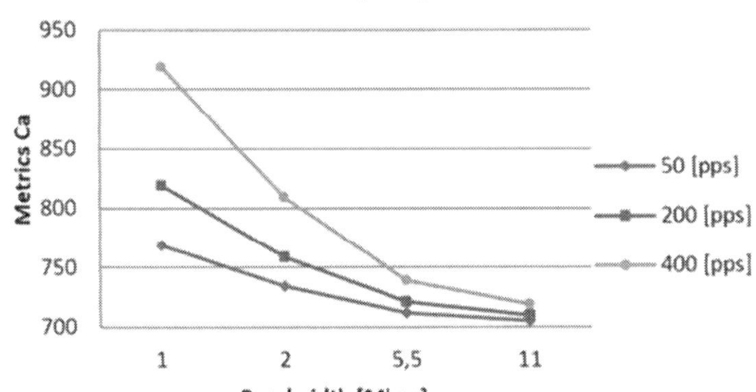

Fig. 3. Airtime link metric – IEEE 802.11b load package.

The tables below: Table 2 and Table 3 include metrics value considered in a broader range of connection overload. Table 2 refers to the IEEE 802.11a standard and Table 3 contains values for the IEEE 802.11b standard. These values significantly diverge from each other at a lower bandwidth connection. The important part of the proposed metric is the part responsible for the connection overload.

Table 2. The value of the metrics depending on the load package – IEEE 802.11a.

[Mbps]\[pps]	100	800	4200	7500	10000
6	205	355	888	1438	1855
9	198	298	654	1021	1298
12	195	270	537	812	1020
18	192	242	419	603	742
24	190	228	361	498	603
36	188	213	302	394	463
48	188	206	273	342	394
54	187	204	263	324	371

Table 3. The value of the metrics depending on the load package – IEEE 802.11b.

[Mbps]\[pps]	50	100	200	300	400
1	769	819	919	1019	1119
2	734	759	809	859	909
5,5	712	721	739	757	775
11	705	710	719	728	737

The following charts present the variability of quality. Fig. 4 refers to the IEEE 802.11a standard and Fig. 5 presents the value for the IEEE 802.11b standard. The parameter responsible for the number of packets received and sent is constant and its value is 400pps. The parameter responsible for the reliability of the connection is also constant and its effectiveness is 100%.

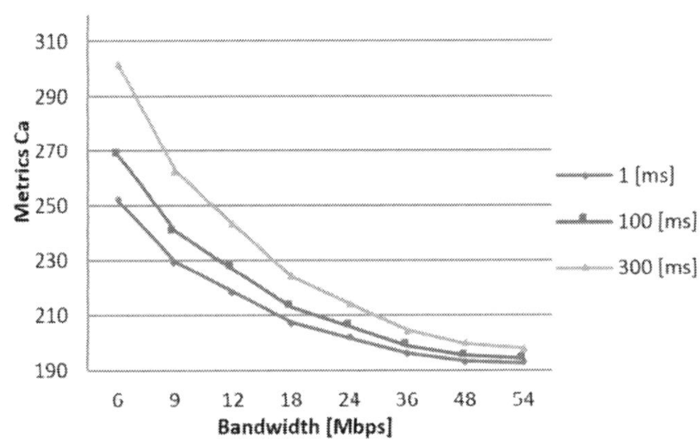

Fig. 4. Airtime link metric – IEEE 802.11a link quality.

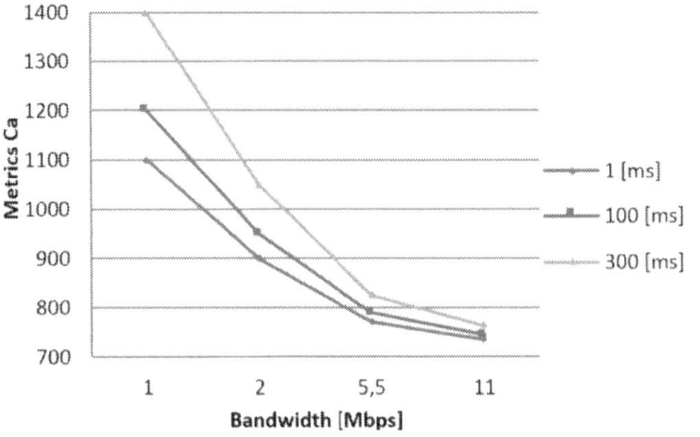

Fig. 5. Airtime link metric – IEEE 802.11b link quality.

The above charts present metrics variation which depends on the bandwidth parameters and the connection delay. The tendency is also declining, resulting from the increase in bandwidth and the decline in the value responsible for the connection delay.

The following tables: Table 4 and Table 5 include values of metrics dependent on the bandwidth and connection delay. Table 4 refers to the IEEE 802.11a standard and Table 5 contains values for the IEEE 802.11b standard. Here the metric was checked in a wider range of time response. Its change affects the change of the oveall value of the metric to a lesser extent than the change values responsible for the connections overload.

Table 4. The value of the metrics depending on the load time – IEEE 802.11a.

[Mbps]\[ms]	1	50	100	300	500
6	252	260	268	302	335
9	230	235	241	263	285
12	218	223	227	243	260
18	207	210	213	224	235
24	202	204	206	214	223
36	196	198	199	204	210
48	193	194	195	200	204
54	192	193	194	198	202

Table 5. The value of the metrics depending on the load time – IEEE 802.11b.

[Mbps]\[ms]	1	50	100	300	500
1	1100	1149	1199	1399	1599
2	900	924	949	1049	1149
5,5	772	781	790	826	863
11	735	740	744	763	781

By analyzing metric used in the HWMP protocol it can be concluded that the metric does not reflect the influence of the most important properties of the link that should be used to calculate metrics. Properties such as bandwidth, load and delay in connection more precisely reflect its current status.

The following charts: Fig. 6 and Fig. 7 present Airtime metric with the metric values of the proposed solution. By analyzing data presented in the chart, it can be concluded that the proposed metric model takes the current state of the connection overload into account. Thanks to that the routing protocol will select the best path based on their decision on the lowest connection overload at that moment. This metric is in favour of the path with a lower load, not as in the case of the old metric model which takes into account the bandwidth connection as the main element of the formula

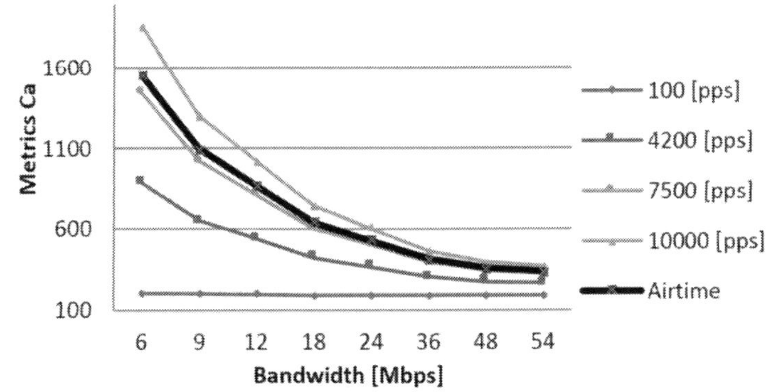

Fig. 6. Compare IEEE 802.11a Airtime link metric with load package.

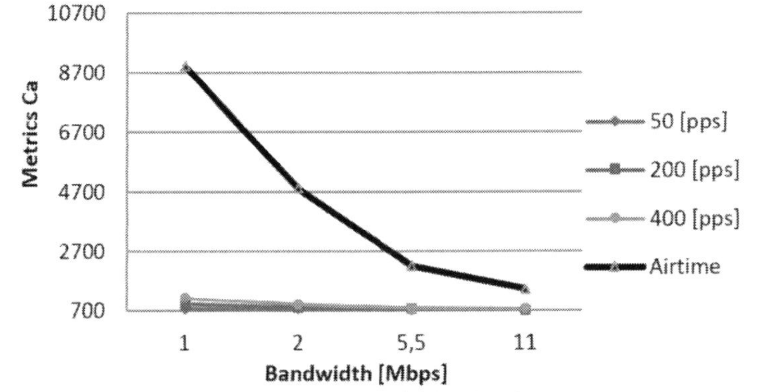

Fig. 5. Compare IEEE 802.11b Airtime link metric with load package.

5 Conclusions

Currently, we are witnessing rapid development and increasing scope of wireless networks application. This fact is affected by many factors such as popularization of mobile devices, the development of new network services, etc. Therefore, it is necessary to search for new solutions and improve existing ones. The modification of route selection methodology for wireless MESH networks proposed in this paper allows for their better adaptation to the current and changing conditions of the network environment. It introduced parameters regarding the connection quality and overload. The obtained simulation results show a close dependence of the metric values on the bandwidth and delay parameters. The proposed metric favours connections with less overload. This approach may be important especially in the case of a converged network. This type of network that combines different types of network traffic, requires the use of links/paths of good quality, high reliability, lack of overload. It seems that the proposed solution takes these requirements into account.

References

1. J.K. Gimzewski, A.Z. Stieg, V. Vesna, *Self-Organization and Emergence of Dynamic Systems. Handbook of Science and Technology Convergence*, part I, 163-180 (2016)
2. C. Prehofer, C. Bettstetter, *Self-organization in communication networks: principles and design paradigms*, IEEE Communications Magazine, **43**, 78-85 (2005)
3. W. Elmenreich, F. Dressler, V. Loreto, *Self-Organizing Systems. Lecture Notes in Computer Science*, **8221** (2014)
4. W. Banzhaf, *Self-Organizing Systems. Encyclopedia of Complexity and Systems Science*, Springer (2009)
5. V.V. Isaeva, *Self-organization in biological systems. Biology Bulletin*, **39**, 110-118 (2012)
6. G.R. Hiertz, D. Denteneer, S. Max, R. Taori, J. Cardona, L. Berlemann, B. Walke, *IEEE 802.11s: The WLAN Mesh Standard*, IEEE Wireless Communications, **17**, 104-111 (2010)
7. A. Sgora, D.D. Vergados, P. Chatzimisios, *IEEE 802.11s Wireless Mesh Networks: Challenges and Perspectives. Social Informatics and Telecommunications Engineering*, **13**, 263-271 (2009)
8. H. Haken, *Information and Self-Organization A Macroscopic Approach to Complex Systems,* Springer (2006)
9. S.M.S. Bari, F. Anwar, M.H. Masud, *Performance study of hybrid Wireless Mesh Protocol (HWMP) for IEEE 802.11s WLAN mesh networks*, International Conference on Computer and Communication Engineering (ICCCE), 712-716 (2012)
10. A. Paszkiewicz, M. Bolanowski, P. Zapała, *Convergent traffic in the environment of wireless MESH technology,* Annales UMCS Sectio AI Informatica, **13**, 84-95 (2013)
11. J. Guerin, M. Portmann, A. Pirzada, *Routing metrics for multi-radio wireless mesh networks*, Telecommunication Networks and Applications Conference, 343–348 (2007)
12. S. Misra, S.Ch. Misra, I. Zhang (Eds.), *Guide to Wireless Mesh Networks*, Springer (2009)

A research on the impact of encryption algorithms on the quality of VPN tunnels' transmission

Dariusz Strzęciwilk[1,*], *Krzysztof* Ptaszek[2], *Paweł* Hoser[1] and *Izabella* Antoniku[1]

[1]Department of Applied Informatics, University of Life Sciences, Nowoursynowska Street 159, 02-787 Warsaw, Poland
[2]Central Anti-Corruption Bureau, al. Ujazdowskie 9, 00-583 Warsaw, Poland

Abstract. The following article presents the results on the impact of encryption algorithms and the cryptographic hash function on the QoS (*Quality of Service*) transmission in a computer network. A network model supporting data encryption using the AES algorithm and the MD5 and SHA hash functions used in VPN tunnels was designed and tested. The influence of different data length on the quality of transmission in a secured network was studied. The measurements and tests of networks were performed according to two methodologies ITU-T Y.1564 and RFC 2544. The impact of the data encryption mechanism on bandwidth, data loss and maximum delays was examined. The secured network tests were performed with different combinations of encryption algorithms and hash functions of the VPN tunnel in the ESP (*Encapsulating Security Payload*) transport mode.

1 Introduction

The Quality of Service as well as network security and information transfer are among the most important challenges emerging during the design and maintenance of modern computer networks and the next-genaration networks [1, 2]. Guaranteeing adequate quality of service is of particular importance in case of real-time applications such as Voice over IP [3] and video - IPTV [4]. The quality of services can be understood as the network's capability of providing a particular service in a better or special way for a group of users or applications, at the expense of other users and applications. Guaranteeing proper quality of service is of big importance in case of real-time applications [5]. These services are particularly sensitive

* Corresponding author: dariusz_strzeciwilk@sggw.pl

to delay and require perfect bandwidth [6]. For this reason, they must have a higher priority and require special management in the network, in comparison with other services and applications, such as e-mail or HTTP traffic. The aim is to provide the desired QoS packages for the entire route from the sender to the recipient, which has been the subject of research for many years [7-9]. The second, but also important, is the issue regarding security of modern computer networks. One of the commonly used methods of increasing network and transmission security is the use of VPN (*Virtual Private Networks*), which is an alternative solution to traditional WAN (*Wide Area Network*) of service providers. VPNs allow you to create private, virtual network connections, so-called tunnels through an unsecured external network - such as public Internet network. However, due to the fact that communication takes place through an unsecured network, there are two problems: no guarantee that the information sent is secured or whether the network is exposed to external attacks. For this reason, adequate protection of the communication channel and access to the internal network should be of great concern, which is why various solutions are sought, such as secured IPSec (*Internet Protocol Security*) tunnels, the use of hardware or software firewalls and systems for detecting and preventing intrusions and attacks on the network. Due to the variety and level of network security advancement as well as data transfer methods, there is a question of how the network security can affect the quality of services available. Thus, the aim of the following research is to examine the impact of network security on the quality of service, using one of the leading Cisco Systems network equipment. A network has been designed and tested that can serve as backbone of a corporate network. The network built is based on Cisco routers and ASA 5510 (*Adaptive Security Appliance*) firewalls, using QoS technology and OSPF (*Open Shortest Path Protocol*). The designed and configured network underwent transmission quality tests using the EXFO FTB-860 measuring platform, which supports the RFC 2544 [10] and ITU-T Y.1564 measurement methodology [11]. Although security is the main priority, the performance of VPN must also be considered. This paper presented how performance of VPN affected by choosing different encryption algorithms used by VPN devices.

2 QoS Model

Along with applications requiring different levels of service quality, various QoS models are available, i.e. ways or strategies according to which the QoS mechanisms designed and implemented within the network. At the current stage of research done by IETF concerning QoS, two architectures have been defined in IP networks, which enable the division of traffic into classes with differentiated quality of services. The first class is Integrated Services (*IntServ*) as described in RFC 1633 [12], and the second class is the Differentated Services (*DiffServ*) described in RFC 2475 [13]. These structures allow for extension of the default Best Effort (BE) model [14] currently applied via the Internet. BE is the default model used in computer networks, which neither does it require package delivery nor configuration. It does not use any QoS mechanisms, but all traffic in the network is treated identically - on the principle of FIFO (*First In, First Out*). This means that packets are sent by a given network device in the order they arrive, regardless of traffic type or priority. In this model, packages are delivered to the destination without guaranteed bandwidth, packets transfer latency, jitter and packet loss at a given level. For this reason, it can only be used by applications not susceptible to latency and not requiring guaranteed bandwidth. The service classes of the IntServ model support all types of applications for which the Guaranteed Service is intended, but they relate to the reservation of resources and scalability problems in backbone networks. For this purpose, the RSVP (*Resource Reservation Protocol*) protocol [15] is used, which deals with a large signaling overhead required for information transfer on reservation parameters and dedicated processor resources for handling packets from a given reservation stream. The Int-Serv model provides a guaranteed bandwidth, however it has low scalability, resulting from a large number of reservations, which is caused by a lack of free bandwidth of network. The scalability problem found in the IntServ model has been eliminated in the DiffServ architecture, which provides the most extensive and appealing solution for QoS support in current IP networks. An important advantage of this model is also the fact that it does not require any signaling protocol. The 8-bit ToS (*Type of Service*) field in the IP packet header (Fig. 1) is used to label the packets, which depending on the value assigns the packet to a specific traffic class - the service type. The DS field value associated with DSCP (DS codepoint) is the label used to classify packages in the DiffServ architecture.

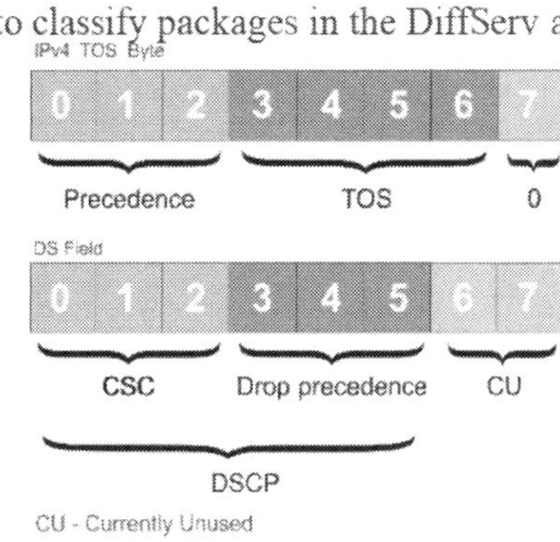

Fig. 1. ToS and DSCP fields

3 IPSec policy components

IPSec is a standard developed by the IETF (*Internet Engineering Task Force*) as a set of protocols and methods that defines configuration of a VPN using the IP protocol. It has been described in RFC documents - among others 2402, 2406, 4301 [16, 17]. The overall IPSec implementation is guided by "*Security Architecture for the Internet Protocol*" RFC 2401[18]. It is not limited to specific security algorithms, encryption, authentication or key exchange, but it is an open standard based on existing algorithms and protocols, in order to implement encryption, authentication and key exchange. The protection offered by IPSec to certain traffic is based on requirements defined by security policy rules defined and maintained by the system administrator [19]. IPSec is a collection of protocols and algorithms used to protect IP packets at layer 3. IPSec consists of five blocks:

- first block - represents the IPSec protocol. You can choose between ESP (*Encapsulating Security Payload*) or AH (*Authentication Header*),
- the second represents encryption algorithms to ensure confidentiality of transmitted data. This can be, for example, DES (*Data Encryption Standard*), 3DES (*Triple DES*), AES (*Advanced Encryption Standard*) or SEAL (*Software-Optimized Encryption Algorithm*),
- the third block represents the algorithms used for ensuring data integrity - the choice is MD5 (*Message Digest 5*) or SHA (*Secure Hash Algorithm*),
- the fourth represents the methods for selecting a shared key used for authentication. It can be PSK (*Pre-shared Keys*) or using a digital signature using the RSA algorithm (from the names of the creators - *Ron Rivest, Adi Shamir, Leonard Adleman*),
- the last block represents DH (*Diffie-Hellman*) key exchange algorithms. There are so-called DH1, DH2, DH5 and DH7.

IPSec defines two modes. It's worth to remember that the IPSec header follows the IP header because it is reference by an IP Protocol number. When IPSec headers are just interested into an IP Packet after the IP header (transport mode). In this mode, the original header is exposed and unprotected. The second mode is known as tunnel mode. In this mode an external IP header is created and the IP addresses are replaced with the tunnel endpoints (Fig. 2).

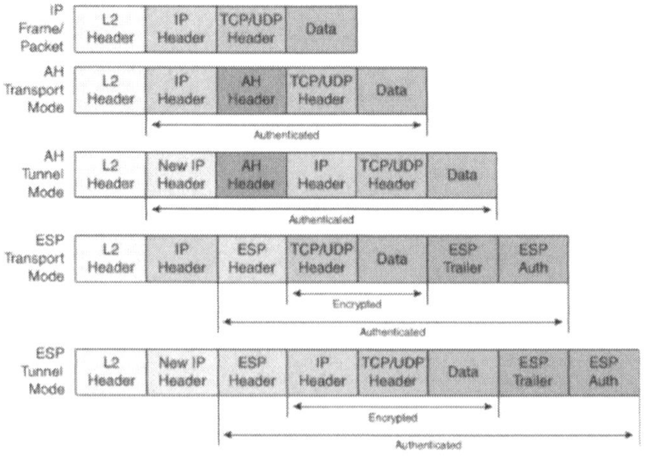

Fig. 2. IPSec header

Confidentiality of data sent in the VPN is ensured by encryption. The level of security depends on the key length of the encryption algorithm. The most commonly used algorithms are:

- DES - fast, symmetrical algorithm using a 56-bit key,
- 3DES - a higher cryptographically DES variant, it uses 3 independent 56-bit keys for each subsequent 64-bit data block, thus providing a much higher level of security,
- AES - symmetric algorithm, safer and more efficient than 3DES. It offers 3 key lengths: 128, 192 and 256 bits,
- SEAL - a symmetric stream algorithm using a 160-bit key.

DES currently does not provide high level of security required in some applications, however, you can artificially increase the length of the key by encrypting the data with the DES (3DES) algorithm. AES was created as a successor of DES at the request of NIST (*National Institute of Standards and Technology*). The AES cipher can operate on a variable length block using variable length keys. The specification allows the use of 128, 192 or 256-bit blocks, encrypted with 128, 192 or 256-bit keys, where all 9 combinations are allowed. The encryption process takes place in N rounds, where N depends on the key length, for a 16-byte key it is 10 rounds, for 24-bytes it is 12 rounds, and for 32-bytes it is 14 rounds. In each round (except for the last one) four transformations are performed successively, with three substitutions and one permutation among them:

- Subbytes - byte substitution using the S-box,
- ShiftRows - simple permutation,
- MixColumns - substitution using arithmetic over $GF(2^8)$,
- AddRoundKey - adding a symmetric (XOR) part of the key to the block.

The encryption and decryption process starts with the AddRoundKey operation, followed by nine four-stage rounds and the tenth three-stage round. The structure of the four-stage round is shown in Fig. 3.

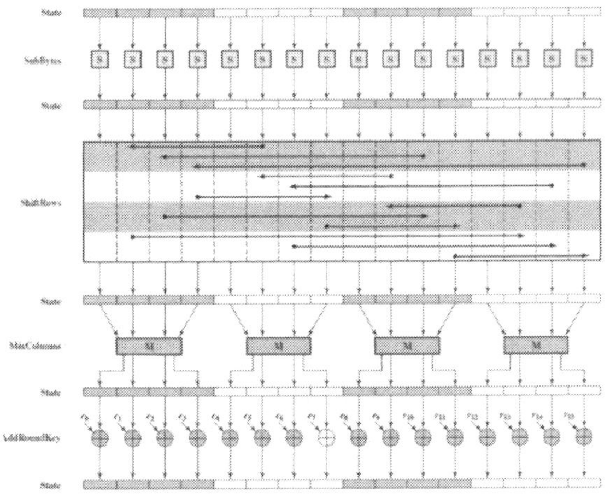

Fig. 3. The course of a single round encryption in the AES algorithm [22].

Another important function of IPSec is data integrity. To ensure the integrity of data during transmission, the HMAC (*Hashed Message Authentication Code*) algorithm is used. Its job is to perform calculations by the device responsible for sending hash values based on the message and the secret key by attaching it to the sent message. Then the receiving device calculates the hash of the received message and compares it with the received one. If the values are equal, then the integrity of the data is preserved. Otherwise, the content of the message changes during transmission and is rejected. Currently, two HMAC algorithms are used:

- messages of any length using 128-bit shared secret key and results in 128-bit hash messages,
- HMAC-SHA-1 - calculates the hash of messages of any length using a 160-bit shared secret key, the calculated hash has 160 bits,
- HMAC-SHA-1 is stronger in cryptographic terms and it is recommended for networks that require a higher level of security.

4 The results of research and discussion

In order to perform tests, two networks were designed - unsecured (as a reference level) and secured one (with different parameters of VPN tunnel). The physical topologies of the networks used are shown in Fig. 4.

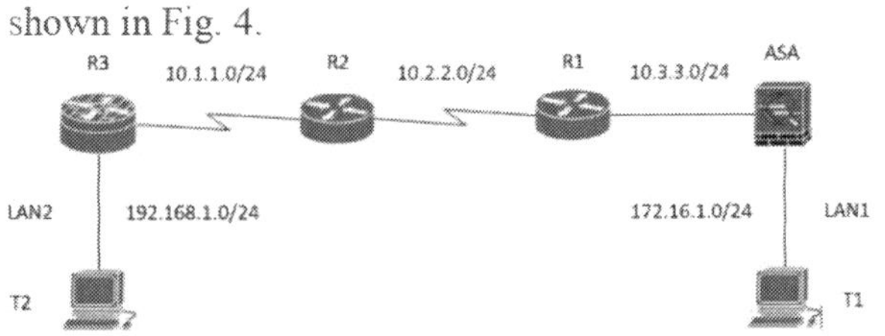

Fig. 4. Topology of the research network

Both networks were implemented using Cisco technology. Cisco 2801 routers with operating system versions IOS 12.4 (13r) T and Cisco 2811 with IOS 12.4 (13r) T (R3). In addition, the Cisco ASA 5510 firewall with operating system 9.1 (2) (ASA), network research and tests were carried out using EXFO FTB-860 *NetBlazer* testers.In the unsecured network, only the basic configuration of all devices was carried out as well as the OSPF routing protocol and NAT address translation on R1 and R3 routers were configured. In the secured network, in addition to the configuration mentioned earlier, the IOS firewall was implemented to R3 router and Intrusion Prevention System (IPS) to guard the network. In addition, in the LAN1 network, a software ASA firewall was used. A site-to-site tunnel IPsec VPN was configured between LAN1 and LAN2 (with different combinations of encryption algorithms and hash functions), while the function of VPN gateways is performed by ASA firewall and R3 router. Traffic in both networks was generated by network testers. These generators were also used to measure QoS parameters in networks. Network tests were carried out according to the RFC 2544 [20] methodology and ITU-T Y.1564 [11], also known as EtherSam. Tests according to RFC 2544 were carried out for frames with 7 sizes defined in the standard - 64, 128, 256, 512, 1024, 1280 and 1518 bytes, while the measured QoS parameters were the following:

- bandwidth,
- frame loss,
- maximum latency (from the moment of sending from the source, until the receiving device collects the frame).

According to the EtherSam methodology tests were performed simultaneously for 3 different services, i.e. types of network traffic, generated at speeds of 3 Mb/s (service-1), 5 Mb/s (service-2) and 2 Mb/s (service-3) and frames about randomly generated size. The secured network tests were performed with the following combinations of encryption algorithms and hash functions used in the IPSec. VPN tunnel in the ESP transport mode. In both test methodologies, network traffic with a total speed of 10 Mb/s was generated from the testers - at the entrance. As a result of the conducted tests, it was found that network bandwidth for frame 64 - 512 bytes increases with the size of the frame, and after reaching the value of 512 bytes remains at a similar level. The exception is a 1518-byte frame in a secured network, where one can observe a significant increase in bandwidth. The measured bandwidth values of frames of different sizes and different encryption algorithms and hash functions are shown in Fig. 5.

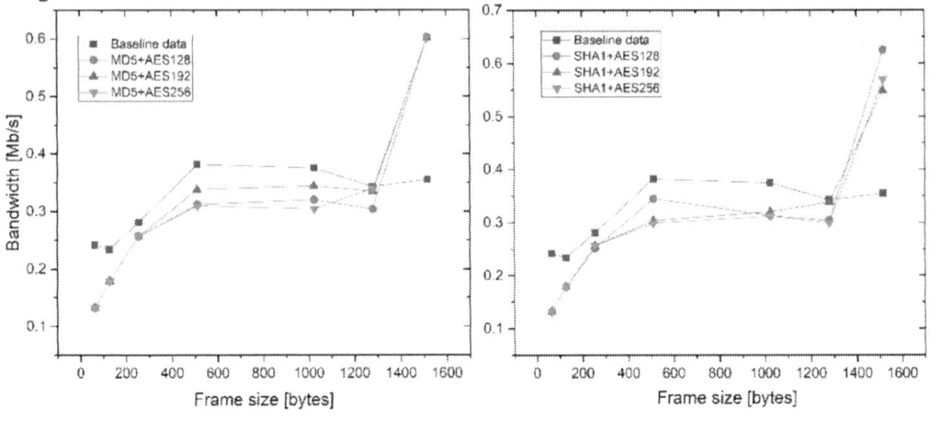

Fig. 5. Network bandwidth values for different frame sizes and AES algorithms as well as MD5 and SHA hash functions

The resulting latency values for frames in the range of 64 to 512 bytes increase with the increase of the frame size, and after reaching the value of 512 they remain at a similar level, except for a 1518 byte frame in a secure network for which the latency value is more than doubled (Fig. 6). In addition, the test showed that the values of network capacity measured for individual services are the highest for unsecured networks, however the secured network remains at a similar level regardless of the security method. The obtained jitter values for different services are the smallest in case of unsecured network, while for the secured network there are slight fluctuations of values (Fig. 7).

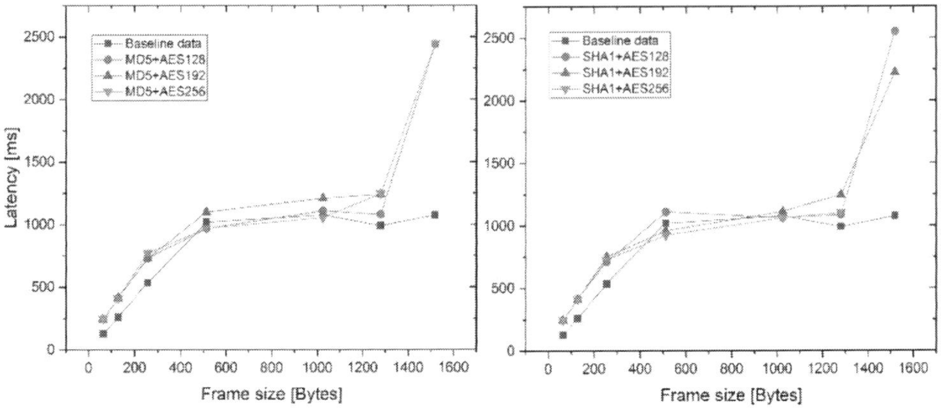

Fig. 6. Latency values [ms] obtained for various network and service protections

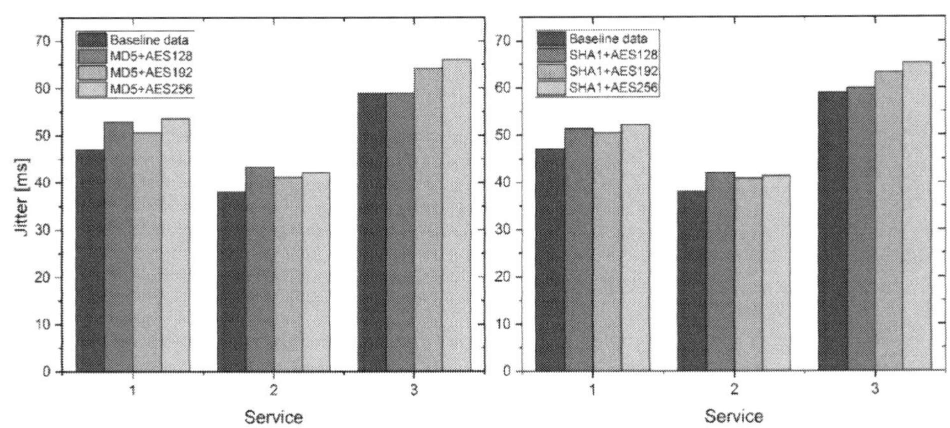

Fig. 7. Jitter values [ms] obtained for various network and service protections

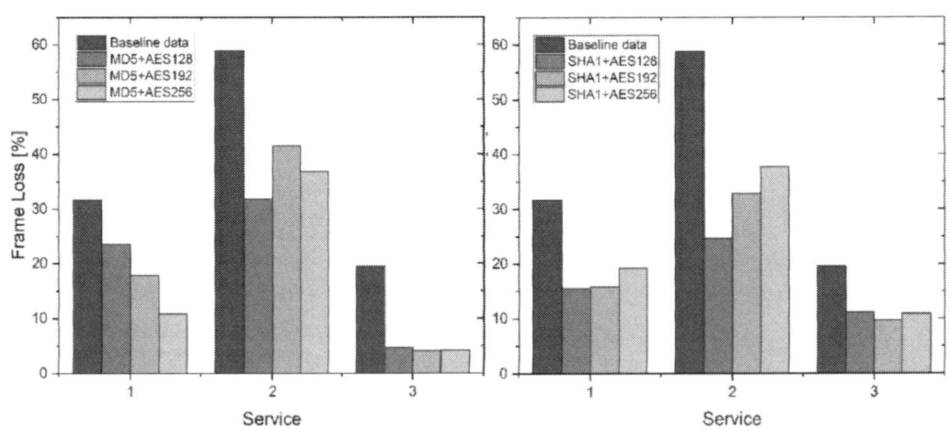

Fig. 8. Percentage of frame loss for various network and service security

The measured frame loss for individual services are the highest for unsecured networks, while for the secured network a clear measured parameter dispersion is noticed (Fig. 8). The analysis of test results according to the RFC 2544 methodology showed that the rise in frame size increases throughput and latency, while the number of frame loss decreases. In case of bandwidth, this is due to the fact that additional bytes are added to each transmitted Ethernet frame - a preamble and a frame interval. The mentioned information overhead causes that the actual network bandwidth decreases, which is much more visible for frames with a smaller payload, because a large part of the transmitted bytes are additional bytes not belonging to stored area. For large frames, additional bytes absorb less bandwidth, as the frame payload is larger. Comparing the obtained bandwidth values of unsecured networks with a secured network, one can observe that the bandwidth of the secured network is smaller. This is due to the encapsulation of IP packets transmitted in the IPSec VPN tunnel. As a result of ESP encapsulation, additional bytes are added to the original packet - ESP header, training sequence, authentication bytes and a new IP address. This is typical for smaller frames. In case of larger frames, the difference between the unsecured and secured network bandwidth is almost unnoticeable due to the large frame payload. It can be concluded that the effect of choosing the AES key length and the hash function is not perceived. Analyzing the results on the key length dependency for the AES algorithm, it can be stated that key length does not have a significant impact on the measured parameters. In AES, depending on the key length used - 128, 192 or 256 bits, the numbers of cipher rounds in the algorithm change, with the value of 10, 12 and 14 respectively, making a small difference in AES speed for various keys. Analyzing the impact of the hash function used, it can also be said that its choice has an nonmeasurable effect on the obtained values of QoS parameters. In addition, the small differences in measured parameters for different algorithms and key lengths used in the tunnel are certainly influenced by hardware support for algorithms implemented in Cisco devices. Tests made in accordance with ITU-T Y.1564, confirm the results obtained for RFC 2544. For all measured parameters common to both methodologies, analogous relations are seen. For all services, the bandwidth values are lower in respect to the secured network, similar with latency - it is greater for secured network. It can be noticed, however, that latencies measured according to ITU-T Y.1564 are much higher, which is due to the fact that they were measured from the moment the frame was sent until the return frame was received by the tester and not one-way like in case RFC 2544. The only parameter, not measured according to RFC 2544 - average jitter, is also lower for all services of unsecured networks. The reason for this is the introduction of additional jitter by means of firewalls and IPS implemented in the secured network. When analyzing the results of the EtherSam tests it is difficult to notice, similarly to the RFC 2544 tests, the dependency of the measured parameter values on the level of security, thus the encryption algorithm, key length or cryptographic hash function used.

5 The results of research and discussion

Information security is a trade-off between ease of use and convenience and restriction for protection from misuse. The conducted research and tests have shown that the use of network security methods offered by Cisco such as IPSec VPN, firewall or IPS causes slight deterioration of service parameter quality. For IPSec VPN, the deterioration of QoS parameters results from an additional information overhead - encapsulation of IP packets and the time needed for encryption, decryption and calculation of the hash function. However, as the results show, the differences in the obtained values for various combinations of VPN tunnel algorithms are insignificant, which proves the high efficiency of Cisco technology. The quality parameters in the network are also influenced by the use of security systems that analyze packets continuously, i.e. firewalls and IPS systems, because the operation of these systems introduces additional latency and jitter to transmitted packets.

References

1. H. Tarasiuk, et al., The IPv6 QoS system implementation in virtual infrastructure, *Telecommunication Systems* **61.2**, 221-233, (2016)
2. G. Schollmeier, Ch. Winkler, Providing sustainable QoS in next-generation networks, *IEEE Communications Magazine* **42.6,** 102-107, (2004)
3. D. Strzęciwilk, Examination of Transmission Quality in the IP Multi-Protocol Label Switching Corporate Networks, International Journal of Electronics and Telecommunications. **58**(3), 267-272 (2012)
4. H. J. Kim, S. G. Choi, A study on a QoS/QoE correlation model for QoE evaluation on IPTV service, Advanced Communication Technology (ICACT), 2010 The 12th International Conference on. **vol. 2**. IEEE (2010)
5. D. Kyriazis, et al., A real-time service oriented infrastructure, *GSTF Journal on Computing (JoC)* **1.2** (2018)
6. W. Zuberek, D. Strzęciwilk, Modeling Quality of Service Techniques for Packet–Switched Networks, Dependability Engineering, ISBN 978-953-51-5592-8 (2018)
7. D. Strzęciwilk, W. M. Zuberek, Modeling and Performance Analysis of Priority Queuing Systems, *Computer Science On-line Conference*. Springer, Cham, pp 302-310 (2018)
8. J. Carmona-Murillo, et al., QoS in Next generation mobile networks: an analytical study, Resource management in mobile computing environments, Springer Int. Publishing. 25-41 (2014)
9. D. Strzęciwilk, W. M. Zuberek, Modeling and performance analysis of QoS data, Photonics Applications in Astronomy, Communications, Industry, and High-Energy Physics Experiments 2016. International Society for Optics and Photonics (2016)
10. R. Bolla, R. Bruschi, RFC 2544 performance evaluation and internal measurements for a Linux based open router, *High Performance Switching and Routing, 2006 Workshop on*. IEEE (2006)
11. T. Diallo, M. Dorais, EtherSAM: The new standard in Ethernet service testing, *EXFO Applicartion Notes*, 4-6 (2001)
12. R. Braden, D. Clark, S. Shenker, *Integrated services in the internet architecture: an overview*, No. RFC 1633 (1994)
13. D. Grossman, New terminology and clarifications for diffserv, No. RFC 3260 (2002)
14. P. Gevros, et al., Congestion control mechanisms and the best effort service model, *IEEE network* **15.3**, 16-26 (2001)
15. L. Zhang, et al., Resource reservation protocol (RSVP)--Version 1 functional specification, *Resource* (1997)
16. S. Kent, R. Atkinson, RFC 2402, *IP Authentication Header* (1998)
17. S. Kent, K. Seo, *Security architecture for the internet protocol,* No. RFC 4301 (2005)
18. S. Kent, R. Atkinson, RFC 2401, Security architecture for the Internet Protocol, November (1998)
19. N. Doraswamy, D. Harkins, *IPSec: the new security standard for the Internet, intranets, and virtual private networks,* Prentice Hall Professional (2003)
20. S. Bradner, J. McQuaid, *Benchmarking methodology for network interconnect devices,* No. RFC 2544 (1999)
21. W. Stallings, *Cryptography and network security: principles and practice,* Pearson Education India (2003)

The use of the power law for designing wireless networks

Andrzej Paszkiewicz[1,*]

[1]Department of Complex Systems, The Faculty of Electrical and Computer Engineering, Rzeszow University of Technology, al. Powstańców Warszawy 12, 35-959 Rzeszów, Poland

Abstract. The paper concerns the use of the scale-free networks theory and the power law in designing wireless networks. An approach based on generating random networks as well as on the classic Barabási-Albert algorithm were presented. The paper presents a new approach taking the limited resources for wireless networks into account, such as available bandwidth. In addition, thanks to the introduction of opportunities for dynamic node removal it was possible to realign processes occurring in wireless networks. After introduction of these modifications, the obtained results were analyzed in terms of a power law and the degree distribution of each node.

1 Introduction

The last half a century is a period of an intensive development of different types of networks. Initially it was communication and energy infrastructure, but in the next step phone networks appeared as well, and currently computer networks exist. We should also remember about social networks. The importance of this type of structure has increased along with the development of the Internet network. The modeling and methods of supporting of the design process are therefore an important part of the work area of engineers and scientists. The paper is primarily focused on designing wireless networks and using a power law for this purpose.

Computer networks like other natural and artificial systems should be treated like complex systems [1-3]. This group includes both biological organisms, social relations and infrastructure including computer networks. For many years such systems have been treated as simple systems and specific methods and means designed for these systems have been applied to them. However, the properties of complex systems require the utilization of suitable mechanisms and models based on fractal structures, power law, non-extensive statistics, etc. [4, 5]. Of course, we must be aware that due to the complexity of the complex systems design problem, their individual properties in the proposed solutions, algorithms and models should be gradually taken into account [6-8].

Unfortunately, for many years, the complex networks have been treated as regular or random structures. In case of regular structures, it was assumed that the degree of each node is the same. Thanks to these properties, the regular networks are characterized by a high clustering coefficient, but have a long average distance between nodes. Such an approach

* Corresponding author: andrzejp@prz.edu.pl

could make sense only in rarely met special cases. However, such an assumption made it easier to formulate statements and achieves the appropriate topological parameters. This approach recommended and even enforced using specific structures e.g. rings, grids, binary trees, etc. for computer networks and their many variations and modifications. The other, different way to create merging structures was the adoption of the random model. This was the result of Paul Erdos and Alfred Renyi's statement in 1959 that such systems can be modeled by random connecting nodes between each other and they have a short average distance between the vertices [9]. As a consequence of this, such a model was generally used, and moreover it turned out that the systems based on this model were characterized by the Poisson distribution in relation to the degree of each vertex (network node) [10, 11]. That system had the symptoms of a democratic one in which majority of nodes have a similar number of connections. As a result, despite the randomness, it wasn't possible to have structures with specific centers or nodes having much more connections than other vertices. This resulted from the assumption that together with the increase of edges attached to the vertex, the probability of joining other ones is decreasing. One of the variants of the random model are mechanisms based on genetic algorithms, in which a set of selected individuals from the population is put to the pseudo random operations of crossover and mutation [12]. During the study of functioning of unnatural systems and the behavior of many natural systems, it was found that their connection, communication structure and social relations as well, they have the characteristics described by the power law [13-15]. The use of this phenomenon in the design of the network infrastructure was initiated by the preferential attachment algorithm presented by Albert-László Barabási and Albert Réka [16]. This algorithm applies to so-called scale-free network, in which the increase of the node's value depends on its current value – this is exactly described in the following part.

This paper presents the results of simulations connected with the introduction of improvements in the form of a modification of the classical preferential attachment algorithm. The purposes of these actions were to make the process of modeling of computer networks, especially wireless networks, more realistic.

2 Power Law and scale-free networks

The power law has accompanied us from the beginning of the time. However, relatively recently it has been used to describe phenomena occurring in artificial systems such as e.g. computer networks. For the first time, the power law was observed in the science by B.G. Buelnger in 1729 during research on stress relaxation in the materials. A significant contribution to the research in the field of power law was made by the Italian sociologist and economist Vilfredo Pareto, who studied, among others, distribution of income and size/level of salaries in society. According to the power law, the degree distribution of vertices is a strongly decreasing function with the so-called heavy tail. However, in the double logarithmic scale, they form straight lines (Fig. 1).

Thus, in the contrast to the democratic distribution of connections known from the random networks, the power law describes systems in which several centers of the so-called hubs are dominators. This type of networks are called scale-free networks [17]. In these networks the probability of connection between the new node and each node belonging to the network depends very much on the number of edges possessed by these nodes and for the k-th vertex is expressed by:

$$P(k) \sim k^{-\gamma}. \quad (1)$$

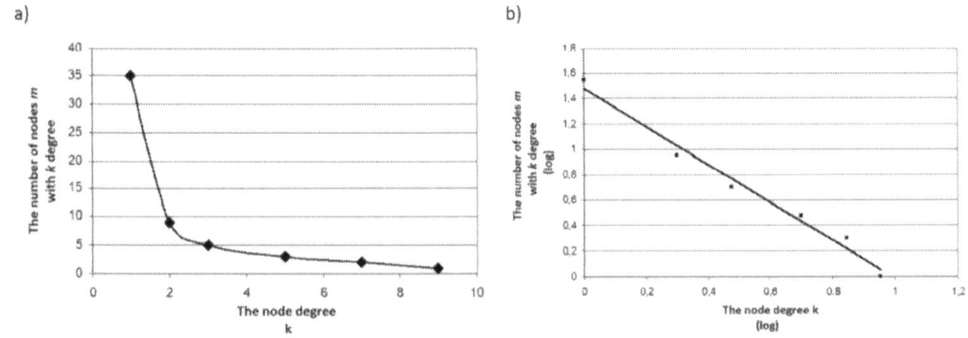

Fig. 1. The probability distribution of connecting to the node: a) the distribution corresponding to the power law; b) the distribution corresponding to the power law in a double logarithmic scale.

The use of relations coming from a power law in computer science was initiated in 1998 in Hawoong Jeong and Réka Albert's works from the University of Notre Dame [18]. These scientists began project of website network mapping. Initially, they assumed that results they obtained would confirm dependences that are characteristic for a random network. However, researches has shown that a small number of pages have multiple connections. Whereas, more than 80% of pages had four connections. From this perspective, it turned out that the system of links between Web pages perfectly fits into relations compatible with a power law. The result of this discovery was showing scale-free feature other networks, which similarly show the power distribution of vertex degrees. This relationship can be very easily observed in a social network, in which a person with a large number of friends is attracting new ones faster [19, 20]. The same is observed in the structure of e-mail connections [14] between different domains, and in the structure of the Internet as well. There are nodes (hubs) in this network that have a particularly large number of connections with others, and also represent the intermediate point for a large number of flows between autonomous systems [13]. These are, of course, selected examples from the area of computer science, where power law and scale-fee networks are visible. Similar examples can be found in other areas of life and also in different fields of science. The income of states, the income of citizens, the distribution of earthquakes as well as the frequency of words in the text, etc. are shaped according to the power law. Taking it into account, relations resulted from a power law should form the basis of currently created models and algorithms of designing connection structures.

An important advantage of systems built in accordance with the power law is their resistance to accidental failures. Due to the fact that many nodes have a small number of connections with other nodes, their accidental damage will not significantly affect the functioning of the entire structure. On the other hand, what is the advantage may be some kind of threat, so there are particularly important centers, which damage will cause the degradation of the entire system. Therefore, they should be especially well protected. However, the problem of protection of these nodes is not the subject of this work.

3 Random structures vs. the preferential attachment algorithm

Wireless networks are characterized by very large dynamics of changes in the structure. At first glance it would seem that the appearance of new nodes (users) in the wireless network has a random character. However, after a deeper analysis, it turns out that also in wireless networks there are specific centers (hubs), which link a much larger number of users than others. Therefore, it appears reasonable to use models based on a power law during designing a wireless network.

At the beginning, experiments were carried out, in which the degree distribution of vertices for the random mechanism and based on preferential attachment (the power law) was compared. For the first case, the obtained results are shown in Fig. 2.

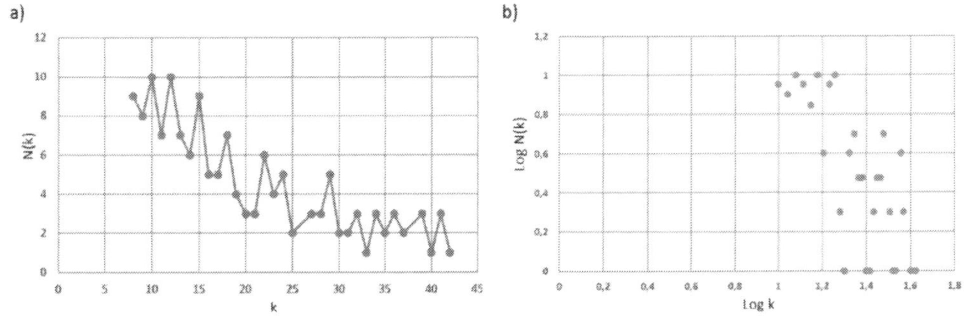

Fig. 2. The probability distribution of connecting to the node (for the random mechanism): a) the distribution corresponding to the power law; b) the distribution corresponding to the power law in a double logarithmic scale.

The process of preferential attachment consists in binding nodes based on the rule that the higher probability, the greater the chance that more will be attached to a given node. This phenomenon is characteristic for scale-free networks. This mechanism was proposed by Barabási and Albert [21]. On its basis, a program generating a graph was created, which presents a scale-free network. The classic algorithm of modeling scale-free network is presented below:

- Initially, we create the relatively small number of nodes (corresponding APs).
- We introduce another new node (representing a client). Probability that the new node (client) is connected with the *i*-th node (access point) depends on the degree of node (k_i): $P(k_i) = k_i / \sum_j k_j$.
- We continue to add new nodes (clients), until requested quantities.

Examples of wireless network designing results obtained by the action of the classic preferential attachment algorithm were illustrated on Fig. 3.

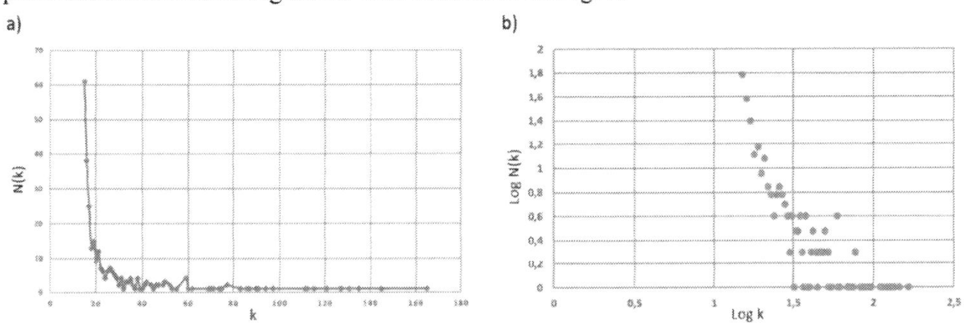

Fig. 3. The probability distribution of connecting to the node (for the classic preferential attachment algorithm): a) the distribution corresponding to the power law; b) the distribution corresponding to the power law in a double logarithmic scale.

As shown in the charts above, the values of individual nodes degrees are close to each other in the random model. Thus, the standard deviation is small in this case. On the other hand, in the case of a model based on preferential attachment the obtained results fit perfectly into relations resulting from the power law.

However, the adoption of the classical Barabási-Albert algorithm for creating scale-free networks does not take many important factors into account. Therefore, this model does not correspond to the real limitation of wireless networks.

4 The proposed solution

In this paper a new approach to the designing of wireless networks based on the power law is proposed. This approach takes additional factors into account, such as limiting the bandwidth and dynamic removal of added nodes. Thanks to this, the modeled system is close to real conditions. The classic model based on the Barabási-Albert algorithm belongs to a group of incapacitated models [22]. These models assume that the hubs (concentrators) have no capacity limitations. In the case of the proposed solution, the limitation for both the available capacity for each node and the capacity (weight) of end users was introduced. Therefore, this approach is consistent with capacitated models [22]. This mechanism is based on an assumption that is compatible to the expression:

$$C_i^{\max} \leq \sum_j c_j, \tag{2}$$

where $C_i^{\max}$ indicates the maximum capacity (weight) of the given node and c_j is a value of traffic (weight) generated by the user (node). Thus, exceeding the sum of the edge weights of the added vertex relative to the specified value stops the adding of further edges. This situation corresponds to the maximum possibilities of transferring data through the node, that is, its capacity. Fig. 4 shows examples of wireless network design results obtained on the basis of operating of the improved preferential attachment algorithm that takes the capacitated model into account. The results confirm that the introduction of the capacitated model for designing wireless networks based on the preferential attachment algorithm has not changed the nature of the network. Still it has the character of scale-free network consistent with the power law.

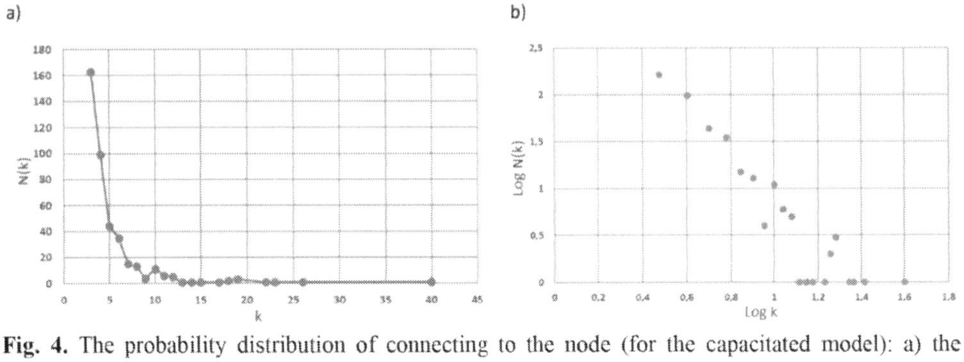

Fig. 4. The probability distribution of connecting to the node (for the capacitated model): a) the distribution corresponding to the power law; b) the distribution corresponding to the power law in a double logarithmic scale.

Another improvement in the proposed solution is consideration of both the appearance of dynamics nodes and their disappearance. Wireless networks are characterized by high dynamics of changes as to the number of current users and devices available (active) at the moment. The classical algorithm for creating scale-free networks does not take this factor into account. The aim of the simulations was to observe whether this change will influence the character of the modeled network. Despite the introduction of randomness of removal nodes, the network still retained its character compatible with the power law as shown in Fig. 5.

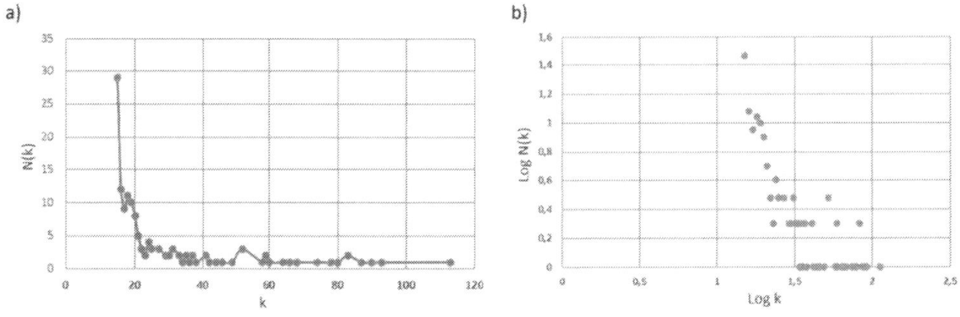

Fig. 5. The probability distribution of connecting to the node (by randomness of removal nodes): a) the distribution corresponding to the power law; b) the distribution corresponding to the power law in a double logarithmic scale.

So far, local wireless networks have usually been a form of a gateway that allows end users to communicate with the remaining network infrastructure (mostly wired) or to provide access to the Internet. However, more and more often wireless networks are an extensive network structure enabling communication between its elements. Individual wireless users (or stations) can provide various services to each other. Very often such services require stable transmission parameters over the entire data path. In this case, one should strive to ensure the best conditions for communication, especially with a large number of active devices/users. One of the possible mechanism to be used in this case is load balancing. Based on an algorithm of preferential attachment some modifications were made. The amount of flows between any pair of users passing through individual access nodes were analyzed. Thus, in this case a higher probability to establish new connections had those nodes through which the least number of paths passes between any pair of vertices. Of course, keeping all other assumptions resulting from the classical preferential attachment algorithm. The described modification is based on the expression:

$$\min \sum_{(i,j)\in V} p_{ij}(x), \tag{3}$$

where p_{ij} represents the existence of the data flow path between any pair i and j in a given node. p_{ij} can be set as 1 if there is a flow, and 0 if it is not. This assumption takes into account the mechanism of load balancing, and such an approach may have a positive effect in the case of networks with medium or high density of wireless nodes.

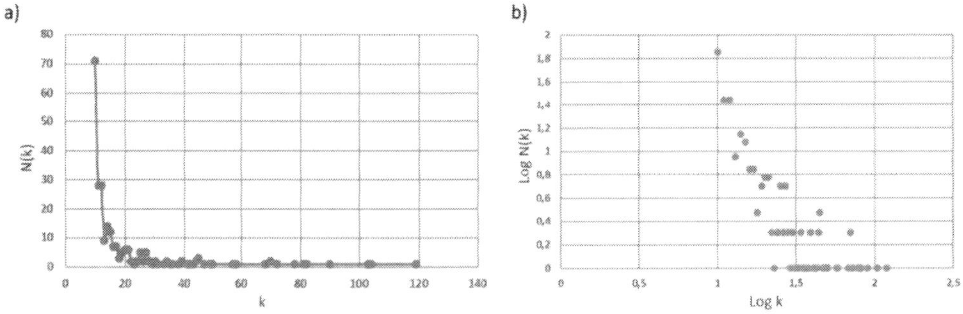

Fig. 6. The probability distribution of connecting to the node (by the mechanism of load balancing): a) the distribution corresponding to the power law; b) the distribution corresponding to the power law in a double logarithmic scale.

Moreover, Fig. 6 presents the results of a sample simulation of the modified algorithm. The results confirm that the introduction of modification taking into account the flow degree of the node to designing of wireless networks based on the preferential attachment algorithm has not changed the nature of the network.

5 Conclusions

The development of mobile technologies causes that it is necessary to search for effective models and mechanisms to support the design and analysis of the functioning of wireless networks. Wireless networks are complex systems. Therefore, appropriate models should be used for these systems, and they are taking into account the actual phenomena occurring in these systems. One of the mechanism that describes these phenomena is the power law. This law can be observed in many naturally occurring effects such as earthquakes, rainfall, topography as well as many human relationships, such as professional links, quoting articles, or wealth distribution in society. It was also noticed in many aspects of the operation of computer systems including software systems and computer networks. Therefore, it should be used during designing of wireless networks. As shown in this paper, the values of individual nodes degrees are close to each other in the random model. Thus, the standard deviation is small in this case. On the other hand, in the case of a model based on preferential attachment, the obtained results fit perfectly to relations resulting from the power law. However, the classical preferential attachment algorithm based on the power law, does not take into account many factors that affect the functioning of the real wireless networks. Thus, the bandwidth of limitations and the number of active users, and the load balancing mechanism were included into the algorithm. Therefore, the solutions proposed are some kind of an approximation of applied models to real conditions. Additionally, as a result of the simulations, it was shown that the changes do not modify the nature of the scale-free network. In future works, queuing mechanisms can be included, and the limitations of the power of mobile devices in developed models and algorithms.

References

1. J. Ladyman, J. Lambert, K. Wiesner, *What is a complex system?* European Journal for Philosophy of Science, **3**(1), 33–67 (2013)
2. F. Grabowski, *Nonextensive model of self-organizing systems. Complexity*, Wiley, **18**(5), 28-36 (2013)
3. G.M. Dimirovski (Ed.), *Complex Systems. Relationships between Control, Communications and Computing. Studies in Systems*, Decision and Control, **55** (2016)
4. G. Nicolis, C. Nicolis, *Foundations of Complex Systems: Emergence, Information and Predicition* (2012)
5. F. Grabowski, A. Paszkiewicz, M. Bolanowski, *Wireless networks environment and complex networks*, Analysis and Simulation of Electrical and Computer Systems, **324**, 261-270 (2015)
6. Z. Gomółka, B. Twaróg, J. Bartman, B. Kwiatkowski, *Improvement of Image Processing by Using Homogeneous Neural Networks with Fractional Derivatives Theorem*, AIMS, Discrete and Continuous Dynamical Systems, Journal of American Institute of Mathematical Sciences, 505-514 (2011)
7. T. Pełech-Pilichowski, *A hybrid algorithm for detecting changes in diagnostic signals received from technical devices*, Proceedings of the Federated Conference on Computer Science and Information Systems, 321–327 (2011)
8. T. Pełech-Pilichowski, J.T. Duda, *A two-level detector of short-term unique changes in time series based on a similarity method*, Expert Systems 2015, **32**(4), 555–561 (2015)
9. P. Erdős, A. Rényi, *On Random Graphs I*, Publicationes Mathematicae, 290–297 (1959)

10. M.E.J. Newman, *Random graphs as models of networks*, Santa Fe Institute (2002)
11. M.E.J. Newman, S. Strogatz, D. Watts, *Random graph models of social networks*, Proceedings of the National Academy of Sciences of the United States of America, **99**, 2566–2572 (2002)
12. S.N. Sivanandam, S.N. Deepa, *Introduction to Genetic Algorithms*, Springer-Verlag Berlin Heidelberg (2008)
13. G. Siganos, M. Faloutsos, P. Faloutsos, Ch. Faloutsos, *Power laws and the AS-level internet topology*, IEEE/ACM Transactions on Networking, **11**(4), 514-524 (2003)
14. H. Ebel, L. Mielsch, S. Bornholdt, *Scale-free topology of e-mail networks*, Physical review E, **66**(3) (2002)
15. S. Redner, *Citation Statistics From More Than a Century of Physical Review*, Physics Today, **58**, 49-54 (2005)
16. R. Albert, A.L. Barabási, *Statistical mechanics of complex networks*, Review of Modern Physics, **74**, 47-91 (2002)
17. A.L. Barabási, *Scale-Free Networks: A Decade and Beyond*, Science Magazine, **325**, 412-413 (2009)
18. R. Albert. H. Jeong, A.L. Barabási, *Diameter of the world-wide web*, Nature, **401**, 130-131 (1999)
19. L. Muchnik, S. Pei, L.C. Parra, H. Makse, *Origins of power-law degree distribution in the heterogeneity of human activity in social networks*, Scientific Reports 3, 1783 (2013)
20. S. Virinchi, M. Pabitra, *Link Prediction in Social Networks: Role of Power Law Distribution*, Springer International Publishing (2016)
21. A.L. Barabasi, E. Bonabeau, *Scale-Free Netwroks*, Scientific American, **288**, 50-59 (2003)
22. A. Claus, S. Kratzig, *Optimal planning of network structures within an exchange area*, European Journal of Operational Research, **7**(1), 67-76 (1981)

Measure and compare the convergence time of network routing protocols

Marek Bolanowski[1,*], *Tomasz* Byczek[2]

[1]Department of Complex Systems, Faculty of Electrical and Computer Engineering, Rzeszow University of Technology al. Powstańców Warszawy 12, 35-959 Rzeszów, Poland.
[2]tbyczek92@gmail.com, Poland.

Abstract. Currently, IT systems require more and more reliability. It can be guaranteed only by using redundancy both in the connectivity and network devices. The authors attempted to measure the convergence time for EIGRP and OSPF routing protocols after link or network nodes failure. Research have been conducted with the real devices and hardware traffic generator. In case of both protocols, failures have been simulated in various places in the network topology. On this basis, time in which tested protocol restored full connectivity for a specific topology with backup links have been precisely determined. Knowledge of the time required to restore the network after a failure can be useful during designing services based on networks with implemented routing. This can improve a tolerance of connectivity interruptions.

1 Introduction

Reliability is the key to proper work of modern Information and Communications Technology systems. The MTBF (Mean Time Between Failures) value for devices of critical infrastructure are getting longer and the reliability of a network devices (availability) reaches 99,999%. However this level of reliability, in some cases, is still not sufficient enough [1]. The formula of improving network availability by improving the device production process and improving the reliability parameters of network nodes seems to be reaching its limit. Another idea to improve the reliability of computer networks was the use of devices with modular structure for the construction of network nodes. Devices made with that type of architecture have duplicated management and power supply systems. Sometimes redundant switching matrix have also been used [2, 3]. Market's tendencies and customer expectations clearly indicate, the best network model is based both on redundant network devices (in single node) and redundant links[5]. Protocols which can create a single virtual device from a separate devices are used in local network (MC-LAG, Virtual Chasiss)[6]. There are also protocols which are widely used in the creation of redundant connections e.g.: RSTP, MSTP, ERP, etc. The network achieves convergence below 50 ms after a failure in the optimal scenario[7,8]. Such solutions are characteristic for campus or corporate networks with dedicated fibre optical links. As you can see, network reliability is ensured in the second layer

* Corresponding author: mb@prz.edu.pl

of ISO/OSI model with switching techniques. Mapping of such convergence mechanisms with layer three protocols is unimaginably expensive, and nearly impossible in some cases. However, routing protocols are widely used and the key element for the authors of this article is to measure the convergence time after a failure for selected routing protocols. In case of a node or link failure, knowledge about time required to restore network connection is essential. It allows to configure the rest of the IT system to tolerate this kind of breaks. This knowledge allows to manage computer system in a holistic way and consider it as a complex system [9,10] and use e.g. advance prediction algorithms[11].

Preliminary research of routing protocols with popular network simulators and emulation programs encountered the following problems:

- Difficulties in mapping correctly links and operating systems of network devices (e.g. small capabilities of heterogeneous environments simulation).
- Some of the advanced configurations of routing protocols algorithms (e.g. OSPF) did not work in simulators, however, worked correctly on physical devices.
- It is not possible to precisely configure all parameters of a given routing protocol available on the devices.
- The problem with the precise representation of the real environment with use of the mathematical models [12].

Therefore, the authors of this article have decided to carry out convergence tests in the real environment of network devices. The following programs were used for preliminary configuration tests: Omnet ++, Riverbed Modeler, PacketTracer. As a part of a preparatory work, the authors chose two most popular protocols for further analysis: EIGRP and OSPF[13,14]. Wider analysis, with larger amount of routing protocols is possible to perform, and such research will be conducted in the future.

2 The architecture of measuring system

A real network device environment located in the laboratory of Department of Complex Systems has been used to perform the measurements. Two groups of devices were used during this work: auxiliary and test ones. Alcatel-Lucent OmniSwitch 6850E switches were used in the first group, while Cisco 2901 and Cisco 2800 routers were used in the second group. The test traffic was generated by JDSU Testpoint TS-170. The hardware traffic generator allowed to perform the exact measurements of lost frames and the convergence time, as well as to define test stream parameters to the fourth layer (ISO/OSI). The core test network was built with Cisco routers. The entire device failure or link failure were simulated on these routers and they will be used to route traffic in the laboratory network. OS6850E switches were used as transit devices to transmit traffic between JDSU generator and routers. They were used to split the stream created by the traffic generator on a fiber optic interface, into a set of outbound streams in copper interfaces. The entire inbound and outbound streams on the switch were duplicated for its error analysis. The dedicated stations analysed them. Two of that switches were used during the tests. Their switching topology will be discussed in the next chapter. Wireshark programme was also used to analyse the traffic. First, the authors planned to use hybrid traffic generation, described in this work[15]. In this approach, the resultant test traffic is a component of the traffic coming from the hardware and software generator as well as the real part of the previously recorded network traffic. Such a network traffic has similar statistic parameters to the network flow in real environment. The initial tests shows that traffic flow which has come only from the hardware generator is sufficient to examine routing protocols convergence time. The use of more complicated flow had no impact on received results.

https://doi.org/10.1051/itmconf/20182100013

2.1 System topology

Two test topologies were created to perform the research, one of them to test a multiarea OSPF protocol, another one to test EIGRP protocol.

OSPF protocol. Redundant links between devices and routes were necessary for test network configuration. The network, which was using OSPF routing protocol was divided into areas. Therefore, measurements of new routes propagation and convergence time, are not limited to one area. In this case time of route propagation is related to the place where the failure occurred. Redundant links should have been provided in every place irrespective of the area.

The topology was designed to test an OSPF routes propagation time, while simulating network device's ports failure is located in a different areas. First, port on the device in area 0, which was the core area, was disabled during the tests. The next step was to measure the convergence time for area next to the backbone area. The final measurement tested the convergence time for an area which was not close to the backbone area. Fig. 1 shows the network topology, which was used to perform the measurements.

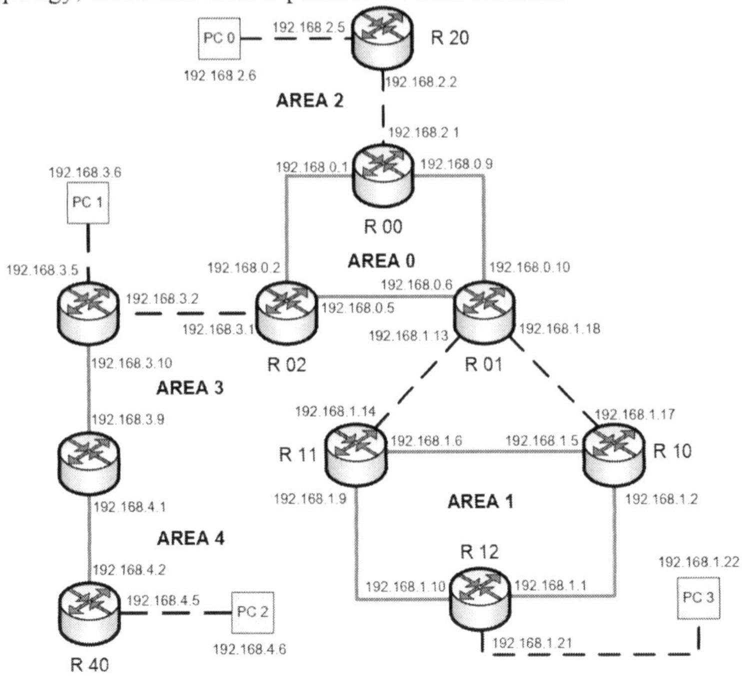

Fig. 1. OSPF protocol measurement topology.

The more complicated network was designed to avoid the need for creation of new networks for each further measurements. Changing of a network point in which frames were sent and received was sufficient to perform another tests. Cisco 2901 devices were mostly used in the design. The amount of devices which was necessary to perform the tests was larger than the held test equipment and that is why Cisco 2800 series were used as the R20 and the R40 devices. Routers with less computing power were used at the edge of the network, because in this places they had less impact on the results. The researches assumed that faults would be simulated in the zero area, the first area and the fourth area, which was set behind the virtual area. Unfortunately, the lack of additional devices forced the modification of the topology for the last measurements. The devices from the first area were used to modify the fourth area. The traffic flow would avoid the first area, so it will would not participate in the new routes propagation. It was possible to use devices with better parameters in the fourth area by eliminating one of the existing area. After performing the modification R40 was replaced with the Cisco 2800 series to 2901. Fig. 2 shows modified network topology for measurements performed for the fourth area.

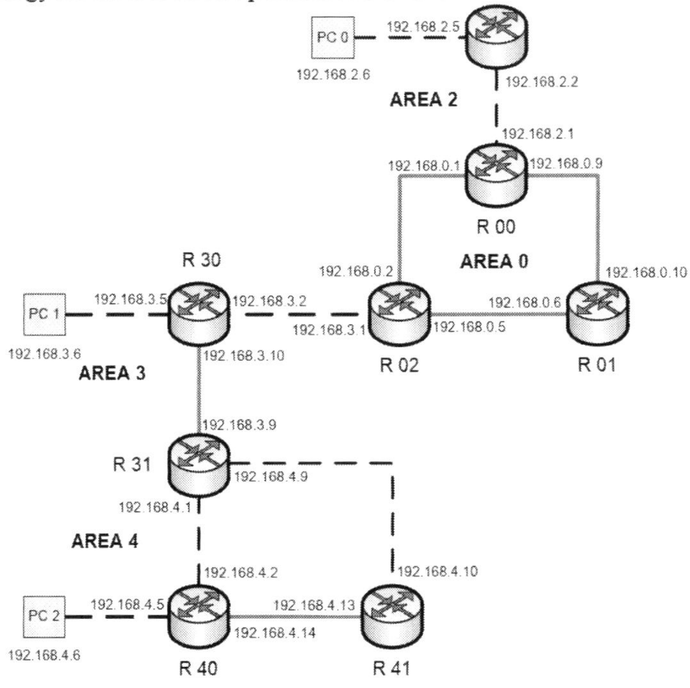

Fig. 2. AREA 4 measurement topology (OSPF protocol).

EIGRP protocol. Another protocol that was tested in this article was EIGRP. OSPF configuration is much more complex. It is not required to use functional areas with EIGRP protocol. That is why the applied topology can be much simpler. Fig. 3 shows the created topology for EIGRP, in which network convergence and routes propagation were tested.

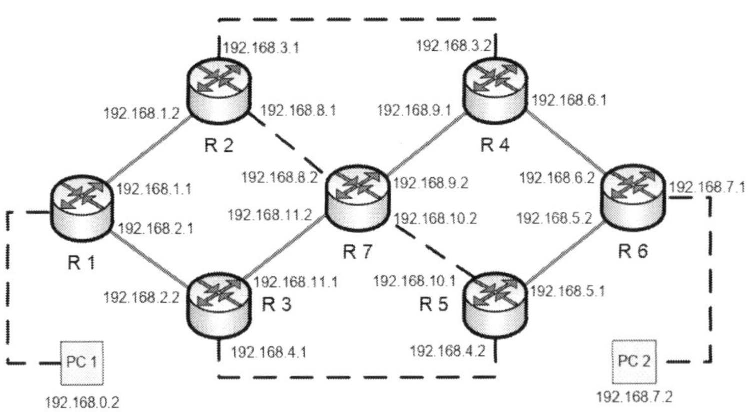

Fig. 3. EIGRP measurement topology.

Seven Cisco 2901 routers were parts of the showed topology. The end devices, which were to send and receive packets were represented by the computers.

JDSU traffic generator. Traffic flow generator was used as two end devices placed in the different endpoints of the network. Traffic was generated by Slot 1 and send to the nearest router, which route it via next nodes to the generator's Slot 2. Slot 2 was configured as the looping traffic device. Sender and recipients' addresses were reversed in every frame, then Slot 2 sent them to the nearest router which routed the frames to the Slot 1.The data were collected by the computer with packet sniffer, which was set between Slot 1 module and the nearest router. Current analysis of collected traffic allowed to determine if frames and packets was sent and received correctly. Generator and computer's connecting schema was showed in fig. 4.

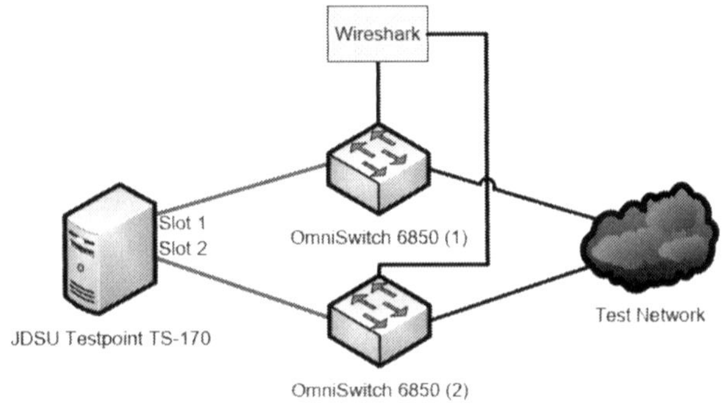

Fig. 4. Generator and computer's (frame collector) connecting schema.

3 Tests and results

The tests in case of both protocols were performed in a similar way. Packets from JDSU generator were send and received simultaneously. During the failure simulation (link disconnection or router shutdown), the routers did not know the route to a specific module (Slot 2 which reflected packets) for some time. Only outbound packets from the generator were registered by the sniffer. Every registered datagram had a time stamp. The value of a time stamp at the start of the each measurement was zero. The difference between the last packet which was returned before the breakdown and the first packet, which was registered after the failure determined the amount of time which network devices needed to learn new routes after the error occurred.

For the OSPF protocol, times were measured in four simulated network failures and then the obtained results were compared. The connection between two routers in the backbone area was dropped during the first test. It was performed by plugging out the used cable in one of the devices. A port failure or another single link connection drop was simulated in this test. The second test was performed in the same way, however, the devices between which connection was dropped were located in none backbone area. Another test was also performed in none backbone area and forcing the selection of a new route was also initiated by disconnecting two devices. However, an entry to the next node, for tested network destination, was already in the router's routing table. This simulation was possible because two interfaces had the same OSPF costs. The final test was the simulation in which the connection was dropped beyond the area adjacent to the backbone area.

Five measurements were carried out for each test. Fig. 5 shows the time needed to get a network convergence for each of the measurement for all of the performed tests.

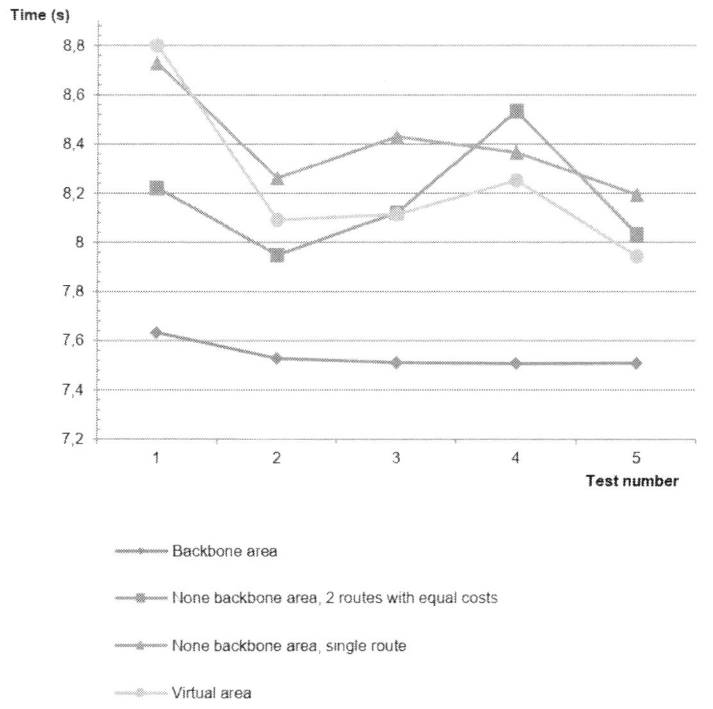

Fig. 5. Summary of measurements for each test for OSPF.

The first test in the fig. 5 which was performed in the backbone area is represented by the blue chart (marked with diamonds). Tests for none backbone area with two routes with equal cost are represented by the orange chart (marked with squares), whereas grey chart (marked with triangles) represents test for the same area, however, with a single route's entrance to the desired subnet in the routing table. The last test in the area which was not next to the backbone area is represented by the yellow chart (marked with dots).

Analysis shows that if the failure occurs in the backbone area, the OSPF protocol would learn and broadcast new route to recover a lost connection in the shortest time. From the protocol topology's point of view, backbone area is located in its centre and is the key to the entire network's proper work. Much higher convergence times can be observed for the rest of the tests, however, the differences between them are not significant. The fig. 6 shows the average convergence time for all of the configurations.

Based on the analysis, we can tell that the best convergence time for none backbone areas during the failures simulation were achieved for two equal routes to the same subnet in the routing table. The device in which the connection loss was initialized had already had an alternate route entry, thereupon switching and propagating new route information to another devices did not take as long as in the other tests. Propagating information and achieving network convergence for failure in the area which was not adjacent to the area 0 was a bit longer. The longest measurement times were achieved for a single route entry in a routing table in a device located in the first area.

EIGRP protocol could not be tested in the same conditions as the OSPF. The differences in the configurations forced changes in the network topology. The redundant network was designed for the Cisco routing protocol, in which various failures could be made. Lack of division into areas simplified the routing implementation, however, it also decreased the amount of performed measurements. The authors decided to perform tests to check whether the failure of a single link is significantly different from the failure of the entire device. In case of a device breakdown, the protocol had to choose the longer route, which could affect the measured propagation time and network convergence. To achieve more reliable results five measurements were performed for each of the EIGRP test (fig. 7.).

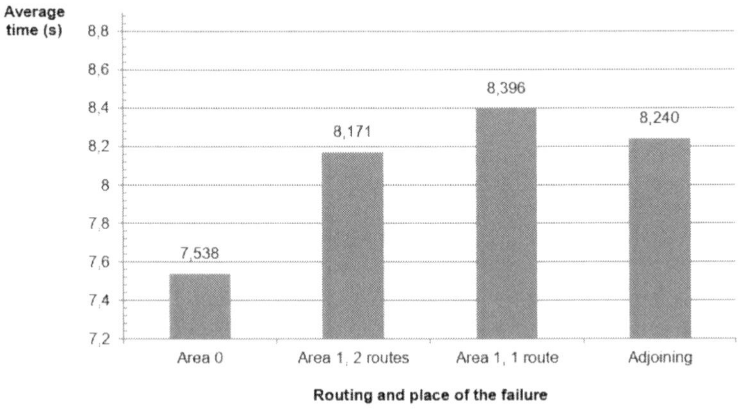

Fig. 6. Average measurements' times for OSPF protocol tests.

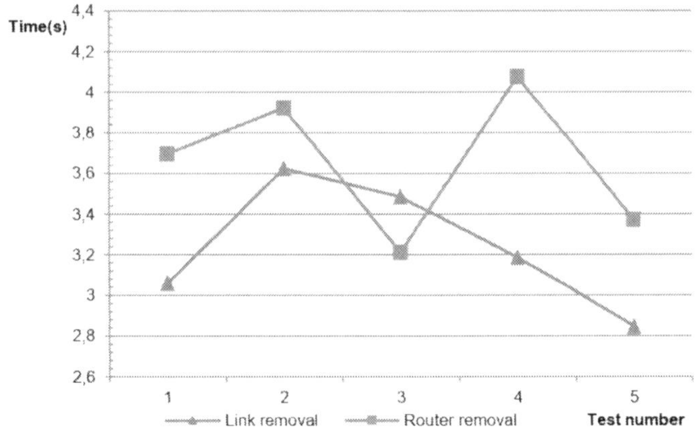

Fig. 7. Juxtaposition of each test for EIGRP protocol.

Orange data (marked with squares) show the measurements when during simulations, an entire device was broken, while blue (marked with triangles) data shows EIGRP network convergence time for a single link failure. The results were not similar to each other, so the average times of convergence were calculated for each of the tests. For measurements performed during simulation of a single link failure, the first measurement gave a value close to 3 seconds, while for the remaining three measurements longer times were recorded. Analysis of the time of the last measurement shows that the network learned the new route the fastest. For the test in which the failures of the entire device were simulated, most of the collected times were longer than in the previous test. For the third and the fifth measurements, faster route learning was noticed than for the first and the second measurement for a single link failure. To compare the performed tests, the average values were calculated and showed in fig. 8.

The presented results show the EIGRP protocol chose a new route quicker if a failure occurred only on a single link. If an entire device fail a new neighbourhood relation has to be established between routers. It means that more devices had to learn new routes. What is more, a bypass via the same device could be used for a link failure. When router stopped working, routing protocol had to find a new route without a broken equipment. It took more time, but the protocol set a new, longer route with gigabit connections instead of serial ones.

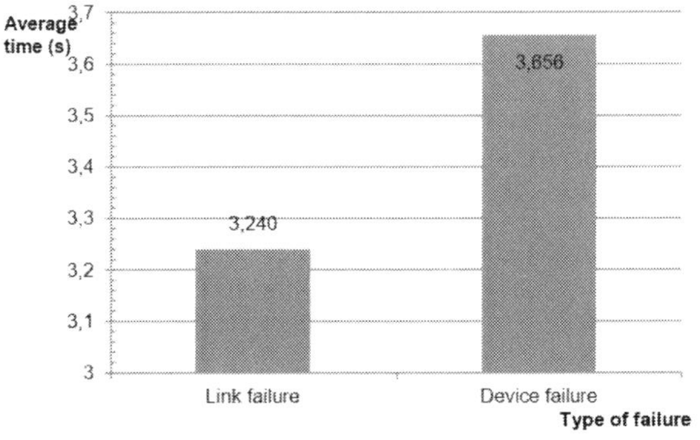

Fig. 8. Average convergence time after an interface failure and equipment for EIGRP.

Performed tests showed, that EIGRP allows for faster times of route reelection after its failure. Although EIGRP was characterized by better convergence time it is not a solution based on an open standards. This protocol can be used only with Cisco Systems devices, which limits the variety of devices in network's design. EIGRP is easier to configure and does not require as much planning as the OSPF, however, more options available in configuration can improve network's management. If one of the OSPF devices stops working, and it is not the autonomous system border router, we are certain that in the worst case scenario access to the network resources will be lost only for the devices in a specific area.

4 Summary

Methods and means for determining the times of convergence and learning alternate routes with physical laboratory's devices were presented in this paper. This type of research is often performed with simulating programs, in which consideration of the large enterprise network's specification may not be possible or leads to unreliable results. Therefore, our study focuses on the implementation of two main routing protocols in the real test network, including physical devices, to determine the amount of time needed to achieve the convergence of the network with use of redundancy mechanisms applied in the third layer. Knowledge of these times allows to modify applications, which use higher layers of ISO/OSI model (from 4 to 7) to tolerate longer breaks in the network's service, e.g. by increasing the buffering time of video streams or by enlarge session's hold time in case of virtual channel connections. Further works will be undertaken in two ways: extending the size of test networks and testing for other routing protocols; developing simulation models and their verification for known routing protocols.

References

1. M. Taifi, J. Shi, Y. Celik, *JENERGY: A Fault Tolerant Stateless Architecture for High Performance Computing*, Service-Oriented System Engineering (SOSE), 2015 IEEE Symposium on, (2015).

2. Vendor Documentation: OmniSwitch 9900 Series, Hardware Users Guide. Alcatel-Lucent Enterprise, Part No. 060409-10, Rev B, (2016).
3. Vendor Documentation: OmniSwitch 10K Hardware Users Guide. Alcatel-Lucent Enterprise, Part No. 060310-10, Rev. J, (2016).
4. F. Burda, P. Havrila, M. Knězek, and others, *Optimization of Network Redundant Technologies Collaboration in IMS Carrier Topology*, Lecture Notes of the Institute for Computer Sciences, Social Informatics and Telecommunications Engineering, **46**, 705-712, (2011).
5. Fenge-Wang, Chang-xing-Zhu, *HSRP Protocol Based on High Reliable Redundant Campus Network Design*, Communications and Information Processing, Communications in Computer and Information Science, **289**, 107-114, (2012).
6. H. Birkholz, I. Sieverdingbeck, *Supporting Security Automation for Multi-chassis Link Aggregation Groups via the Interconnected-Asset Ontology*, Availability, Reliability and Security (ARES), 2014 Ninth International Conference on, 126-133, (2014).
7. M. Nurujjaman, S. Sebbah, C. Assi, *Design of Resilient Ethernet Ring Protection (ERP) Mesh Networks With Improved Service Availability*, Journal of Lightwave Technology, **31**(2), (2013).
8. J. Lopes, S. Sargento, A. Zúquete, *A Dependable Alternative to the Spanning Tree Protocol. Dependable Computing*, Lecture Notes in Computer Science, **7869**, 148-164, (2013).
9. M. Bolanowski, A. Paszkiewicz, *The Use of Statistical Signatures to Detect Anomalies in Computer Network*, Analysis and Simulation of Electrical and Computer Systems, Lecture Notes in Electrical Engineering, **324**, 251-260, (2015).
10. F. Grabowski, A. Paszkiewicz, M. Bolanowski, *Wireless Networks Environment and Complex Networks*, Analysis and Simulation of Electrical and Computer Systems, Lecture Notes in Electrical Engineering, **324**, 261-270, (2015).
11. J.T. Duda, T. Pełech-Pilichowski, *Enhancements of moving trend based filters aimed at time series prediction*, Advances in systems science, eds. Jerzy Świątek, Advances in Intelligent Systems and Computing **240**, 747–756, (2014).
12. B. Twaróg, R. Pękala, J. Bartman, Z. Gomółka, *The changes of air gap in inductive engines as vibration indicator aided by mathematical model and artificial neural network*, Discrete and Continous Dynamical Systems, Journal of American Institute of Mathematical Sciences, 1005-1012, AIMS (2007).
13. G. Kanti Dey, M. Ahmed, K. Tanvir Ahmmed, *Performance analysis and redistribution among RIPv2, EIGRP & OSPF Routing Protocol*, Computer and Information Engineering (ICCIE), 2015 1st International Conference on, (2015).
14. C. Wijaya, *Performance Analysis of Dynamic Routing Protocol EIGRP and OSPF in IPv4 and IPv6 Network*, First International Conference on Informatics and Computational Intelligence (2011).
15. M. Bolanowski, A. Paszkiewicz, *Performance test of network devices*, Annales UMCS Sectio AI Informatica **13**(1), 29-36 (2013).

The possibility of using LACP protocol in anomaly detection systems

Marek Bolanowski[1,*], *Piotr* Cisło[2]

[1]Deptartament of Complex Systems, Faculty of Electrical and Computer Engineering, Rzeszow University of Technology, al. Powstańców Warszawy 12, 35-959 Rzeszów, Poland
[2] piotrekcislo@gmail.com, Poland

Abstract. This article presents the use of the Link Aggregation Control Protocol (LACP) for detection of anomalies in network traffic. The idea itself is based on checking the representativeness of a single LACP link for the whole traffic transmitted by the aggregation. This approach allows to reduce the requirements for the performance of threat detection systems, and thus reduce their implementation costs and the gives a possibility of using probes (IDS or IPS) directly in the core of the network. The authors also examine the influence of hashing algorithms used for the particular LACP link on the possibility of using of developed method and on the level of intrusion detection.

1 Introduction

Detection of threats in modern information systems is an important issue both in science and engineering. This results in the use of more and more advanced filters in the communication channels that are capable to analyze traffic up to and including the seventh layer of ISO/OSI model. The bandwidth of the links in which they are used increases with the increase in the number of probes IDS and IPS. Unfortunately, increasing throughput significantly affects the performance requirements of the implemented solutions for threats detection. It often limits their use, in particular for core links and connection points at the edge of large computer networks. Therefore, recently the concept of rough identification of the suspicious traffic expands greatly, which leads consequently to the separation of the suspicious traffic and to passing it to further, more sophisticated inspection. An identification of suspicious traffic is often performed based on the analysis of statistical properties of the traffic [1-7]. In [1] the authors present a method that allows to identify anomalies in the network traffic based on the change of the selected set of parameters of network traffic. An important aspect of this case is not only the change of parameters but also the value of these changes. The authors propose the use of statistical signatures to detect the anomalies and they confirm their effectiveness by analyzing the results for the real network attacks. Of course, other statistical method can be used in anomaly detection process, which are dedicated to change detection in non-stationary time series [8]. In [9-10] the authors propose the network systems architectures for implementing the anomaly detection system in real network system.

* Corresponding author: marekb@prz.edu.pl

In [11] the authors examine the statistical properties of a traffic sent through each link of the LACP aggregation, and check whether they can be representative of the whole transferred traffic. The results obtained in this work show that the traffic on a single LACP link, from the viewpoint of anomalies detection, is representative of the entire channel. The results obtained in these works encouraged the authors to try to check the implementation possibilities of this class of systems using the tools available on the market and check their effectiveness. An important question that arose at the initial stage of the work was to check the influence of load balancing algorithms of individual links in the LACP on the effectiveness of threats detection.

2 The LACP protocol

Compliant with IEEE 802.3ad link binding offers a method of aggregating many Ethernet links into a single logic LAG channel. This function helps to improve the efficiency of the device, increasing the total throughput of a single channel without the need of a hardware upgrade. In addition, IEEE 802.3ad standard offers the ability to dynamically assign, manage and monitor various aggregated links and enables interoperability between different devices from different vendors.

LACP supports the automatic creation of aggregating LAG groups by exchanging LACP-PDU packets between the physical interfaces. LACP packets are exchanged only between ports in active mode and are received by the ports operating in passive mode. The LACP switch thus "learns" the possibility of aggregation of ports dynamically, simultaneously diagnosing the state of the established connection with the LACP-PDU frame. LACP identifies correctly dedicated Ethernet links, what greatly simplifies the grouping of the links into the LAG group. LAG logical interfaces are added to the spanning tree (STP) as a single logic interface of the LAG group.

The IEEE 802.3ad protocol redirects the flows to the particular link of the LACP aggregation using specially implemented hash algorithms for this purpose. We get two methods available. The first hashing method is using a packet header of the second layer and of the third of ISO/OSI model. The second method is using a packet header of the third layer and of the fourth. In the case of IPv4 traffic the hashing may for instance run as follows:

- In the case of "bridged" aggregation, the hash is built with the following variables: L2 MAC source/destination and L3 IP source/destination.
- In the case of "routed" aggregation, the hash is built as follows: L3 IP source/destination and L4 PORTS source/destination.

In the case of IPv6 traffic hashing is carried out as follows:

- In the case of "bridged" aggregation, the hash is built with the following variables: L2 MAC source/destination and L3 IPv6.
- In the case of "routed" aggregation, the hash is built with the following variables: L3 IPv6 source/destination and L4 IPv6 source/destination.
- For Non-IP traffic, the hash is built with the following variables: L2 MAC source/destination.

Depending on the particular vendor of network switches we very often have different options of the configuration. Let us consider an example of a hash value configuration for the switch [12]:

```
forwarding-options {
    hash-key {
        family inet {
            layer-3;
            layer-4; }}}
```

We can choose in a detailed way the dedicated values of the hash calculation:

```
forwarding-options {
    hash-key {
       family inet {
            layer-3 {
                destination-address;
                incoming-interface-index;
                protocol;
                source-address;
            }
            layer-4 {
                destination-port;
                source-port;
                type-of-service; }}}}
```

The tests have shown that the more configuration possibilities of hashing algorithms we have - the more efficient the use of LAG is. If you choose only two or more hashing components you get bigger saturation of the individual interfaces of the aggregating group. If you choose a single method, for example "source-mac" or "source-ip", a particular device connected to the LAG unit will take into account only the single features of the packets of the second layer ISO / OSI (MAC address) or of the third (the IP address of the machine) so that all packets will be sent by a single interface of the aggregation group. However, if you choose layer 4 additionally, and the source port method, it is possible for a single device to use the full capabilities of all aggregation interfaces. Depending on the implementation and configuration in a given type of switch or in a given operating system, you can receive different performance.

3 The physical and virtual structure of test environment

The environment for network anomaly detection has been created in accordance to the concept of universal hardware-network environment, with high capability of scaling, taking into account the idea of future migration to more efficient hardware environment. The guiding idea was to use opensource tools, and tools based on "for non - commercial use" licenses. In order to manage flexibly the server and network infrastructure on the server, the virtualization environment by using of VMware was installed. Within the virtual environment the following virtual switches have been created:

VS-IF-1 to **VS-IF-4** with a transmission capacity of one gigabit per second, which included the virtual cards of threat detection systems, aggregation hubs, and the physical interface used in case of mirroring LAG-IF1 to LAG-IF4 (respectively) traffic from an external switch.

VS-STREAM-IN - with a transmission capacity of one gigabit per second, which included the virtual cards of network traffic generators, and physical interfaces for transparent forwarding the traffic coming from the physical network devices.

VS-STREAM-OUT - with a transmission capacity of one gigabit per second, which included the virtual cards of network traffic generators, and physical interfaces for transparent forwarding the traffic coming from the physical network devices.

PENTEST-LAB - with a transmission capacity of one gigabit per second, isolated network created to manage virtual machines used for the network attacks.

VM-MGMT - with a transmission capacity of one gigabit, used for VMware system managing.

VM-Kernel - with a transmission capacity of one gigabit, used to perform the migration processes of the VMware system.

In the next step the following virtual machines have been created:

IDS-0 - the system of network threats detection, having six virtual cards, four virtual processors and four gigabytes of RAM. Additionally, resources was reserved, ie. a critical level of access to the processor time, memory, and a required space in data store resources.

LACP-0 and **LACP-1** aggregation traffic hub, having six virtual cards, two virtual processors and two gigabytes of RAM.

TXGEN-0 - network traffic generator, having sixteen virtual cards, two virtual processors and two gigabytes of RAM.

RXGEN-0 - network traffic generator, having sixteen virtual cards, two virtual processors and two gigabytes of RAM.

PEN-0 - network threats generating system having seventeen virtual cards, two virtual processors and two gigabytes of RAM.

Resources have been allocated to each of the machines depending on the planned load level and the tasks to be performed. Fig. 1 presents the structure of the test virtual environment taking into account interconnections and names of the machines, switches and network interfaces.

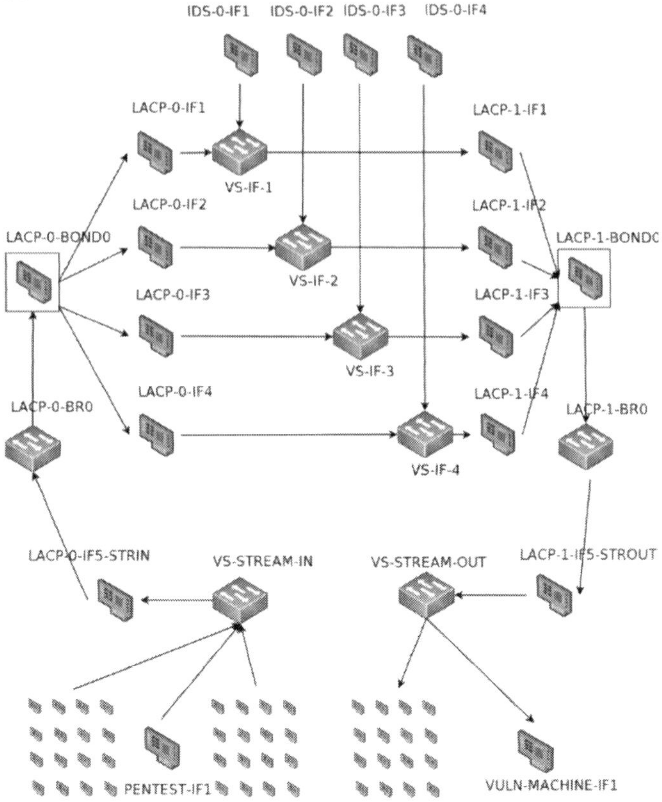

Fig. 1. Virtual structure of test environment.

The whole path leading from the virtual VS-STREAM-IN switch to the virtual VS-STREAM-OUT switch had the VLAN-s service at every point, so it was possible to transfer the TRUNK traffic (802.1q), and the normal ACCESS traffic. To the virtual VS-IF-1,2,3,4 switches the virtual IDS cards have been connected. Virtual and physical server interfaces have been connected to virtual VS-STREAM switches. The last step was the test of the configuration, which clearly confirmed the operation of the whole system. The virtual switch VS-STREAM-IN and VS-STREAM-OUT are connected with two physical interfaces of the server with a bandwidth of one gigabyte, and then the traffic from the ISP router was redirected to them. The traffic from the ISP had following attributes:

- The clients connected to PPPoE authentication server used the dedicated VLAN.
- IP-Multicast (TV) and VOIP used the dedicated VLANs.
- The average load of the client router was fifty megabits.
- Default VLAN (MGTVLAN) was not tagged with the standard identifier "1"

As a result of the performed test, the following parameters were changed: MTU to 9000 bytes and a dedicated resource disk was created to serve the queues and output files (tcpdump). The environment built this way enabled to run tests using both real traffic and traffic coming from the program generator.

4 The logical structure of test environment

In order to carry out the necessary statistical analysis of IEEE 802.3ad standard and of LACP protocol, it was necessary to run tests with previously prepared network and server environment, with particular traffic hashing methods. The study was divided into two stages. The first stage was to configure bound interfaces of the network switches so as to forward network traffic using the hashing algorithm of the second and the third layer. The second stage was to configure the network switches so that they serve the forwarding of network traffic using a hashing algorithm of the third and the fourth layer.

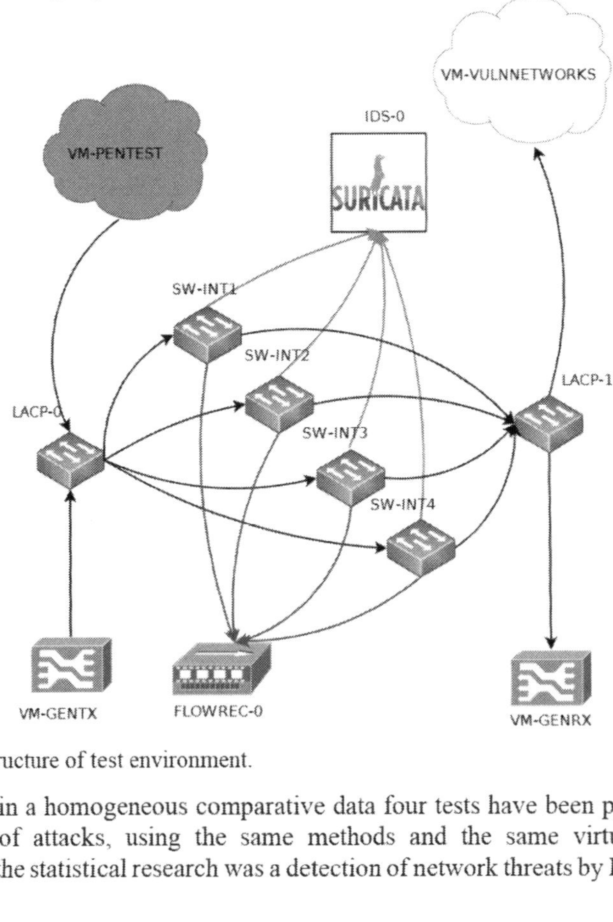

Fig. 2. Logical structure of test environment.

In order to obtain a homogeneous comparative data four tests have been planned, based on the same sets of attacks, using the same methods and the same virtual machines. A supplement for the statistical research was a detection of network threats by IDS system based

on Suricata software[13]. The Suricata system worked in inline mode, connected to virtual network switches operating between LACP switches. The logic diagram is shown in Fig.2. The VM-GENTX and VM-GENRX machines were responsible for traffic generated through LACP switches. The generated TCP traffic had the task to increase network load artificially between switches, in order to generate a traffic close to the real load in high-throughput networks. The task for the FLOWREC-0 machine was to copy periodically the traffic recorded in the particular time cycles from incoming attacks, from all connected interfaces. The collected data were then used to detect anomalies using statistical analysis.
The task of IDS-0 (2) machine was to detect network threats based on standard emergency signatures [14]. In the area of VM-PENTEST network, responsible for generating of sequent network attacks, there were machines based on Kali distributions, and there was a machine based on Debian distributions with installed and configured pytbull software. In the VM-VULNNETWORKS network there were standard Debian machines with running services of ftp, ssh, mysql, www, which were the objects of further attacks.

5 Results

In the first study the LACP network environment has been configured so that the hashing algorithm used only the properties of the second and the third layer. In order to determine the effectiveness of the proposed solution, a number of attacks was carried out. The results will be presented on the basis of four examples, it is: Brutaforce attack, Serverside attack, ClientSide attack, DoS attack. The test results have been shown in Fig. 3 Using hashing algorithms for L2 and L3 layers, all the traffic is directed to one interface and only on it the traffic analysis is possible - both in the case of detection using the statistical signatures, or in the case of detection using the Suricatta program. Samples of the traffic on particular interfaces are not statistically representative for the total flow, and their use for the anomaly detection is not possible.

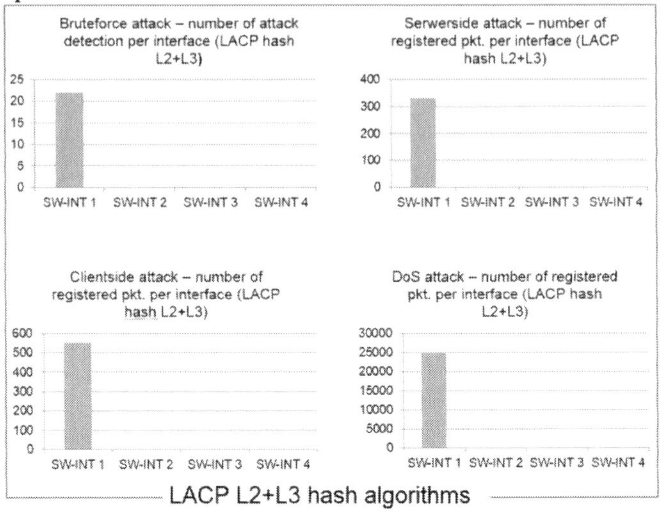

Fig. 3. Anomaly detection or number of packet per interface in case of using the LACP L2+L3 hash algorithms.

In next study the LACP network environment was configured so that the hashing algorithm used only the features of the third and the fourth layer. The test results are shown in Fig 4. Thanks to the use of hash algorithms L3 + L4 for LACP protocol, the traffic spread evenly on particular interfaces. Such a situation allows to carry out the detection using the statistical signatures, and using the Suricatta program on any interface. Number of successfully verified attacks on a single interface was in the range of 60% to 80%.

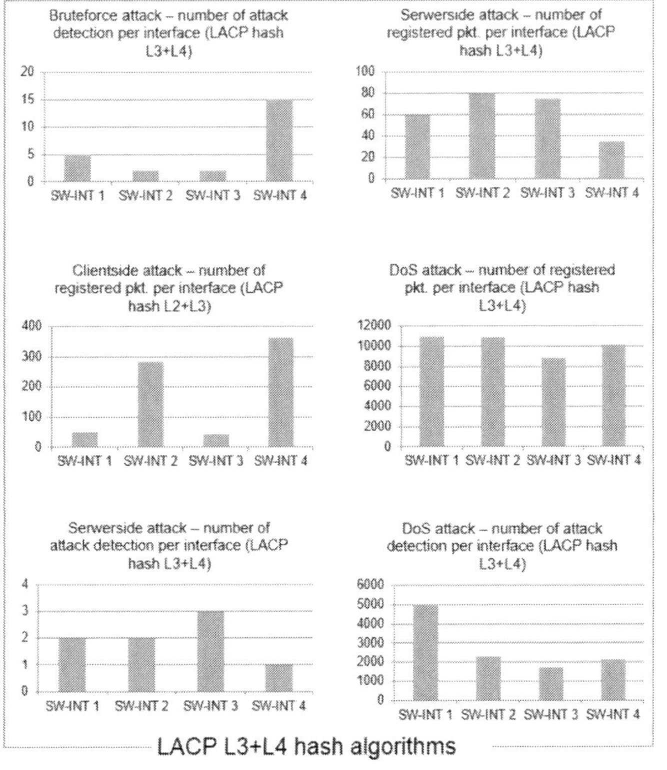

Fig. 3. Anomaly detection or number of packet per interface in case of using the LACP L3+L4 hash algorithms.

6 Conclusion

Detection of threats in computer networks is an important and current subject. A large number and intensity of attacks on modern information systems forces the producers of protection systems to a multistage process of detecting and blocking threats. In the study, the authors propose a method of rough identification of the attack based on a separate part of the flow. The LACP standard is an open standard and allows to divide a single communication channel into maximum eight logic channels. The tests have shown that with the use of hashing algorithms of L3 + L4 layer it is possible to identify 60 to 80% of attacks based on a single logic link. Thanks to this solution financial spendings for detection systems can be reduced, especially in the area of hardware performance. It should also be noted that the whole proposed solution was built on the basis of existing and widely implemented protocols and open source system. The described solution can also be easily implemented in a network environment of SDN type.

References

1. M. Bolanowski, A. Paszkiewicz, *The use of statistical signatures to detect anomalies in computer network,* Lecture Notes In Electrical Engineering, **324**, 251-260, (2015).
2. F. Simmross-Wattenberg, J. Asensio-Perez, P. Casaseca-de-la-Higuera, M. Martin-Fernandez, I. Dimitriadis, C. Alberola-Lope, *Anomaly Detection in Network Traffic*

Based on Statistical Inference and alpha-Stable Modeling, IEEE Transactions on Dependable and Secure Computing, **8**(4), 494-509, (2011).

3. W. Zhang, Q. Yang, Y. Geng, *A Survey of Anomaly Detection Methods in Networks*, Computer Network and Multimedia Technology, CNMT 2009, International Symposium on, 1-3, (2009).
4. S. Oshima, T. Nakashima, *Computational Complexity of AnomalyDetection Methods,* Seventh International Conference on Broadband, Wireless Computing, Communication and Applications, 664-649, (2012).
5. P. García-Teodoro, J. Díaz-Verdejo, G. Maciá-Fernández, E. Vázquez, *Anomaly-based network intrusion detection: Techniques, systems and challenges*, Computers & Security, **28**(1-2), 18-28, (2009).
6. W. Han, W. Xiong, Y. Xiao and others, *A class of Non-statistical Traffic Anomaly Detection in Complex Network Systems*, 32nd International Conference on Distributed Computing Systems (ICDCSW), 640-646, (2012).
7. F. Palmieri: *Network anomaly detection through nonlinear analysis*, Computers & Security, **29**(7), 737-755, (2010).
8. T. Pełech-Pilichowski, J.T. Duda, *Low-frequency signal reconstruction and abrupt change detection in non-stationary time series by enhanced moving trend based filters*, Studies in Computational Intelligence **579**, 111–125, (2015).
9. M. Bolanowski, B. Twaróg, R. Mlicki, *Anomalies detection in computer networks with the use of SDN*, Measurement Automation Monitoring **61**, 443-445, (2015).
10. M. Bolanowski, A. Paszkiewicz, *Nowy model detekcji zagrożeń w sieci komputerowej*, Przegląd Elektrotechniczny, **89**, 308-311, (2013).
11. M. Bolanowski, A. Paszkiewicz, M. Wroński, R. Żegleń, *Representativeness analysis and possible applications of partial network data flows*, Measurement Automation Monitoring, **62**(01), 29-32, (2016).
12. http://www.juniper.net/us/en/.
13. https://suricata-ids.org/.
14. https://rules.emergingthreats.net/open/suricata/rules.

Load balancing algorithms in cluster systems

Andrzej Imiełowski[1,*]

[1]The State Higher School of Technology and Economics in Jarosław, Poland

Abstract. The beginning of XXI century brought dynamic rise in popularity of the Internet. It was connected with the development of telecommunications technology, especially the spread of broadband access to the global network. The key issue became ensuring satisfactory access to the services available through the network. Therefore, the challenge caused the development of various clusters. The paper presents an overview of algorithms for load balancing used in modern cluster systems. Load balancing is a key issue in cluster systems. It is a method that uses multiple nodes (servers) and dynamically distributes the load between them so that no node is not overloaded. The main goal of load balancing is the optimal use of resources, thereby enhancing system performance and minimizing resource consumption. This allows for reducing operations costs of information systems and is also compatible with Green Computing. The paper focuses on analysis of existing algorithms in terms of load balancing and comparing them on basis of various quality indicators, such as throughput, reliability, energy saving, performance, scalability, etc. The paper takes into account the specificities of different solutions, from the classic cluster through systems of blade servers with virtualization to cloud systems.

1 Introduction

The modern world is more and more dependent on information systems. It is due to both the rapid development of the Internet and services made available through it and with the common application of solutions for information processing in all spheres of life from business through administration to private information resources (documents, photos, correspondence, etc.). The widespread use of IT systems implies ever greater demands on the quality of services that are provided by these systems. An important parameter determining the quality of IT solutions is their efficiency. This factor has a significant impact on the comfort of use and in extreme situations may result in the inability to use a given solution. For the above reasons, actions aimed at improving the efficiency of IT systems are of great importance for the development of IT applications. In recent years, it has become common to use cluster systems to support IT systems requiring high performance. At the same time, solutions that use virtualization as a working environment of server systems have become very popular (for many reasons). The above two factors, the development of cluster systems and the widespread use of virtualization have enabled the popularization of services related to cloud systems (cloud clomputing). This article focuses

* Corresponding author: andrzej.imielowski@pwste.edu.pl

on the development of load balancing algorithms in multi-server systems from classic clusters to cloud systems.

2 Architecture of cluster systems

Research and development works aimed at improving the efficiency of IT systems are multidirectional. These works cover all areas that can affect performance. This applies to the development of the software itself, both application and system. The second direction of work concerns the development of hardware solutions that increase efficiency. In connection with the development of equipment, the important issue is, in addition to performance, also increasing the reliability parameters of computer systems.

The proposed solutions are aimed in the following directions:

- dedicated multiprocessor solutions (generally aimed at improving performance through new hardware solutions within a single computer)
- solutions for improving the parameters of both application software and operating systems
- distributed solutions - systems based on multiple computers.

Independently from work related to the development of application software, the work on the scalability of the applied solutions depending on the current needs has the decisive influence on improving the efficiency of IT systems [1]. Scalability is most often achieved through the use of multi-server systems. The classification of methods to improve the performance of scalable systems is shown in Figure 1.

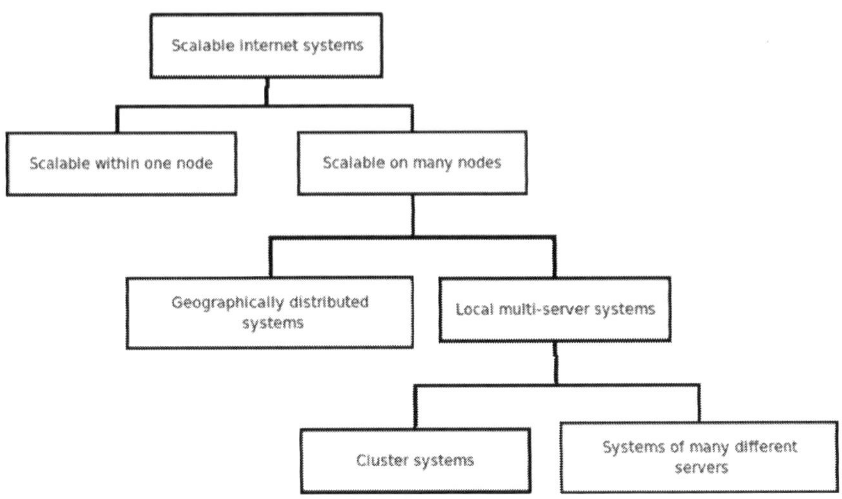

Fig. 1 Methods of improving internet applications performance

Scalable solutions based on the use of multiple servers can be divided into two types:

- systems consisting of servers located in different locations, but functioning in such a way that for the client they form one system
- systems consisting of multiple servers located in one location:
    - cluster systems consisting of multiple servers visible outside as one system (common IP address)
    - systems consisting of multiple servers between which system tasks are distributed (the client can distinguish between individual servers, they have different IP addresses)

This article focuses on the solutions from the second group, i.e. on local cluster systems. The architecture of the classic server cluster is shown in Figure 2. In the simplest case, such a cluster consists of a number of identical servers and a dedicated device called dispatcher

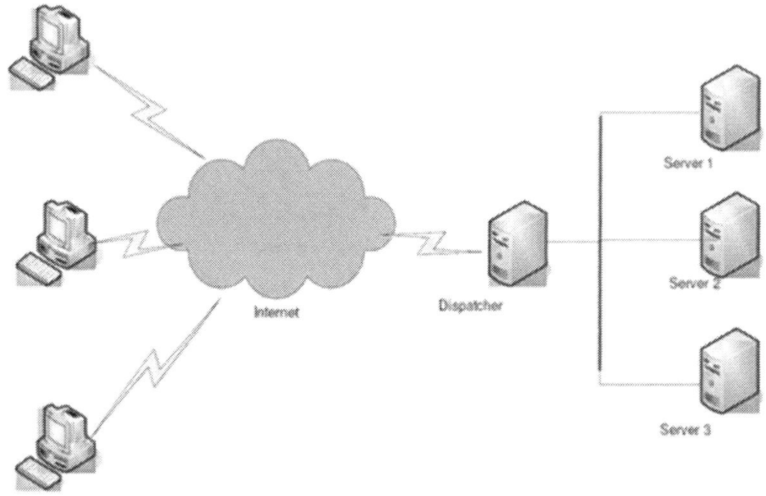

Fig. 2 Architecture of cluster

or load balancer. Cluster switch is a term sometimes used in Polish, but it does not occur too often. Dispatcher has the task of distributing tasks between servers constituting cluster nodes. In this solution, the load balancer can be a dedicated network device operating in layer 3 of the OSI network model. Devices of this type are provided by most manufacturers of network hardware. The role of the dispatcher can also be performed by a dedicated server included in the cluster - such solutions are provided by system software producers. They are available for both Windows (Windows Azzure) operating systems and most UNIX / Linux operating systems. Yet another group of solutions is software for a node managing a cluster at the level of application software, e.g. managing the database system or web servers, also in this case the software producers provide such solutions (MS SQL Failover Cluster, MySQL Cluster, Oracle RAC).

Another approach allowing to increase the system's efficiency is to split the system's functionality into a larger number of servers. Figure 3 shows the idea of this solution. In contrast to the solution described above, in this case it is necessary to adapt the application

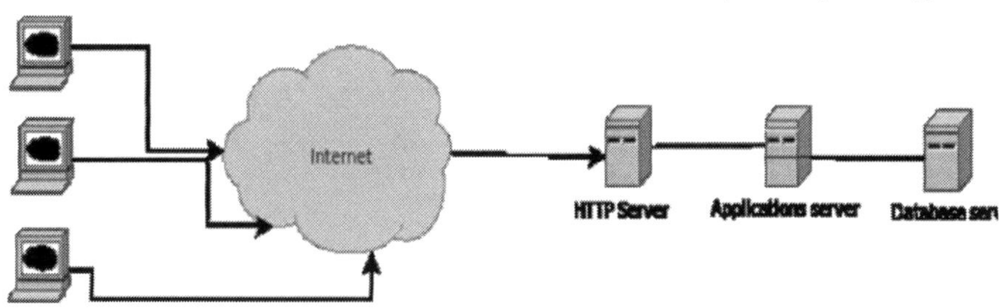

Fig. 3 Cluster with the division of server functions

software to such an organization of task division. For typical application solutions, this is possible without any special restrictions. The figure presents cluster organizations for web applications, but it is often used in other areas, e.g. for highly available GIS applications. Often for applications requiring high performance, the two above solutions are combined, i.e. after a functional division, a cluster with duplicate nodes is used as part of a given function. The further part of the article focuses on solutions concerning clusters with nodes without division of functions.

3 Load balancing algorithms in classical cluster systems

Work of task switches in the cluster has a significant impact on system performance. The basic tasks that are set before the cluster switch are the following:

- maximizing system efficiency
- efficient use of resources
- reducing energy consumption in a case of low load
- reducing costs of use of resources

While maximizing efficiency is obviously the main task, the remaining ones listed above are the result of high cost-consumption of cluster solutions not only at the level of investment but also ongoing maintenance. Ensuring proper working conditions of the cluster due to the power quality and climatic conditions of the system is very expensive. In addition, there is a factor related to ecology, which is called Green Computing in recent years.

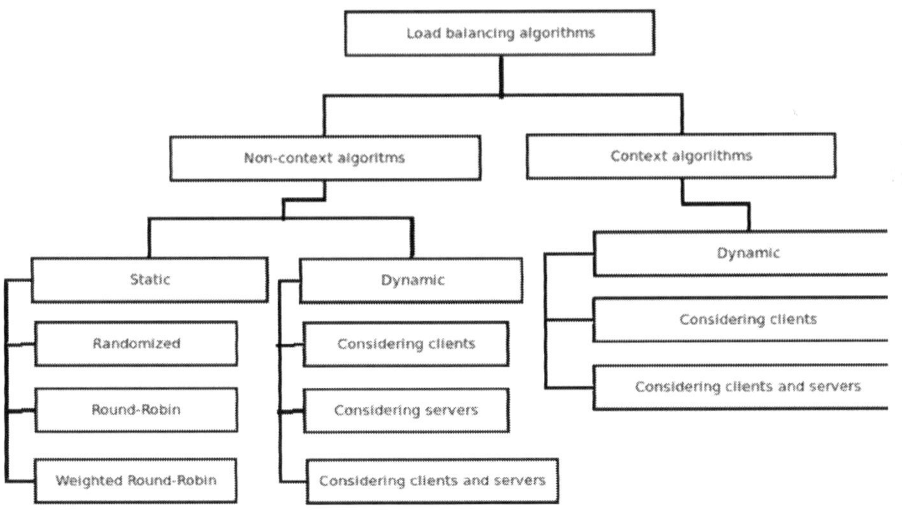

Fig. 4 Systematic of load balancing algorithms

The main task performed by a switch is to distribute loads of individual servers in a way to obtain the best performance indicators of the entire system. Dispatchers work on the basis of various task allocation algorithms. The division of task distribution algorithms in cluster systems is shown in Figure 4. For several years, works have been underway related to the development of algorithms allowing for better alignment of tasks to dynamically changing cluster working conditions such as server load, relative number of requests incoming to the system and others. Task distribution algorithms must meet one basic condition - they must have very low complexity, because the decision to choose a server must be made in real time. Two main types of algorithms are distinguished:

- contextual - taking into account the content of queries
- context-free - not taking into account the content of queries.

Among the context-free algorithms we distinguish:

- static: algorithms that operate independently of external factors, they do not use any information about the system state
- dynamic: algorithms that take into account information about the system state in their operation

Typical and most commonly seen in practice static algorithms are the algorithm that randomly assigns tasks to servers and the Round Robin algorithm [2]. The typical Round Robin algorithm is often extended to a form that takes into account the performance of individual cluster servers (in a situation where they are different), the so-called Weighted Round Robin (WRR). In this case, the servers, depending on their performance, are assigned appropriate weights that affect the frequency of task allocation.

Dynamic contextless algorithms can be divided into:

- taking into account clients
- taking into account the state of servers
- taking into account both clients and the state of servers.

Dynamic algorithms usually take into account the state of servers. This is due to the fact that they work in OSI layer 3 and 4 switches [3]. The result is that the only information about the clients that the switch has is those included in the TCP / IP packet headers - the address and port to which the connection is directed. In some cases, this information is used to divide clients into groups and to assign them specific resources within the cluster. More information is available about the status of the cluster, although the information about the load of individual servers is not directly available, but the switch has information about the status and number of active connections. Another method of determining the status of individual servers in the cluster is periodically checking by the switch the response times of individual servers and directing new connections to the servers with the shortest response time. A common solution is to modify the WRR algorithm by updating the weights of individual servers with the number of connections or response times taken into account.

A separate group of algorithms are contextual algorithms operating in OSI layer 7 switches [4]. These switches analyze the content of HTTP requests, which allows for:

- increasing the efficiency of cache usage by directing tasks with the same content to servers that have handled similar requests recently
- using specialized servers, e.g. for delivering video content
- partitioning server content and distributing functions within the service

4 Architecture of cluster systems with virtualization

In the last dozen or so years we have been observing the intensive development of server systems based on virtualization. It is connected with many other new solutions regarding both hardware and software solutions. The key from the point of view of this article is the combination of server system virtualization technologies with cloud solutions. Virtualization is a technique that allows you to separate the software layer (at the application or operating system level) from the hardware layer. This allows you to freely manage hardware resources and assign them to tasks depending on your needs. The simplest solution from this point of view is the static allocation of resources to individual virtual machines based on the forecasted load. This type of virtual system organization is found mainly in smaller systems with a limited and known number of users [5]. Possible modifications to the allocation of resources can be made relatively rarely based on the observation of the system load. In systems with greater complexity, solutions allowing for dynamic allocation of resources are used, this will be the subject of the further part of the article.

Solutions providing mechanisms for virtualization vary on many levels, but the basic idea and principles of operation are similar. The main virtualization solutions are currently:

- VMware vSphere
- Citrix XenServer
- Microsoft Azure / Hyper-V

A detailed description of solutions used in server virtualization is not the subject of this article, but it is necessary to present the general principle of operation of such a system. An example of the Vmware vSphere solution has been used for this purpose.

The cluster system architecture with the use of virtualization is based on the use of a dedicated server to manage the system. The system manager (different terminology is used in different solutions) is to supervise the operation of virtual systems and direct service requests to selected virtual machines. The physical servers in such a system are managed by specialized software that provides virtualized resources (in the case of VMware ESX software). The resources of individual physical servers are allocated to virtual systems, one physical machine can be part of a larger virtual machine, but it can also host multiple virtual systems. The whole cluster can be treated as a common pool of virtual resources that can be allocated depending on the needs. Modern solutions allow for dynamic allocation of resources depending on the current load, it requires the use of advanced mechanisms that allow the migration of virtual systems between physical servers. Another mechanism that improves the efficiency of the virtual cluster is the ability to temporarily freeze the

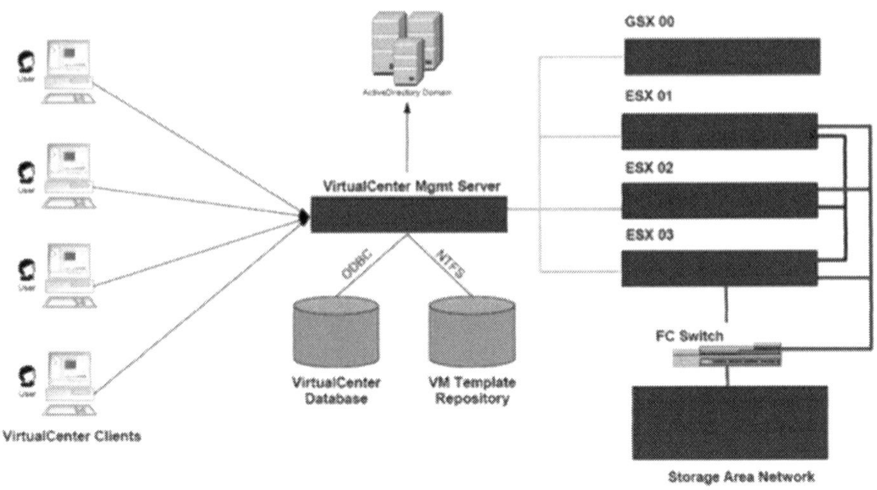

Fig. 5 Architecture of cluster with virtualization [6]

operation of unloaded systems and recreate them as needed.

5 Load balancing algorithms in cloud systems

The previous chapter presents the basic mechanisms occurring in a cluster of servers with virtualization applied. All of these mechanisms have a negative impact on system performance. It should be noted that the main benefits that are obtained from virtualization are [7]:

- consolidation of resources
- increasing the efficiency of hardware resources utilization
- centralized management

- increased resilience to critical situations
- improvement and reduction of failure removal costs

The above benefits are unquestionable, however they also cause an additional system load. Therefore, balancing the burdens in such systems becomes so important. Chapter 4 presents algorithms for load balancing in classical cluster systems. The solutions for clusters mainly concerned static context-free solutions. Dynamic contextless algorithms, in the case of classical clusters, can take into account the state of the system usually only to a small extent. This is due to the lack of information about the status of individual servers. This situation changes fundamentally for clusters with virtualization. The correct operation of the virtual system requires ongoing monitoring of the status of its components. This opens up wide possibilities of using this information to balance loads in the system. The tasks set before the balancing mechanisms will also be greater. In addition to the basic task of separating tasks between physical servers included in virtual machines, the load balancing subsystem should decide on the distribution of virtual resources within the cluster, including the deciding on migrations. Due to the above, research into algorithms optimizing the efficiency of such systems has been dynamically developing in recent years.

The tasks that are placed before the load balancing subsystem [8]:

- resources are readily available (at the desired time)
- cluster resources are used efficiently (taking loads into account)
- energy consumption is minimized (particularly in the case of a small load)
- resource utilization cost is reduced

In connection with the above tasks, the algorithms used in load balancing vary widely and are used depending on the configuration of a cluster system. Therefore, several types of load balancing algorithms can be distinguished.

- in a static environment: algorithms similar to those used in classical clusters (described in Chapter 4) are used, mainly the Round Robin algorithm with different additional weights available to the cluster management software
- in a dynamic environment, three types of algorithms are distinguished depending on which node is responsible for load balancing:
    - Centralized Load Balancing - in this case, one designated node is responsible for all tasks related to load balancing, it reduces the time necessary to make decisions but also causes a higher load on the node and reduces the system's resistance to failures
    - Distributed Load Balancing - in this case all nodes store the information needed to make decisions, which allows to ensure a high level of resistance to failures
    - Hierarchical Load Balancing - in this case to manage tasks a hierarchical structure of nodes in the cluster is used, decision making is spread over several levels (a three-level structure is most common)

Regardless of the above-described systematics, load balancing mechanisms use various kinds of algorithms. Artificial intelligence methods are increasingly in use. Table 1 shows the comparison of algorithms and their use.

Table 1 presents a comparison of algorithms that are used in various types of cloud systems. It is not the purpose of this article to provide detailed information about individual algorithms, information about them is widely available in the literature. The list above has been cited mainly to demonstrate the huge variety of currently proposed solutions.

6 Summary

The article presents basic information on issues related to load balancing in cluster systems. The tasks and limitations applicable to the algorithms in use are presented. Due to the popularization of solutions based on virtualization, there was a significant development of load balancing mechanisms, their role and their tasks increased significantly. Currently, mechanisms that come from various fields of computer science are used to build effective solutions that will allow meet the requirements. Optimization mechanisms using artificial intelligence has gained very much importance in the development of load balancing in cluster systems.

References

1. V. Cardellini, E. Casalicchio, M. Colajanni and P. S. Yu, "The state of the art in locally distributed web-server systems," ACM, (2002)
2. H. Bryhni, E. Klovning and O. Kure, "A comparison of load balancing techniques for scalable web servers.," Network, IEEE, (2000)
3. M. Colajanni and E. Casalicchio, "Scalable web clusters with static and dynamic contents.," in In Cluster Computing, 2000. Proceedings. IEEE International Conference on, (2000)
4. K. Gilly, N. Thomas, C. Juiz i R. Puigjaner, „Scalable qos contentaware load balancing algorithm for a web switch based on classical policies.," w Advanced Information Networking and Applications, 2008. AINA, (2008)
5. Q. C. Zhang and R. Luand Boutaba, "Cloud computing: state-of-the-art and research challenges," Journal of Internet Services and Applications, pp. 7--18, (2010)
6. www.vmware.com
7. M. Xu i W. Tian, „An Online Load Balancing Algorithm for Virtual Machine Allocation with Fixed Process Intervals," Journal of Information & Computational Science, p. 989–1001, 10 February (2014)
8. P. A. Pattanaik, S. Roy i P. K. Pattnaik, „Performance study of some dynamic load balancing algorithms in cloud computing environment," Signal Processing and Integrated Networks, (2015)
9. M. Katyal and A. Mishra, "A Comparative Study of Load Balancing Algorithms in Cloud Computing Environment," International Journal of Distributed and Cloud Computing, (2013)

ITM Web of Conferences **21**, 00016 (2018) https://doi.org/10.1051/itmconf/20182100016
CST 2018

Multifractal Analysis Of Selected Multicast Routing Protocols In IP Networks

Paweł Dymora[1,*], and *Mirosław* Mazurek[1], and *Dominik* Strzałka[1]

[1] Rzeszów University of Technology, Department of Complex Systems, Al. Powstanców Warszawy 12, 35-959 Rzeszów, Poland

Abstract. The article presents results of studies using simulations on computer network devices, designed to examine the effectiveness of routing protocols with the video streaming and generated traffic for Jperf applications. In order to demonstrate the effectiveness of the selected protocols several simulation scenarios were made using different sized UDP packets. The traffic was analyzed in terms of statistical self-similarity. Multifractal analysis has also been made, using two kinds of spectrums. The study determined the relationship between them. These tasks were designed to determine the multifractal and long-term relationship for a given process.

1. Introduction

Live streaming content such as video, Internet radio broadcasts, VoIP are ones of the most promising services among the many possibilities offered by IP networks [1]. Unfortunately, the network traffic of these services is problematic from the point of view of taking congestions [2] and traffic patterns recognition [3]. The main reason is the large size of the required bandwidth, in particular for video streaming. This band may increase as with the popularity of the service [4]. In addition, the traffic will be irregular because the data are received by the random recipients [5]. It is expected that the live streaming will dominate traffic in IP networks [6, 7]. This means that the above traffic problems become critical at this moment. Given the nature of the service, the implementation of multicast techniques seems to be the best solution to solve these problems [8]. A key element of live video traffic is simultaneous distribution of information to multiple recipients. Therefore, it can be assumed that during operation of such a service network resources are wasted. The multicast techniques can effectively reduce the size of such a traffic [9]. In order to reduce implementation problems, we can implement standard multicast protocols or other multicast techniques.

[*] Corresponding author: dymora.pawel@prz.edu.pl

Although these opportunities are widely available, it becomes important to determine how effectively multicasting can reduce the intractability of traffic caused by the live content. As it was written above a video network traffic is usually caused by congestions. Their existence lead to enlargement of response time and reduced network throughput. Usually they occur if the bandwidth is insufficient and the amount of data traffic exceeds available capacity. Starting from pioneer work of Leland and his cooperators [10] it is known that network traffic congestions can be omnipotent as an emergent phenomena [11, 12] and we cannot avoid them, but we can reduce their number taking into account different techniques and methods, among them there are: monitoring network traffic, use network segmentation, use a content delivery network, reconfigure TCP/IP settings, use backpressure routing, prioritize network traffic, use network redundancy, use multicast techniques. The existence of congestions is also related to the bursty traffic and statistical self-similarity [10, 13] thus it is important to determine all possible phenomena that allow better understanding the complex nature of video stream network traffic.

A paper consists of seven sections. Section 2 gives a discussion about goals and multicast routing mechanisms used in routing protocols. We describe used protocols: PIM-DM (Protocol Independent Multicast -- Dense Mode) and PIM-SM (Protocol Independent Multicast -- Sparse Mode). Section 3 is a presentation of analysed network specification with topology based on five Cisco routers and two or three computers, depending on the type of scenario. Section 4 presents the methodology for determining the Hurst coefficient and the tools used for the test of streaming video (Selfis application). Section 5 gives details about carried experiment and Section 6 shows multifractal spectrum for the studies using a multicast server and one recipient. We presented long-term relationships in the test process. Section 7 gives conclusions and research for the future.

2. Multicast Routing

Multicast routing refers to the creation of trees distribution that provide a path from the multicast source to a multicast group members. Multicast routing protocols can be divided into types with respect to the type of network. In a wired network routing protocols are identified based on two types of trees [14]:

- Source trees;
- Shared trees.

In contrast, wireless networks multicast routing protocols can be divided into three types of trees created:

- The source tree;
- Shared Tree;
- Based on the grid.

PIM-DM (Protocol Independent Multicast – Dense Mode) is relatively simple implementation of the flood-and-prune protocol. It is a multicast routing protocol that uses the underlying unicast routing information base to flood multicast datagrams to all multicast routers and uses dense multicast routing. Prune messages are used to prevent future messages from propagating to routers without group membership information. To illustrate (in Fig. 1), host S1 is the source of a multicast group G and a host H2 is a member of the group. When the source S1 starts sending IP datagrams to a group G, the datagram floods all routers [15, 17].

Each router that processes the packet, creates entry (S1, G) in multicast routing table, where the input interface is set as the RPF interface for the source S1,and set of output interfaces include all other interfaces (Table 1). E.g., multicast routing table of the router R2, is as follows [15]:

Table 1. Description of multicast routing table R2 router

Source IP	Multicast group	Input interface	The set of output interfaces
S1	G	I1	I2, I3

According to the algorithm flood-and-prune, the router R4, that is not connected to the network and members of the group, sends a Prune message through his RPF interface to the router R2. The message contains the address of the group G and address severed source node S1 (Table 2). When the R2 receives a message Prune selects the appropriate output interface as cut off:

Table 2. Description of the multicast routing table - cut off of the output interface

Source IP	multicast group	Input interface	The set of output interfaces
1	G	I1	I2, I3(cutting)

PIM-SM (Protocol Independent Multicast – Sparse Mode) is more complex than PIM-DM. PIM-SM initially builds a tree core for multicast group, which is common to all sources and generally scales fairly well for wide-area usage. When traffic from a source exceeds the threshold, PIM builds source tree for the source. The following will be discussed how core tree is constructed, how a source transmits data and PIM-SM turns them into the source tree.

In PIM-SM, the core router is called the *rendezvous point* (RP), and the core tree is *rendezvous point tree* (RPT). It is one-way, i.e., packets are forwarded only down trees, and sources send packets to the RP. RP can either be statically configured or dynamically determined by a broadcast mechanism, which is part of the PIM-SM. Moreover, the network may have a different RP for each multicast group [16]. A Rendezvous Point (RP) is a router in a multicast network domain that acts as a shared root for a multicast shared tree. Any number of routers can be configured to work as RPs and they can be configured to cover different group ranges. For correct operation, every multicast router within a Protocol Independent Multicast (PIM) domain must be able to map a particular multicast group address to the same RP [24].

In PIM, the router can have both entry (S, G) and (*, G) in the routing table for the same multicast group. In this case, when a packet arrives with a source address S for the group G, the router at the beginning is trying to find a match in the routing table for an entry (S, G). If such a match does not exist, then searches for the entry (*, G). If also it doesn't exists, the router attempts to forward the packet to the RP for that group. If it is not aware of any of RP, the datagram is discarded. When there is a match, the router performs checking of the RP, i.e. verifies if the datagram has been received by the input interface, which is recorded in the routing table entry, and then transmits the data to a set of output interfaces.

https://doi.org/10.1051/itmconf/20182100016

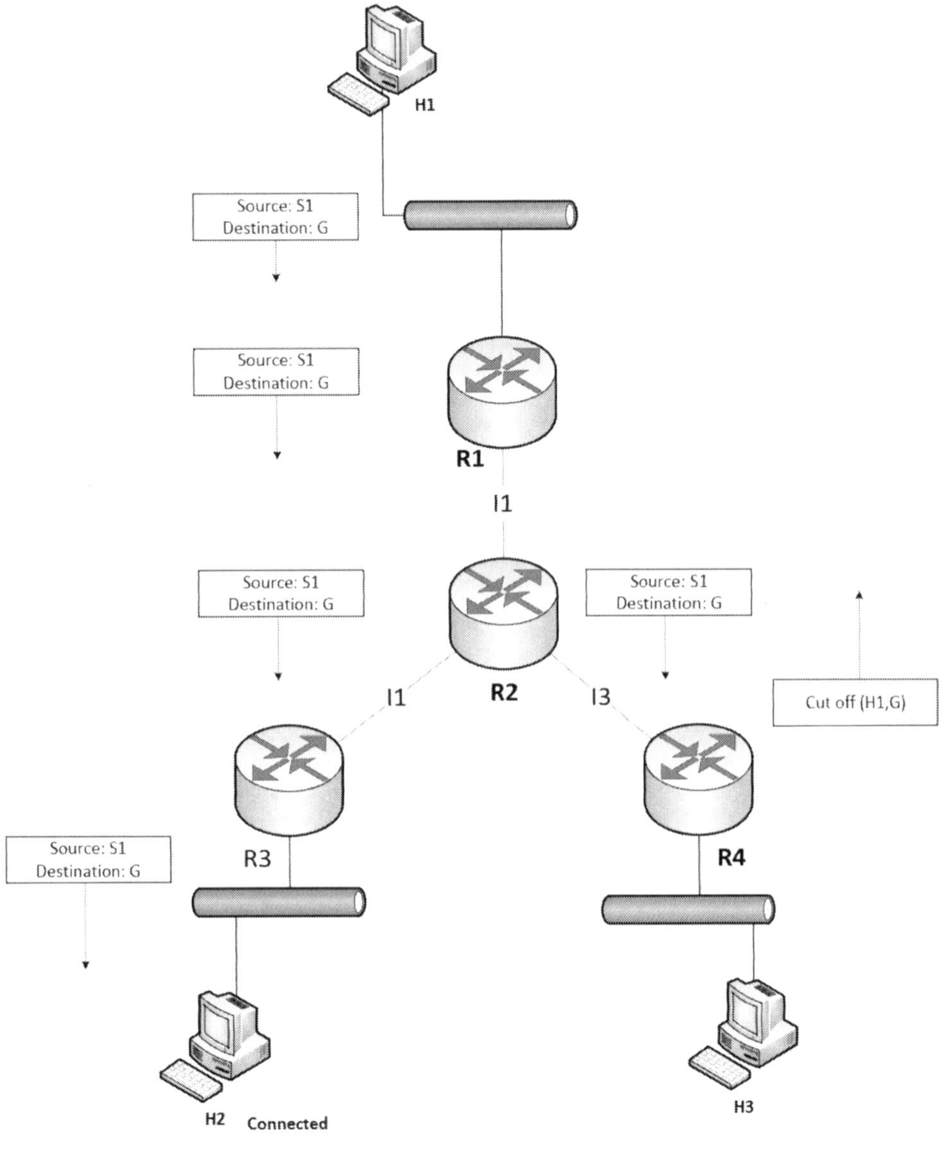

Fig. 1. RPF and cut off in PIM-DM

In multicast, the router forwards the packet away from the source to make progress along the distribution tree and prevent routing loops. The router's multicast forwarding state runs more logically by organizing tables based on the reverse path, from the receiver back to the root of the distribution tree. This process is known as reverse-path forwarding (RPF). The router adds a branch to a distribution tree depending on whether the request for traffic from a multicast group passes the *reverse-path-forwarding* check (RPF check). Every multicast packet received must pass an RPF check before it is eligible to be replicated or forwarded on any interface. The RPF check is essential for every router's multicast implementation. When a multicast packet is received on an interface, the router interprets the source address in the multicast IP packet as the destination address for a unicast IP packet. The source multicast address is found in the unicast routing table, and the outgoing interface is determined. If the outgoing interface found in the unicast routing table is the same as the interface that the multicast packet was received on, the packet passes the RPF check. Multicast packets that fail the RPF check are dropped because the incoming interface is not on the shortest path back to the source [24].

When a host joins a multicast group, the *Designated Router* (DR) for that host sends a message: Join the reverse path to the RP. DR for the host H2 or router R3 (Figure 2a) sends a Join (*, G) to R2, its neighbour RPF for RP. Assuming that R2 does not have an entry (*, G) in the routing table when it receives Join message, it creates such an entry and sends a Join(*, G) to R5. When RP gets Join message, it adds the output interface, that connects with R2 to the entry (*, G) in the routing table. Just like with messages Prune Join messages are sent periodically, about once every minute. Entries in the routing table created by a message Join have a limited lifetime and router removes the entry if it does not receive any new message Join for some time [16].

When a host H3 joins the multicast group G, as shown in Fig. 2 (b), the router R4 sends a Join(*, G) to R2. Because R2 already has an entry (*, G) the routing table does not send a Join message to RP and simply adds the I2 interface to a set of output interfaces for the entry (*, G) in the routing table [16].

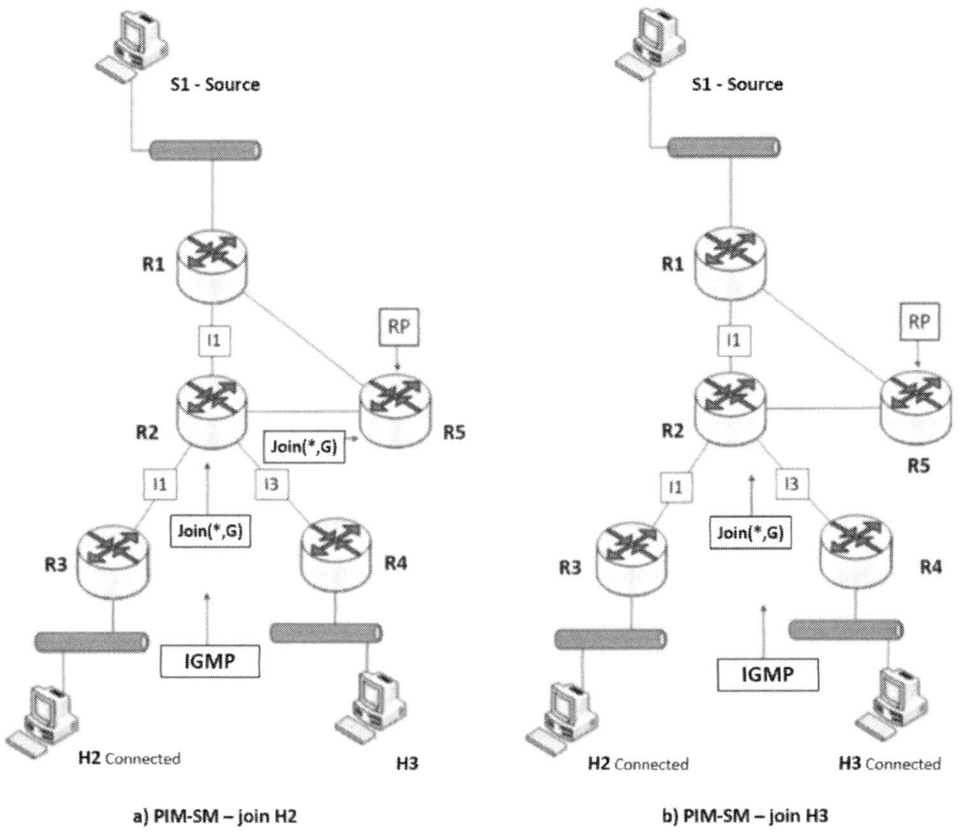

Fig. 2. RPF and cut off in PIM-DM Cut off and join messages

When a source wants to transmit data to the multicast group, the DR for the source sends a Register message to the RP of that group and includes multicast packet in this message. RP which receives the Register message, receives the packet and sends it down the RPT tree. If the RPT has no node down, RP discards the packet. When the Register message with datagram reaches the RP, it sends a Join (S, G) to the source. Join message travels to RP shortest reverse path and creates entries (S, G) in the routing tables of all routers between the source and RP [18].

When the Join message reaches the source DR, DR sends packets from the source to the RP. When the RP receives packets from the reverse path, it sends a Register-stop message to the DR to stop the transmission containing datagrams. For a time between receiving messages Join and Register-stop source DR receives two copies of each packet from the source, one in the Communication Register and one in the parent package. Host S1 sends a multicast packet to its DR, that is R1. This includes the datagram in a Register message and send it as a unicast message to the RP [19].

RP receives the packet and forwards it to the RPT. In Fig. 2, we assume that host H1 only joined to the group G and the RPT consists of a path R5 -> R2 -> R3. Then, RP sends a message Join (S1, G) to DR source. When R1 receives a Join message, creates an entry (S1, G) in the routing table and starts to stem the transmission of packets, i.e. normal IP datagrams with destination address G, to the RP. As shown in Fig. 2 (b), R1 continues to send packages in the message Register to RP. As soon as the first parent packet arrives to R5, the router sends a Register-stop to R1. This stops the transmission of messages Register with packets [18].

3. Study

For the analysis of multicast traffic in this work an experiments on computer networks with multicast routing protocols: PIM-DM and PIM-SM were carried out. The study used five Cisco routers and two or three computers, depending on the type of scenario.

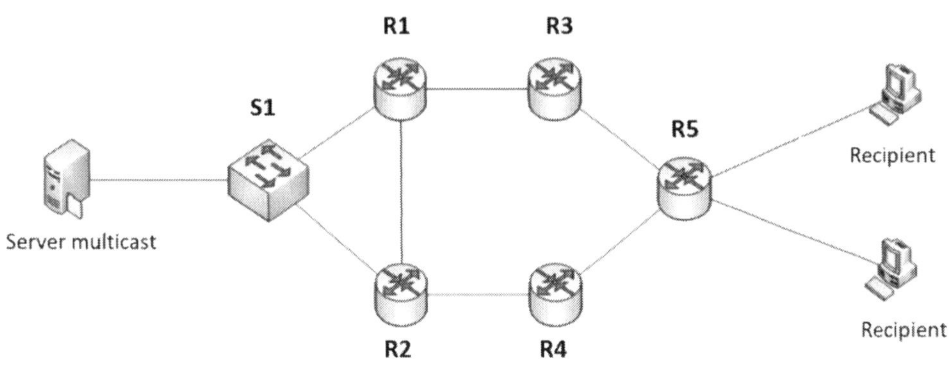

Fig. 3. Tested network topology

During the first simulation one of the computers was a multicast server, which transmits video using VLC media player program, while in the entire network was only one recipient. This experiment was conducted for a network with separately implemented two above-mentioned multicast routing protocols.

The second study was to transmit streaming video from the multicast server to two recipients included in the test network. Like the previous study this one was also carried out for both multicast routing protocols.

The third study was to generate traffic using a Jperf generator, from the server to the one or two recipients. In this study the main objective was the highest load capacity of the network and the analysis of load resistance of two multicast routing protocols. The different sizes of UDP packets were transmitted. The test may have allowed to verify that network bandwidth can be obtained for a variety of UDP packets in two types of multicast routing protocols deployed in the network. There were sent packets of different lengths 1359 kb and 1470 kb.

4. Self-similarity statistical analysis

Statistical self-similarity analysis was performed using a Selfis application [25]. This software is based on the source code written in the Java programming language. The main parameter in the analysis of statistical self-similarity was the number of transmitted packets per second. To determine the statistical similarity, Selfis uses the Hurst coefficient. The Hurst coefficient allows to specify the nature of the process, long-term dependencies, direction of change and stationarity. To determine these properties the relation H > 0.5 was used. However, if the Hurst coefficient is smaller than 0.5, it is considered that in the according process occurs short term dependencies, the process is not persistent and do not occur stationarity dependencies [10, 18, 20].

The fractional Brownian motion (fBm) is the basis of long-range dependent statistical models. This model is a natural expansion of Brownian motion and was proposed by Mandelbrot and Van Ness [21] as an association with a Hurst parameter H. Mandelbrot and his followers proposed many natural phenomena which can be described by fBm. A process (term of 'process' doesn't mean a program that is executed or processed in a computer system) can be considered as self-similar if for some H>0.

$$X(at) \overset{d}{\approx} a^H X(t) \text{ for every } a > 0. \quad (1)$$

Equation (1) means that the process is invariant under translations of time and scale. If variable t is considered as a time and $X(t)$ as a process space then, according to Eq. (1), every change of time scale by factor $a>0$ corresponds to change of space scale by factor a^H. The H exponent shows the process memory effects and also gives information of time series persistence. In Gaussian processes $H=0.5$ denotes the probability that process will stay in its trend and it equals $p=0.5$; if H changes the p also. If H is under 0.5 value a sequence has a tendency to return to the mean and is called an anti-persistent [22]. There is also another type of self-similar processes - Lévy α-stable processes where $H = 1/\alpha$. Then the existence of a memory effect is described by d in range $<-1/2,1/2>$ parameter and finally $H = 1/\alpha + d$ (if $d=0$ than $H = 1/\alpha$).

In 1994, according to famous paper of Leland [10], the existence of long-range dependences in computer networks was noted. The existence of statistical self-similarity leads to many important features of computer network traffic including flow burstines and congestions.

5. Long-range dependencies in analyzed data

We assume that the analysed time series are stationary; our experiments were carried under stable and do not changing conditions. However, it should be remember that some methods used to estimate H in fact give d parameter. Then the overall information about the process self-similarity should be obtained with the analysis of probability distribution. Generally, is not easy to obtain the real value of time series statistical self-similarity factor thus a few methods can be used:

- *Variance of Residuals* (VR) – it calculates the d value,
- *Aggregated Variance* (AV) – it calculates the d value,
- *Mean Value Analysis* (MVA) – it calculates the H value,
- *R/S* – it calculates the d value,

- *Detrended Fluctuation Analysis* (DFA) – it calculates the *H* value,
- *Periodogram* – it calculates the *d* value,
- *Whittle Estimator* – it calculates the *d* value,
- *Waveled Method* – it calculates the *d* value.

The description of each method can be found for example in [23]. Most of these methods were used, because calculations of *H* parameter is not easy, and strong confirmation of investigation result was required.

5.1. PIM-DM and PIM-SM protocols - video streaming

After the test of streaming video to a single recipient with the use of both protocols it can be stated that this process has long-term dependencies. All statistical methods for determining the Hurst coefficient for PIM-SM protocol (Table 3) designated this ratio above 0.5, while for the protocol PIM-DM only Absolute Moment method set the Hurst coefficient below 0.5.

Table 3. Description Analysis of Hurst coefficient for the PIM-DM and PIM-SM protocols - streaming video - one recipient

Estimation method	PIM-DM	PIM-SM
Variance Method	0.506	0.605
R/S Method	0.621	0.682
Absolute Moment Method	0.201	0.540
Variance of Residuals	0.858	0.764
Periodogram	0.641	0.782
Whittle Estimator	0.928	0.659
Abry-Weitch Estimator	0.702	0.794

After connecting to the multicast group a second recipient, we can see that the values of the Hurst coefficient determined by the majority of methods for both protocols: PIM Dense Mode and PIM Sparse Mode are below 0.5. Multicasting of video transmission to more than one recipient does not lead to deepening the long-range dependencies, but even decreases the intensity of this phenomena. Detailed results are included in the Table 4.

Table 4. Analysis of Hurst coefficient for the PIM-DM and PIM-SM protocols – streaming video - two recipients

Estimation method	PIM-DM	PIM-SM
Variance Method	0.406	0.562
R/S Method	0.086	0.072
Absolute Moment Method	0.024	0.240
Variance of Residuals	0.471	0.602
Periodogram	0.410	0.323
Whittle Estimator	0.906	0.799
Abry-Weitch Estimator	0.171	0.359

5.2. PIM-DM and PIM-SM – Jperf

Table 5 shows a comparison of Hurst coefficient for studies using Jperf traffic generator for one server and one recipient. The Hurst values clearly show that processes with implemented routing protocols: Multicast PIM-DM and PIM-SM, are characterized by long-term dependencies.

Table 5. Analysis of Hurst coefficient for the PIM-DM and PIM-SM protocols – Jperf - one recipient

Estimation method	PIM-DM	PIM-SM
Variance Method	0.562	0.771
R/S Method	0.720	0.590
Absolute Moment Method	0.640	0.200
Variance of Residuals	0.602	0.557
Periodogram	0.623	0.828
Whittle Estimator	0.799	0.684
Abry-Weitch Estimator	0.839	0.845

For the second case, in the Jperf traffic generator only one method does not calculate the Hurst coefficient above threshold value 0.5. For other methods the Hurst coefficient was greater than 0.5 and sometimes even greater in the case of one recipient (see Table 5), which indicates comparable long-term dependencies occurring in the process. Detailed results are included in the Table 6.

Table 6. Analysis of Hurst coefficient for the PIM-DM and PIM-SM protocols - JPerf - one recipient

Estimation method	PIM-DM	PIM-SM
Variance Method	0.671	0.856
R/S Method	0.640	0.589
Absolute Moment Method	0.351	0.451
Variance of Residuals	0.656	0.804
Periodogram	0.678	0.625
Whittle Estimator	0.871	0.822
Abry-Weitch Estimator	0.699	0.859

As a summary it can be stated that program traffic generators not always lead to a real traffic nature and obtained results can be different from those gathered in real cases.

5.3. The performance analysis of multicast routing protocols

To complete this research the JPerf traffic generator was used. The study was designed to test bandwidth with implemented two multicast routing protocols. The packet that has been set in the program had value 1359 bytes and 1470 bytes. The data collected in the Wireshark were used to obtain graphs as shown in Fig. 4 and 5.

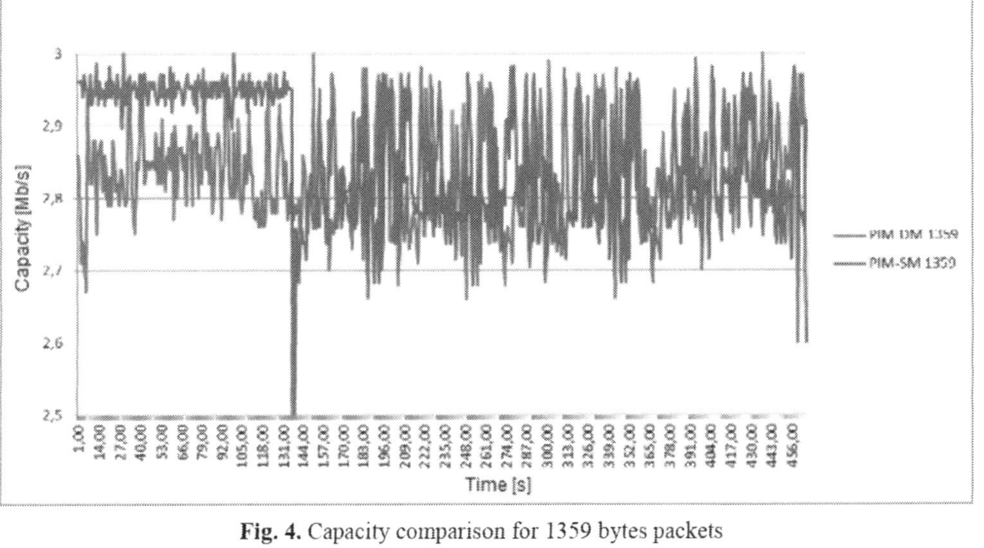

Fig. 4. Capacity comparison for 1359 bytes packets

Fig. 4 shows a comparison of the capacity for the two routing protocols using multicast streaming 1359 bytes. In the initial period of the audit it may be noted that the capacity of network protocol implemented with PIM Sparse Mode was higher than the PIM Dense Mode protocol. However, in later studies the performance of both protocols was similar.

In the case of streaming 1470 bytes it can be seen that for a half the time of the experiment time PIM Dense Mode protocol showed higher performance (details are in Fig.5).

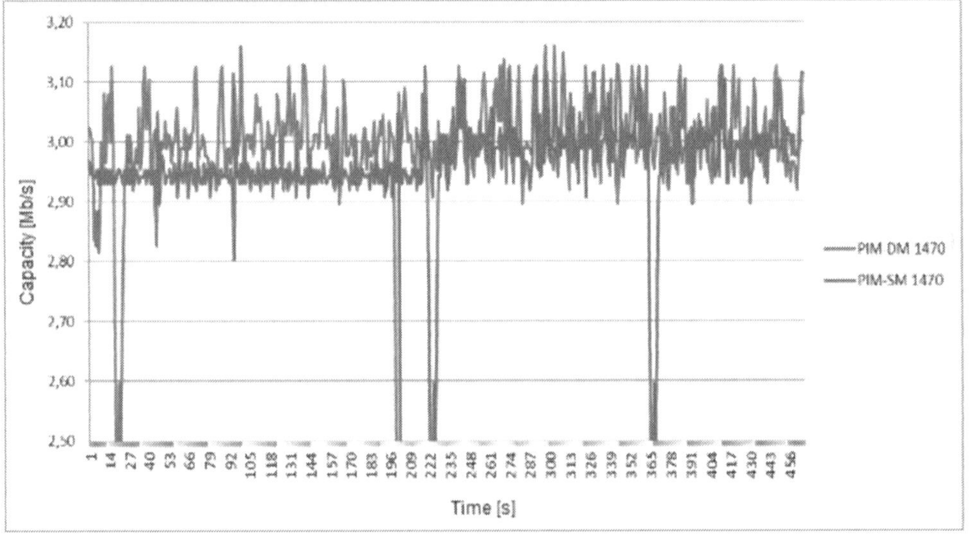

Fig. 5. Capacity comparison for 1470 bytes packets

The flow capacity in this period was in the range of 2.9 Mb/s to 3.15 Mb/s. While at the same time PIM Dense Mode protocol the capacity was in the range of from 2.92 to 2.96 Mb/s. In the second half of the experiment time the capacity for both multicast routing protocols was at the same level. It was in the range of 2.9 Mb/s to 3.12 Mb/s.

6. Multifractal of Analysis

For multifractal analysis the FracLab tool has been used which is written in Matlab [26]. Before the multifractal spectrum analysis was done a polynomial synthesis of the collected data was performed. Multifractal spectrum was determined by two methods. The first method is using Legenrde'a transform, which is determined by the classical method. The second way to determine the spectrum is the kernel density estimation [22]. When we compare the two spectrum at the same time, and the result will be similar, it means that the process is characterized by multifractal dependencies.

Data collected for statistical self-similarity analysis was used to analyse the multifractal analysis. As shown in Fig. 6 the two multifractal spectrum for testing video streaming with implemented PIM Dense Mode routing multicast protocol are given.

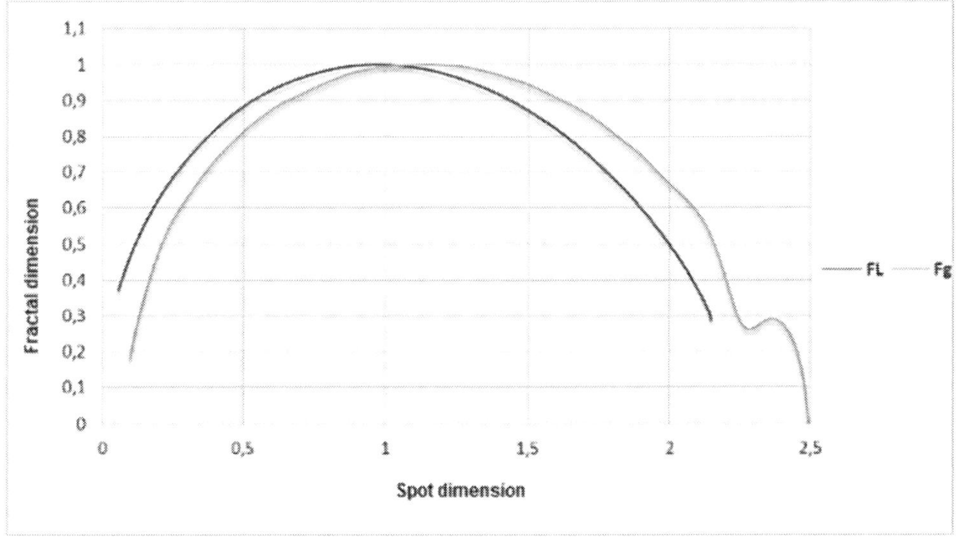

Fig. 6. The multifractal spectrum analysis for PIM-DM protocol - video streaming

The apparent similarity of multifractal spectrum shows that in the studies using a multicast server and one recipient, in the process occurred multifractal dependency, and former long-term relationships in the test process.

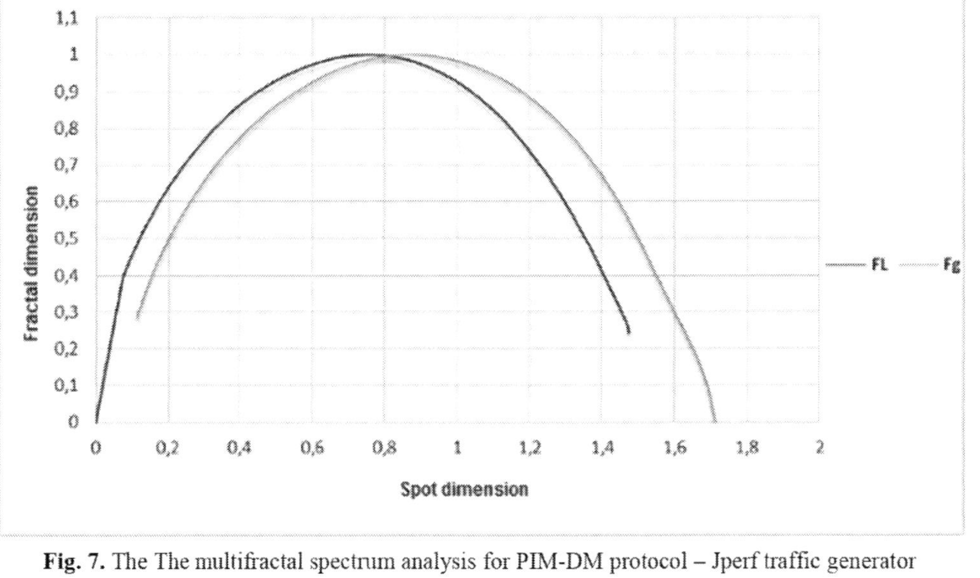

Fig. 7. The The multifractal spectrum analysis for PIM-DM protocol – Jperf traffic generator

Another study subject of multifractal analysis was the JPerf traffic generation. In the case of this experiment a multifractal spectrum can be noted; the spectrum using Legenrde'a transform with major deviation (Fig. 7) which also shows signs of similarities. It can be concluded that also in this process the multifractal dependencies exist, which means that process is also based on long-term dependencies.

The multifractal spectrum analysis was also used to determine the multifractal relationship for networks with implemented PIM Sparse Mode multicast routing protocol.

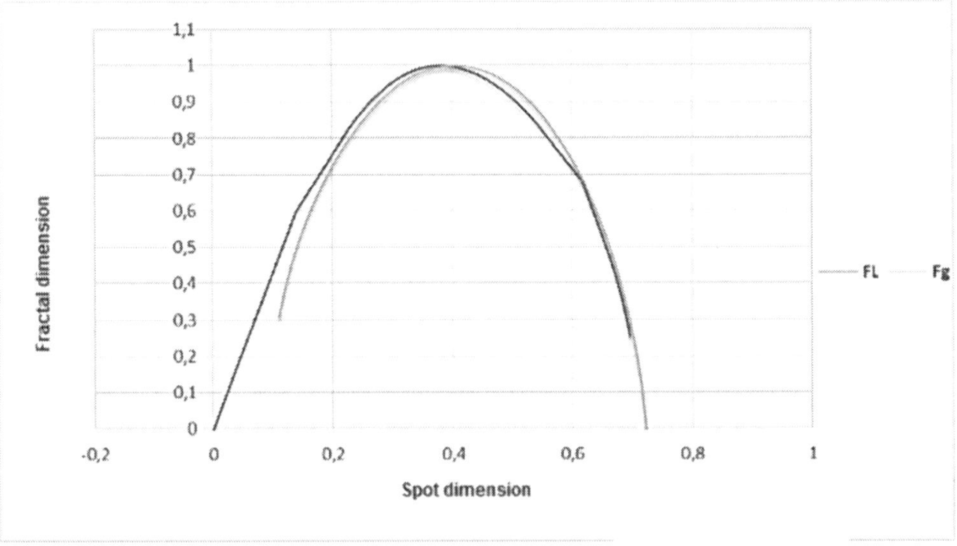

Fig. 8. The multifractal spectrum analysis for PIM-SM protocol - video streaming

In Fig. 8 two multifractal spectrum are presented; they were obtained from the data collected during the streaming video traffic. The results confirm that in a study using a multicast server and one recipient with implemented PIM SM routing multicast protocol, a process occurred with multifractal dependencies and this proves the occurrence of long-term dependencies.

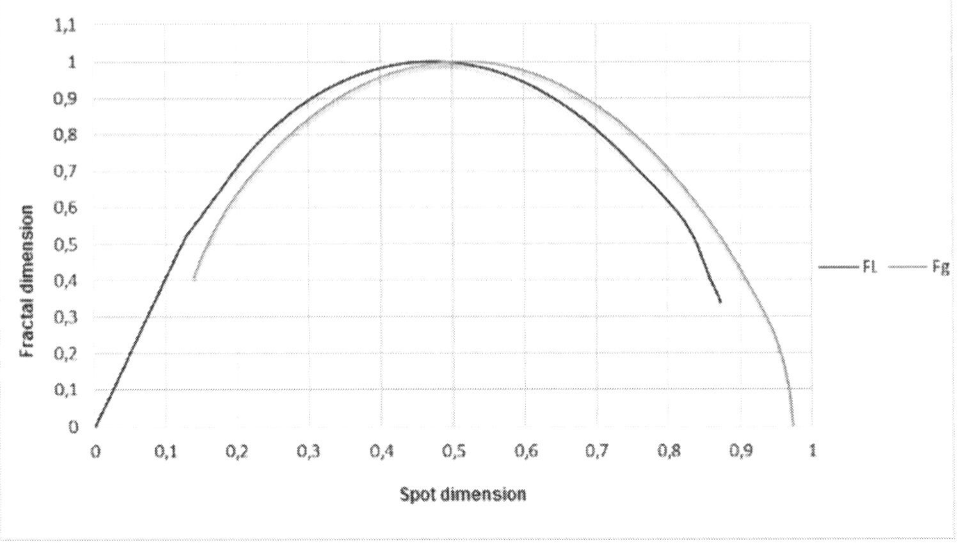

Fig. 9. The multifractal spectrum analysis for PIM-SM protocol – Jperf traffic generator

The last case of multifractal analysis was to study UDP traffic generated by JPerf traffic generator. In this case, it can be seen that the shape of the spectrum does not vary; generated process was characterized by multifractal properties.

7. Summary

The carried out tests to determine the multifractal and long-term dependencies as well as the analysis of the routing protocol performance has been implemented in network with two multicast routing protocols: PIM Dense Mode and PIM Sparse Mode. For each of these protocols various studies have been carried out in order to gather enough data for analysis.

Implementation of multicast technology over IP networks involves choosing the appropriate multicast routing protocol. A major significance in the design of this type of network is awareness of large data to be transmitted. The comparison of multicast routing protocols presented in this work was done for a small network in which there were 5 routers, 1 and 2 multicast customer servers and showed that not each size of the packet in routing protocol is fully efficient.

During the study of statistical self-similarity, in the case of video streaming server and one recipient, Hurst coefficient for both protocols had values above 0.5. With this relationship, it could be stated that the process has long-term dependences.

In the case of studies in which a multicast server and two customers were implemented not all methods of the Hurst coefficient calculation give H value above 0.5. This relationship leads to the conclusion that in this type of experiment based on real stream the existence of long-term dependencies is not so obvious due to the use of multicast protocols.

It was also found that in the network with implemented multicast routing protocols and traffic generated by Jperf occurred multifractal dependencies which largely confirms that in the network either with streaming video content or with generated UDP traffic long-term dependences take place.

References

1. R. Pantos, W. May, *HTTP live streaming*, IETF, Informational Internet-Draft 2582, (2011),
2. M. Seufert, et al., *A survey on quality of experience of HTTP adaptive streaming*, IEEE Commun Surveys Tuts , 17(1): 469-492, (2015),
3. N. A. Saqib, Y. Shakeel, M. A. Khan, H. Mehmood, M. Zia, *An effective empirical approach to VoIP traffic classification*. Turk J Elec Eng & Comp Sci , 25: 888-900, (2017),
4. C. Sieber, A. Blenk, M. Hinteregger, W. Kellerer, *The cost of aggressive HTTP adaptive streaming: Quantifying YouTube's redundant traffic*, In Proc. IFIP/IEEE IM'15, pp. 1261–1267, (2015),
5. E. Essaili E, et al, *QoE-based traffic and resource management for adaptive HTTP video delivery in LTE*, IEEE Trans Circuits Syst Video Technol, 25(6): 988–1001, (2015),
6. J. Samain, G. Carofiglio, L. Muscariello, et al., *Dynamic Adaptive Video Streaming: Towards a Systematic Comparison of ICN and TCP/IP*, IEEE transactions on Multimedia, 19(10): 2166-2181, (2017),
7. Cisco. *Visual networking index: Global mobile data traffic forecast update*, 2016–2021, White Paper, (2017),
8. I. Santos-Gonalez, A. Rivero-Garcia, J. Molina-Gil, P. Caballero-Gil, *Implementation and Analysis of Real-Time Streaming Protocols*. Reindl LM, ed. Sensors (Basel, Switzerland), 17(4): 846, (2017),

9. T. Zinner, O. Abboud, O. Hohlfeld, T. Hossfeld, P. Tran-Gia, *Towards QoE management for scalable video streaming*; Proc. of ITC Spec. Sem. on Multimedia Applications-Traffic, Performance and QoE; Miyazaki, Japan, pp. 64–69, (2010),
10. W. W. Leland, M. S. Taqqu, W. Willinger, D. V. Wilson, *On the self-similar nature of ethernet traffic (extended version)*. IEEE/ACM Trans on Netw, 2(1):1–15, (1994),
11. S. Vig, *Network Congestion as an Emergent Phenomena in Internet Traffic*, (2011),
12. E. Manley, T. Cheng, *Understanding Road Congestion as an Emergent Property of Traffic Networks,* Proc. of 14th World Multi-conference on Systemics, Cybernetics and Informatics, pp. 25-34, (2010),
13. A. Popescu, *Traffic self-similarity*, In Proc of the IEEE ICT2001, pp. 20-24, (2001),
14. M. Da Silva, A. Correia, *Transmission Techniques for Emergent Multicast and Broadcast Systems*, CRC Press, (2010),
15. R. Wittmann, *Multicast Communication: Protocols & Applications*, MK, (20010,
16. S. S. Manvi, M. S Kakkasager, *Multicast routing in mobile ad hoc networks by using a multiagent system*, Infn Scien, 178(6): 1611–1628, (2008),
17. B. Williamson, *Developing IP Multicast Networks*, Volume I, Cisco Press, (1999),
18. E. Rosenberg, *A Primer of Multicast Routing*, Springer, (2012),
19. M. Mazurek, P. Dymora. *Network Anomaly Detection Based on the Statistical Self-similarity Factor,* Analysis and Simulation of Electrical and Computer Systems, LNEE*; 324*: 271-287, (2015),
20. P. Dymora, M. Mazurek, K. Zelazny, *Operating system efficiency evaluation on the base of measurements analysis with the use of non-extensive statistics elements*, Annales UMCS, Informatica, 14(3): 65-75, (2014),
21. B. B. Mandelbrot, J.W. van Ness, *Fractional Brownian Motions*, Fractional Noises and Applications. SIAM Review, 10: 422-437, (1968),
22. M. Mazurek, P. Dymora, *Network anomaly detection based on the statistical self-similarity factor for HTTP protocol,* Electr Rev, 90(1): 127-130, (2014),
23. R. J. Adler, R. E. Feldman,M. S. Taqqu, *A Practical Guide to Heavy Tails: Statistical Techniques and Applications (Eds.)*. Birkhauser, Boston, (1998),
24. https://www.juniper.net/documentation/en_US/junos/topics/concept/multicast-pim-overview.html, (2018),
25. http://alumni.cs.ucr.edu/~tkarag/Selfis/Selfis.html, (2018),
26. https://project.inria.fr/fraclab/, (2018).

ITM Web of Conferences **21**, 00017 (2018) https://doi.org/10.1051/itmconf/20182100017
CST 2018

Open data – an introduction to the issue

Paweł Dymora[1,*], and *Mirosław* Mazurek[1], and *Bartosz* Kowal[1]

[1] Rzeszów University of Technology, Department of Complex Systems, Al. Powstancow Warszawy 12, 35-959 Rzeszów, Poland

Abstract. Rapidly developing of internet technologies and digitalization of government generate more and more data. Databases from various public institutions and private sectors, e.g. in the fields of economics, transport, environment and public safety are publishing in the global Internet network, so that any user can browse them without additional charges. Most of this data is published on the open data portals. Open data - that is, "open", public data can allow the processing and analysis of information contained in them completely free of charge. This article is an introduction to a fairly new area of issues such as "open data" or "open government", presents the main mechanisms of accessing to data in public open data portals and also propose a conceptual open data/government model.

1 Open Data

The term of "open data" was best defined by the Open Knowledge International non-profit organization [1]. It assumes that open data means the free data that can be freely used, re-used and distributed by anyone for any purpose [2]. This is a somewhat idealized definition of open data. Most published databases do not have all the listed properties [2 - 4]:

- *Free* - access to data must be free,
- *Availability* - data must be available as a whole without any intentional errors. These data must also be available in a convenient and modifiable form, e.g. CSV, JSON, GeoJSON, KML, XML, RSS or RDF Turtle,
- *Re-use and redistribution* - the data provider must allow work on the contents of the database and the ability to publish these data with other databases,
- *Use of open data* - every user has the opportunity to work on data, reuse and redistribute them regardless of their purpose.

A large part of the available open data is published by government institutions. The most of them publish in categories [5]:

- social issues, law, political life,
- science, education and communication,
- geography, environment,
- economic life, agri-food sector,
- employment and work,

* Corresponding author: dymora.pawel@prz.edu.pl

- finance and trade,
- energy, industry, production, technology and research,
- agriculture, forestry and fishing,
- European Union, international relations, international organizations,
- transport, enterprise and competition.

1.1 Open Government Data

Open Government Data (OGD) is a social initiative that refers to the public disclosure of information created by public offices. Most public offices collect large amounts of data during routine activities. The main purpose of OGD is to allow free reading of data to any user who would be interested in such information. This initiative is based on the same principle as open data. Data must be available free of charge and access to data has to be unlimited and one can use and redistribute data [7].

The governments of many countries, not only the European Union, have introduced the OGD concept aimed at providing the citizens of the country with access to the collected data by public institutions. The main purpose is often to enhance the knowledge of citizens on how public administration works. It is worth to emphasize that actually most of the data collected by offices is not published because the law does not allow the publication of certain data. Most of them are covered by various security clauses. OGD is to enable residents to analyze data and consequently allows better decisions, suggestions regarding the functioning of a given unit, or detection of irregularities [6 -7].

Referring to the OGD, in the European Union from 2012 the open data portal was created to collect data from the public sector of the EU member states. All collected data is in accordance with the terms of open data. Only a small portion of the data is subject to the conditions for their use and processing. The initiative to create a portal with the open data concept was the stimulation and economic development of the each of the EU member states, as well as the European Union itself. The main objective was to improve the transparency of operation of the state institutions that generated a large amount of data. The advantage of entering open data was the possibility of using them, e.g. in applications promoting a given city, increasing the city's reputation [8 -11]. Depending on the base category, the update time of the records varies. In the case of the finance category, specifically the budget arrears database, the updates are carried out every six months, while the agricultural information, for example about fruit and vegetable prices, is updated every month [6, 11 - 13].

1.2 Socrata - open data portal

Open data are placed on the Internet. According to the dataportals.org service [5], over 524 different open data portals have been created. Most of these types of databases can be found on specially designed portals. For Europe, the largest portal providing open data is the European Union Open Data Portal (EU ODP) containing the official open databases from all of its member countries [10]. The Polish equivalent of EU ODP is a "dane publiczne" portal [6], containing data only from the territory of Poland. It is worth mentioning the Socrata portal [14], which stores existing official data, mainly from the United States. It enables easy downloading of data from the portal using specially written libraries for various applications, e.g. the Socrata package for the language R.

Socrata is already mentioned as one of the providers of open data browsing services. Socrata is a widely used government solution to work on open data. It provides a data platform and services in the cloud for government organizations in the United States, i.e. urban, state, federal, etc. The advantage of using this portal is automation of the public sector data flow to a commonly accessible website so that the interested people can easily find and use government data. Socrata has developed the application programming interface for open data (API). Access to public data in their database can be obtained through a common, standards-based application interface. Socrata allows to check the type of database columns and data stored in them. It has ready-to-use functions for downloading data for various applications and environments, e.g. PhpSoda, .NET, Java, PHP, Python, Ruby, R and many others [14].

There are two methods of downloading data from the portal without the specialized programming or analytical environments. The first one allows to write to the disk the database in a format: CSV, JSON, RDF, RSS, TSV and XML. Table 1. presents example of a part of Active Trademark Registrations database saved in .csv format and Fig. 1 shows the data according to the SoDA standard. The disadvantage of using this method is the necessity of manually downloading updates every time [14].

Table 1. Example of a part of Active Trademark Registrations database saved in .csv format [7]

Registration Number	Registration Date	Trademark Description	Correspondent Name	Address
102	03/15/1968	"SR" MONOGRAM	SUNRIVER RESORT LIMITED PARTNERSHIP	11777 SAN VICENTE STE 900
103	03/15/1968	"SUNRIVER"	SUNRIVER RESORT LIMITED PARTNERSHIP	11777 SAN VICENTE STE 900
158	01/24/1969	THREE TENNIS BALLS AND FOUR TENNIS RACQUETS	WEST HILLS RACQUET CLUB	-------------
3957	04/21/1936	"CORNING"	MICHELE N KEEFER-MEHLENBACHER	CORNING INCORPORATED
4020	08/29/1936	"MOLY-KROME"	PACIFIC MACHINERY & TOOL STEEL CO	3445 NW LUZON ST

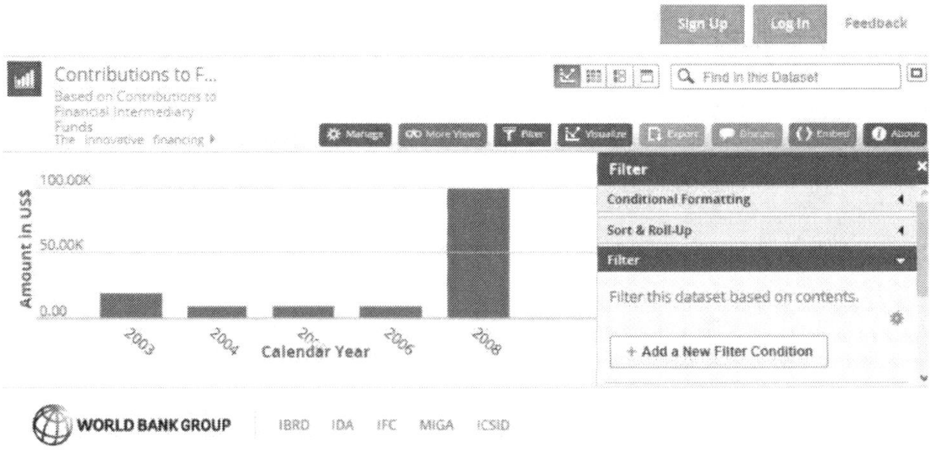

Fig. 1. Graphical presentation of data according to the SoDA standard [15].

The second method of collecting data is API. Any unauthorized user can send a small number of requests to databases that come from one shared address pool within an hour. Own API allows to make up to 1000 requests per hour, allowing for dynamic operation over data [14].

1.3 Open databases - statistics of selected portals

There is a very large number of open data databases in the Internet. To facilitate browsing and selecting the right database in the Socrata format, the data.json standard is used, containing entries for each database in the portal. From it one can read the name of the data set, the format of the record and whether the database is public.

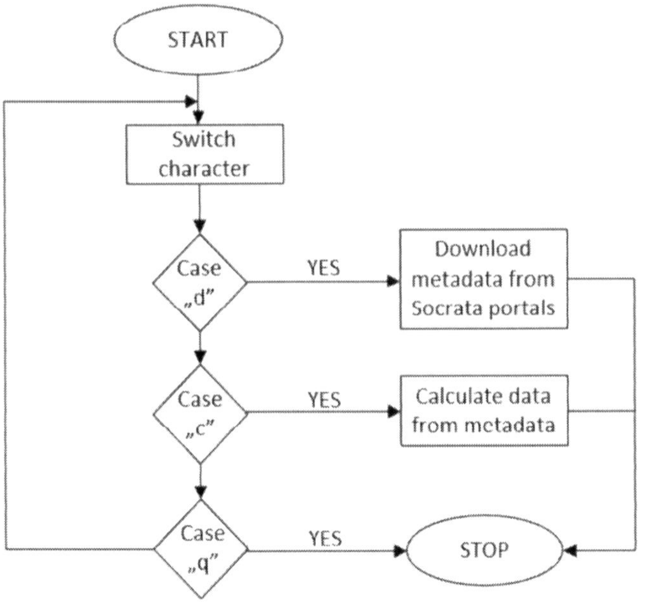

Fig. 2. Block diagram of a script that processes data from available Socrata portals.

The study analyzed selected features of Socrata's portals. A script was created to load a list of all available Socrata portals located on the opendatanetwork.com portal and its metadata. Fig. 2 presents the diagram describing the prepared script. There are currently 241 portals available. There is a possibility to download metadata about portal data sets containing, for example, information about the purpose of databases, date of creation and last modification, types of formats, etc. An additional option in the script is the ability to calculate the number of data sets and data formats that individual portals offer.

Each database may have several data formats at the same time, e.g. csv, rdf, PDF, etc. Fig. 3 shows that more than half of the databases come from government (gov) or state (edu) websites. Depending on the specificity of the portal, the number of open databases it collects is different (from 2 to 397 different sets of data).

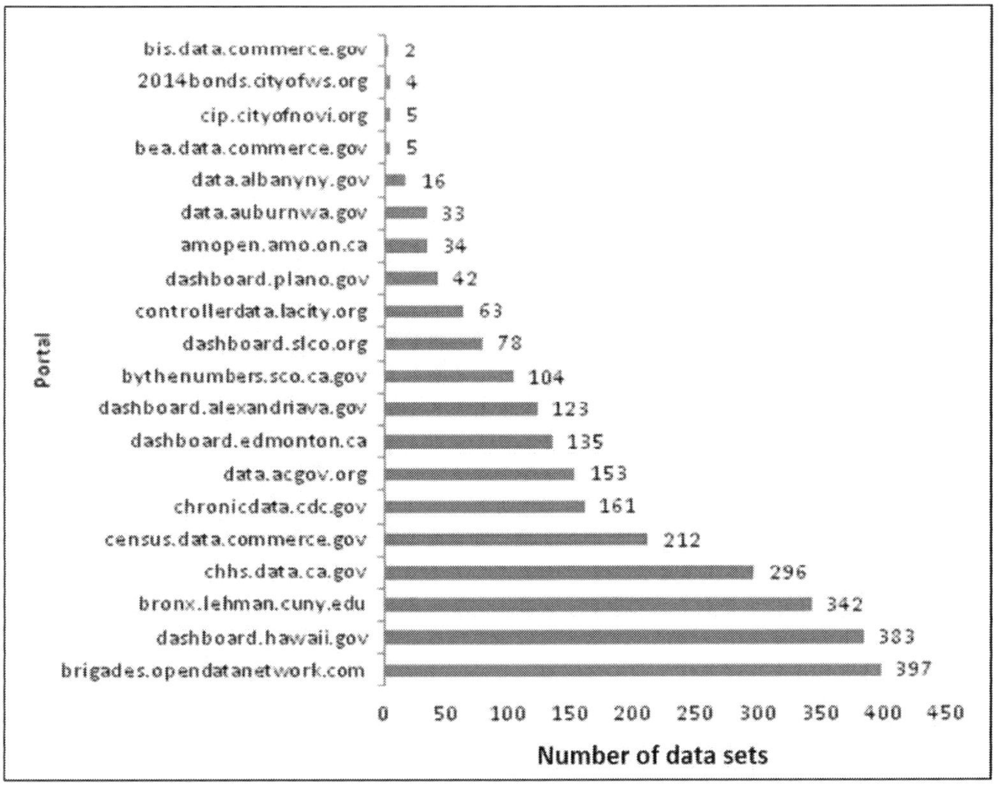

Fig. 3. Number of datasets provided by the first 20 Socrata portals based on files data.json (as of 30/06/2018) [14].

Analyzing the data.json file in terms of data formats, it can be seen that the most frequently used format is csv (49.90%), rdf (39.4%) and xml (41.5,%). The less frequently used data formats are PDF (12.1%), html (13.9%), octet stream (32.5%), vnd.ms-excel (0.2%) or zip (14.4%). The CSV type (comma delimited) is a very common format that allows to import data from a file into one's own API or your own database.

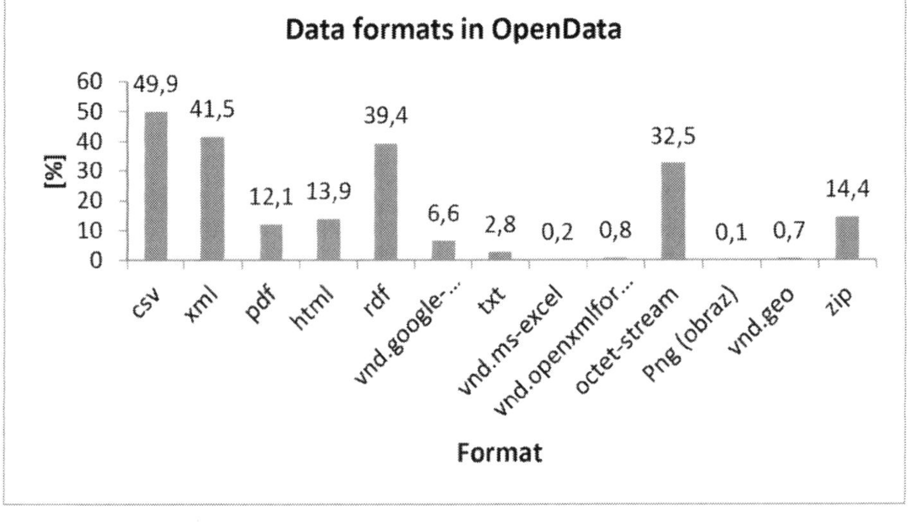

Fig. 4. The most commonly used data formats of Socrata portal databases [14].

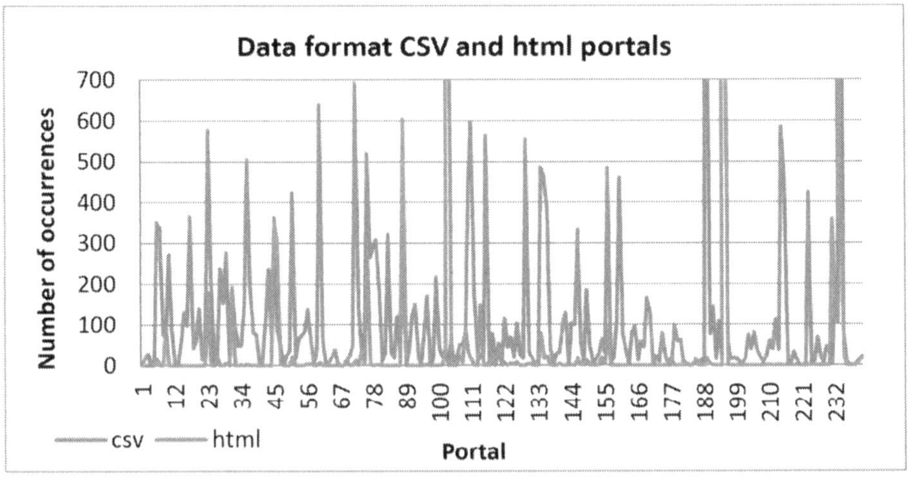

Fig. 5. Comparison of the frequency of using CSV and html data formats on Socrata portals.

Table 2 shows the number of open databases provided by various global portals, e.g. Socrata or the European EU Open Data Portal. The Socrata portal allows access to a large amount of open data, mainly from the United States (over 69,000 different sets of data). The main portal in the European Union is the EU Open Data Portal, containing over 11,000. databases from Member States' portals. Table 3 shows the number of open databases provided by various Polish portals, e.g. Local Data Bank or Local Tourist Organizations in Poland.

Table 2. Statistics of various open databases of Open Data portals (as at 30/04/2018).

Portal (name of the portal)	Number of databases
Socrata	91210
Dallas Open Data	78
New York Open Data	1430
Oregon Open Data	540
EU Open Data Portal	12313
Polskie Dane Publiczne	905
London Datastore	706

Table 3. Selected attributes of the Polish Public Data portal (as at 30/04/2018).

The name of the database	Availability	The number of columns	Time update	Average number of record changes	Recording format
Reports of the Insurance Ombudsman	Public	Not specified	Annual	All document	PDF
Local Tourist Organizations in Poland	Public with specific conditions	22	If necessary	Not specified	CSV
List of inventions	Public with specific conditions	14	Daily	1	CSV
Local Data Bank	Public with specific conditions	Not specified	Quarterly	Not specified	HTML
Register of plant protection products	Public with specific conditions	16	Annual	2035	XLS

Information on the number of applications submitted in CEIDG	Public with specific conditions	7	Monthly	30	CSV, XLS, ZIP

2. Data access methods

There are three main methods of accessing to data sets available on open data portals, not only from Socrata, but also on other portals [14]:

- Access to data by the API,
- Export of the data set (csv, html, xml, xls, rdf, etc. formats),
- Reading data by the html browser.

2.1 Access by API

One of the ways to read data from open data portals is the API - Application Programming Interface, which allows communication of our written application with open data servers. Depending on the chosen portal, various API creation systems are used - CKAN [16] for the EU Open Data Portal or SODA for Socrata [14]. The format of queries and answers is JSON. API is very often used in network applications, where, for example, the http query is written on the server address, and the corresponding value is returned in response. Fig. 6 shows part of the settings of the sample API written in the SODA system [14].

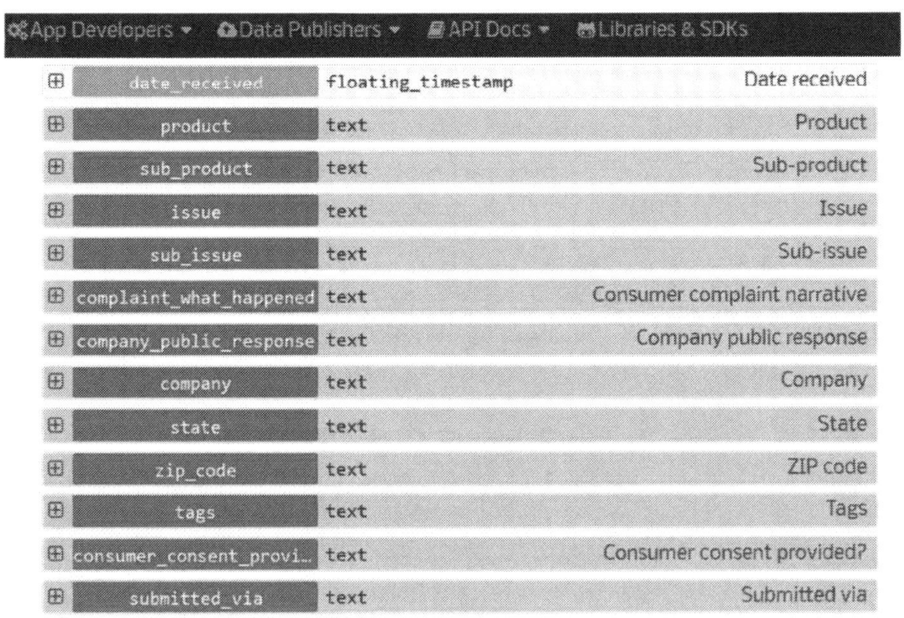

Fig. 6. Part of the settings of the sample API written in the SODA system [14].

Very often when writing API for specific data sets, only interesting data are selected, e.g. only records from the time interval or containing a sequence of characters. For SODA API queries, for example can search by column name:

```
https://data.consumerfinance.gov/resource/jhzv-
w97w.json?product=Tekst do znalezienia
```

We must include query limits when creating the API. Most portals set a quota limit for their data sets that can be used within an hour. For users who do not have a token, the maximum number of queries usually does not exceed 100 queries per hour. API has two methods of accessing to its data: authorization and token. Authorization allows for data management, e.g. adding, deleting, and modifying data sets. The token allows the application to read data from data sets. Access to data sets using the Token in the SODA system is carried out by function shown below [14]:

```
https://data.consumerfinance.gov/resource/jhzv-
w97w.json$$app_token=APP_TOKEN
```

2.2 Database export to available formats

The second way to work on data sets is export of databases to available formats, or to download and analyze databases using program frameworks [3, 14]:

- RS for the R language;
- SoDA-php, Ckan_client for PHP language;
- Socrata, CKAN for the Ruby language;
- SODA, Ckan_client for Java;
- SODA2, ckanjs for JavaScript.

Depending on the portal e.g. Socrata or EU Open Data Portal, the data set provider determines which data format will be made available to the user. These can be various data formats such as: JSON, CSV, HTML, XML, RDF, MS-ACCESS, MS-EXCEL, TXT, OCTET-STREAM or ZIP. Most of applications, e.g. R, can work on JSON, XML or CSV formats but cannot handle the OCTET-STREAM format. If one is using Python for the SoDA format, the following functions should be used [14]:

```
import pandas as pd
from sodapy import Socrata
client = Socrata("domena_zestawu-danych", None)
results = client.get("identyfikator_zestawu-danych",
limit=99999)
results_df = pd.DataFrame.from_records(result_list)
```

For the .NET platform, the data set in SoDA format can be read using [14]:

```
using System;
using System.Linq;
using SODA;
var client = new SodaClient("domena_zestawu-danych ",
"TOKEN");
var dataset = client.GetResource("identyfikator_zestawu-
danych ");
var rows = dataset.GetRows(limit: 99999);
Console.WriteLine("Dumping first results:",
rows.Count());
foreach (var keyValue in rows.First())
{    Console.WriteLine(keyValue);    }
```

Depending on the data format being viewed, the same data is presented in a different ways. When working on a CSV data set, the first line contains the column names (Fig. 7a), whereas in the JSON file each column is saved in value lists (Fig. 7b).

a)


```
1  Registration Number,Registration Date,Trademark Description,Correspondent Name,.
2  102,03/15/1968,"""SR"" MONOGRAM",SUNRIVER RESORT LIMITED PARTNERSHIP,11777 SAN
3  103,03/15/1968,"""SUNRIVER""",SUNRIVER RESORT LIMITED PARTNERSHIP,11777 SAN VIC
4  158,01/24/1969,THREE TENNIS BALLS AND FOUR TENNIS RACQUETS,"WEST HILLS RACQUET
5  ",C/O NORTH PACIFIC MANAGEMENT INC,1905 SE 10TH AVE,PORTLAND,OR,97214,http://re
6  272,10/26/1970,G.I. TYPE CHARACTER OF A MAN WITH A JARHEAD - TAKE OFF OF A M
7  3606,02/01/1935,"""PYREX""",MICHELE N KEEFER-MEHLENBACHER,CORNING INCORPORATED,
8  3957,04/21/1936,"""CORNING""",MICHELE N KEEFER-MEHLENBACHER,CORNING INCORPORATE
9  4020,08/29/1936,"""MOLY-KROME""",PACIFIC MACHINERY & TOOL STEEL CO,3445 NW LUZO
10 4622,10/06/2000,"THE WORDS ""CAPPUCCINO COWBOY"" WITH A LOGO OF A BUCKING HORSE
```


b)


```
"meta" : {
  "view" : {
    "id" : "ny3n-dx3v",
    "name" : "Active Trademark Registrations",
    "averageRating" : 0,
    "category" : "Business",
    "createdAt" : 1296662567,
    "description" : "(Updated 1/2/2018) (Must use
    "displayType" : "table",
    "downloadCount" : 6993,
    "hideFromCatalog" : false,
    "hideFromDataJson" : false,
```


Fig. 7. Data saved in CSV (a) and JSON (b) format [14].

2.3 Data access by the html browser

The third, and the least used method of reading and managing data is accessing data through a browser offering the so-called human readable format. It is simply the ability to preview the whole set of data in the html browser without downloading it. For each set of data there is a description and type of each database column with example values. This method is used only to check whether ones are interested in the data contained in this set, or want to look at what type of columns/records is interested in to copy data to the API. Fig. 8 shows a sample data available throughout the html browser.

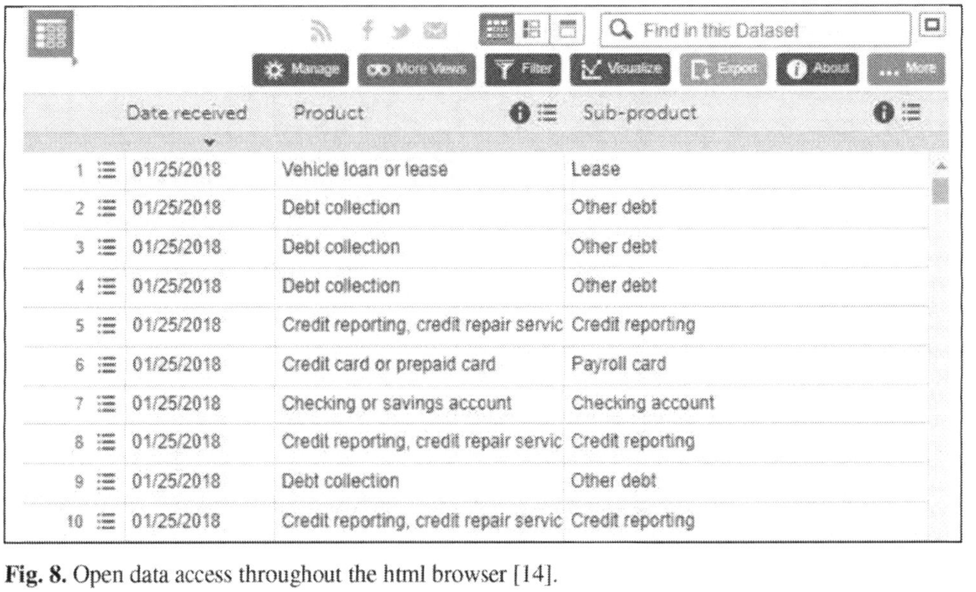

	Date received	Product	Sub-product
1	01/25/2018	Vehicle loan or lease	Lease
2	01/25/2018	Debt collection	Other debt
3	01/25/2018	Debt collection	Other debt
4	01/25/2018	Debt collection	Other debt
5	01/25/2018	Credit reporting, credit repair servic	Credit reporting
6	01/25/2018	Credit card or prepaid card	Payroll card
7	01/25/2018	Checking or savings account	Checking account
8	01/25/2018	Credit reporting, credit repair servic	Credit reporting
9	01/25/2018	Debt collection	Other debt
10	01/25/2018	Credit reporting, credit repair servic	Credit reporting

Fig. 8. Open data access throughout the html browser [14].

3. Conceptual model of the open data system

There are specific models to represent Open Data Systems (ODS). UML diagrams are used for it. However, a context diagram is of great help. Such a model is shown in Fig. 9 and is based on the analysis of existing ODS and OGS in Rzeszów, Poland.

Models are built to better illustrate existing or future systems but model will never fully correspond to reality. Modeling is designed to highlight certain features and ignore others; and there is no universal answer to the question of what to distinguish and what to omit. A context diagram is characterized by the following features:

- is a set of actors who are interacting with a given system treated as a single process,
- is a tool used to get to know the scope of system operation and presents the designed system as one process with events taking place,
- defines the system area (system boundary - environment),
- includes persons/organizations/systems - communication (external premises),
- determines data from outside - for processing (flows),
- defines the data generated by the system and transmitted to the environment (flows).

The context diagram shows the general connections between the different subsystems and the external terminators. Functional flows between system functions (in the functional architecture) correspond to physical flows between modules in the physical architecture. Based on the analysis of available sources, many important components can be distinguished that allow the development of a conceptual model for a comprehensive ODS/OGS, as shown in Fig. 9.

In general, we may consider the ODS model in many dimensions. The model depicts the knowledge about the basic functional blocks. One of them is its architectural design. In case of Rzeszów city, it is client- server model. The primary function of the architectural model is to split the entire system into subsystems or components.

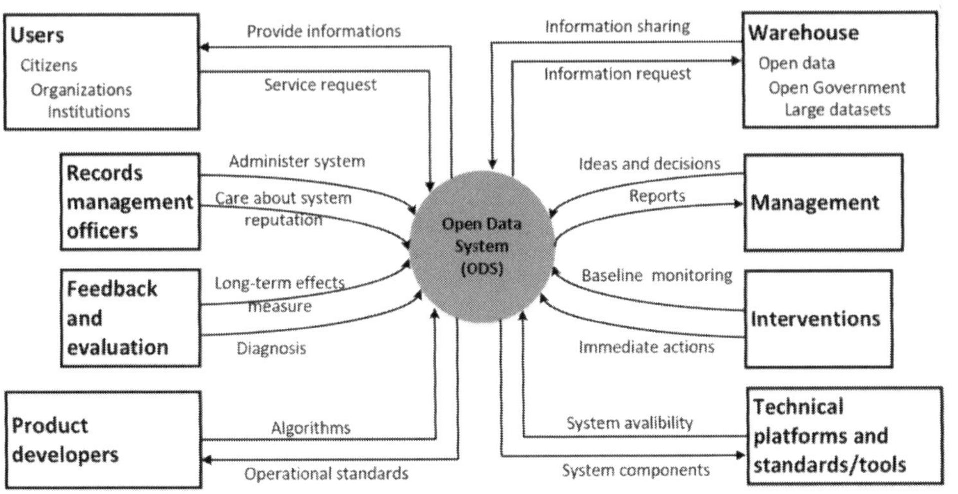

Fig. 9. Main components of the conceptual Open Data/Government System.

The identification of the subsystems and their communication is depicted by Fig. 10. The architectural model for ODS shows transport layer - data is hosted on servers that use HTTP and exchange data throughout the Internet. Clients use the system through an interaction layer that uses the interface and the services generated by the presentation layer. An important part of the system is the access layer because it authenticates to the users and allocates access to the system and thus to the data layer itself, which stores the information resources.

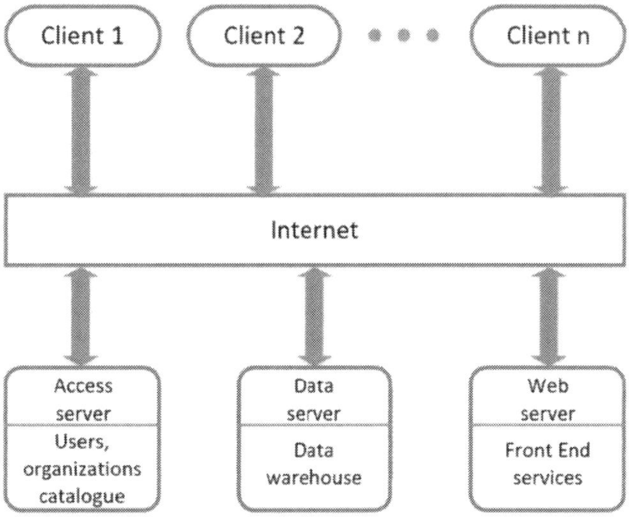

Fig. 10. Architecture of the Open Data/Government System.

The ODS supports business procedures and functions, flow of data, documentation managers, terminators (entities) and databases as well as repositories therefore the repository architecture can be also used. The individual modules of the entire system can be implemented as microservices. It is a proven solution. It enables scalability and flexibility to be achieved without limiting the speed of system development. The main component of the entire system is the database. The data base is a component, which is used to collect, store and process data. Data are usually entered by the staff of individual organizational units. However, some data may be collected directly from the external devices, i.e. sensors using wireless communication solutions. The service is carried out through a client application adapted to various types of user devices - stationary or mobile. The structure of the data warehouse creates further data layers. The lowest layer is made up of data sources. Each subsequent layer is based on the previous one. It is a basic place for storing non-volatile information collected from sources, as well as partial summaries useful in OLAP tasks and decision support. This fits in with the concept of the Big Data solutions discussed previously and the related data processing, advanced data analysis, and decision making support. The data warehouse records the history of the data source, its modifications, and is periodically updated with new condensed information about the current state of the data source, saved alongside previous data sources. Data in data warehouses may be present for the specified time period. The warehouse also performs archival functions.

Another important component of the system is data mart. Data marts are created for the needs of analytical departments, containing selected data in a highly aggregated form, allowing for quick presentation of summaries used in management, long-term planning, historical analyzes, trend analysis, information processing and integrated analyzes. Data warehouses are called thematic wholesalers (data marts, departmental warehouses). Due to the smaller size and the possibility of local work, thematic wholesalers allow for more efficient data handling. They can be implemented as relational databases or special multidimensional structures. Processing of collected data in accordance with analytical algorithms specified by the user (in relation to the source data) is characterized by a delay. It results from the batch process character. The update layer complements the results of batch data processing with data flowing online.

An important part of the entire architecture is the appropriate communication's structure. It is a set of measures enabling the exchange of information between various parts of the system and external entities. To determine the requirements for a communication system, we have to consider two aspects. Communication channels should ensure adequate speed, bandwidth and cost of transmission. The information will be transmitted without distortion such that it will be properly understood. This aspect concerns the security communication system and transmission protocols. Designing IT systems, we have to fulfill the basic requirements for system and data transfer security. It is necessary to develop a security policy for the system.

Al-Garadi et al. 2018 warns us that "online social networks (OSNs) are structures that help users to interact, exchange, and propagate new ideas [17]. The identification of the influential users in OSNs is a significant process for accelerating the propagation of information that includes marketing applications or hindering the dissemination of unwanted contents, such as viruses, negative online behaviors, and rumors." An important issue of improving the system is obtaining feedback in the Open Data/Government System. The feedback can result in improving its front end, transparency, the speed of work and task handling as well as the possibility of combining data from multiple sources and reusing them. In order to complement internal analytics with information from external sources, system administrators or supervisors may use output data from the open data users as an important source of feedback. It can help them to identify areas in which public services can be improved. This is information of particular importance to the public sector and research institutions. Users can receive more matched offers, data or interface features, as well as a useful analysis of their data by specialized filters and microservices. Data is a resource, and its value and quality are often determined by feedback and validation. Opening data to public may be a way to complement its own analyzes with observations from external sources. A quick and correct response is important in the case of system problems or data security threats. It has a deep sense and influence to product and process improvement. It is also advisable to create an appropriate point of contact for data users or services. It provides assistance and consultation for receiving feedback. It can be used to further improve access to data innovation.

4. Summary

The paper presents current trends in the development of open data portals. Progressive digitalization contributes to more and more effective management of time and resources. An example is the growing number of services available under open government systems. Publishing data in the network are activities aimed at increasing the transparency of the work of offices or institutions. The user can get access to information created by public administration, search and use them in any way. The article aims not only to present ways of accessing open data, the open data system's model or architecture but also to raise the awareness of Internet users about the possibilities that the open data portals provide. The choice of a particular method of accessing data depends on the level of advancement and the needs of a given user. The presented analysis of the danepubliczne.gov.pl or Socrata portals shows that the upward trend is maintained. The number of "open data" is constantly increasing. The increase concerns not only Poland, but also the world. These portals publish credible and confirmed data by the institutions, therefore it is necessary to ensure the confidentiality, accessibility and integrity of such data. It should be remembered that before such data becomes public they must undergo appropriate anonymization processes. It is necessary to adapt the data to ensure the privacy of individuals or institutions. Access to the data requires acceptance of the conditions for the re-use of information, which may differ for each data set.

References

1. J. Gurin, *Open Data Now: The Secret to Hot Startups, Smart Investing, Savvy Marketing, and Fast Innovation*, Published by McGraw-Hill Education, (2014)
2. https://okfn.org/opendata/, (2018)
3. A. Young, S. Verhulst, *The Global Impact of Open Data*, Published by O'Reilly Media, (2016)
4. https://www.europeandataportal.eu/pl/resources/training-companion/open-data-formats, (2018)
5. B. Ubaldi, *Open Government Data: Towards Empirical Analysis of Open Government Data Initiatives*, OECD Working Papers on Public Governance, No. 22, OECD Publishing, (2013)
6. https://danepubliczne.gov.pl, (2018)
7. https://www.opendatanetwork.com/, (2018)
8. Z. Gomolka, E. Dudek-Dyduch, Y.P. Kondratenko, From Homogeneous Network to Neural Nets with Fractional Derivative, Lecture Notes in Computer Science, vol 10245 (2017)
9. Z.Gomolka, B.Twarog, E. Zeslawska, A. Lewicki, T. Kwater, Using Artificial Neural Networks to Solve the Problem Represented by BOD and DO Indicators, Water 2018, 10(1), 4
10. http://dataportals.org, (2018)
11. P. Colpaert , S. Joye, P. Mechant, E. Mannens, R. Van de Walle, *The 5 stars of open data portals. In Proceedings of the 7th International Conference on Methodologies,* Technologies and Tools Enabling E-Government (MeTTeG13), University of Vigo, Spain (pp. 61-67),
12. Z. Gomolka, B. Twarog, J. Bartman, Improvement of image processing by using homogeneous neural networks with fractional derivatives theorem, Discrete and Continuous Dynamical Systems- Series AI, ssue SUPPL., Pages 505-514, (2011)
13. Z. Gomolka, B. Twarog, E. Zeslawska, Cognitive Investigation on Pilot Attention During Take-Offs and Landings Using Flight Simulator. Lecture Notes in Computer Science, vol 10246. (2017)
14. http://socrata.com, (2018)
15. http://worldbank.org, (2018)
16. http://docs.ckan.org, (2018)
17. M. A. Al-Garadi, K. D. Varathan, S. D. Ravana, E. Ahmed, G. Mujtaba, M. U. Shahid Khan, S. U. Khan. *Analysis of Online Social Network Connections for Identification of Influential Users*. Comput. Surveys 51, (pp. 1–37), (2018)

Time Complexity of an Distributed Algorithm for Load Balancing of Microservice-oriented Applications in the Cloud

Marian Rusek[1,*] and *Joanna* Landmesser[2]

[1,2]Warsaw University of Life Sciences – SGGW, Nowoursynowska 159, 02-776 Warsaw, Poland

Abstract. Microservice architecture is a relatively new cloud application design pattern. Each microservice has a single responsibility in terms of functional requirement, and that can be managed independently from other microservices. This is done using automated cloud orchestration systems. In this paper we analyze the time complexity of an simple swarm-like decentralized load balancing algorithm for microservices running inside OpenVZ virtualization containers. We show that it can offer performance improvements with respect to the existing centralized container orchestration systems.

1 Introduction

Monolithic enterprise systems are difficult to scale, difficult to understand and difficult to maintain. Microservices-based architecture is free of these problems [1]. Designed with cloud-based applications in mind it advocates creating a system from a collection of small, isolated microservices, each of which owns their data and uses lightweight HTTP mechanisms for communication with other microservices. These microservices integrate with each other in order to form a cohesive system that is more flexible, scalable and resilient to failure than a corresponding monolithic system. In this way the accidental complexity is shifted from inside of an monolithic application into the cloud infrastructure. Microservices are deployable by fully automated cloud machinery, but there is still a necessity for centralized monitoring and management of an microservces based application. Examples of such microservices orchestration tools are Google Kubernetes [2], Apache Mesos [3], and Docker Swarm [4].

Virtualization containers are ideal for practical realization of the concept of microservices [5]. Virtualization container is a group of processes isolated from the rest of the system. Different containers running on the same machine share the host's operating system kernel. Recent interest in virtual containers is associated with their performance. Public cloud virtual machines have to boot a full operating system and for every time it takes up to several minutes. In contrast to this the startup time for a container is around a second. This technology is not new but before Docker there was no common interface for container management and there was no standard format of how container is described in

* Corresponding author: marian_rusek@sggw.pl

the system. All three orchestration systems mentioned above work with Docker containers. The role of orchestration and scheduling within these container platforms is to match microservices-based application containers to cloud servers resources.

The actual realization of a microservices-based application in the cloud requires that we instantiate and place virtualization containers responsible for individual microservices on real machines forming the cloud. Container live migration allows a user to start a microservice on any node of the cloud after which it can transparently move to other nodes to make efficient use of resources. The basic idea is that overall system performance can be improved if microservices are moved from heavily loaded to lightly loaded machines. However instead of offloading machines we can imagine that code is moved to make sure that a machine is sufficiently loaded. For example, migrating complete virtual machines to lightly loaded machines in order to minimize the total number of nodes being used is a common practice in optimizing energy usage in data centers [6]. Another advantage of live migration is the ability to put the code processing the data close to where the data reside. This allows minimizing communication what is an important issue in today's distributed cloud environments [7]. In this paper we focus on the first from these scenarios (load balancing).

Note, that Docker compatible container systems can not provide live migration. Docker was created for different purpose, an automated application deployment, but there is commonly used, container-based virtualization software, Parallels Containers, which supports live migration [8]. Thus the experimental results discussed in our previous papers were obtained using OpenVZ, an open source version of Parallels Containers. Moreover all the existing container orchestration systems (Google Kubernetes, Apache Mesos, and Docker Swarm) are monolithic applications running as daemons on dedicated nodes of the cloud. They orchestrate containers in a centralized fashion. Usually decentralized orchestration systems offer performance improvements [9]. For example, decentralized orchestration of composite web services yields increased throughput, better scalability, and lower response time. In connection to this, in this paper we analyze the performance of a completely decentralized microservice management system based on swarm algorithm.

This paper is organized as follows: In Sec. 2 the distributed algorithm for load balancing of containerized microservices in the cloud proposed in our previous paper [10] is recalled. In that previous paper a "cloud" consisting of 18 servers only was studied experimentally. In Sec. 3 a mathematical model is introduced which allows us to investigate arbitrarily large clouds and analyze the time complexity of our algorithm. In Sec. 4 numerical simulations for 1000 servers and 50000 containers are also presented. We finish with a summary and some conclusions in Sec. 5.

2 Distributed Algorithm

The question of the optimal distribution of the containers on the hosts can have multiple variants. One of them is the uniform distribution of the containers on the hosts. This scenario is the following: we have N hosts (cloud servers) loaded with virtualization containers (containing microservices). At the start containers are arranged in a way that there is not the same number of them n_i on i-th host. Uniform distribution means that the targeted number of containers on every host is equal to n_0, and the goal of the algorithm is to achieve this state of balance. A decentralized algorithm for controlling the uniform distribution of tasks between nodes of a simple computational cloud was presented in our previous paper. In that approach, each host is described by a pheromone p_i which can be either repulsive $0 < p_i < 1$ or attractive $p_i < 0$. Attractiveness or repulsiveness is associated with the number of containers already n_i on the host and the number of containers queued for migration in the kernel queue Q_i:

$$p_i = \frac{n_i - Q_i - n_0}{n_i - Q_i}, \quad i = 1,\dots,N \tag{1}$$

Note, that during migration the container's files are present on both source and destination hosts. Therefore the total number of containers calculated as sum of n_i over all hosts is not conserved. To prevent the containers from being counted twice, what in Eq. (1), we subtracted from the number of containers n_i present in the file system of the i-th hosts the number of containers Q_i queued for migration from this host. In this way the migration process of a container appears to be instantaneous to its neighboring containers on the same host. As shown in our previous paper [11] this prevents the unstable behavior of the algorithm without this subtraction.

In addition to cloud application microservice each container runs an additional process implementing it's swarm-like mobile agent intelligence. It executes the following pseudocode [11]:

```
loop
  Compute the pheromone value p of the current host.
  Generate a random number 0 < r < 1.
  if r < p
    repeat
      Randomly choose a new host.
      Get the pheromone value of the chosen host.
    until chosen host has an attractive pheromone
    Ask the current host to migrate to chosen host.
    Wait until migration to another host is complete.
  end if
end loop
```

Thus the pheromone value p_{ij} of the host is equal to migration probability of a container.

In the following it will be assumed for simplicity that the containers are identical and have almost the same memory, disk, and processor requirements. An analogous assumption will be made for the hosts: the memory, disk, and processing performance of each host is the same.

3 Mathematical Model

The distributing of a robot swarm among multiple tasks can be described using delay differential equations [12]. Let us write a similar system of equations for the swarm of containers from Sec. 2. The main difference is that in [12] the migration probabilities between hosts are constant, and it can be shown that the system has a unique, stable equilibrium point. In contrast we dynamically adjust the migration probabilities (see Eq. (1)) so the system reaches not some equilibrium point, but an equilibrium point that is interesting to us (i.e., $n_i = n_0$).

Let us assume that it takes a time T to migrate a container between any pair of hosts. The change in time of the number of containers Q_i queued for migration on the i-th host is due to new containers entering it with probability p_i and containers leaving it due to migration to other hosts. Thus

$$\frac{dQ_i(t)}{dt} = p_i(t) n_i'(t) - Q_i(t-T), \quad i = 1,\dots,N \tag{2}$$

where $n_i^{'}(t) = n_i(t) - Q_i(t),\ i = 1,\ldots,N$ is the number of containers still undecided to migrate, i.e., generating random numbers r and comparing them to p_i in the loop from Sec. 2. The change in this number is due to containers entering the migration queue on the same host and migrating randomly from other hosts with probability $1/(N - 1)$:

$$\frac{dn_i^{'}(t)}{dt} = -p_i(t)n_i^{'}(t) + \frac{1}{N-1}\sum_{j \neq i} Q_j(t-T), \quad i = 1,\ldots,N \tag{3}$$

A finite number of containers will usually be en route between hosts, but it follows from Eqs. (2) and (3) that the total number of containers is conserved: $\frac{d}{dt}\sum_i n_j(t) = 0$.

Note, that the delayed differential Eqs. (2) and (3) model can not take into account the finite network bandwidth. The containers migrate during time T but infinitely many of them can migrate in parallel. This will be corrected in the numerical simulation presented in the next section.

Usually a solution of delayed differential equations is not possible using elementary functions. Therefore in this section we will limit ourselves to the solution of a simpler linear model. It assumes that containers instantaneously migrate from one host to another. The system of equations governing the dynamics of the system reads as:

$$\frac{dn_i^{'}(t)}{dt} = -p_i(t)n_i^{'}(t) + \frac{1}{N-1}\sum_{j \neq i} p_j(t)n_j^{'}(t), \quad i = 1,\ldots,N \tag{4}$$

After substituting Eq. (1) and introducing a new notation $n_i^{''}(t) = n_i^{'}(t) - n_0,\ i = 1,\ldots,N$, Eqs. (4) reduce to the system of linear equations:

$$\frac{dn_i^{''}(t)}{dt} = -n_i^{''}(t) + \frac{1}{N-1}\sum_{j \neq i} n_j^{''}(t), \quad i = 1,\ldots,N \tag{5}$$

which can be easily solved using diagonalization. There are N - 1 eigenvectors

$$[-1,1,0,\ldots,0], \quad [-1,0,1,\ldots,0], \quad \ldots \quad ,[-1,0,0,\ldots,0,1] \tag{6}$$

corresponding to eigenvalues - $N/(N - 1)$, and one eigenvector [1, ..., 1] corresponding to eigenvalue 0. Thus all solutions decay exponentially in time. Interestingly, a system of two hosts decays twice as fast as a system of a large number of hosts.

Also as opposed to the algorithm from Sec. 2 the choice of the destination host in Eqs. (5) (and (3)) is random. However this choice is less effective than the choice of the host with an attractive pheromone. Therefore the solution of Eq. (6) should predict a correct upper bound on the pessimistic time complexity of the swarm algorithm from Sec. 2. The initial state of the system $n_i^{''}(0),\ i = 1,\ldots,N$, can be expanded into eigenvectors from Eq. (6). They then decay exponentially.

First we consider a limiting case of one empty host at the initial time:

$$\begin{aligned} &n_1(0) = 0 \\ &n_i(0) = n_0 + 1, \quad i = 2,\ldots,N, \\ &n_0 = N - 1 \end{aligned} \tag{7}$$

In order to reach the final state $n_i = n_0$ the number of N - 1 containers need to be migrated. It is readily seen that $n''(0) = [-(N-1),1,...,1]$. This vector is equal to the sum of all eigenvectors from Eq. (6) corresponding to the same eigenvalue. Let us denote by τ the time for which $n_i''(\tau) < 1$. For $t > \tau$ it is already decided which containers should move where in order to bring the system into the desired equilibrium state $n_i(t_0) = n_0$. The time τ depends on the size of the cloud as log(N). Thus the time t_0 at which equilibrium is reached grows in the worst case linearly with N. Thus the time complexity of our distributed algorithm should be O(N) or better. We will check this prediction in the next section.

Interestingly the second limiting case of one non empty host at the initial time:

$$\begin{aligned} &n_1(0) = N \\ &n_i(0) = 0, \quad i = 2,\dots,N, \\ &n_0 = 1 \end{aligned} \tag{8}$$

correspond to the same initial vector $n''(0) = [N-1,-1,...,-1]$. And also N - 1 containers need to be migrated. In the next section using a more realistic numerical model, we will show that surprisingly this case behaves different from the previous one.

4 Numerical Simulation

In this section results given by a simple cellular automaton-like simulator are presented. The simulation operates on two arrays: n_i' and Q_i — thus the containers are identical and indistinguishable from each other. The simulator is single-threaded but nevertheless is able to reproduce the experimental distribution of stabilization times t0 for a system of 18 hosts presented in our previous paper [11]. At each time step all the active (i.e., not waiting in the migration queue) containers calculate their migration probability according to Eq. (1), decide to migrate or not to migrate, and chose their destination host with an attractive pheromone like in the pseudocode presented in Sec. 2 (and not randomly like in the mathematical model from Sec. 3). Than one container from each migration queue is allowed to transfer itself to another host. Each time step has a duration of the migration time T. Thus as opposed to the model from the previous section in takes into account finite network bandwidth.

First we performed 10000 simulations of situation corresponding to Eq. (7). The parameters were chosen in accordance with the presentation of Docker Swarm at DockerCon 2015 Conference: $n_0 = 49$, $N = 1000$ (at that conference a system of 1000 hosts with 50000 containers was demoed). The experiment ended when the numbers of the containers reached equilibrium $n_i = n_0$ and all the migration queues were empty $Q_i = 0$. In Fig. 1 we have a histogram of times needed to reach equilibrium t_0. We see that although 49 containers need to be transferred to reach the desired final state the average stabilization time is around 85 T. This is due to the fact, that the algorithm presented in Sec. 2 is probabilistic and sometimes more than one container chooses to migrate. Such containers interact with each other by entering the same migration queue.

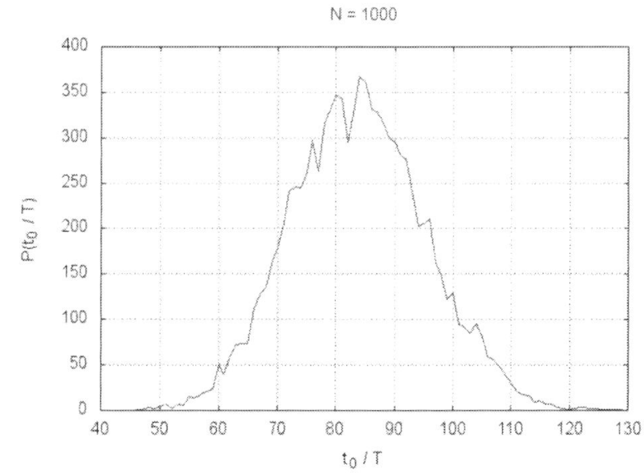

Fig. 1. Histogram of times needed to reach equilibrium t_0 for a system corresponding to Eq. (7).

Next the experiment was repeated for increasing number of hosts. The initial state was: one host in 50 empty and the remaining had 50 containers each. Therefore for $N = 50$ one host was initially empty, for $N = 100$ —two hosts, for $N = 150$ —three hosts, and for $N = 1000$ —fifty hosts were initially empty. The scaling behavior of the average value of t_0 is depicted in Fig. 2. We see, that the time complexity of the algorithm is of the order of O(N) in this case. Therefore although the mathematical model from Sec. 3 predicts time of the order of O(log N) to predict which container should migrate where, the majority of time in the case of Eq. (7) is spend on emptying the migration queues (this process is obviously of linear order).

Let us now present the same plots calculated for the second case corresponding to Eq. (7). They are presented in Figs. 3 and 4. Again sometimes more than one container chooses to migrate — this is the reason why the histogram from Fig. 3 is not centered around 49 T. Surprisingly the time complexity as depicted in Fig. 4 in this case is a logarithmic one. Thus the mathematical model from Sec. 3 in specific cases can very well describe reality.

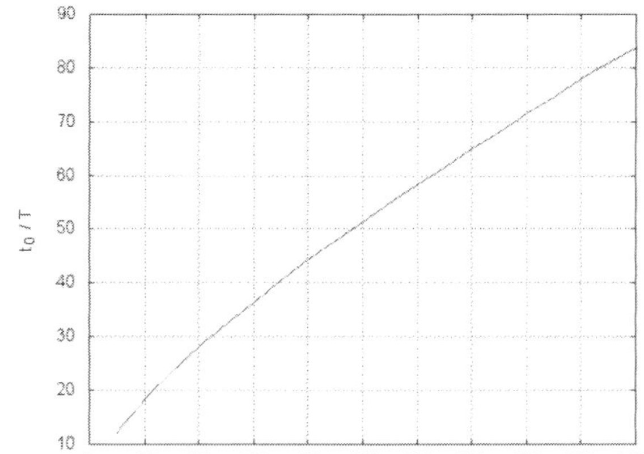

Fig. 2. Scaling of the average time needed to reach equilibrium t_0 with the number of hosts N. Initial conditions are given by Eq. (7).

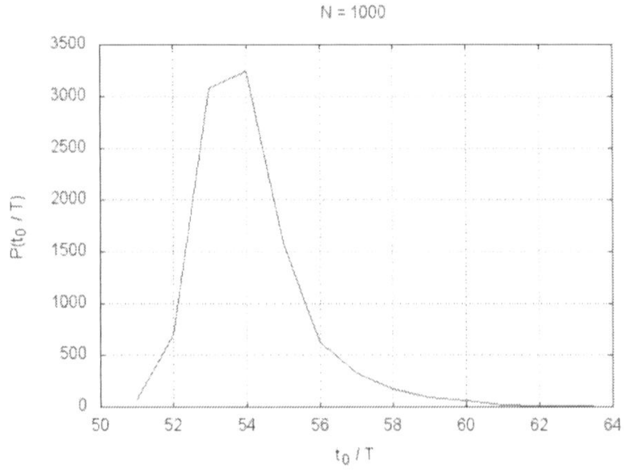

Fig. 3. Histogram of times needed to reach equilibrium t_0 for a system corresponding to Eq. (8).

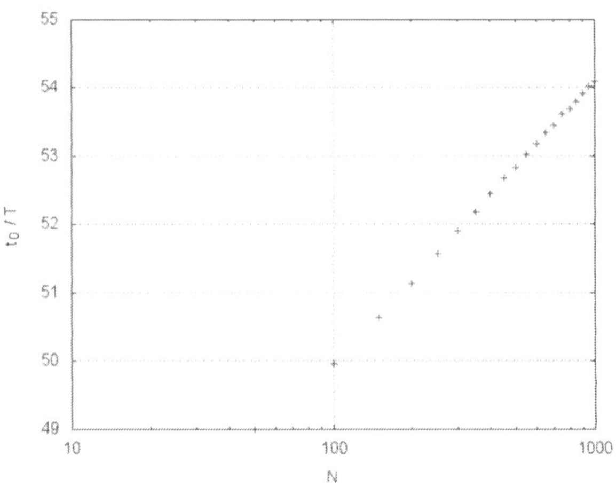

Fig. 4. Scaling of the average time needed to reach equilibrium t_0 with the number of hosts N. Initial conditions are given by Eq. (8).

5 Summary

In summary, an decentralized algorithm for load balancing of containerized microservices in the cloud was studied theoretically and numerically. Each container includes an additional mobile agent process which governs its migration to another nodes of the cloud. Thus the tasks running on the nodes of the cloud self-organize to maintain a constant load among the servers. The resulting system is resilient on server failures: a failing server can take down only a minimal number of tasks.

The performance of a similar centralized algorithm is of the order of O(N log N). First the numbers of containers on all hosts are sorted. Next the list is traversed from both sides and decision is made which containers should be migrated where. The decentralized algorithm studied in this paper gives the worst case time complexity of the order of O(N), and in specific cases even O(log N).

Swarm systems consisting of multiple autonomous agents exhibit complex behaviours. The interaction between the robots and its environment is very important to achieve the overall group performance. The analyzing of the system's behaviour using real and simulated experiments is often expansive and time-consuming. Therefore, the observation of, for example, social insects can help in the extraction of ideas and models underlying natural systems and apply them to artificial problems. Using mathematical models we can efficiently study the swarm systems in order to better understand them as a whole.

In our paper, the problem of designing control policies that enable the swarm of agents (virtualization containers) to distribute themselves between multiple sites (servers) was solved using a system of differential equations that summarize the state transitions. However, one should not forget that in more sophisticated cases, interactions among the agents may lead to the transition probabilities that are a function of the number of agents in other states, and thus yield a system of differential equations that are time delayed and nonlinear. Hence, there are many directions for the future work. We would like to extend our linear model and implement nonlinear transition rules as well as time delays. The other idea could be to model large agent populations using partial differential equations. Also the use of stochastic differential equations should be considered.

References

1. J. Thönes, IEEE Softw., **32(1)**, 116 (2015)
2. E.A. Brewer, *Proceedings of the Sixth ACM Symposium on Cloud Computing*, 167 (2015)
3. B. Hindman, B., A. Konwinski, M. Zaharia, A. Ghodsi, A. D. Joseph, R.H. Katz, S. Shenker, I. Stoica, *Proceedings of the 8th USENIX Symposium on Networked Systems Design and Implementation*, 295–308 (2011)
4. J. Stubbs, W. Moreira, R. Dooley, *7th International Workshop on Science Gateways (IWSG)*, 34–39 (2015)
5. C. Pahl, IEEE Cloud Comput., **2(3)**, 24–31 (2015)
6. M. Zhao, R.J. Figueiredo, *Proceedings of the 2nd International Workshop on Virtualization Technology in Distributed Computing*, 5 (2007)
7. N. Kratzke, *CLOUD COMPUTING 2015: The Sixth International Conference on Cloud Computing, GRIDs, and Virtualization*, 165–169 (2015)
8. A. Mirkin, A. Kuznetsov, K. Kolyshkin, *Proceedings of Linux Symposium*, **2**, 85–90 (2008)
9. A.Y.U. Gital, A.S. Ismail, H. Chiroma, A. Abubakar, B.M.A. Abdulhamid, I.Z. Maitama, A. Zeki, *Information and Communication Technology for The Muslim World (ICT4 M 2014)*, 1–6 (2014)
10. M. Rusek, G. Dwornicki, A. Orłowski, *Advances in Systems Science, ICSS 2016. Advances in Intelligent Systems and Computing*, **539**, 142–152 (2017)
11. M. Rusek, G. Dwornicki, A. Orłowski, *Proceedings of 36th International Conference on Information Systems Architecture and Technology – ISAT 2015 – Part III. Advances in Intelligent Systems and Computing*, **431**, 75–85 (2016)
12. S. Berman, Á. Halász, M.A. Hsieh, *Bio-inspired Computing and Networking* (2011)

Analysis of the influence of selected non-linear devices on the waveform of supply voltage

Jacek Bartman[1,*], and , and *Dariusz* Sobczyński[2]

[1]Department of the Computer Engineering, University of Rzeszow, 35-959 Rzeszow, Poland
[2]Department of Power Electronics and Power Engineering, Rzeszow University of Technology, 35-959 Rzeszow, Poland

Abstract. The paper presents research on the influence of selected non-linear devices on the shape of supply voltage. It has been assessed how current distortion, expressed by THD_I, and rms current $||i||$ influence voltage distortion, represented by THD_U. For this purpose, an induction generator with a power comparable to that of the loads was used to power the loads. The devices were selected in such a way as to increase current distortion with the decrease of rms current. The measurements were made with a class A energy quality analyzer.

1 Introduction

The influence of non-linear loads on electrical systems has been of concern to the scientific community for many years. Harmonic distortion caused by non-linear energy consumers is the main cause of problems with the quality of electricity [1 - 3]. Electrical devices such as regulated induction drives, controlled rectifiers, arc furnaces, induction heaters, LED lamps, personal computer power supplies and many modern electronic devices are typical examples of non-linear and parametric loads widely used in industry, office, municipal and household applications [4 - 6]. The number of non-linear electrical devices is systematically increasing [3, 7] because they usually offer lower energy consumption and better working conditions. Non-sinusoidal harmonic currents caused by non-linear devices may lead to significant distortion of supply voltage [8, 9], which may cause disturbances in the operation of other equipment, particularly sensitive electronic equipment, worsening the energy consumption, and cause additional thermal effects [10, 11]. Harmonic distortion reduces the power factor. The flow of inactive energy caused by harmonic currents and voltages has become a major problem today [1, 8]. Even electrical equipment with a relatively low power, when added, can constitute an important harmonic source [2, 3], especially if they are devices of the same type, e.g. computers, pumping units, LED lighting, etc.

* Corresponding author: jbartman@ur.edu.pl

2 Non-linear load impact assessment

Standards and regulations define the parameters to be taken into account when assessing energy quality, including [12]:

- frequency,
- voltage value,
- light flicker coefficient for rapid voltage changes,
- short and long power outages,
- short-time overvoltage,
- transient overvoltage,
- voltage unbalance,
- supply voltage sags and interruptions,
- content of higher harmonics in the voltage waveform,
- content of inter-harmonics in the voltage waveform,
- voltage signal for data transmission.

In most cases, the interaction of non-linear electrical devices can be limited to the analysis of the content of higher harmonics in the voltage waveform. The content of each harmonic can be individually determined by giving the relative amplitude of the U_h hth harmonic related to the voltage of fundamental component U_1:

$$w_h = 100\% \cdot \frac{U_h}{U_1}. \tag{1}$$

However, it is more common to give the total harmonic content in the form of total harmonic distortion (*THD*). According to IEEE 1459-2010 [13], the distortion factors for voltage and current harmonics can be determined from the equation:

$$THD = \sqrt{\frac{\sum_{h=2}^{\infty} U_h^2}{U_1}} \tag{2}$$

The PN-EN 50160 standard [12] specifies that when assessing voltage quality, higher harmonics up to the 40th order should be taken into account when calculating the total harmonic distortion of voltage (THD_U). In works [14, 15] the author showed that such a limitation may lead to incorrect assessment of waveform distortion, therefore in the present paper both THD_I - total harmonic distortion of current and THD_U - total harmonic distortion of voltage were calculated taking into account 127 and 511 components respectively. The number of components results from the measurement capability of the equipment used

3 Measurement and analysis of distorted waveforms

Measurement and analysis of distorted electrical waveforms caused by non-linear devices is not an easy task. Difficulties result from the nature of waveforms in which both harmonic and inter-harmonic components, slow- and quick-variable components are present, and waveforms themselves are often non-stationary [16, 17]. For harmonic analysis, the signal must be measured at the Nyquist frequency and the signal measured must meet the Dirichlet conditions. The measurement methodology and the requirements for the instruments used for energy quality testing, including distortion of currents and voltages, are described in IEC 61000-4-30 [18] and IEC 61000-4-7 [19]. Many literature items [20, 21] explain the recommendations and suggestions contained in the standards for the analysis of waveform distortion. As recommended by the standards, the frequency analysis of waveforms should include 40 harmonics determined by the DFT/FFT method. In order to quantify the waveform distortion, IEC 61000-4-7 [19] introduces the concept of grouping. According to this concept a DFT-based spectrum with a resolution of 5 Hz is subjected to grouping. The standard defines: a harmonic group, a harmonic subgroup, an inter-harmonic group, and an inter-harmonic subgroup.

Since the samples obtained from a measurement are specified in the time domain, it is necessary to transform the signal into the frequency domain. This task is usually performed with the use of the fast Fourier transform (FFT) [14, 22 23], although there are also other alternative methods [24 - 27]. The Fourier transform decomposes a periodic waveform into the Fourier series (a series of periodic functions) so that the resulting transform provides information on how the individual frequencies make up the original function:

$$Y(f) = \int_{-\infty}^{\infty} y(t)e^{-j2\pi f t}df \tag{3}$$

where: t – time,

f – frequencies,

$y(t)$ – waveform in the time domain,

$Y(f)$ – Fourier transform of a waveform.

As mentioned above, transformation consists in converting the signal domain from time to frequency, as a result of which the frequency spectrum of the signal is obtained from a time waveform. The transform can be interpreted as determining the correlation of the analyzed signal with individual harmonic components, the frequencies of which are a multiple of the frequencies of the analyzed signal f_0 (they are distributed every $f_0 = 1/T_0$). When $T_0 \rightarrow \infty$ then $f_0 \rightarrow 0$ and harmonics are distributed more and more densely over the frequency domain.

4 The scope of research

The literature extensively describes the effects of the operation of non-linear loads and the effects of their influence on the power supply [2, 3, 28, 29], especially highlighting their negative impact on the quality of energy supply. For example, paper [3] presents the problem of the influence of low-power non-linear loads on the distortion of supply voltage in statistical terms. The authors stated that in the case of household appliances and lightning, in about 40% of cases changes in the recorded average current *THD* values (THD_I) affect the voltage *THD* values (THD_U). The authors also noted that the *THD* value is higher in agglomeration centers than on the outskirts, which they attribute to the interaction of non-linear loads installed in various buildings, e.g. commercial, office and industrial housing. On the other hand, the authors of paper [28] assess the change of the *THD* of supply voltage under the influence of non-linear household appliances. Their research shows that the operation of non-linear household appliances increased the distortion factor THD_U by 4.9%. The authors note that the cumulative effect produced by a large number of small non-linear electrical devices (harmonic sources) can be so significant, because the current distortion factor (THD_I) reaches high values of up to 130%. Such large distortion generates additional losses of power and energy in electrical networks.

Authors of most studies analyze the impact of a non-linear load on the power source, i.e. the public network. Therefore, they focus mainly on the assessment of the THD_I current distortion factor and its impact on the THD_U voltage distortion factor, treating the power of the devices they test as a parameter of negligible importance. Such an approach, taking into account the relation between the power supply output and the power output of a load seems reasonable. In the present study, the source of power in the form of a 12 kW induction generator was used. The effects of a vacuum cleaner, a DC motor supplied by a rectifier and a set of LED lamp on the supply voltage waveform were analyzed. The devices the impact of which on the source was tested have the power from several watts to several kilowatts, and therefore comparable to the power of the power source, therefore the assessment of the impact also took into account the effective current of the devices in operation. Because the apparent power S depends only on the values of voltage U and current I:

$$S = f(U, I) \tag{4}$$

at a symmetrical load and constant voltage value, the power changes are proportional to the current changes, therefore the influence of the effective current value was taken into account in the tests, and not the power

5 Results of experimental tests

The tests were performed on a laboratory stand equipped with an energy quality analyzer by Elspec, BlackBox G4500 model. The BlackBox is a class A device that performs measurements at a frequency that allows for the analysis of up to 512 harmonic voltage components and up to 128 harmonic current components.

The equipment tested was powered from a three-phase asynchronous symmetrical generator with a rated power of 12 kW and a rated voltage of 230 V. The effective value for the test voltage was 220.3 V to 227.7 V. The shape of the voltage waveform in each phase, during idle operation of the generator, is shown in Fig. 1a, while their spectra are shown in Fig. 1b. The share of higher harmonics in the supply voltage is very small (Fig. 1b.), THD_U=0.9%. After the generator was loaded with successive loads of electrical energy, the changes taking place in the shape of the voltage waveform were analyzed.

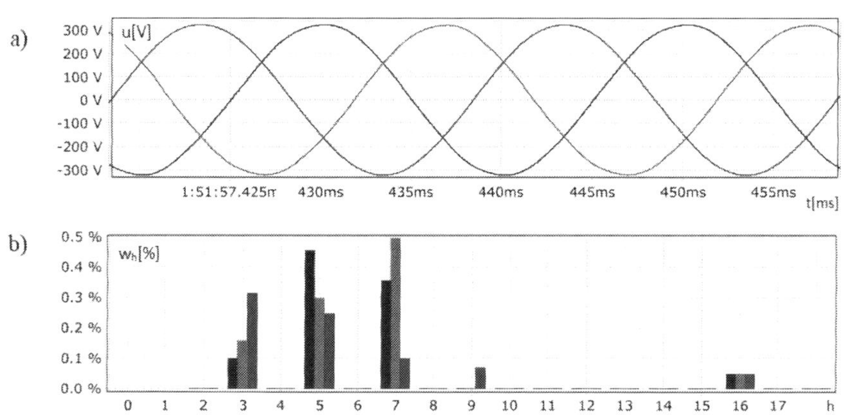

Fig. 1. Shape of the supply voltage waveform (a) and the harmonic spectrum (b) for phases L1 (brown), L2 (green), L3 (blue) when the generator is idle.

5.1 Analysis of the impact of a vacuum cleaner

The influence of the Jupiter 4000.0 M67H T vacuum cleaner by Zelmer with the rated power of 1950W on the shape of the supply voltage supplied from the generator was tested. The test of the interaction of the vacuum cleaner was performed with four different values of suction power, the change of the suction power corresponds to the change of the active and apparent power consumed by the appliance.

Fig. 2 shows the shape of the current flowing through the appliance (blue line) and the shape of the supply voltage (red line) for different values of suction power of the vacuum cleaner. The analysis of the figures shows that the current is highly distorted and its distortion increases with the decrease of the power of the vacuum cleaner (effective current). You can also see distortion of the voltage waveform which indicates that the vacuum cleaner has a negative effect on the power supply.

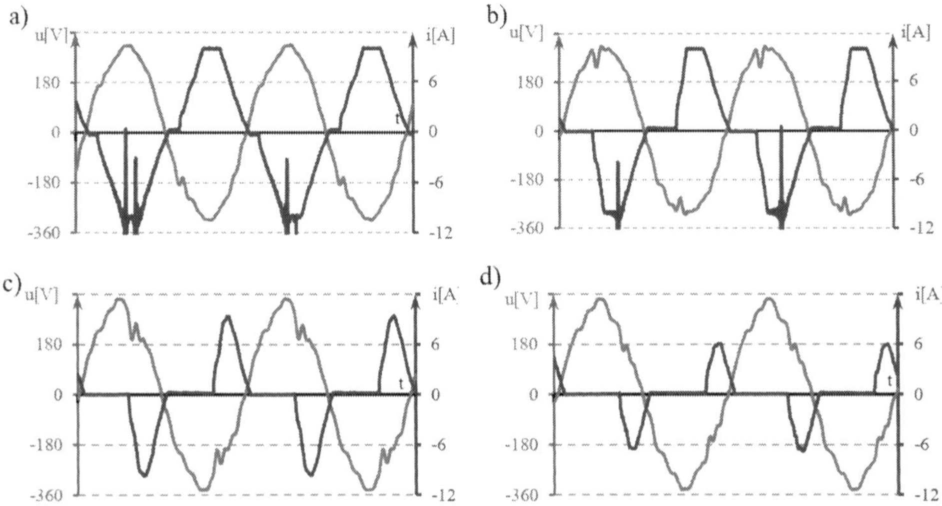

Fig. 2. Shape of the voltage and current of the vacuum cleaner during tests: a) $\|i_a\|$=6.51 A, b) $\|i_b\|$=5.88 A, c) $\|i_c\|$=4.23 A, d) $\|i_d\|$=2.61 A.

The changes in the current distortion factor (*THD*I) shown in Fig. 3 confirm the observation that current distortion increases as the power of a working vacuum cleaner decreases. The value of the voltage distortion factor (*THD*U) changes during tests (Fig.3), however, it is not possible to indicate a simple dependence of its change in the function of current distortion factor (*THD*I) or the effective value of current (consumed power). However, it can be stated that the *THD*U value increased in relation to the situation when the generator was not loaded (then *THD*U=0,9%), this indicates that the operation of the vacuum cleaner, as a non-linear appliance, affects the power supply, deteriorating the quality of supply voltage.

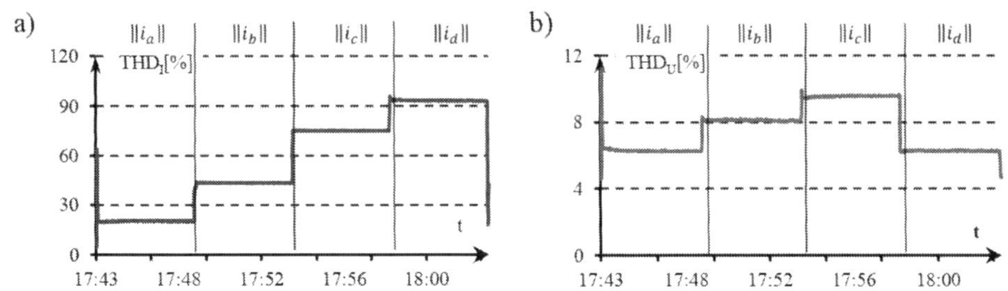

Fig 3. Changes in the current *THD* value (a) and voltage *THD* value (b) during operation of the vacuum cleaner with different suction power.

5.2 Testing the impact of LED lighting

The analysis included the influence of LED lamps on the shape of the supply voltage supplied by the generator. Six different lamp power values - six different effective current values - were tested: $\|i_a\|$=0.24 A, $\|i_b\|$=0.60 A, $\|i_c\|$=0.92 A, $\|i_d\|$=1.23 A, $\|i_e\|$=1.54 A, $\|i_f\|$=1.82 A. The power changes were obtained by switching on successive lamps, all lamps used during the study were of the same type.

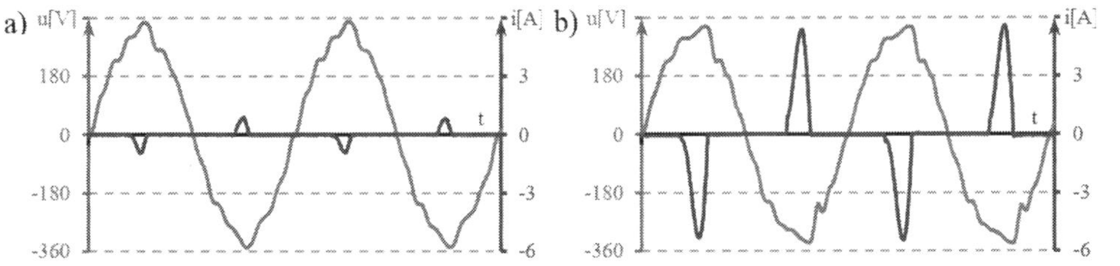

Fig. 4 Shape of the voltage and current of the lamps during tests: a) $\|i_a\|$=0.24 A, b) $\|i_f\|$=1.82 A.

Fig. 4 shows the current and voltage waveform for the smallest current consumed by the lamps ($\|i_a\|$=0.24 A) and for the largest current ($\|i_f\|$=1.82 A). There is high distortion of the current and clear distortion of the voltage waveform. This observation is confirmed by Fig. 5, which shows changes in the value of THD_I current distortion factor and THD_U voltage distortion factor. Analyzing the values of both factors, it can be noticed that with the increase of the current value, its distortion decreases, while the voltage distortion increases. The increase in voltage distortion indicates that the load affects the power source, causing distortion of the source voltage due to its non-linearity.

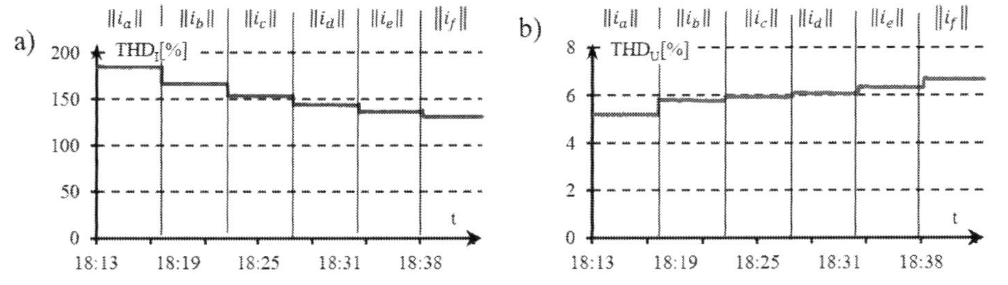

Fig. 5. Changes in the current *THD* value (a) and voltage *THD* value (b) during operation of the LED lightning with different power.

5.3 Analysis of the impact of a DC motor

Another appliance, the influence of which on the power source was investigated, was a DC motor with a rated power of P=1.5 kW. The tests were carried out at three different engine speeds for the motor running at no load. Changes of the rotational speed caused that the effective value of the current flowing through the motor and the apparent power consumed were changing: $\|i_a\|$=5.05 A, S_a=3.4 kVA, $\|i_b\|$=5.33 A, S_b=3.6 kVA, $\|i_c\|$=5.64 A, S_c=3.8 kVA.

Changes in the current and voltage waveforms in individual phases during the test of the influence of the motor operation on the supply voltage waveform are shown in Fig. 6. The rectifier, which works with the motor, introduces a strong non-linearity which is much visible in the waveform of the phase currents (blue line in Fig. 6). The flowing current influences the shape of the voltage causing its distortion (Fig. 6), the voltage distortion increases with the increase of the effective current value, at the same time the current distortion decreases (Fig. 7).

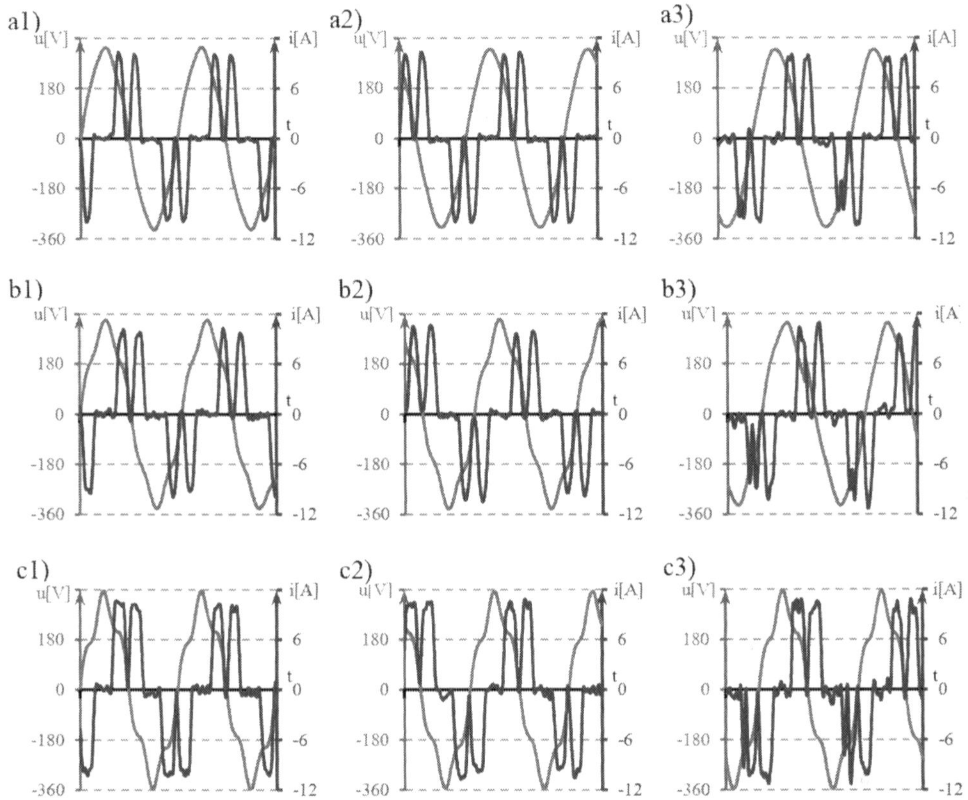

Fig. 6. Shape of the voltage and current of the DC motor during tests: a) $\|i_a\|$=5.05 A, S_a=3.4 kVA, b) $\|i_b\|$=5.33 A, S_b=3.6 kVA, c) $\|i_c\|$=5.64 A, S_c=3.8 kVA, 1) phase L1, 2) phase L2, 3) phase L3.

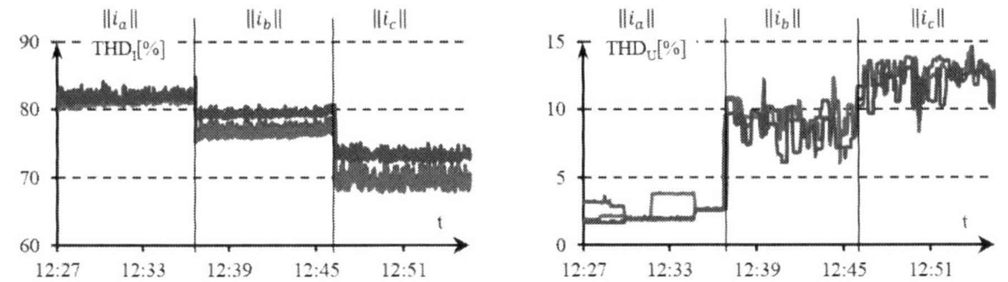

Fig. 7. Changes in the *THD* current factor (a) and THD voltage factor (b) values for phases L1 (brown), L2 (green), L3 (blue) when the motor is running at different rotational speeds.

6 Conclusion

The tests presented in this paper are used to assess the influence of non-linear loads on the waveform of supply voltage. It has been assessed how current distortion, represented by THD_I, and rms current $\|i\|$ influence voltage distortion, represented by THD_U, for this purpose the loads were supplied with voltage from a source of relatively low power (comparable to the power of the loads). The devices were selected in such a way as to increase current distortion with the decrease of rms current. The research has shown that an increase in current distortion does not necessarily increase voltage distortion. This indicated that the degree of distortion of the supply voltage as a result of the operation of non-linear devices depends both on the effective value of the current drawn ($\|i_a\|$) and on the degree of distortion of the current expressed by the THD_I factor.

References

1. J. Arrillaga, N. R. Watson, *Power System Harmonics*, (John Wiley&Sons, West Sussex, 2003)
2. M. Maciążek, M. Pasko, Prace Instytutu Elektrotechniki, **242**, 149 (2009)
3. K. Kamuda, D. Klepacki, K. Kuryło, W. Sabat, Przegląd Elektrotechniczny, **91**, 19 (2015)
4. K. Buczek, J. Bartman, A. Koziorowska, Przegląd Elektrotechniczny, **83**, 9 (2007)
5. C. Ciufudean, F. Neri, WSEAS Transactions on Systems, **13**, 457 (2014)
6. T. Binkowski, K. Buczek, Kazimierz, D. Sobczynski, Przegląd Elektrotech-niczny, 87, 30 (2011)
7. M. Pawłowski, Mechanizacja i Automatyzacja Górnictwa, **7**, 17 (2010)
8. H. Farooq, C. Zhou, M. E. Farrag, International Journal of Smart Grid and Clean Energy, **2**, 46 (2013)
9. H. E. Mazin, E. E. Nino, W. Xuand J. Yong, IEEE Transactions on Power Delivery, **26**, 1592 (2011)
10. A. Kot, W. Nowak, W. Szpyra, R. Tarko R., Przegląd Elektrotechniczny, **88,** 144 (2012)
11. P. Gnaciński, M. Pepliński, IET Electric Power Applications, **8**, 287 (2014)
12. PN-EN 50160 (2010)
13. IEEE 1459 (2010)
14. J. Bartman, Revue Roumaine des Sciences Techniques - Serie Electrotechnique et Energetique, **61**, 355 (2016)
15. J. Bartman J., Lecture Notes in Electrical Engineering, **452**, 305 (2018)
16. J. Rezmer, Z. Leonowicz, R. Gono, Przegląd Elektrotechniczny **87**, 254 (2011)
17. J. Bartman, Journal of Electrical Engineering, **68**, 194 (2017)
18. IEC61000-4-30
19. IEC 61000-4-7
20. M. Bollen, M. Olofsson, A. Larsson, S. Ronnberg, M. Lundmark, IEEE Electromagnetic Compatibility Magazine, **3**, 114 (2014)
21. P. Otomański, G. Wilczyński, Przegląd Elektrotechniczny, **8**, 38 (2015)
22. Z. Hanzelka, A. Bień A, *Harmonics, Interharmonics*, (Power Quality Application Guide, 2004)
23. H. C. Lin, IEEE Transactions on Industrial Electronics, **59**, 1184 (2012)
24. J. Zygarlicki, J. Mroczka, Metrology and Measurement Systems, **21**, 521 (2014)
25. I. Taranenko, R. Pawełek, O. Gorpynych, Przegląd Elektrotechniczny, **91**, 69 (2015)
26. L. Alfieri, G. Carpinelli, A. Bracale, P. Caramia, *12th International Conference on Environment and Electrical Engineering*, Wroclaw, 562 (2013)
27. C. F. Nascimento, A.A. Oliveira, A. Goedtel, A.B. Dietrich, Applied Soft Computing, **13**, 475 (2013)
28. A. Iagar, G. N. Popa, C. M. Dinis, WSEAS Transactions on Systems, **13**, 357, (2014)
29. S. Czapp, Acta Energetica, **1**, 25, (2009)
30. A. Koziorowska, K. Kuryło and J. Bartman, Przegląd Elektrotechniczny, **86**, 279 (2010)

The influence of power electronic converter passive filter parameters for flicker in LED lighting

Dariusz Sobczynski[1,*]

[1]Rzeszow University of Technology, Department of Power Electronics and Power Engineering, The Faculty of Electrical and Computer Engineering, 35-959 Rzeszow, Poland

Abstract. The light emitting diodes (LEDs) are ever more used, and their price is getting lower year on year. Although, exchanging traditional light sources for the LED lamps does not seem to be complicated, we need to remember to maintaining high–quality of light. One of the aspects we should be worry about is a light's flickering. Due to the shape of the current–voltage characteristics of the LED diode and their dependence on temperature, the value of the luminous flux – but also the lifetime – depends to a large extent on the stability of the supply voltage. Therefore, correct power system should be a thermally stable current source. Unfortunately, the simple power systems, equipped with passive filters are often used as cheap commercial solutions. In those types of systems stability of the output voltage is heavily dependent on the load conditions. Passive filters – usually consisting of coils and capacitors – are placed in the output circuit. This paper presents research carried out to show of filter capacitance influence on flickering phenomenon, and practical light's flickering measuring technique for the LED lamps.

1 Introduction

The light emitting diodes (LEDs) is a type of semiconductor diode that emits light when voltage is applied. LED's diode light flux is a function of physical properties of the construction material and the value of the current flowing through the semiconductor. LED chips – commonly used in lamps – consists of two basic blocks: power and optical. Power electronic converter system and control system are part of the power block. While, the optical block can be divided into LED diode, heat sink, lens system, and in some cases a phosphor layer. So, besides temperature, stability of the light flux depends on the power block [1].

1.1 Light Flickering

Flickering of lighting is fast, periodic changes in light intensity, so it can become a hazard to health. Flickering caused by inadequate power supply of LEDs is an undesirable

* Corresponding author: dsobczyn@prz.edu.pl

phenomenon which has negative impact on human comfort. Besides slow flickering of the LED light sources (components with a frequency not exceeding 80 Hz) it is important that emitted light do not contain higher frequency components which are causing the phenomenon of the so called „spectral matrix". This phenomenon is based on the impression of serial, spatial extension of the point light source after a step change of observed object (leaves impression of the trace of light) [2]. Many LED light sources flickers with frequencies from 100 to 500 HZ, which is not noticeable if eye does not move. However during fast eye movements (saccades) images of the LED lights sources appear in different places on the retina which are causing the impression of the image traces.

1.2 Human Effects of Light Flickering

The most unfavourable flicker effect occurs in the frequency range from 3 to 70 Hz – in 1 out of 20000 cases it can lead to epileptic seizures. Although most of the flickering effects occur on the level equal or twice higher than AC input frequency and is invisible to the human eye, nevertheless this phenomenon can still be a threat. Flickering for the frequencies from the range of 100 to 500 Hz are causing headache and eyestrain in large part of the population. Invisible flickering is forbidden in certain places such as Hospitals and offices [3]. The cause of invisible flickering are the low harmonic components of the output voltage of the switched power supplies used to power the diodes. Also, there can be other factors as well such as incorrectly working feedback loop, incorrect filter or converter working with current's discontinuity in inductance.

1.3 LED supply and flickering

Various types of power supplies and integrated electronic circuits can be used to power supply LED lamps. LED lightning requires constant current – so the key to eliminating light flickering is the right type of the power electronic converter used for power supply. Cheaper, power supplies of lower quality do not provide current stabilization for LED. Instead of providing constant current cheaper versions simply rectify current from AC to DC using a passive filter with LC elements. As a result voltage and current with relatively large ripple – usually with twice the input voltage – will be generated. That generate 100 potential flickers per second.

2 Mathematical definition of flicker index

The light flickering is mainly characterized by the depth of luminance changes. The depth of flicker can be quantified using mathematical formulas. There are many differently defined indicators of ripple depth in literature [4,5]:

$$W_1 = (Amax - Bmin)/(Amax + Bmin) \tag{1}$$

$$W_2 = (Amax - Bmin)/Amax \tag{2}$$

$$W_3 = (Amax - Aav)/Aav \tag{3}$$

$$W_4 = (Amax - Bmin)/Aav \tag{4}$$

$$W_5 = Bmin/Aav \tag{5}$$

$$W_6 = 0{,}5\ (Amax - Bmin)/Aav \tag{6}$$

Where, *Amax*, *Bmin*, *Aav,* marks successively: maximum, minimum and average luminance. The W_1 index is most often used but expressed as a percentage:

$$W_{1\%} = 100\%\ (Amax - Bmin)/(Amax + Bmin) \tag{7}$$

The quantification methods of $W_1 - W_6$, $W_{1\%}$ and *FI* was shown in Fig. 1.

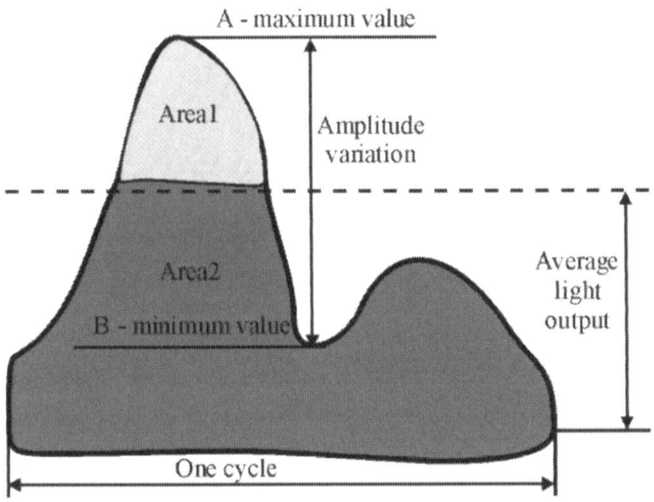

Fig. 1. Flicker quantification methods.

The $W_{1\%}$ factor does not take into account the shape, fill factor and frequency of the signal. Hence the flicker index (*FI)* has been used which – in contrast to the percentage of the flicker $W_{1\%}$ – also takes into account the shape and duty ratio. This coefficient is a better way to describe irregularly shaped courses because of it is able to account for differences in waveform shape [7]:

$$FI = (Area1/(Area1 + Area2)) \tag{8}$$

The light flicker factors assumes values from 0 to 1. The value of this coefficient depends on the type of light source used, as well as on its supply system. The flickering of light with the value W_1=0, can be considered harmless. In practice, this value is greater than zero. It was assumed that the light sources used to illuminate the work areas should have a flicker factor not greater than W_1=0.05.

In spot lighting, flicker index should be in the range of $0.1<W_1<0.15$, while in other illuminated areas this coefficient should be less than 0.2 [7]. As cited before, flicker factor allows for simply and rapid comparison of different LEDs' drivers.

3 Flicker measurements - experimental setup

The measuring device uses a digital, light to voltage sensor TSL250R, powered from a lithium-polymer battery. The sensor supply system is additionally equipped with a battery charging module using a micro USB port. The output voltage of the sensor, which is directly proportional to changes in light intensity, is given to one of the oscilloscope channels (Fig.2).

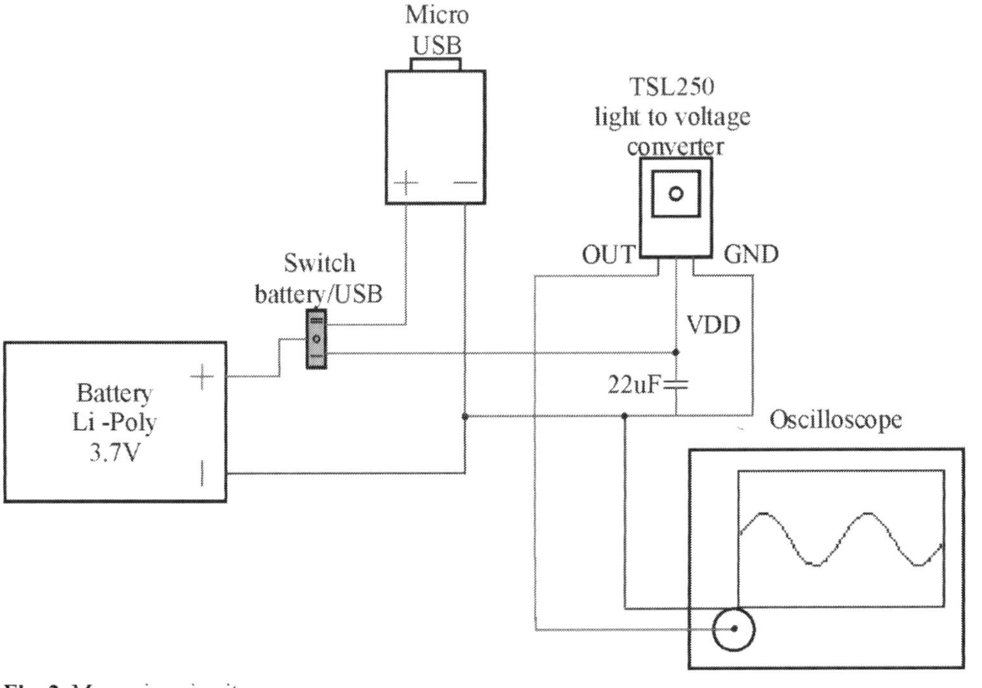

Fig. 2. Measuring circuit.

The LED power converter consists of the following elements (Fig. 3):
- KBPC5010 bridge rectifier.
- Capacitors with capacities of 110μF, 220μF and 470μF.
- 2-position switch.

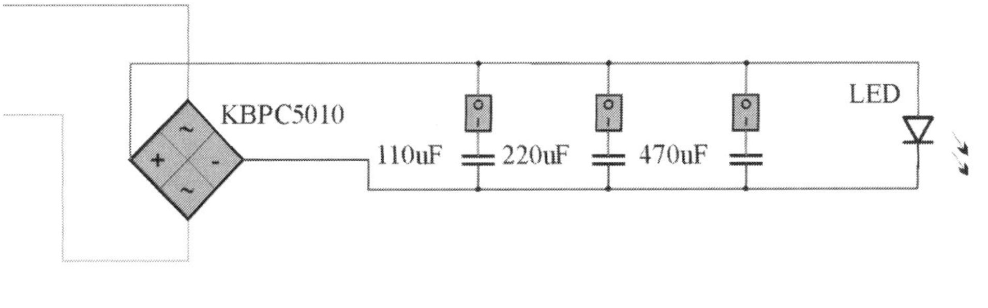

Fig. 3. LED supplier with adjustable capacitor filter.

4 Laboratory test

The measurements were carried out in experiment setup presented in Fig 4. The laboratory stand consists of:
- measuring module TSL250,
- amperemeter for measuring LED current,
- voltmeter for measuring the LED supply voltage,
- oscilloscope.

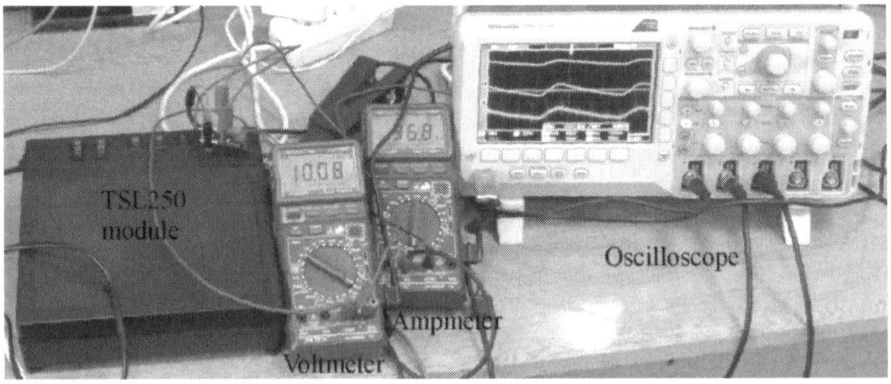

Fig. 4. Experimental setup.

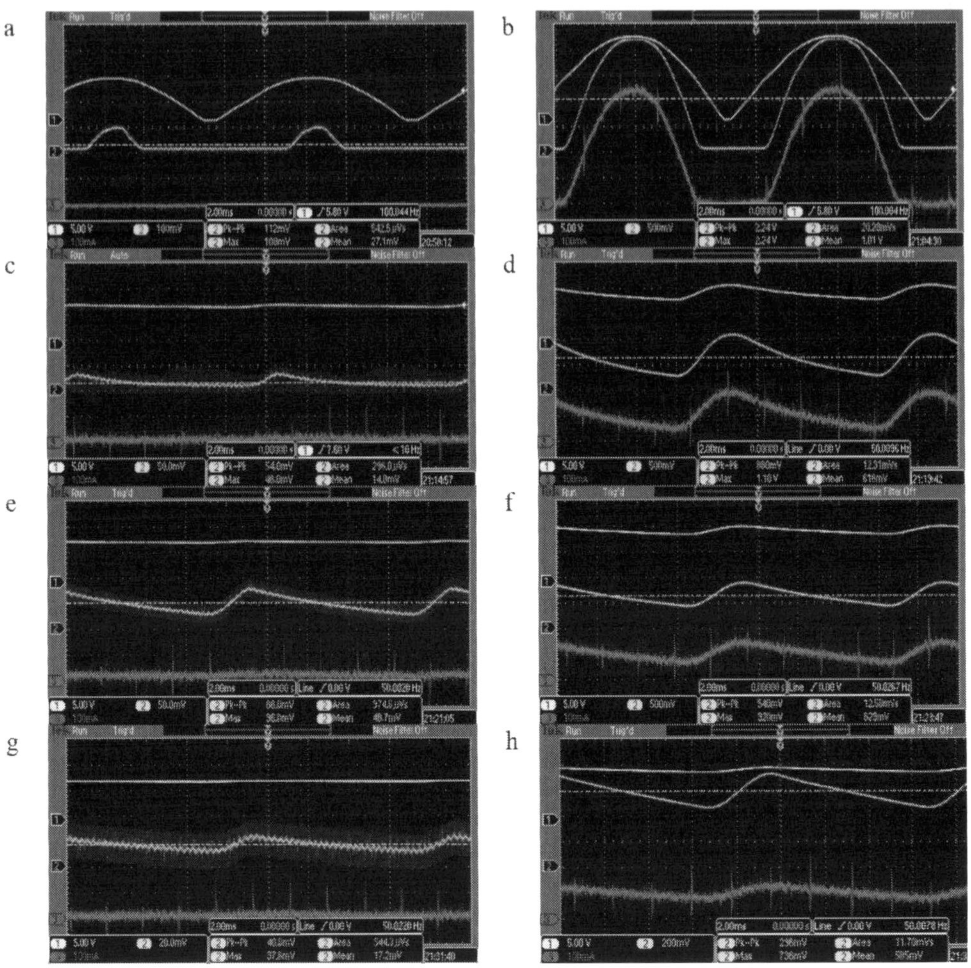

Fig. 5. Waveforms of: diode voltage (Ch1), TSL250 sensor output voltage – proportional to light intensity (Ch2), diode current (Ch3) for different value of supply voltage and filter's capacitor. (a) U= 7,5V; C=0µF, (b) U= 10V; C=0µF, (c) *U*= 7,5V; *C*=220µF, d) *U*= 10V; *C*=220µF, (e) *U*= 7,5V; *C*=470µF, f) *U*= 10V; *C*=470µF, (g) *U*= 7,5V; *C*=800µF, h) *U*= 10V; *C*=800µF.

The LEDs' chips and TSL 250 module were mounted in a black box. Each measurement experiments, have been done in order to determination of the light flicker coefficient for different value of passive filter capacitor capacitance. The first aspect that can be analyzed from the tests is a comparison between the all LED flicker indexes for several capacitor filter values. The Fig. 5a to Fig. 5h show qualitatively that some discrepancies in flicker index rise when using various voltage level.

During the measurements, the values of current and voltage supplied to the LED strip were read. On the oscilloscope, the voltage and current waveforms as well as the signal output of the TSL250 transducer proportional to the luminous flux were observed. Measurements have been made during LED strip supplying by converter without an output filter and when filter has been connected subsequently with capacitance vary from 110μF up to 800μF. The peak-to-peak, maximum and average values of the light to voltage TSL250 converter output signal have been read. The *Area*1 and *Area*2 necessary to designate the *FI* are read from the oscilloscope waveforms (Fig. 5a – 5h), similarly as was shown in Fig. 1.

Table 1. List of values of $W_1 - W_6$, $W_{1\%}$, FI for different values of filter capacitance.

Filter capacitance (uF)	W_1	W_2	W_3	W_4	W_5	W_6	$W_{1\%}$	FI
0	1	1	1.22	2.22	0	1.11	100	0.402
110	0.94	0.97	1.16	2.1	0.06	1.05	94	0.333
220	0.67	0.8	0.79	1.43	0.36	0.71	67	0.195
330	0.53	0.69	0.6	1.11	0.49	0.55	53	0.141
470	0.42	0.59	0.46	0.86	0.6	0.43	42	0.113
580	0.34	0.5	0.36	0.69	0.67	0.34	34	0.089
690	0.28	0.44	0.3	0.57	0.72	0.29	28	0.075
800	0.25	0.4	0.26	0.51	0.75	0.25	25	0.063

The indexes $W_1 - W_6$, $W_{1\%}$, provided in Chapter 2 are intended to describe an alternating signal. In the considered case the LED was powered by rectified voltage, which had the variable component, and therefore a description of the phenomenon used those indicators. On the basis of the realised research it can be concluded that the values of $W_1 - W_4$, W_6 coefficients, and $W_{1\%}$, start to decrease with increasing voltage and current supplying the LED, while the W_5 coefficient starts to increase.

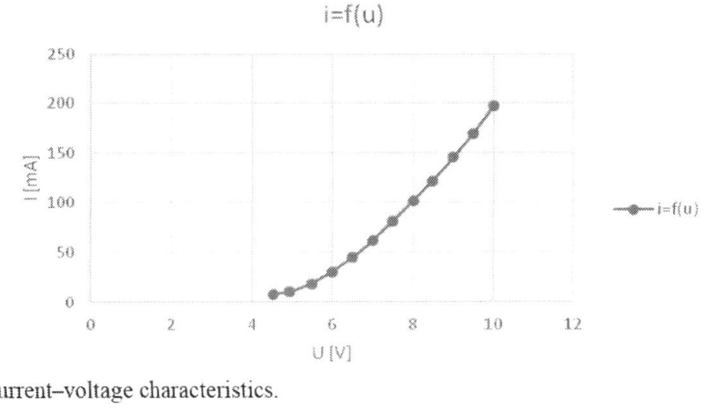

Fig. 6. Diode current–voltage characteristics.

The flicker indexes have been calculated according to the relationship (1 – 8) from Chapter 2. Table 1 shows such comparison.

Relating the values of the mentioned factors to the diode current–voltage characteristics, one can also observe a relationship (especially for the $W_3 - W_6$ coefficients) that the changes of those values are getting smaller and smaller from the point where the operating point on the current–voltage characteristics begins to enter linear area (a current of around 30–40mA). Analyzing the *FI* index can be notice that its value (similar to the $W_1 - W_4$ and W_6 coefficients) decreases with the increase of current and LED voltage, however these changes in relation to other coefficients are so small that one can accept that this ratio is constant for a given capacity. The factors values are decreasing together with the increase of voltage and supply current. That may confirm necessity of proper voltage supply parameter sets which were given by the producers.

The calculated indexes from $W_1 - W_6$ have a value greater than 1. After attaching subsequent capacities, the values of the indices are within the range given in the literature, from 0 to 1. Below, the values of flicker at measuring points at voltage of 10V are presented, where the values are the smallest for individual capacities and they are presented in Fig. 7.

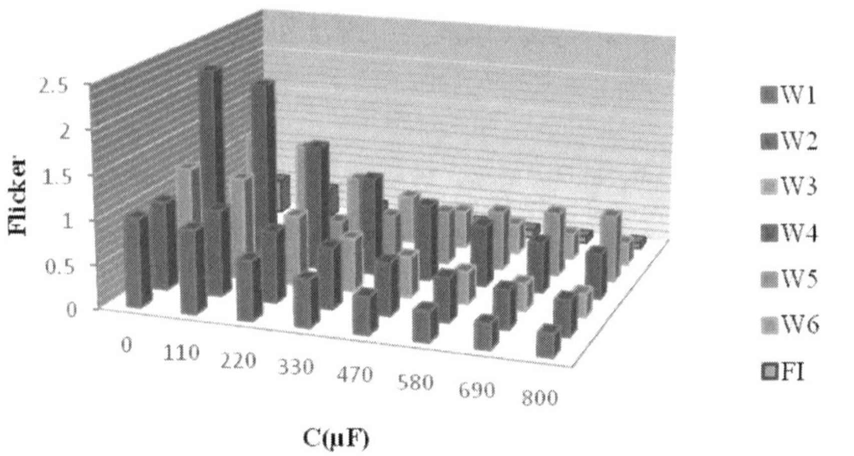

Fig. 7. List of flicker indexes for different capacitances.

As can be seen in the case under consideration, the flicker light indexes have reach the lowest values for the largest volume of capacitor, equal to 800 μF.

5 Conclusion

After analyzing obtained flicker index values it has been concluded that increasing the output capacity of LED power supply filter (reducing voltage ripples) results in reducing the ripple of light. The flicker index values from W_1 to W_6 and $W_{1\%}$ do not fit into acceptable limits specified in the Chapter 2. Assuming that values of the flicker index *FI*, are also regulated by quoted limited values, so can be conclude that given LED can be used as a light source with the filter capacity of 220 μF (*FI*<0.2). Using diode lamp in local lightning would require to attach a minimum capacity of 330 μF (*FI*<0.15). For the capacity value of 800 μF flicker index *FI* equals 0.063 which exceeds acceptable value of 0.05 used to illuminate exact workplaces. In reference to maximum flicker indexes provided by IEEE, given value meets the condition with the capacity of 690 μF or higher (*FI*<08). As mentioned in Section 2, *FI* takes into account the shape and duty ratio of the signal which contrast with the other factors that as pointed in literature on the subject are used to describe the ripples of light caused by AC power supply. Obtained values of the factors W_1 – W_6, $W_{1\%}$, *FI* differ from the values given in Chapter 2. Test results confirm the validity of utilizing FI factor – especially for the rectified voltage shape. It can be noticed that this coefficient was within the limits defined in the theoretical part of this article, differently than other factors.

References

1. X. Cao, D. Zheng, 11th China Int. For. on Solid State Lighting, *Inteligent LED lighting system and sensor technology*, (2014)
2. W.A. Hershberger, J.S. Jordan, The Psych. Rec., *The Phantom array: a perisaccadic illusion of visual direction*, **48**, 21-32 (1998)
3. A. J. Wilkins, J. Veitch, B. Lehman, IEEE standard PAR1789 update, in Proc. IEEE Energy Conversion Congr. Expo., *LED lighting flicker and potential health concerns*, 171–178 (2010)
4. R. Roy, Richtek Application Note AN022, *Minimizing Light Flicker in LED Lighting Applications*, (2014)
5. M. Poplawski, N.J. Miller, Pacific Northwest National Laboratory Tech. Rep., (2013)
6. J. Gomez, M. Morcos, IEEE Power Engineering Review, *Flicker measurement and light effect*, 11-15, (2002).
7. A. Wiśniewski, Przegląd Elektrotechniczny, *Tętnienie światła wytwarzanego przez Tuby LED – zamienniki świetlówek liniowych*, **7** (2015)

The impact of mutual position of joints that generate a bipolar field on the decay of the components of the electromagnetic field's vector

Bogdan Kwiatkowski[1,*], *Jacek* Bartman[1], *Paweł* Krutys[1]

[1]*University of Rzeszow, Faculty of Mathematics and Natural Sciences Department of Computer Engineering, ul. Pigonia 1, 35-959 Rzeszow, Poland*

Abstract. In the article the influence of mutual position of the upper joint in relation to the lower one on the decay of the electromagnetic field was presented. Moreover, the indirect measurement method was depicted, by means of which the measurements were taken on the surface of the contact circuit. This method enables the simultaneous measurement of all the components of the vector of the electromagnetic field.

1 Methods of measurement of the electromagnetic field

The axial magnetic field generated by the coil's joints can be measured by concentrically arranged coils placed in the spaces between the joints. In these coils during the flow of the current through the contact circuit (fig.1) the tension is induced. The value of the tension measured in the particular coils allows to calculate, on the basis of relations (1) the value of the electromagnetic induction B in relation to the radius of the coil on the joint's surface [1]. Analysing the equation (1), it can be observed that the tension, or more precisely the difference of tensions between the subsequent coils, is the measure of the electromagnetic field and can be described with the formula:

$$V_n = -S_n d \frac{B_n}{dt} \tag{1}$$

where: Vn-the tension induced on the n-coil, Sn-the surface of the joint comprised by the n-coil, Bn-the density of the electromagnetic field's stream. The examples of the arrangement of the coils and measuring systems are presented in picture 1. While measuring the joints were connected with copper rod and the coils were arranged concentrically in such a way, so the field does not influence on the measured value of the tension. (fig.1a) [2] [3]. The calibration of coils was made in the field generated by the special and big enough solenoid in such a way, to obtain a homogenous field on the surface of embraced by the calibrated coil.

*Correspondingauthor: bkwiat@ur.edu.pl

https://doi.org/10.1051/itmconf/20182100021

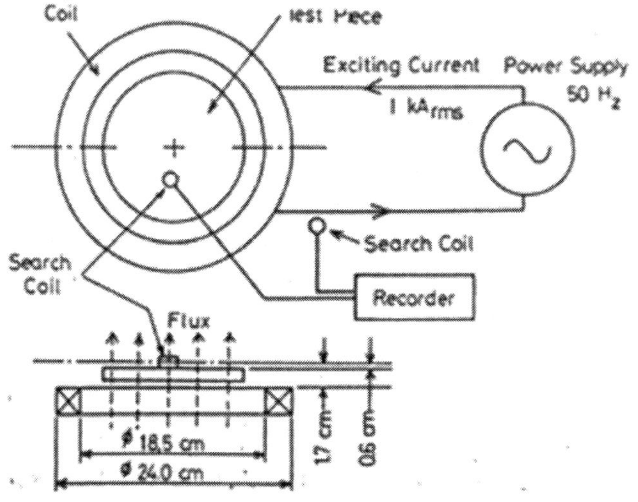

Fig 1a. The examples of measuring the electromagnetic field: with the use of concentrically placed coils.

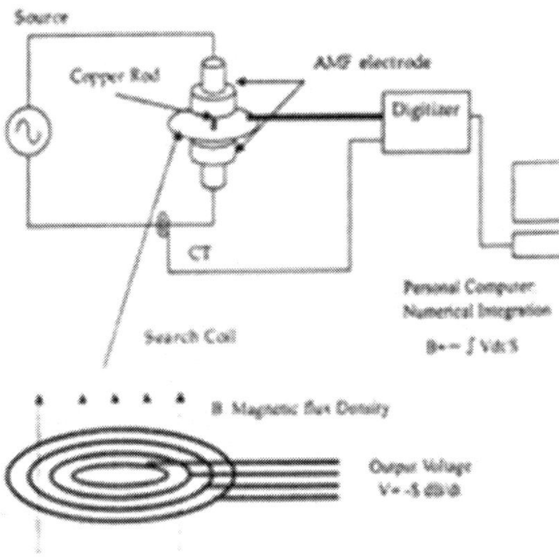

Figure 1b. The examples of measuring the electromagnetic field with the use of the so called measuring probe.

The endings of the coil were screwed in a way to eliminate the unfavourable impact of the wires connecting the coil with the measuring system [4]. The other method to measure the decay of the electromagnetic field between the surfaces of the coils was presented in pic.1b. In this case to measure the decay of the field the probe was used. The measurement was taken by the use of the probe placed on the surface of the joint, and the measured tension was compared with the tension of the coil of the reference system, which was placed outside the measuring system [5]. In the case of measuring the field for the coil systems generating the bipolar field it is crucial to use the method from pic. 1b, the so called 'the measuring probe method'. To the laboratory measuring a recorder HIOKI type „8841/42 MEMORY HiCORDER was used. The parameters of this device allow to collect the appropriate amount of the measuring and satisfying accuracy of the measurements taken [6]. With the view to measuring the electromagnetic induction in the spaces between the joints, the measuring probe was constructed, which consisted of three coils. (fig.2).

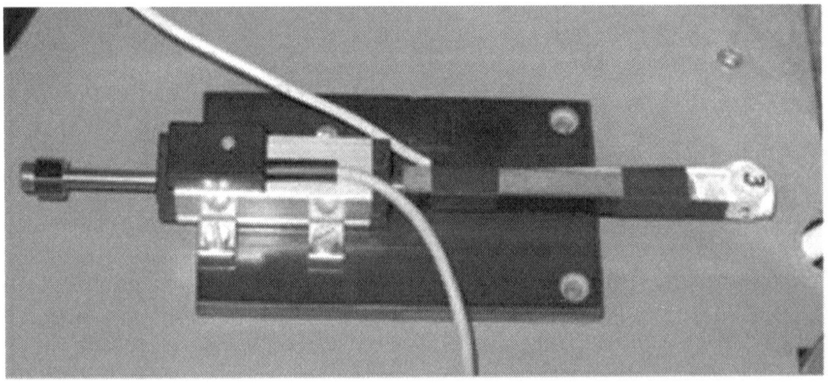

Fig 2. The measuring probe.

The measuring system with probes was placed in the Faraday's cage in order to eliminate the influences from the outside [7] [8]. In the used measuring methods, the quantity which is directly measured is the tension induced in the measuring coils. These coils, during the flow of the current through the coil system, are placed in spaces between the joints and are put from the outside to the centre of the joint plate. The measurement of the tension induced on the coil is made by HIOKI recorder with the frequency of 100 ms. It allows to get approximately 25 thousand measuring points for each position of the measuring probe. This probe in the initial phase of measuring each of the joint system is placed in the zero position (0^0) and is moved successively every 15^0 around the joint plate [9].

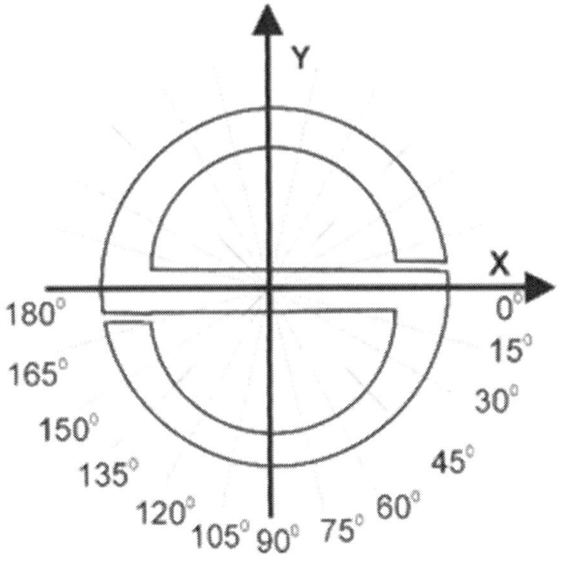

Fig 3. Diagram of contact with angles.

In case of measurements of the joint systems the measured quantity is the tension induced in the measuring coils and the desired quantity is the value of the electromagnetic induction, precisely the decay of the electromagnetic induction on the surface of the joint plate [10 -11]. While taking measurement, the frequency of the recorder was of 100 ms, which with mains power supply gives 200 samples per period. We can count the electromagnetic induction by transforming the formula 1 [12]. The final formula to calculate the electromagnetic induction measured for 50kA is presented below:

$$B = \frac{\sum_{i=1}^{200} abs(u - offset) * f_p}{4 * z * S} * \frac{\sqrt{2} * 50 * 10^3}{\max(abs(I))} \quad (2)$$

$$offset = \frac{\min_{1 \div 200}(u) + \max_{1 \div 200}(u)}{2} \quad (3)$$

Where: u- the tension measured in the measuring coils, z=50 – the number of measuring coils rolls, S=59 mm2 – the surface of the measuring coil, fp – the frequency of recorder, s sampling, I- the current flowing through the coils system.

2. The results of measuring of particular coil systems

The main goal of the measuring is to point that there is a possibility of improving the evenness of the decay of the electromagnetic field thanks to the choice of construction and placing the joints to each other in the vacuum chamber of the off switch in a way to get possibly the best conditions of the decay of the electromagnetic field as well as the conditions of extinguishing of the arc [13]. Three components of the field were measured: axial component, perimeter component and the radius component, measuring them by three probes simultaneously from the outside edge of the joint to its center. Picture 3 shows the joints constructions which had undergone the research.

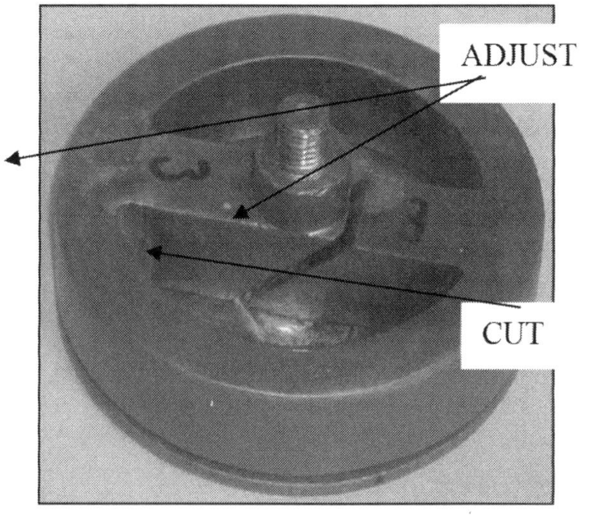

Fig 4. The joint constructions used in the research the bipolar joint no.1.

For the joint in picture 4 there was a measurement taken for four positions. In picture 5 there are presented the positions of joints in which the channeling of the upper joint is precisely above the channeling of the lower joint.

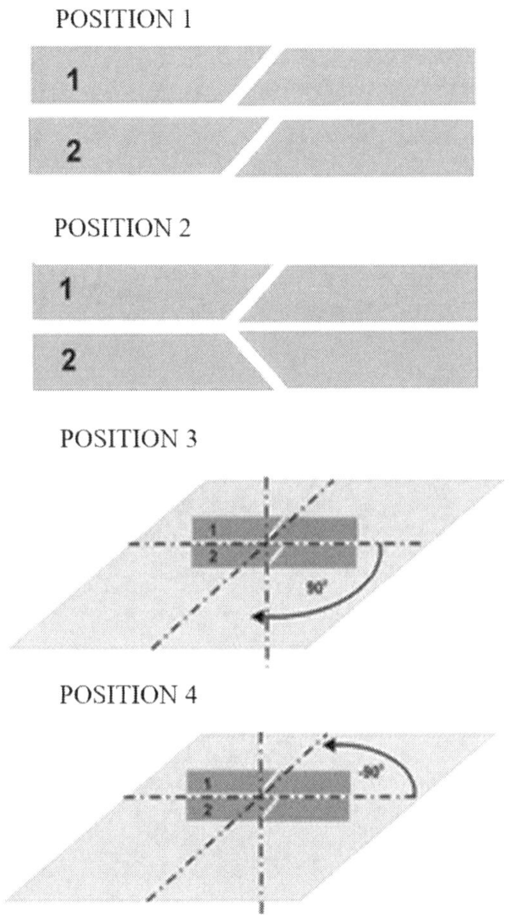

Fig 5. The positions of the joint system for which the measurements were taken.

Position 1. The highest values for this position is reached by the radius component, and the smallest by the perimeter component of the electromagnetic induction B. The axial component of the induction has an even decay on the surface of the joint. The highest values are reached for the central angles of measurement, that is from 60^0 to 120^0. The smallest values are reached by the angles of 0^0 and 180^0. While the values of the maximum courses increase, these points (maxima) come to the central part of the joint plate. The courses for the perimeter component are increasing when moving to the centre of the joint plate. In the central part of the measured area the value of the induction are slightly smaller and they create something like a 'saddle'. On the external part of the joint plate from 30 to 20 mm, the values of the induction increase in the course of moving from 0^0 to 180^0. In the central part of the joint the system is changing and the highest values are reached by the angles from 0^0 to 30^0. It was also observed that the smallest differences between the values on the outer side of the joint occur for the angles from 90^0 to 180^0. The highest values are for the course of 180^0, that is from 100 mT on the outer part of the joint to 300 mT in the central part of the joint.

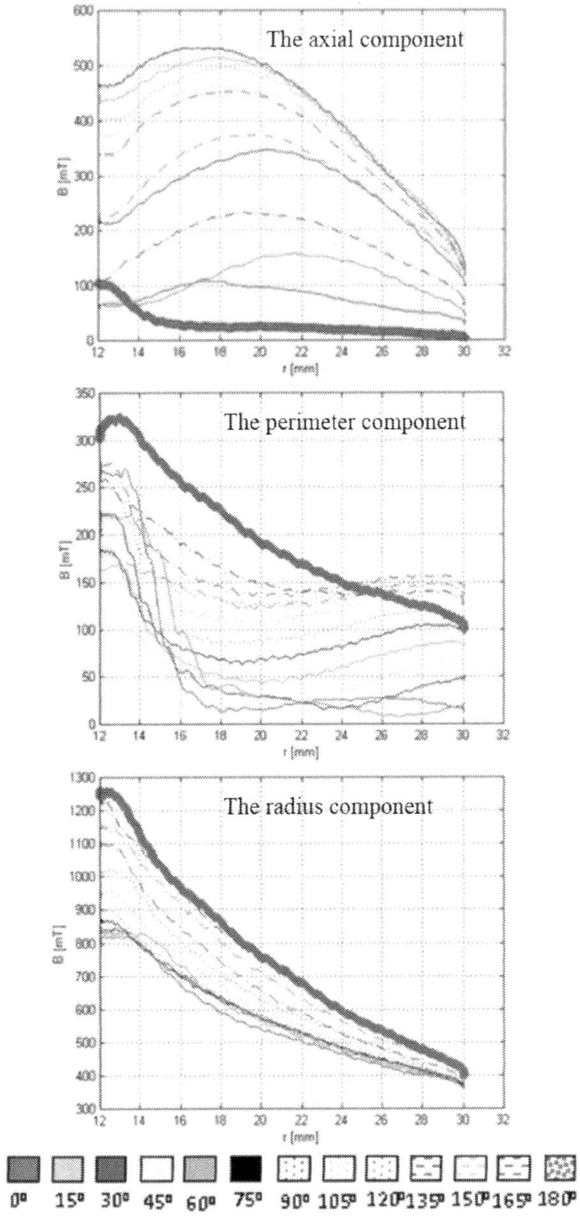

Fig. 6: The course of the components of the vector of electromagnetic induction for all the measurement angles – joint pic.3a, arrangement 1.

As it was mentioned before the axial component of the induction reaches the highest values. The courses for all the measuring angles begin with almost one and the same point. The values of induction have their increasing character (almost linear) in the direction from the outer to the central part of the joint. The value of the induction is increasing alongside with the measuring angle from 0^0 to 180^0.

Position 2. All the courses for the axial component start with the same value of the induction (approx. 25-30 mT). The highest values are observed for the 135^0 angle. When crossing this point, the courses subsequently decrease in their values. In the range of measurement, which is 12 mm to 30 mm (pic. 3), in the courses for the starting measuring angles – 0-75⁰ – there is a point of inflexion. For the bigger angles the inflexion points are of increasing character.

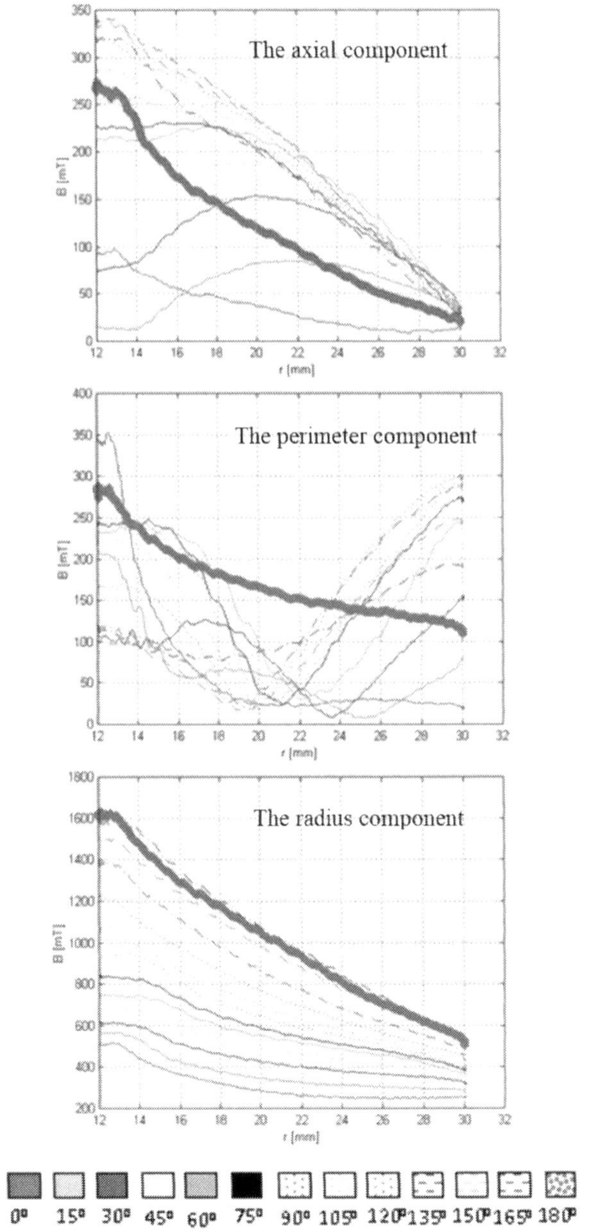

Fig. 7: The course of the components of the vector of electromagnetic induction for all the measurement angles – joint pic.3a, arrangement 2.

For the majority of the measuring angles the perimeter component of electromagnetic induction reaches its minimal value in the central part of the measuring area, in the distance of 19 to 22 mm. However, there are exceptions for angles of 0^0 and 180^0. The majority of courses will reach their maximal value on the external part of the joint plate. The radius component, just as in the previous cases reaches its highest values in comparison with the rest of the components of this position. The lowest values are for the 0^0 angle, later with the increase of the angle, the courses reach higher values. The maximal are for the angles of 180^0.

Position 3. The courses for the axial component reach maximal values in the central part of the measuring area. The highest are for the initial measuring angles; 0^0, 15^0 and 30^0. The lowest course was for the 90^0 angle. From 0^0 to 90^0 the courses were gradually decreasing their values, to increase again when crossing the point of 90^0 angle.

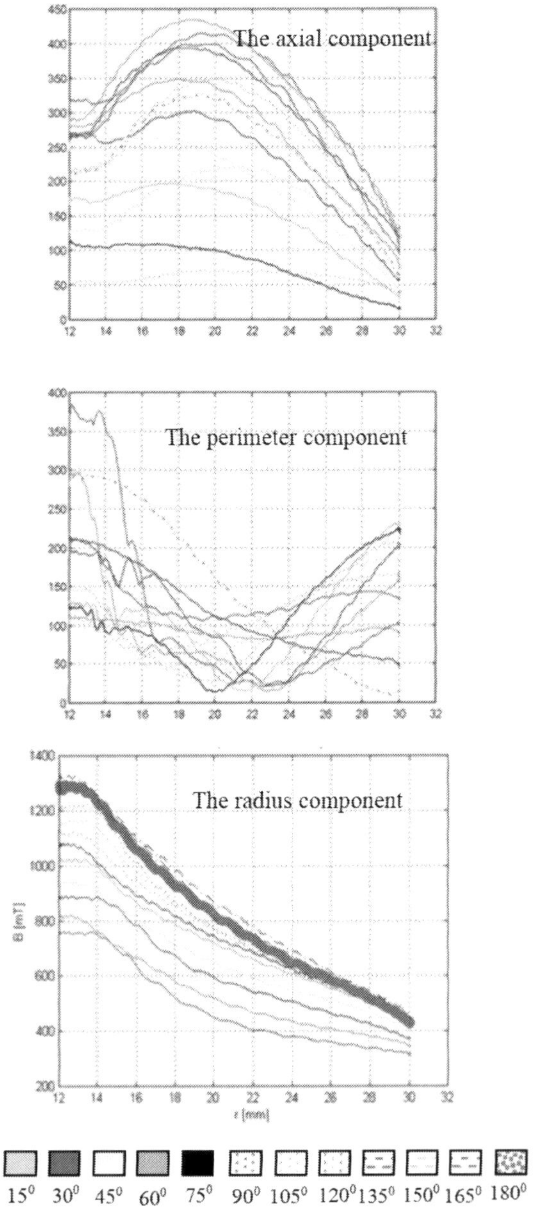

Fig. 8: The course of the components of the vector of electromagnetic induction for all the measurement angles – joint pic.3a, arrangement 3.

Similarly to the position depicted above, here the perimeter component has the most irregular courses. In the central part of the measuring area, the majority of courses reach their minimums. The highest values for this position were reached by the radius component, however these are still lower than in position 2. The lowest values are for the course of 0^0, then with the increase of the measuring angle the value of induction rises, to reach its maximum in 180^0 angle.

Position 4. The axial component for this position is similar as in position 3. The values reaches by this component are slightly higher in comparison with position 3. Thus in this case the perimeter component of the electromagnetic induction has its minimum point in the centre of the measuring sphere.

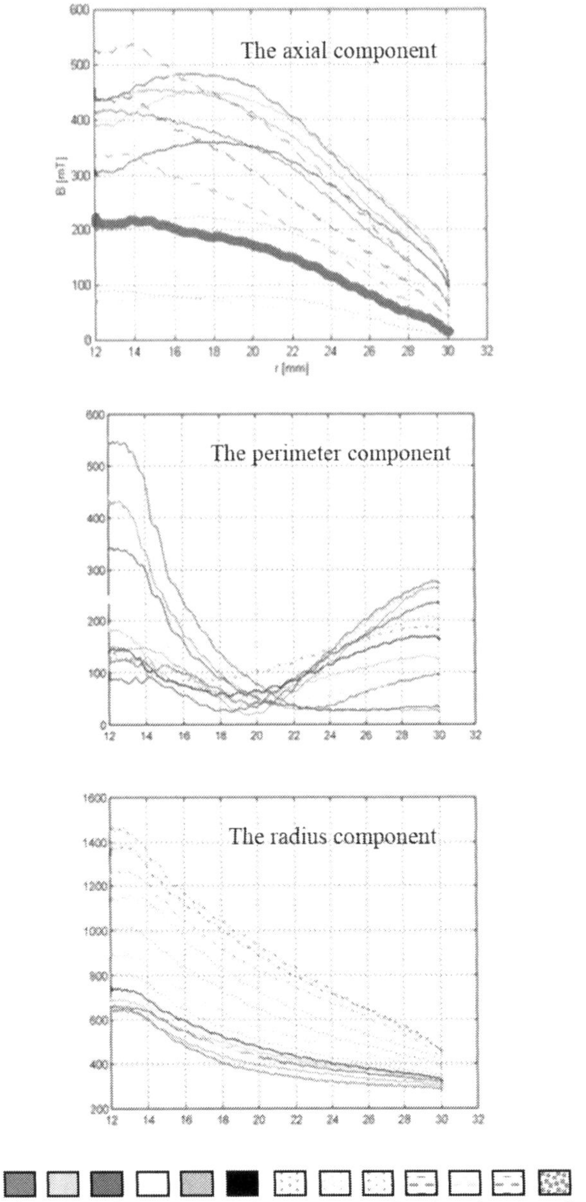

Fig. 9: The course of the components of the vector of electromagnetic induction for all the measurement angles – joint pic.3a, arrangement 4.

The radius component behaves likewise as in position 3. In the whole measuring area it is increasing. The values taken by the particular measuring points on the joint plate increase alongside with the increasing measuring angle. Thus it can be concluded that for both position 3 and 4 the axial component of induction has even decay on the whole surface of joint and reaches its maxima at the moment when perimeter component has its minimal values.

3. Remarks and conclusion

The results of the measurements taken on particular joints used in the off switches of vacuum chambers proved that there is a considerable influence of the arrangement of joints among each other on the decay of the components of the electromagnetic field among the joints. In case of bipolar joints, the influence if the joint's arrangement is visible and there is a possibility to choose the decay of the electromagnetic field in the post favourable way. The bipolar joints (acc.pic. 3). The measurements were also taken for their arrangement 'supply-supply', and 'supply-supply+90^0'. It was unanimously agreed that the arrangement of the joints among one another, especially of such a construction, has a crucial impact on the decay of the vector of the electromagnetic induction. It was also observed in the courses of the axial component of the electromagnetic field. In the further research it is hoped to carry out measurements for other contact circuits, e.g. from pic. 3b, contact circuits generating SADE field and other new constructions.

References

1. Sikora R.: Teoria pola elektromagnetycznego, Wydawnictwo Naukowo-Techniczne, Warszawa 1985.
2. Dahlquist G., Björck A.: Metody numeryczne, PWN, Warszawa 1993.
3. B. Fenski, M. Lindmayer: Vacuum Interrupters with Axial Magnetic Field and Contacts, 3-d. Finit Element Simulation and Switching Experiments, IEEE Transaction on Dielectrics and Electrical Insulation Vol.4 1997 pp. 407.
4. Grodziński A., Szymański A., Sibilski H., Dzierżyński A., Borowski P., Hejduk A., Krasuski K., Badania styków z osiowym polem magnetycznym w rozbieralnej komorze próżniowej. Elektronika Konstrukcje, Technologie, Zastosowania, nr 8 (2011), 42-44.
5. Z. Gomolka, B. Twarog, J. Bartman, Improvement of image processing by using homogeneous neural networks with fractional derivatives theorem, Discrete and Continuous Dynamical Systems- Series AI, ssue SUPPL., Pages 505-514, (2011).
6. Brandt S.: Analiza danych. Metody statystyczne i obliczeniowe, Wydawnictwo Naukowe PWN, Warszawa 1998.
7. Harald Fink, Marcus Heimbach, Wenkai Shang: Vacuum Intrerrupters with Axial Magnetic Field Contact Based on Bipolar and Quadropolar Design, IEEE 19 International Symposium on Discharges and Electrical Insulation in Vacuum, Xian-2000.
8. Z.Gomolka, B.Twarog, E. Zeslawska, A. Lewicki, T. Kwater, Using Artificial Neural Networks to Solve the Problem Represented by BOD and DO Indicators, Water 2018, 10(1), 4

9. Sibilski H., Dzierżyński A., Hejduk A., Krasuski K., Grodziński A., Szymański A., Badanie właściwości magnetycznych styków komór próżniowych, Materiały konferencyjne - Łączniki 2010, 7-16.

10. Z. Gomolka, B. Twarog, E. Zeslawska, Cognitive Investigation on Pilot Attention During Take-Offs and Landings Using Flight SimulatorArtificial Intelligence and Soft Computing, vol 10246. (2017).

11. Z. Gomolka, Neurons' Transfer Function Modeling with the Use of Fractional Derivative. DepCoS-RELCOMEX 2018. Advances in Intelligent Systems and Computing, vol 761. (2019)

12. Sibilski, H. Dzierżyński, A. Berowski, P. Błażejczyk, T. Hejduk, A. Krasuski, K. Grodziński, A. Szymański, A. Badanie styków dla łączników próżniowych średniego napięcia, Przegląd Elektrotechniczny 2012, 193-196.

13. J. Bartman "Accuracy of reflecting the waveforms of current and voltage through their spectrum determined by the standards regulating measurements" in Revue Roumaine des sciences techniques - Serie Electrotechnique et Energetique, vol 61/4, 2016, pp. 355-360.

Operation analysis of a spiral ground heat exchanger functioning as a lower heat source in a pressurizing heat pump

Damian Mazur[1,*], and *Robert* Smusz[2]

[1]Rzeszow University of Technology, Department of Electrical and Computer Engineering Fundamentals, ul. Wincentego Pola 2, 35-959 Rzeszow, Poland
[2]Rzeszow University of Technology, Department of Thermodynamics and Fluid Mechanics, al. Powstańców Warszawy 8, 35-959 Rzeszów, Poland

Abstract. The main aim of the study is to identify functioning of a ground, spiral heat exchanger co-functioning with a pressurizing heat pump. The heat pump is connected with a heat battery and works periodically during the heating period. The analysis was made by means of numerical modelling and using the finite element method.

1 Introduction

A common solution for lower heat source in low-power, pressurizing heat pump installations are horizontal, ground heat exchangers. Horizontal exchangers are usually installed at the depth of 1.5-1.6 metre in relation to the ground level. The main limitations connected with using such solutions are:

- the efficiency is strongly dependant on the degree of base ground moisture;
- there is strong influence of atmospheric air temperature on the efficiency of a ground heat exchanger;
- large ground area is required in order to provide appropriate efficiency of the exchanger;
- there is a possibility of freezing the ground surface layers, which leads to hindering plant vegetation;
- high investment costs connected with laying pipes of the exchanger in the ground.

The so-called spiral ground heat exchangers are free from these disadvantages.

* Corresponding author: mazur@prz.edu.pl

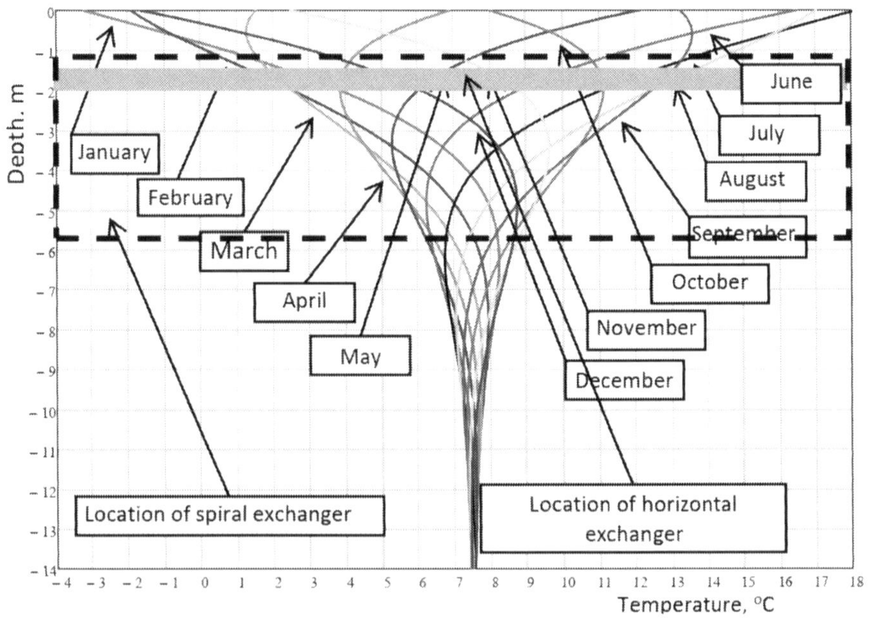

Fig. 1. Ground temperature distribution.

Figure 1 shows temperature distribution in ground for particular months. The closer to the surface the higher amplitudes of temperature changes in the ground can be observed. It is the effect of temperature wave penetrating the ground, which results from seasonal changes of atmospheric temperature. In the case of a spiral exchanger, which is installed at the depth of 1.8-5.5 m beneath the ground level, one can observe a significantly lower amplitude of temperature change than in the case of a horizontal exchanger. This enables to provide much more stable working conditions of a spiral exchanger during whole year and its smaller influence on temperature in the area just below the ground surface. It has significant influence on plant vegetation. Apart from that, in deeper parts grounds have lower moisture, which has positive impact on heat transfer from the ground to the working medium in the ground heat exchanger [6, 8].

2 Model

In order to conduct the analysis of a ground heat exchanger in the conditions of non-determined heat exchange, the measurement data were approximated to average monthly temperature of atmospheric air on the basis of many-year meteorological research of Rzeszów [10], Table 1, by using Hillel's model, fig. 2:

$$T(x,t) = T_a + A_o \cdot exp\left[-\frac{(x+x_{gr})}{d}\right] \cdot sin\left[\frac{2\cdot\pi\cdot(t-t_o)}{d} - \frac{(x+x_{gr})}{d} - \frac{\pi}{2}\right] \quad (1)$$

where:
x-depth, m
$x_{gr} = \frac{k_{gr}}{h}$,
k_{gr}- coefficient of ground conductance , W/mK,
h-heat transfer coefficient, W/m^{2}K,

$d = \sqrt{\frac{2 \cdot D_{gr}}{\omega}}$ – penetration depth,

D_{gr} - ground thermal diffusivity, m^2/day

$\omega = \dfrac{2 \cdot \pi}{T}$

T=365 days,

t - time, h

t_o - phase shift, h

A_o - amplitude, K

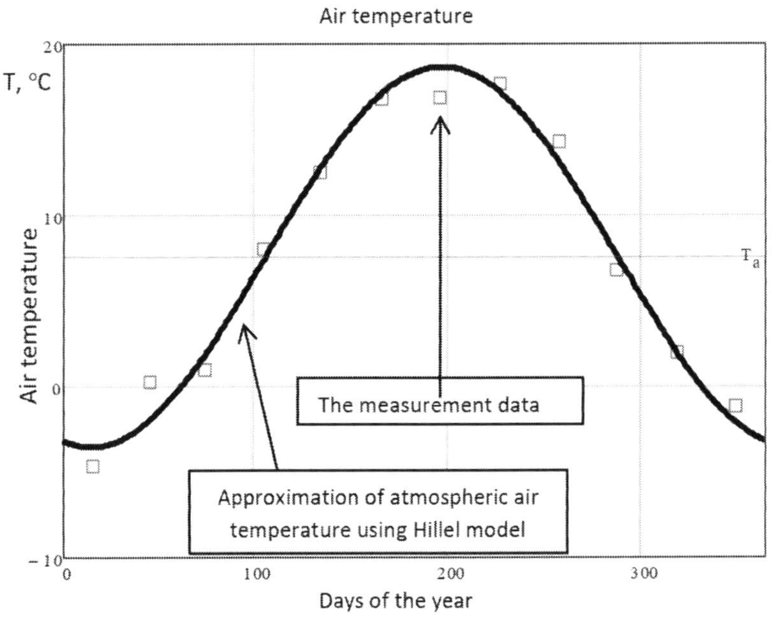

Fig. 2. Approximation of atmospheric air temperature.

The amplitude of atmospheric air was determined on the basis of meteorological data [10]. Constant values of specific heat, density and ground conductance coefficients were assumed for the analysis of lower heat source operation. Boundary conditions at the ground surface were also determined on the basis with Hillel's model, assuming the coefficient of atmospheric air transfer of 16 W/m^2K.

Table 1. Meteo data for Rzeszów [10].

Month	Average monthly temperature of external air, °C
1	-4.6
2	0.3
3	1
4	8
5	12.5
6	16.8
7	16.9
8	17.7
9	14.3
10	6.8
11	2
12	-1.2

Table 2. Thermal properties of ground.

Ground heat transfer, W/mK	Ground density, kg/m^3	Specific heat, J/kgK
1.5	1742	1175

The data for December were assumed as an initial condition for numerical calculations. On this basis, as well as by using Hillel's model, the initial profile of temperature in ground was determined, fig. 3.

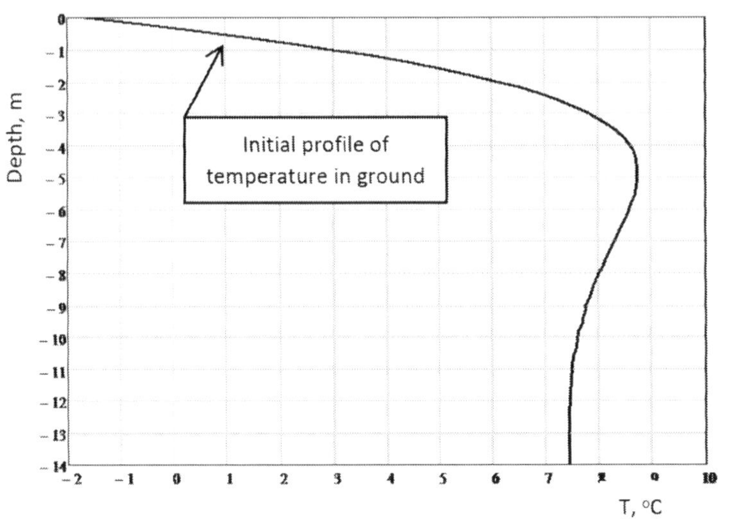

Fig. 3. Ground temperature profile for December.

The calculation model consisted of two spiral coils placed in the ground. The calculation domain was the ground area together with the exchanger, the dimensions of which were 15 m x 24 m x 14 m.

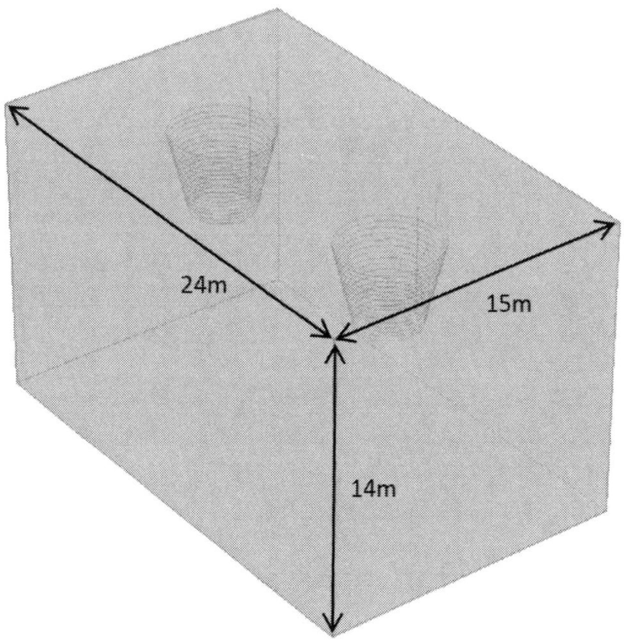

Fig. 4. Calculation domain.

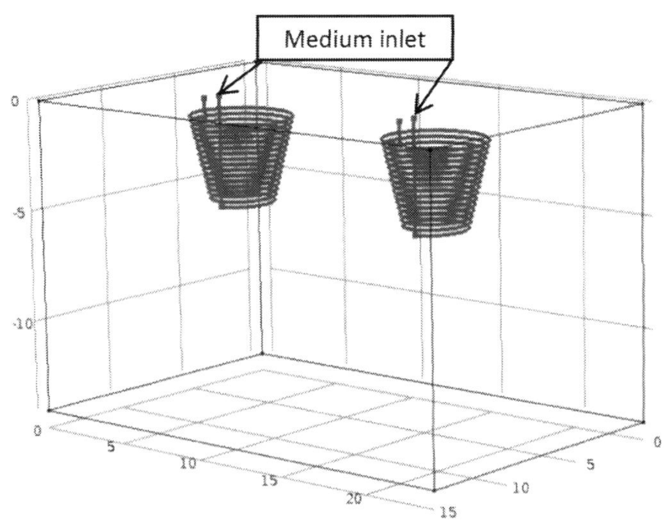

Fig. 5. Spiral exchangers.

The exchangers were placed at the depth of 5 m below the ground surface, in the distance of 12 m from each other. The height of the exchangers was 4 m, and minimal and maximal diameter amount, respectively, 3 m and 5 m. The scale of coils was 25 cm. The coils were made of a pipe made of polymer with the conductivity coefficient of 0.4 W/mK and the external diameter of 36 mm and wall thickness amounting 3 mm. The working medium flowing through the coils is water solution of propylene glycol of the concentration of 20%. The flow of the medium through each coil is constant and amounts 0.25 l/s. The exchangers are connected with the heat exchanger of the power of 3 kW. The exchanger works periodically, due to the fact that the heat pump is integrated with a pop tank, fig. 6.

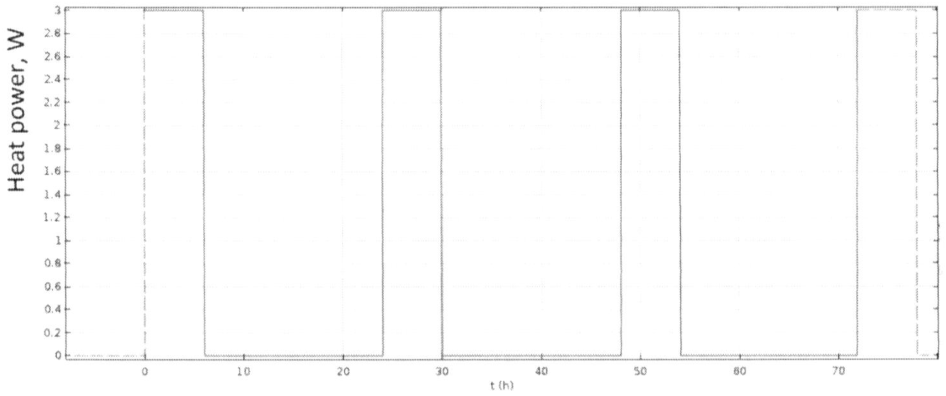

Fig. 6. Duty of a heat exchanger.

3 Numerical model

The computational domain was divided into: 148774 3D prismatic elements, 6296 triangular elements of 2D surface and 940 boundary elements. The numerical calculations encompassed the analysis of the unsteady temperature area in the ground, the temperature of the working medium flowing in coils of ground heat exchangers. The flow of the medium and the unsteady heat exchange in coils were analysed by using 1 D-time models, and in the ground by means of the 3D-time method. Comsol Multiphysics software was used for calculations [1,7].

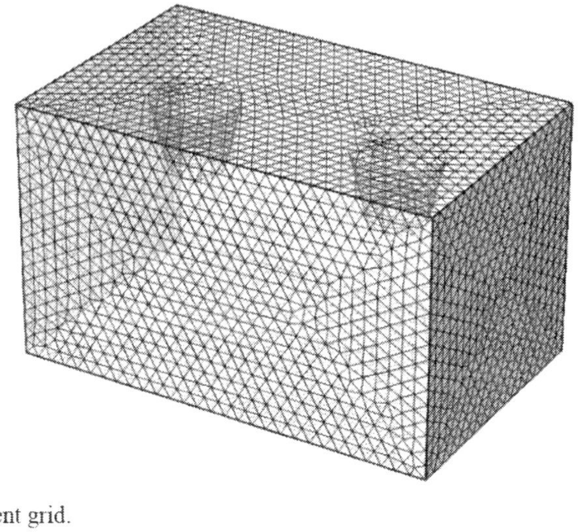

Fig. 7. Finite element grid.

4. Results

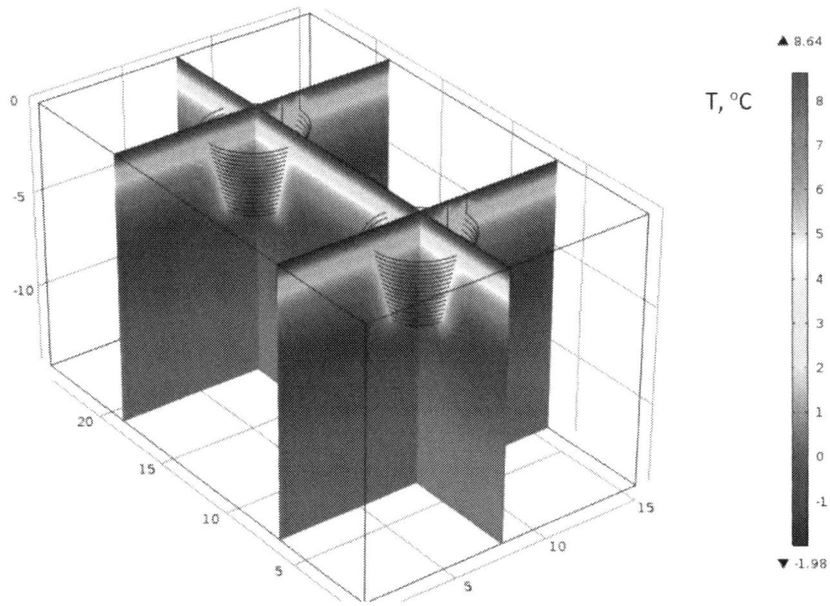

Fig. 8. Temperature distribution in the ground on the 5th day of operation.

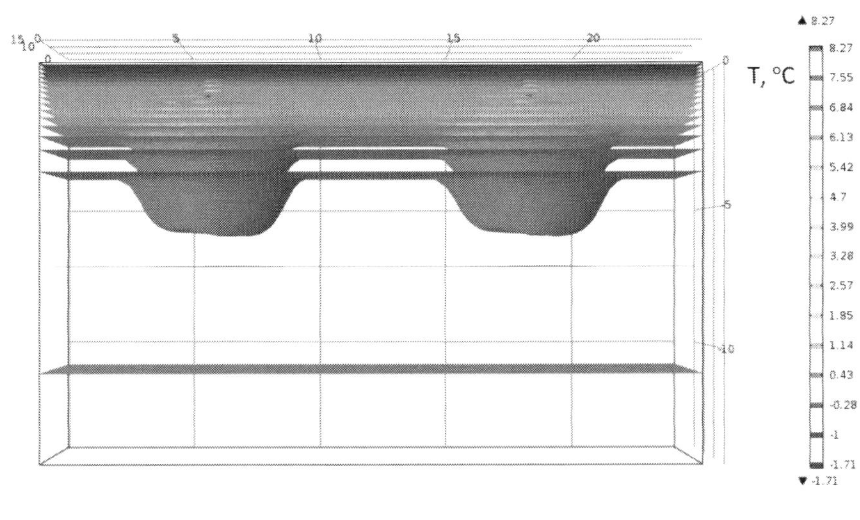

Fig. 9. Isotherms around the ground heat exchanger on the 5th day of operation from its start.

Figures 8 and 9 show the temperature field in the ground around coil-spiral heat exchangers. As one can notice, the area of the influence of heat exchanger on the temperature field encompasses a small area around the exchanger. Additionally, heat is transported to the medium from deeper parts of the ground [3]. It provides the possibility to increase condensation of coils in the given area. It enables to increase unit heat power when comparing to horizontal ground heat exchangers. Additionally, absorption of heat from deeper parts of ground by spiral heat exchangers allows for lower cooling in the surface layers of soil and hence improvement of plant vegetation.

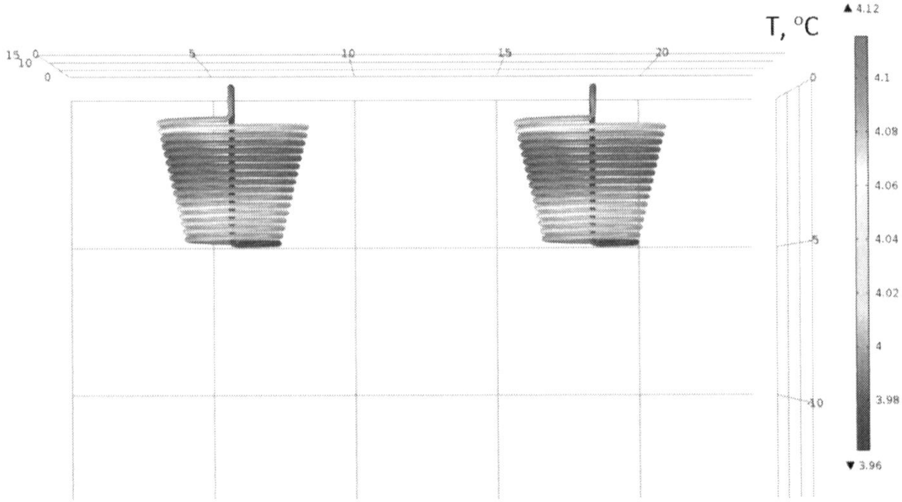

Fig. 10. Temperature distribution of the working medium in coils on the fifth day of operation.

Figure 10 presents temperature distribution of the working medium in the coil. Cold working medium flows in at the lowest point of the coil and then is transported upwards. As one can notice the medium gradually heats up, but in the upper part of the coil that is placed below the ground surface it is cooled down. It is due to lower ground temperature than the temperature of the medium. It causes deterioration of the efficiency of heat exchanger performance [2, 5]. Therefore, in order to improve the efficiency of operation one should apply an exchanger with variable scale so that it is smaller in the lower part and bigger in the upper part. It enables to increase the efficiency of heat exchangers as the difference between the ground and the medium becomes bigger.

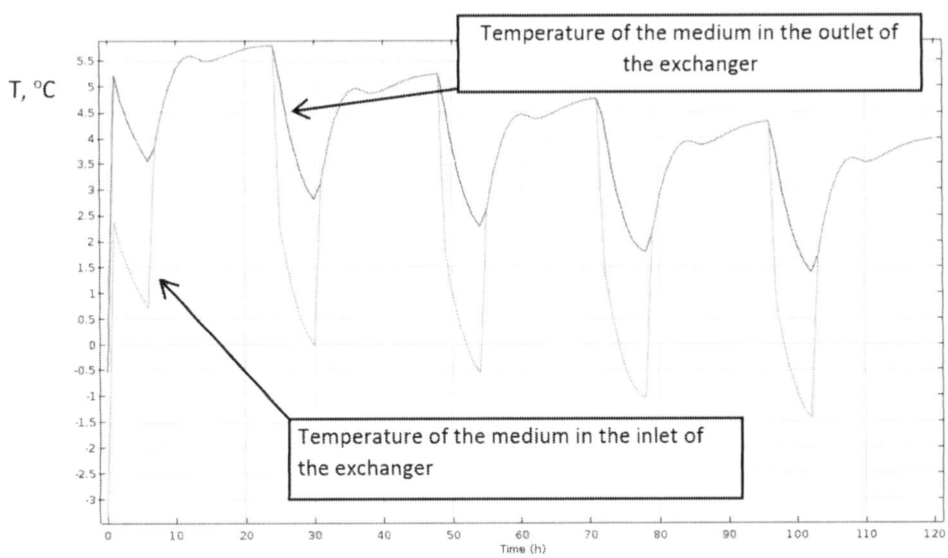

Fig. 11. Working medium temperature waveform.

Figure 11 presents temperature of the medium in the inlet and outlet of the coil heat exchanger. As it can be seen, after some time the waveform of temperature is stabilised and almost reaches a quasi-stastic state. One can notice a small amplitude of the working medium changes, about 2°C, as well as that temperatures above 0°C that are maintained at the outlet of the exchanger. It has positive influence on the conditions of heat exchanger operation as it improves the thermal coefficient of performance.

5. Conclusion

Final effects of the R&D studies in the context of the research results will allow for quantitative and qualitative analysis of the influence of coupling photo-thermal collectors with a heat pump in the lower part of the heat pump on the energy output, as well as productivity and general efficiency of the installation [4, 9]. The economic analysis together with the what-if analysis will enable to consider the influence of control algorithms and characteristics of energy receivers, which should allow to optimize the choice of technological installation scheme selection to the building where it is to be installed.

The result of the R&D research in the implementation aspect will be preparation of the offer for energy system working on the basis of photo-thermal collectors with a heat pump that uses the effect of synergy of their coupling in the lower part of the pump and component elements of such a system.

References

1. D. Butrymowicz, Baj P., K. Śmierciew, *Cooling technique*, PWN, Warszawa (2014)
2. A. Gużda, Selected refrigerants used in a heat pumps, Zeszyty Naukowe Politechniki Opolskiej, Mechanika, z.105, p. 73-76 (2015)
3. D. Hillel, *Introduction to soil physics*. Academic Press, San Diego, CA (1982)
4. Z. Kusto, *Uwarunkowania ekonomicznej efektywności pomp ciepła*. IMP PAN, Gdańsk, (2006)
5. W. Oszczak, *Ogrzewanie domów z zastosowaniem pomp ciepła*. WKŁ, Warszawa, (2009)
6. V. Pisarev, *Projektowanie instalacji grzewczych z pompami ciepła*. Oficyna Wydawnicza Politechniki Rzeszowskiej, Rzeszów (2013)
7. D.M. Ramos, F.R. Cunha, Y.D. Sobral, J.L.A. Fontoura Rodrigues, Computer simulations of magnetic fluids in laminar pipe flows. Journal of Magnetic Materials 289, p. 238-241 (2005)
8. M.R. Richter, S.M. Song, J.M. Yin, M.H. Kim, C.W. Bullard, P.S. Hrnjak, Experimental results of transcritical CO2 heat pump for residential application. Energy 28, p. 1005-1019 (2003)
9. M. Saikawa, S. Koyama, Thermodynamic analysis of vapor compression heat pump cycle for tap water heating and development of CO2 heat pump water heater for residential use. Appl. Therm. Eng. 106, p. 1236–1243 (2016)
10. Typical meteorological years and statistical climatic data for buildings energy calculations: https://www.miir.gov.pl/strony/zadania/budownictwo/charakterystyka-energetyczna-budynkow/dane-do-obliczen-energetycznych-budynkow-1/

One day ahead forecasting of energy generating in photovoltaic systems

Grzegorz Dralus[1,*], *Grzegorz* Dec[2] , and *Damian* Mazur[1]

[1]Rzeszow University of Technology, Department of Electrical and Computer Engineering Fundamentals, 35-959 Rzeszów, Poland
[2]Rzeszow University of Technology, Department of Computer and Control Engineering, 35-959 Rzeszów, Poland

Abstract. The article presents selected methods for forecasting energy generated by a solar system. Short-term forecasts are necessary in planning the work of renewable energy sources and their share in the energy market. Forecasting from the one-day horizon is one of the short-term forecasts. Rear-round prognostic models have been designed using various forecasting methods such as regression, neural networks or time series. On the basis of one day ahead forecasts the accuracy of designed models was assessed. The influence of selected weather factors on forecasts accuracy is also presented, only for models implemented by MLP neural networks. As well as the results of research on the impact of the model structure (as MLP neural network) on the accuracy of forecasts are presented.

1 Introduction

Currently, renewable energy is an important element of the energy market in the world. Its share in the total energy balance is constantly growing. One of the significant sources of renewable energy is solar energy, from which electric energy is generated in solar systems. Solar energy is considered to be inexhaustible, free and clean. For these reasons, photovoltaic systems have gained great acclaim and importance as an alternative to conventional sources. However, the production of energy from photovoltaic cells is characterized by great variability and is strongly dependent on weather conditions. Changes in the volume of this production must be regularly monitored and supplemented with conventional energy sources. Short-term changes in the amount of energy generated from renewable sources as a result of sudden weather changes may be particularly dangerous for the power system. On the other hand, an important problem is improving the control performance of energy transmission from PV sources. Therefore, an important issue in the energy balance is accurate forecasting of energy production in the short term.

Short-term forecasting in the energy sector means forecasting in the time horizon up to several hours. Therefore, forecasting one day ahead, is classified as short-term forecasting.

Except the time horizons, the parameters subject to forecasting are also important. In the case of short-term forecasts, average power values are usually applied in periods from 15

* Corresponding author: gregor@prz.edu.pl

minutes to 1 hour. In the case of predictions with a day-ahead, the average daily power value or quantity of energy produced within 24 hours is used. Forecasts of energy production in PV systems are usually based on the value of solar irradiation during the period considered, weather conditions and others.

For forecasting energy generated in photovoltaic systems, different methods are used, for example, regression, time series, mathematical models, artificial intelligence, hybrid methods and many others. Among the artificial intelligence methods, neural networks achieved great success in forecasting. Therefore, different types of neural networks are used to build forecasting models, as well as combinations of neural networks with fuzzy logic or wavelet transform. The choice of neural network type usually does not depends on the horizon of forecasts, access and scope of data and the availability of numerical forecasts (NWP).

To forecast the amount of energy generated in solar PV installations, feed-forward neural network is usually used [1-4]. Other types of neural networks, such as radial basis function neural network (RBF) [5-6], recurrent neural network (RNN), e.g. the Elman network [6], dynamic neural networks of the type FTDNN and DTDNN [7 -9] are also successfully used. Forecasting can also be used with Support Vector Machine (SVM) [10], physical models [4], time series analysis [11 - 13] with recurrent neural network [14 - 15]. The connection of neural network with fuzzy-logic can also be used in the power forecasting of photovoltaic panels [16].

2 PV systems and methods

This chapter describes the solar system on which our research is carried out. In addition, this chapter presents a brief description of the forecasting methods, as well as a description of the prognostic models designed for research.

2.1 Description of a solar PV system

The photovoltaic system from which the data needed to build forecasting models and for which forecasts will be made is presented in Fig.1. Fig. 1 shows a block diagram of a real low power system, which is located in Rzeszów (50°02'N 22°17'E).

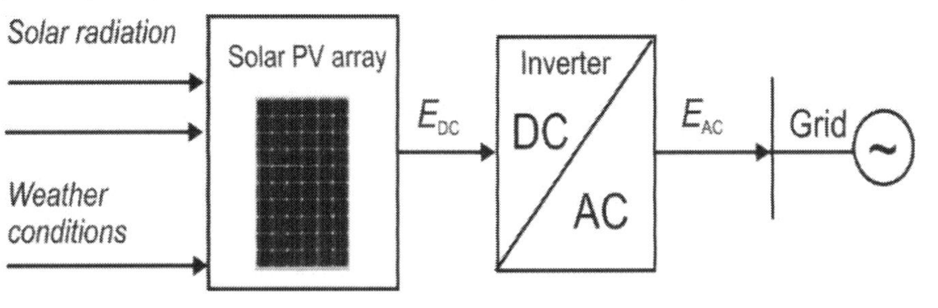

Fig. 1. The solar photovoltaic system.

The presented system consists of three monocrystalline modules with a total peak power of 330Wp, connected to a voltage inverter. Photovoltaic modules mounted at a fixed angle of 30 degree to the horizon. In the PV system the electric power of the solar system before and behind the inverter and the efficiency of the system were measured. A measuring system installed in the solar system collected DC voltage and DC current measurements before the inverter, AC voltage, AC current, and AC power behind the inverter. At the same time, the solar irradiation was also measured. All parameters were measured every 10 seconds and averaged to 1 minute values.

Data from the measurement system were prepared so that they could be used to build forecasting models with the horizon of one day ahead. On the basis of measurements of AC voltage, AC current and AC power, the total amount of AC energy (behind the inverter) generated during one day by the system was determined. Additionally, for the objectivity of the results obtained, the generated energy was scaled to one square meter of the active surface of a solar PV panel. These are measurement data from the PV system and meteorological conditions collected in one year (from November 2013 to October 2014 year). The data set collected for the study covers 340 days (25 days are missing, due to incorrect measurement readings or lack of reading). In addition, the data from the whole year was divided into training and testing data sets.

In order to determine the parameters of the forecasting models, in addition to the electrical data of the PV system, the data on weather conditions at the system's place of work are needed. Data on weather conditions on a given day are input data for models. In this work, seven weather factors taken from the local meteorological station (see Table 1) are used as input data for predicting models. As the eight explanatory factor, the daily value of irradiation in the system's working place is used.

Table 1 contains a list of explanatory factors and their correlation coefficients with the amount of energy generated in the PV system. Correlation calculations were performed for data for the year-round model. Correlation coefficients were calculated separately for the training data set and test data set. The correlation coefficient determines which selected explanatory factor affects the amount of energy produced in the solar PV system.

Table 2. Formatting sections, subsections and subsubsections.

No	Spacing	Correlation coefficient
1	Average daily air temperature	0.570
2	The highest air temperature	0.689
3	Visibility	0.584
4	Daily wind speed	-0.399
5	Daily rainfall	0.164
6	Cloudiness	-0.720
7	Wind direction	-0.070
8	Daily solar irradiation	0.993

2.2 One day ahead forecasting year-round models

Acquisition of renewable energy in solar systems strongly depends on the weather conditions that prevail throughout the year, as well as the seasons and other factors. In different seasons the length of the day changes, that is, the action of the sun, the height of the sun on the horizon, cloud cover and temperature also change. In literature, you can find different strategies for building prognostic models.

Most studies on short-term prediction of power generation in solar systems in the 24-hour horizon. There are works describing the models that generate 24 hour ahead forecastings with a 10-minute step, [7], with a 15-minute step [4, 14] or with a one-hour step [3, 5, 6]. These studies concerned forecasting models designed for selected months [4] or for all months of the year [5, 6, 14].

Forecasts in the 24-hour horizon are performed for the needs of current control and planning of renewable energy source (RES) work. However, such accurate forecasts are not needed for electricity trading in local or regional energy markets. For energy sales operators, forecasts of the daily energy production volume from a given RES source are sufficient to be able to receive this energy to the grid and sell it to another customer. Therefore, the amount of RES energy purchased and sold can be based on forecasts in the horizon one day ahead. There are not many studies in the subject in the literature so far. Few works present methods and forecasting models in the horizon of one day ahead [2, 5]. So, taking this issue at work seems to be justified. Therefore, our goal is to develop several methods to forecast one day ahead of the amount of energy generated in PV systems.

In order to examine the suitability and accuracy of selected predicting methods, it was assumed that the studies will be conducted on a year-round mode.

The following methods of one day ahead forecasting were selected for the research:

- Multiple regression
- Neural network MLP
- Neural network RBF
- Support Vector Machine SVM
- Nonlinear autoregressive model with exogenous inputs and MLP neural networks

2.3 Forecasting models

The following methods and tools are used to build predictive models for the PV system.

2.3.1 Linear regression model

Regression is a statistical method that permit to predict unknown values of a dependent variable based on known values of an independent (explanatory) variable. Regression, in which there is more than one independent variable, is also called multiple regression.

In the case of multiple regression models, where there is a greater number of explanatory variables, the following formula is applied to the regression line [17]:

$$Y = b_1 X_1 + b_2 X_2 + \ldots + b_n X_n + a \quad (1)$$

where: Y is a dependent variable (output), X_1, X_2, X_n, - independent (explanatory) variables, b_1, b_2, b_n -regression coefficients, a - constant, random factor.
In the year-round model using linear regression, the forecasts of energy production in the PV system are adjusted according to the equation (1) for eight explanatory factors listed in Table 1. Optimization of regression coefficients b_1, b_2, ..., b_n of the model was made using the least squares method.

2.3.2 MLP neural network model

Neural networks due to their many features are successfully used in many, very different fields such as finance, medicine, technology or physics. Neural networks can be used wherever tasks related to prediction, classification or control appear. The basic feature of neural networks is the ability to generalize or generalize knowledge for new data previously unknown, i.e. not published during the course of learning. This is also referred to as the ability of neural networks to approximate the value of a function of several variables. Thus, neural networks are also very well-suited for building prognostic models.

Among many types, feedforward neural networks are often used for forecasting tasks, in particular neural network called multilayer perceptron (MLP) [1,2,4].

A feedforward neural two-layers MLP neural network is shown in Fig. 2.

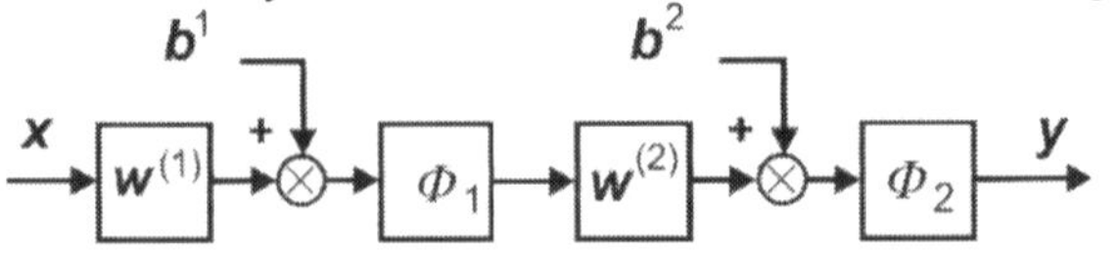

Fig. 2. A feedforward MLP neural network.

The output of j-th neuron in of neural network is given by following formula (2):

$$y_j(t) = f_2\left[\sum_{k}^{K} w_{jk}^{(2)} \cdot f_1\left[\sum_{i=0}^{I}\left(w_{ki}^{(1)} x_i(t) + b_k^{(1)}\right)\right] + b_j^{(2)}\right] \quad (2)$$

where: $\boldsymbol{w}^{(1)} \in R^{KxI}$, $\boldsymbol{w}^{(2)} \in R^{JxK}$, $\boldsymbol{b}^{(1)} \in R^{K}$, $\boldsymbol{b}^{(2)} \in R^{J}$, $\boldsymbol{x} \in R^{I}$, $\boldsymbol{y} \in R^{J}$, $x_i(t)$ is the i-th input of the neural network, y_j is the j-th output of the neural network, $w_{ki}^{(1)}$ and $w_{jk}^{(2)}$ - the weights between neuros, $b_k^{(1)}$ and $b_j^{(2)}$ are the biases of neuros, t is a sample of data.

In the operation of MLP neural networks, an important issue is the selection of the transfer function. In equation (2) there are two transfer functions denoted as $f_1() \in \Phi_1$ in first layer and denoted as $f_2() \in \Phi_2$ in second layer. Typically, the first layer called the hidden layer uses non-linear transfer functions such as log-sigmoid or tan-sigmoid. In the second layer called the output layer, a linear function is usually used, but other functions can be used successfully.

The MLP neural networks was used to build a model for predicting the energy of the PV system. Thus, the neuronal model uses eight explanatory factors (see Table 1), which are inputs the model. The model output is a forecast of the daily amount of energy generated in the PV system.

For the base forecasting model (e.g MLP neural network) was adopted the following structure: 8-7-1 (8 inputs, 7 neurons in the hidden layer, 1 neuron in the output layer). All neurons in hidden layer use the log-sigmoidal transfer function. A linear transfer function is used in the output layer.

The parameters of the forecasting model were determined by minimizing quality criterion such as a Root Mean Square Error (RMSE).

2.3.3 RBF neural network model

FBF neural network is a variation of the MLP neural network, in which neurons in the signal processing uses radial basis functions. RBF neural networks have found application in solving classification problems, tasks of approximation of functions of many variables, as well as in prediction problems.

The architecture of RBF neural networks has a structure analogous to the structure of a multilayer neural network with one hidden layer, which represents a nonlinear mapping carried out by neurons with a radial base function. In practice, several types of radial basis functions are used, but the Gaussian function is most commonly used, which is described by following formula:

$$\phi(r) = \exp(-\beta r^2) \tag{3}$$

where: β is the parameter of smoothness of the Gaussian function.
Other examples of radial basis functions are the polynomial function, the multiquadratic or the inverse multiquadratic function.

RBF neural networks were also used to build a forecasting model, in which eight explanatory factors are used (see Table 1). As the radial basis function, the Gaussian function was accepted.

2.3.4 SVM model

Support Vector Machine (SVM) was also used to build a model for predicting production of electricity by the solar PV system. This method can be successfully used to estimate multidimensional functions, for approximation and prediction.
Based on the knowledge in the field of SVM, a forecasting model was designed, which uses eight explanatory factors as input data (see Table 1). The SVM model uses a polynomial 3rd order kernel function and data normalization.

2.3.5 Nonlinear autoregressive model

The forecasting model of the amount of energy production by a PV system can also be built by using nonlinear autoregressive model with exogenous inputs (NARX). The NARX model is based on the linear aureressive model, which is commonly used in time-series analysis.

The NARX model is defined by the following equation [18]:

$$y(t) = f\big(y(t-1), \dots, y(t-n), u(t-1), \dots, u(t-m)\big) \tag{4}$$

where: $f()$ is some nonlinear function, $y(t)$ is the output of the model at the t time, $y(t\text{-}1)$, $y(t\text{-}n)$ are the past values of the model output, $u(t\text{-}1)$, $u(t\text{-}m)$ are the inputs of the NARX model, n and m are the maximum time lag for the output and input. Therefore, in the NARX model, the next value of the dependent output signal $y(t)$ is regressed on previous values of the output signal and previous values of an independent (exogenous) input signal.

Nonlinear function $f()$ in formula (4) is performed by MLP neural networks with a log-sigmoid transfer function in hidden layers. Two forecasting models with the first and second order recursion were designed.

The first model is the first order NARX model with the structure 5-8-3-1. The model has 5 inputs for 5 explanatory factors (factor from Table 1 e.g.: average air temperature, the highest air temperature, visibility, daily irradiation, and energy generated on the previous day). In addition, the model has two hidden layers, 8 neurons in the first and 3 neurons in the second hidden layer, nonlinear transfer functions of the log-sigmoid type. The model has one output, on which we obtain the forecast of energy production on a given day.

3 Results

In this chapter, errors of energy production forecasts made by the developed models are presented.

To estimate the accuracy of forecasting models a Mean Absolute Percentage Error (MAPE) of the forecasts was determined. The MAPE error was calculated by following formula:

$$MAPE = \frac{1}{T}\sum_{i=1}^{T}\frac{\left|E_i^P - E_i\right|}{E_i}\cdot 100\% \quad (5)$$

where: E_i is measured energy in PV system in the i-th day, E_i^P is prediction of energy generated in the i-th day, T - number of days.

Table 2 presents forecasting errors of energy for all developed models. Forecast errors were estimated by the measure of MAPE error (5). MAPE errors were determined for the training data of the learning phase of the models, as well as for the test data of the verification phase.

Table 2. The errors forecasts of energy generation in the year-round models.

Model	Estimation MAPE [%]	Verification MAPE [%]
Multiple regression	16.2	11.7
MLP neural network(8-7-1)	3.61	3.30
RBF neural network(8-136-1)	4.32	3.67
SVM	5.03	4.65
1st order NARX (5-8-3-1)	4.19	3.16

The complete set of data was divided into a training set containing data from 280 days and a test set containing data from 60 days. The training and testing set contained eight explanatory factors (except NARX' models) and the daily amount of energy produced in the solar PV system. Parameters of the MLP neural model were determined using Levenberg Marquard (LM) learning algorithms [19]. The weights and number of neurons in the hidden layer in the RBF neural network were determined by the least squares method and the back propagation learning algorithm. Thus, RBF neuron model has 8 inputs, 136 neurons in the hidden layer and 1 neuron in the output layer. The parameters of the 1st order NARX model were determined using the LM algorithm. Initial weights were generated randomly in the models, which use neural network.

For the test data, the most accurate is the 1st order NARX model, in which the MAPE error of the forecast is equal to 3.16%. The MPAE error around 3 percent means that year-round model generates accurate forecasts. The MLP neural network model is the second most accurate (MAPE error is 3.30%). The RBF model generates predictions with slightly larger errors than the top two models, but their accuracy is quite good. In the SVM model, the MAPE error is below five percent, i.e. the model can be considered to be sufficiently accurate. A relatively large error in the forecast is generated in the linear regression model (around 11.7%), but this model is the least computationally demanding one.

Fig. 3 presents an example of the forecast of and the real amount of energy production by the solar photovoltaic panels for test data (verification phase) for a selected model, i.e. for RBF neural networks model. The forecast covers 60 selected days of the whole year, includes 15 days from each season.

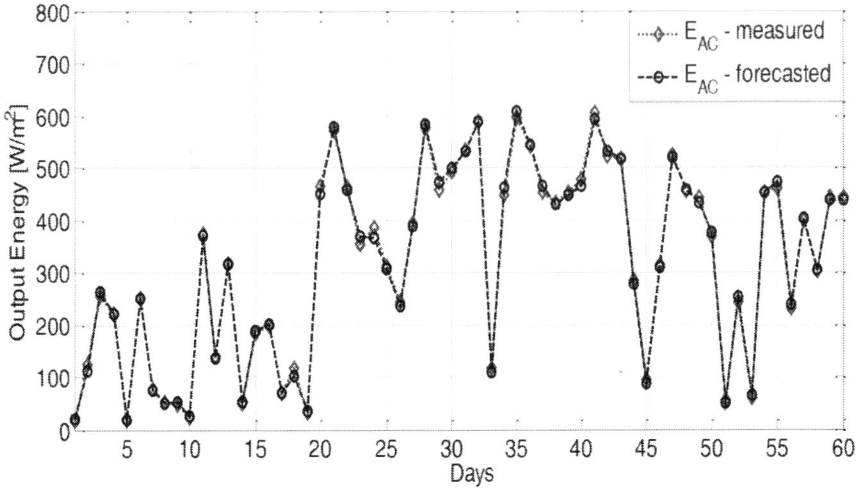

Fig. 3. The course of the AC energy (E_{AC}) forecast generated by RBF neural network model for the test data.

4 Research on the impact of model structure and explanatory factors on the accuracy of forecasts

This chapter describes the results of studies on the impact of the MLP neural network structure on the accuracy of the generated forecasts, as well as on the influence of the number of explanatory factors on the accuracy of forecasts.

Studies on the impact of the neural network structure on the accuracy of the generated forecasts were carried out on six models built of MLP neural networks. Three models were built from a network with one hidden layer and contained 7, 9 and 13 neurons in hidden layer, respectively. The other three models consisted of two hidden layers that contained the following number of neurons in the first and second hidden layer, 5-3, 7-3 and 9-3 neurons, respectively. The basic research on the impact of the model structure on the accuracy of forecasts was carried out for the maximum number of explanatory factors, i.e. up to eight factors (see Table 1). In addition, an impact study was conducted for four and two explanatory factors (see below). The results of these studies are presented in Table 3, which contains MAPE errors of predictions for the test data.

On the six MLP neural models, studied on the influence of the amount of the explanatory factors on the accuracy of the prognostic model was conducted. The point of reference are forecast errors for the 8 input explanatory factors (the first variant). In the second variant, only for four explanatory models generate the forecasts. This four selected explanatory factors have a large correlation coefficient (greater than 0.2) and these are following factors: average air temperature, the highest air temperature, visibility, daily irradiation. In the third variant, the number of explanatory factors was reduced only to two factors, with have the highest non-negative correlation (e.g. the highest air temperature and daily irradiation).

The influence of the number of explanatory factors on the accuracy of forecast in MLP neural network models is shown in Table 3 and Fig. 4.

Fig. 4 shows the influence of the number of explanatory factors on the accuracy of forecasts (i.e. MAPE error values) for six MLP neural networks as predictive models. At the same time, in Fig. 4, it can be observe the influence of the structure of neural models on the accuracy of forecasts.

Table 3. *MAPE* errors of energy forecast in MLP neural network models (x-number of inputs).

Structure of the model	2 factors	4 factors	8 factors
x-7-1	3.35	3.45	3.30
x-9-1	3.64	3.51	3.35
x-13-1	3.34	3.46	3.29
x-5-3-1	3.36	3.57	3.05
x-7-3-1	3.25	3.31	3.25
x-9-3-1	3.38	3.12	3.13

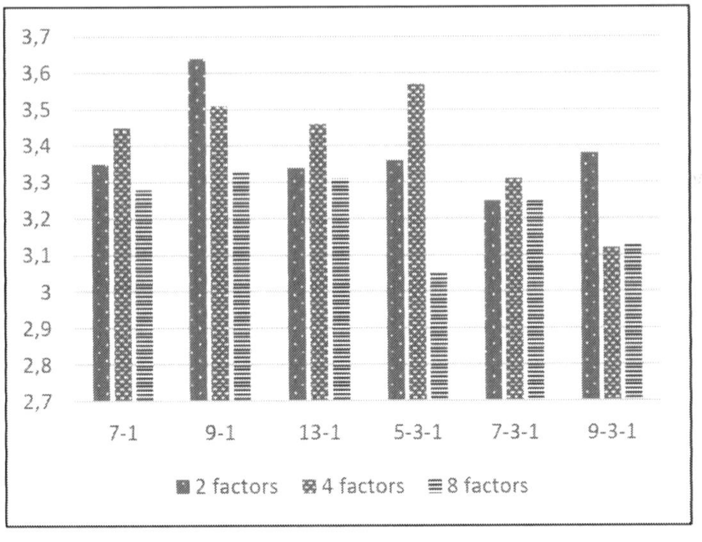

Fig. 4. Values of *MAPE* forecast errors depending on the structure of the MLP neural network model.

The analysis of results obtained shows that the MLP neural network models with two hidden layers generate more accurate forecasts than models with one hidden layer, but only in the case of forecasts for eight explanatory factors. In other cases, models with two hidden layers are usually more accurate.

The analysis obtained results from the fact that a decrease in the number of explanatory factors causes an increase in the errors of forecasts. Models using eight explanatory factors to generate forecasts are the most accurate, but with one exception. The only exception is the model with structure (4-9-3-1) using four explanatory factors.

Conclusions

The work presents the results of research on one day ahead forecasting of electricity production by the solar PV system. For this purpose, various forecasting methods have been developed. The forecasting of AC energy production was generally based on eight explanatory factors (seven weather factors and daily irradiation level). In the NARX models, smaller number of explanatory factors were used. The developed methods and training sets were used to build year-round models. The models were verified using a test set that was 60 days long.

Due to the fact that for MLP neural networks it is difficult to determine the optimal structure in advance, therefore the influence of the model structure (i.e. MLP neural networks) on the accuracy of forecasts was examined in the work. The work also includes the results of research on the influence of the number of explanatory factors (weather factors) on the accuracy of energy forecasting.

The models provide forecasts of energy production by the solar system with satisfactory accuracy. Forecast errors in models using artificial intelligence range from 3.16% to 4.65%. but errors in the regression model are at the level of 11.7%.

The MLP neural networks and the first order NARX model based on MLP neural network are the most effective tool for one day ahead forecasting. However, most of the developed methods can successfully apply the tasks of forecasting of energy generation in photovoltaic systems for practical application.

References

1. F. Almonacid, C. Rus, P. J. Perez, L. Hontoria, Renewable Energy, vol. **34**, pp. 2743-2750 (2009)
2. G. Dralus, Z. Gomółka, D. Mazur, A. Smoleń, *Proceedings of International Interdisciplinary PhD Workshop* (2017),
3. P. Piotrowski, Electrical Review (in Polish), **5**, pp. 162-165 (2015)
4. Y. Huang J. Lu, Ch. Liu, X. Xu, W. Wang, X. Zhou, International Conference on Power System Technology (POWERCON) (2010)
5. Ch. Chen, S. Duan, T. Cai, B. Liu, Solar Energy vol. **85**, Issue 11, pp. 2856-287 (2011)
6. A. Yona, T. Senju, A. Saber, T. Funabashi, H. Sekine, Ch-H. Kim, Power and Energy Society General Meeting - Conversion and Delivery of Electrical Energy in the 21st Century, IEEE (2008)
7. N. Al-Messabi , Y. Li, I. El-Amin, C. Goh, Comput. Intell., pp.10-15 (2012)
8. Z. Gomolka, E. Dudek-Dyduch, Y.P. Kondratenko, From Homogeneous Network to Neural Nets with Fractional Derivative Mechanism. Artificial Intelligence and Soft Computing, vol **10245**, pp 52-63, (2017)
9. Z. Gomolka, B. Twarog, E. Zeslawska, Cognitive Investigation on Pilot Attention During Take-Offs and Landings Using Flight Simulator. Artificial Intelligence and Soft Computing. Lecture Notes in Computer Science, vol **10246**, pp 432-443, (2017)
10. J. Shi, W-J. Lee, Y. Liu, Y. Yang, P. Wang, 2011 EEEI Industry Appl. Society Annual Meeting (IAS), IEEE, pp.1-6 (2011).
11. L. Martin, L.F. Zarzalejo, J. Polo, A. Navarro, R. Marchante, M. Cony, Solar Energy, **84**, pp. 1772-1781 (2010).
12. Z.Gomolka, B.Twarog, E. Zeslawska, A. Lewicki, T. Kwater, Using Artificial Neural Networks to Solve the Problem Represented by BOD and DO Indicators, Water 2018, **10(1)**, 4
13. Z. Gomolka, Neurons' Transfer Function Modeling with the Use of Fractional Derivative. Contemporary Complex Systems and Their Dependability. DepCoS-RELCOMEX 2018. Advances in Intelligent Systems and Computing, vol **761**. Pp. 218 -227 , (2019)

14. M. Cococcioni, E. D'Andrea, B. Lazzerini, *11th International Conference on Intelligent Systems Design and Applications* (2011)
15. T. Cai, S. Duan, Ch. Chen, Power Electronics for Distributed Generation Systems (PEDG), 2nd IEEE International Symposium, pp.773-777 (2010)
16. F. Grimaccia, M. Mussetta, R. Zich, Fuzzy Systems (FUZZ), IEEE International Conference, pp.2454-2457 (2011)
17. D.A. Freedman, *Statistical Models: Theory and Practice* (2005)
18. L. Ljung, *System Identification: Theory for the user* (1987)
19. M.T. Hagan, M. Menhaj, IEEE Trans. on Neural Networks, vol. **5**, No. **6**, pp. 989-993 (1994)

ITM Web of Conferences **21**, 00024 (2018) https://doi.org/10.1051/itmconf/20182100024
CST 2018

Automatically conducted learning from textually expressed vacationers' opinions

Bartosz Jędrzejec[1,*], and *Krzysztof* Świder[1]

[1]Rzeszów University of Technology, Al. Powstańców Warszawy 12, 35-959-Rzeszów, Poland

Abstract. The automatically conducted consumers' opinions investigation is one of the most interesting potential applications of text analytics. In our study we perform a two steps procedure of learning from the textually expressed reviews concerning hotel services offered by a travel company. In the first stage we accomplish the necessary *Extract-Transform-Load* process utilizing one of the available web portals and required language resources. In the second stage each of the suitably pre-processed opinions is "linguistically evaluated", which results in a vector of numeric indicators characterizing its sentiment.

1 Introduction

1.1 Automated text analysis for consumer investigation

Automated text analysis (*text mining*) utilizes analytical methods to learn from collections of text data, like books, newspapers, emails or Web portals. Over the last two decades, we have observed an explosion of continuously growing consumer-generated content including discussions of products, services, hobbies, or brands. There are thousands of product websites which offer forums for consumer comment. Todays receivers of the information do not only consume the available content on the web, but in turn, actively annotate this content and generate new pieces of information. Within all this information lies knowledge about consumer opinions, decision-making, psychology, and culture that may be useful for consumer investigation [1, 2].

Although there are many ways to incorporate automated text analysis into consumer research, there is not much agreement on the standard set of methods, reporting procedures, steps of data inclusion, exclusion, sampling, and, where applicable, dictionary development and validation. Moreover, in order to provide the users, e.g. specialists in web marketing, with a truly operational tool, it seems to be a natural need to be able to develop text analysis applications not only for English but for any other language as well.

In our research, we developed the two steps procedure for learning from the textually expressed vacationers' opinions written in Polish. Essentially, we focused on *sentiment analysis*, which is the field of study that analyses human attitudes and emotions towards

[*] Corresponding author: bartoszj@prz.edu.pl

entities and their attributes expressed in a written text. In the following subsection we specify some significant features of sentiment analysis.

1.2 Sentiment analysis

Sentiment analysis is the computational study that analyses people's opinions, sentiments, emotions, and attitudes toward entities and their attributes expressed in a written text [3]. The entities can be products, services, organizations, individuals, events, issues, or topics. The problem is increasingly attractive in business and society offering numerous research challenges.

1.2.1 Opinions and sentiments

The main objective in sentiment analysis is typically to design effective algorithms and models to extract *opinions* from natural language text and to summarize them suitably. The term *opinion* can be considered as a broad concept that covers sentiment (evaluation, appraisal, or attitude) and associated information such as opinion target and the person who holds the opinion [3]. More formally, opinion O can be considered as the quintuple

$$O = (Entity, Aspect, Sentiment, Holder, Time).$$

The first element *Entity* denotes the opinion target, i.e. an object which the particular opinion refers to. Sometimes an opinion concerns a specific part or attribute of *Entity* called *Aspect*. Then follow: *Sentiment* which reflects an underlying positive or negative feeling implied by opinion, *Holder* – a person who formulated the opinion, and *Time* representing a moment when an opinion was issued. The simple example in Fig. 1 will perhaps be helpful in further clarification of crucial opinion components.

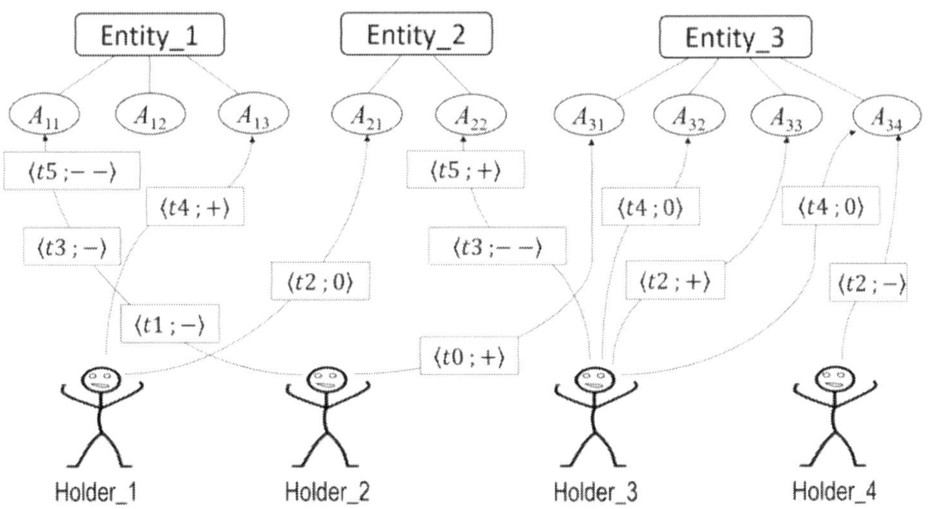

Fig. 1. An intuitive explanation of essential opinion components.

We assume that four persons depicted as *Holder_1, Holder_2, Holder_3*, and *Holder_4* are formulating a number of opinions referring to certain aspects of the three objects: *Entity_1*, *Entity_2*, and *Entity_3*. We further presume that the *Entity_1* is described by three aspects denoted by A_{11}, A_{12}, and A_{13}. Likewise the *Entity_2* has two aspects: A_{21} and A_{22}, etc. The fact that a *Holder_i* (i=1…4) has formulated an opinion about some aspect A_{jk} of an *Entity_j* (j=1…3) is represented by the line with an arrow connecting the opinion holder with the relevant aspect. Each opinion line is marked by one or more labels holding information about an opinion posting time and an assigned sentiment value. For example the label (t4 ; +) informs that at the moment t4 a positive opinion was formulated. Similarly (t3 ; – –) denotes a very negative opinion at the moment t3.

As reported in [3], sentiment analysis research has been mainly carried out at three levels of granularity: document level, sentence level, and aspect level. The task at the document level is to classify whether a whole opinion document expresses a positive or negative sentiment. The next level of granularity is to determine whether each *sentence* expresses a positive, negative, or neutral opinion. This level of analysis is closely related to *subjectivity classification*, which distinguishes sentences that express factual information (*objective sentences*) from sentences that express subjective views and opinions (*subjective sentences*). Neither document-level nor sentence-level analyses discover what people like and dislike exactly. In other words, they do not tell what each opinion is about, that is, the target of opinion. To obtain this level of fine-grained results, we need to go to the *aspect* level. Instead of looking at language units (documents, paragraphs, sentences, clauses, or phrases), aspect-level analysis directly looks at an opinion and its target.

1.2.2 Sentiment lexicon

The most important indicators of sentiments are *sentiment words*, also called *opinion words*. For example, *good*, *wonderful*, and *amazing* are positive sentiment words, and *bad*, *poor*, and *terrible* are negative sentiment words. Apart from individual words, there are also phrases and idioms, as for example, *cost an arm and a leg* in English. Sentiment words and phrases are instrumental to sentiment analysis. A list of such words and phrases is called a *sentiment lexicon* or *opinion lexicon*. Over the years, researchers have designed numerous algorithms to compile such lexicons.

In some cases a sentence containing sentiment words may not express any sentiment. This phenomenon happens in several types of sentences. Question (interrogative) sentences and conditional sentences are two main types, for example, "*Can you tell me which hotel in Crete is good*?" and "*If I can find a good hotel in Greece, I will book it*." Both these sentences contain the sentiment word *good*, but neither expresses a positive or negative opinion about any specific hotel.

1.3 Scope of the study

In order to test and introduce the analytical framework developed in this paper we used the real-world textual opinions posted by Polish speaking holidaymakers on a traveling company Web portal. In our work we concentrated on the *Extract-Transform-Load* process which is crucial for the whole analysis. The row data extracted from numerous websites was appropriately pre-processed and placed into regular structures suitable for analysis. Finally we performed tokenization chopping each review up into bigrams and applied a number of measures to get a numerical summarization of each opinion at the document level.

2 Data acquisition

In order to obtain data appropriate for the consecutive analysis we developed and applied a number of automatic procedures ready to accomplish the task.

2.1 Identifying data source

A number of popular social networking sites, such as Facebook and Instagram, as well as many portals, where users can present their opinions about products or services, are very good sources for developing an analytical database for sentiment analysis. In our study we exercised clients' reviews (opinions) presented on the websites of one of the Polish travel agencies referring to holidays spent in hotels offered by the agency. The general structure of the portal is illustrated in Fig. 2.

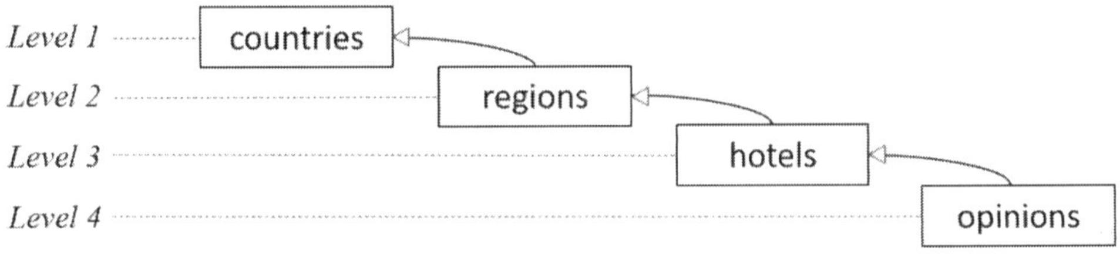

Fig. 2. The overall structure of the travel agency web portal.

Clients have an opportunity of entering the textual comments related to their stay in a hotel, as well as putting an overall numerical rating (1-6) determining the level of satisfaction - with the entire service as well as with selected aspects (room cleanliness, board, animations, etc.). Opinions are published on the website of a particular offer in a separate tab. The reviews are systematised in several levels including: destination (country), region, hotel, and particular opinion.

2.2 Extracting data

In order to create the reviews database i.e. the source repository for forthcoming analysis we used some web data extraction techniques also called *webscraping* (Fig. 3).

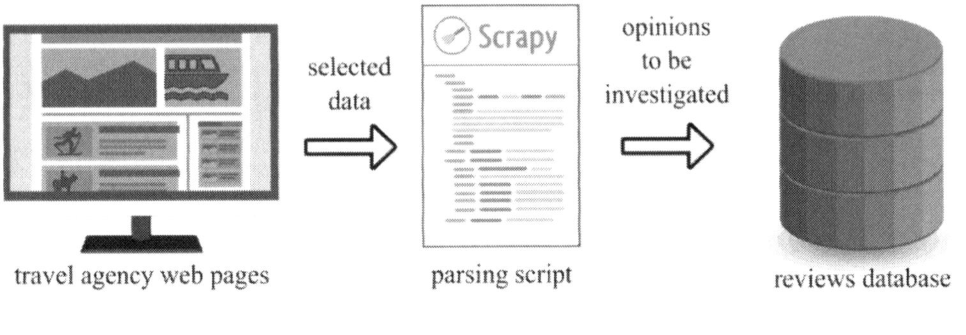

Fig. 3. The data extraction process.

The process of data extraction involves selecting elements related to desired data and parsing particular web pages. The application of this scheme requires a search through the website code consisting of HTML tags which mark relevant data. Very useful tools to accomplish the task are leading web browsers which provide appropriate functionalities and help to investigate even complex websites. After detecting elements responsible for displaying relevant data we need to connect to the websites of the travel agency in order to extract the desired values. For the purposes of this research, a parsing script has been developed to examine the applicable pages. It starts from the page with the list of destinations (countries to spent a holiday in), then deals with different regions in a country, and finally works with the list of hotels in a region. The script was limited to one destination (Greece) and resulted in 38,946 records containing information about hotels, regions, text opinions, and numerical ratings.

To implement the parsing script we used the Python programming language. It provides a number of programming libraries to support the website processing, from which, possibly the most popular one called *Scrapy*, was selected. The library is an open source product for creating website parsers, downloading data and storing it in a structured form. A properly prepared parser is able to process multiple sub-pages, at the same time significantly improving the preparation of the resulting database. The obtained data were saved in a CSV (*comma-separated values*) file, which is a popular format used both in analytical software and in processing with use of programming scripts.

3 Data transformation

Collecting data from external sources is usually only the first step in preparing them for analysis. Such data, especially when entered "manually" by users, is often not suitable for the construction of data mining models and needs to be modified accordingly to the requirements of the method chosen.

The most common operations on numerical data are: standardisation, discretization, identification of erroneous or empty values, etc. The pre-processing of textual data, such as opinions, requires preliminary operations different from those for numerical values. Typical text operations performed in this case are: deleting punctuation marks or case-sensitive unification. In addition, texts in languages other than English may require diacritical character conversion or the use of a basic form of a word. Our reviews database has been pre-processed in a few steps shown in Fig. 4.

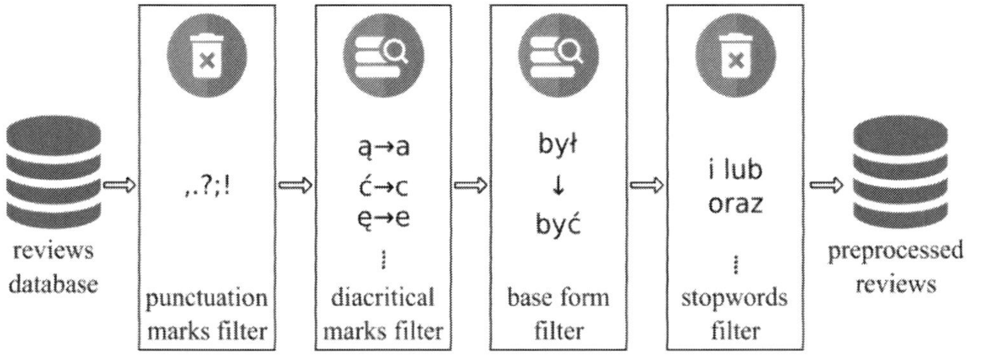

Fig. 4. The data pre-processing operations.

3.1 Removing punctuation and diacritical marks

At the first stage of opinion processing, all punctuation marks were removed from the text. This operation was performed in two sub-stages. First the punctuation marks were replaced by a space character, and then all the excess space marks were replaced by one. In this way, the problem is avoided in the case when the reviewer has forgotten to enter a space character after the punctuation mark, and deleting it would result in two words being merged into one.

The preliminary inspection of the source data was sufficient to discover that some text-based opinions were completed without Polish diacritical marks. This inconsistency needed to be unified so that all functions would work properly regardless of whether an author of any particular review used or not used the language specific characters. That is why we have decided to change the Polish signs to their equivalents without diacritical marks. To this end a necessary Python script was developed, which automatically modified the textually expressed opinions.

3.2 Transforming words into elementary form

Similarly to many other languages, together with the basic word form in Polish there is a number of derivative forms related to the flection. In the text analysis this could cause problems because as the same word can appear in multiple forms and at the same time should be identified as one unit. It is therefore important that the various forms that appear in the text be converted into their basic forms. For this purpose, a freely available dictionary of Polish words with their flection [4] was used. It is a collection created by hobbyists and used for spell-checkers and word games. The flection dictionary was used both to process textual opinions and to prepare a sentiment dictionary which included only basic forms with their emotional marks.

3.3 Eliminating stop-words

There exists a group of words which very often appear in sentences, but do not bring with them any content. This group includes, among others, conjunctions, most grammatical particles, numbers, etc. Such words are often omitted in the process of analysing texts although in the field of sentiment analysis, for example, some of them may have an impact on the emotional image of an utterance. Words that should not be removed in this case include "*not*", which reverses the meaning of the word as in "*not the best*", or "*very*", which enhances an emotional impression, such as "*very beautiful*".

4 Sentiment evaluation

The common and fundamental goal of sentiment analysis of free-text documents is to assign a predefined sentiment label as "positive" or "negative" to each document. Having collected and prepared textual data in section 3 we scheduled and programmed a number of operations aimed at sentiment evaluation and applied them for each of the pre-processed reviews. The result was the list of numerical values describing the review (see Fig. 5).

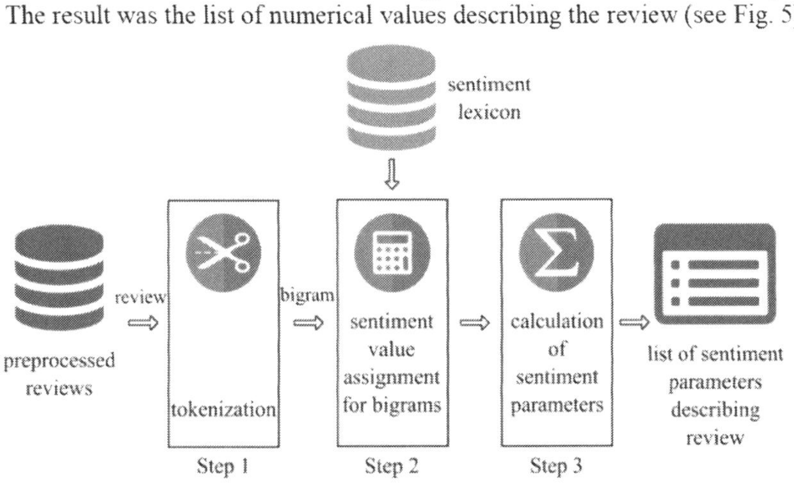

Fig. 5. The main steps of sentiment evaluation.

One of the key components of the schema in Fig. 5 is the sentiment lexicon which consists of sentiment words. As indicated in section 1, sentiment words and phrases are helpful for sentiment analysis. In our project we used the plWordNet 3.0 database [5, 6] which is a semantical vocabulary reflecting the lexical system of the Polish language. For a number of words it provides information about their emotional divergence as: fully negative (-m), slightly negative (-s), neutral (0), slightly positive (+s), and fully positive (+m). The plWordNet 3.0 provided as XML document was used as an input data to form our sentiment lexicon. To accomplish this another Python script was developed and applied. Additionally, in order to include more words we involved another repository introduced in [7]. Merging this two resources resulted in a sentiment lexicon containing 27472 words in their basic form with sentiment marks assigned.

The sentiment parameters summarizing each review were calculated by applying a number of operations forming the three steps in Fig. 5. We shortly explain them in the following subsections.

4.1 Document tokenization

A *token* is an instance of a sequence of characters in some particular document that are grouped together as a useful semantic unit for processing [8]. Thus tokenization in Fig. 5 means chopping each review up into pieces called *tokens*, perhaps at the same time throwing away certain characters.

The major question of the tokenization phase is what are the correct tokens to be used for sentiment analysis. The important disadvantage of using separate words as tokens is that in such a case the negations such as "not bad" and "not good" will be not properly treated during sentiment evaluation. In order to avoid the handling of only single words in a review we decided to use *bigrams* [9-12] which are generally tokens consisting of two consecutive words of the document. We assume, that the application of bigrams will increase the overall accuracy of sentiment evaluation.

4.2 Assigning sentiment to bigrams

In the next step of sentiment evaluation we use the sentiment lexicon to check the sentiment mark of the second word of each bigram. The involvement of bigrams makes it possible to detect such combinations of words in a review where the first word effects the sentiment value of the second one. For example, if we consider "*beautiful*" as the second word in a bigram, the typical cases of such influence are: strengthening ("*very beautiful*") or negation ("*not beautiful*"). If the second word of a bigram in not recorded in lexicon, the bigram is ignored.

4.3 Computing sentiment indicators at the document level

As mentioned in section 1, the document-level sentiment analysis aims to classify an opinion document (e.g. a product review) as expressing a positive or a negative attitude (sentiment). Following the approach we consider each document as a whole and do not study entities or aspects inside the document or determine sentiments expressed about them. Instead, in order to get more information about sentiment of each individual review a number of numerical values were calculated for this review through the third step in Fig. 5. The calculations were performed for each document (opinion) and resulted in 16 numerical indicators referring to sentiment. The examples of the calculated values are:

– number of words with positive, negative, and neutral sentiment,

- mean value of sentiment separately for the positive and negative words,
- (number of positive words) / (total number of words in review) ratio, etc.

Document sentiment classification can be considered as a traditional text classification problem with sentiment orientations or polarities as the classes. It is the relative simple sentiment analysis task and any supervised learning algorithms can be applied directly to solve the problem [3]. In such a case our numerical indicators for each individual review appear to be helpful in preparation the necessary training data.

5 Summary

We investigated the real-life textual opinions formulated by Polish speaking vacationers and published on a traveling company Web portal. The special emphasis was given to the *Extract-Transform-Load* process which is traditionally recognized as crucial for data analysis. The row data extracted from numerous websites was properly pre-processed and recorded as regular forms suitable for exploration. Finally, we applied a number of numerical measures to get a summarization of each opinion at the document level.

In our view, sentiment analysis of free-text documents is a common task but most likely it has to be solved separately for any particular language. This concerns first of all such language-specific issues as document pre-processing and sentiment lexicon generation. At the same time we believe that the parsing and pre-processing schema presented and discussed in this study could be applicable and helpful for a number of particular solutions.

References

1. A. Humphreys, R. Jen-Hui Wang, J Consum Res, **44**(6), 1274–1306 (2018)
2. S. Padmaja, S. S. Fatima, Int J Ad Hoc Sensor Ubiq Co, **4**(1), 21–33 (2013)
3. B. Liu, *Sentiment analysis. Mining opinions, Sentiments, and Emotions* (Cambridge University Press, 2015)
4. Zespół SJP, Lista słów z odmianami (*A repository of Polish vocabulary resources available on* https://sjp.pl/slownik/odmiany/) (2018)
5. M. Maziarz, M. Piasecki, E. Rudnicka, S. Szpakowicz, P. Kedzia, *Proceedings of COLING 2016, the 26th International Conference on Computational Linguistics: Technical Papers*, 2259-2268 (2016)
6. M. Zasko-Zielinska, M. Piasecki, S. Szpakowicz, *Proceedings of the International Conference Recent Advances in Natural Language Processing*, 721-730 (2015)
7. A. Wawer, D. Rogozinska, *2012 IEEE 12th International Conference on Data Mining Workshops*, 724–730 (2012)
8. C. D. Manning, P. Raghavan, H. Schütze, *An Introduction to Information Retrieval* (Cambridge University Press, 2009)
9. S. Young, G. Evermann, M. Gales, T. Hain, D. Kershaw, G. Moore, J. Odell, D. Ollason, D. Povey, V. Valtchev, P. Woodland, *HTK Book* (2005)
10. P. Lamere, P. Kwok, E. Gouvea, B. Raj, R. Singh, W. Walker, P. Wolf, *The CMU Sphinx-4 speech recognition system* (2004)
11. E. Whittaker, P. Woodland, Comput Speech Lang, **17**(1), 87–104 (2003)
12. T. Hirsimäki, J. Pylkkönen, M. Kurimo, IEEE T Audio Speech, **17**(4), 724–732 (2009)

Computer-aided processing of the oculomotor signal

Tomasz Lewandowski[1*], and *Anna* Lewandowska[2]

[1]Institute of Technical Engineering, State School of Technology and Economics, 37-500 Jaroslaw, Czarniecki Street 16, Poland
[2]Institute of Healthcare, State School of Technology and Economics, 37-500 Jaroslaw, Czarniecki Street 16, Poland

Abstract. Specific features of oculomotor signal and availability of high-end measurement equipment, as well as using modern IT techniques and tools creates the possibility of automatic processing of this type of data and extensive use of developed algorithms. Analysis of such data is a tedious and complex process so computer processing of the oculomotor signal makes the process less time-consuming, more precise and effective. The article discusses data filtering and removing noise, detection of saccades and fixations and determination of characteristic oculomotor parameters and then analysis using neural networks (unidirectional, two-layer neural network with backpropagation learning method and Kohonen's self-organising network) and application supporting the analysis process. The proposed test method allows registration of a view path followed by its automatic analysis to obtain objective parameters characterising the movement of the eyeball. The motor apparatus of the eyeball, due to its high sensitivity to changes in the body, can serve as a measure of general health.

1 Introduction

Registration and computer processing of biomedical signals is currently the subject of numerous works in the field of biomedical engineering, with ECG, EEG and EMG being the most frequently examined signals. Other biomedical signals, such as the oculomotor signal, are examined relatively less frequently [1]. However, considering the complex structure and mode of action of the organ of sight, as well as significance of information transferred to the brain, understanding of the substance and determining the characteristic parameters of the oculomotor signal are an extremely important scientific and practical aspect. The most frequently undertaken studies concern the use of the oculomotor signal in usability tests [2-4], tests on reading [5-8] or sleep phase classification [9-11]. The usage of the oculomotor signal in medicine is extremely important, taking into consideration care for human life and health, and specific features of this signal, availability of high-end measurement equipment, as well as using modern IT techniques and tools, creates the possibility of automatic processing of this type of data and extensive use of developed algorithms, e.g. in the diagnosis of neurological diseases.

* Corresponding author: tomasz.lewandowski@pwste.edu.pl

Analysis of such data is, however, a tedious and complex process which necessitates exceptional computational discipline and the use of heuristic computational methods. A medical specialist or an oculography scientist can easily indicate the place of the fixations and saccades in the eye movement chart. However, computer processing of the oculomotor signal makes the process less time-consuming, more precise and effective.

2 Acquisition of the oculomotor signal

Useful signal parameters. On the basis of literature analysis and medical consultations, parameters of eye movement important for the diagnosis of Parkinson's disease were determined, and the method of their acquisition was proposed, e.g. resting amplitude measured during the observation of a static object, spontaneous saccade latency measured during spontaneous transfer of sight between immovable objects.

Visual tasks. In order to obtain relevant measurement data, a set of visual tasks was prepared in terms of duration, resolution, dynamics, readability and the possibility of estimating oculomotor parameters. The oculatory data obtained as a result of the conducted measurements are characterised by high precision, so their processing requires the use of specific calculation tools in order to isolate the characteristic behaviour of the eyeball and the parameters that make it possible to classify the measurement.

Measurement method. The oculomotor signal was obtained by the photoelectric method which is based on the measurement of the beam of light reflected by the surface of the eyeball, generated by an artificial source, most often – infra red radiation. The radiation is emitted by a pair of LED illuminators, placed symmetrically to the eyeball, which, after reflection from the iris, is registered by two IR photodetectors. Due to the scleral and iris reflectivity, the intensity of the reflected radiation is a function of the angle of rotation of the eyeball [12,13]. The main advantages of this method are: non-invasiveness, high measurement accuracy, low interference sensitivity.

Research group. Visual tests were carried out on patients with diagnosed Parkinson's disease, as well as on young and healthy people as a control group. This division was used in order to distinguish between ocular disorders caused by age and those caused by the disease.

3 Stages of processing of the oculomotor signal

Automatic analysis of the oculomotor signal requires the use of appropriate algorithms based on finding a method of distinguishing between real changes in the position of the eyeball from those generated by various types of interference. In the literature several techniques of identifying oculomotor events are described: based on speed, based on variability, based on areas [14].

Every detection algorithm for oculomotor events has three important tasks to perform: removing interference from the signal, detecting fixations and saccades and determining the parameters of eyeball movements (duration of the saccade, speed of the saccade, speed of free movement etc.) that would allow formulation of conclusions concerning the work of the sight organ.

3.1 Filtering and removing noise

The registration of the oculomotor signal is accompanied by the registration of disturbances of various origins (innate eye properties, abnormal measurement conditions, head movements etc.) that have a significant impact on the quality of measurement data. Very often, measuring devices pre-filter the measured signal values, but in most cases it is necessary to perform additional data cleaning.

The most undesirable phenomenon during the measurement, having a huge impact on the quality of the results, was a movement of the head accompanying tracking of the objects moving during the show. The consequence of a sudden head movement is the vestibulo-ocular reflex that negatively affects the value of the collected data.

In order to filter out disturbances of the oculomotor signal, the filtration method was applied to eliminate the samples that go beyond the empirically determined tolerance range [15,16]. The direction and sense of the movement, as well as the reference signal value at every measurement point was known, and this fact was used during the filtration. On this basis, the tolerance range for the signal value can be determined. Above this range, the signal would be considered as a disturbance and removed from further analysis (Fig. 1). This threshold is selected experimentally, depending on the type of visual task.

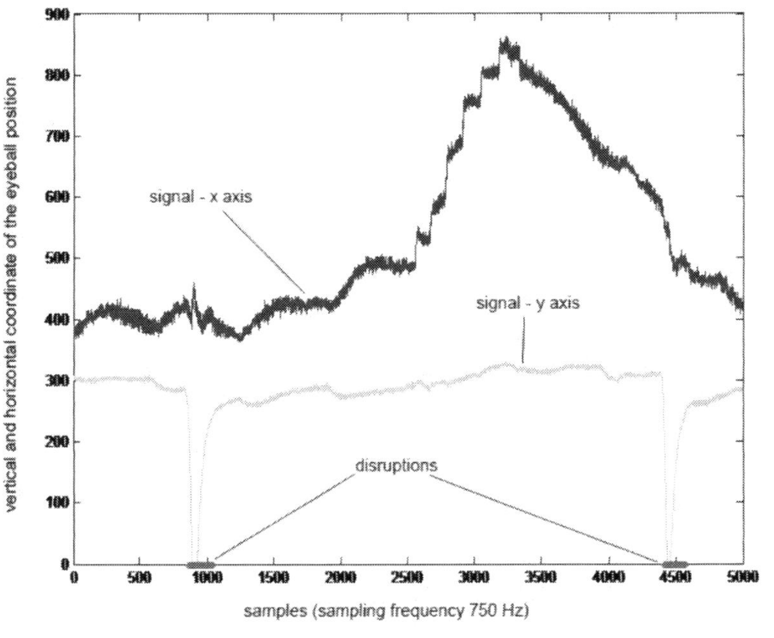

Fig. 1. Results of the filtration of the oculomotor signal by applying a reference signal

The second method of filtration used was identification of the areas containing disturbances by comparing the signal value with the average of signals in the proximity. The selection of the size of the proximity is of great importance in this case – if it is too small, its size causes the omission of disturbances, if too big – it may be the cause of classifying the correct saccade as interfering noise. Signals in each axis were filtered separately and then correlated due to the fact that the disturbance may occur both in the horizontal and vertical axis (Fig. 2).

Both methods of disturbance detection produced good results for the analysed data. In order to confirm the correctness of the selection of areas excluded from the analysis, both methods were applied and the obtained results were compared.

Many researchers in this field state that for the filtration of the oculomotor signal, median filters can be used, as they enable preserving of key signal characteristics while reducing the noise [17,18]. As part of the described test, a one-dimensional median filter was additionally used. By comparison, a low-pass Butterworth filter was used (filter order selected experimentally), obtaining satisfactory results in both cases – the signal was cleared while maintaining its characteristic features (Fig. 3).

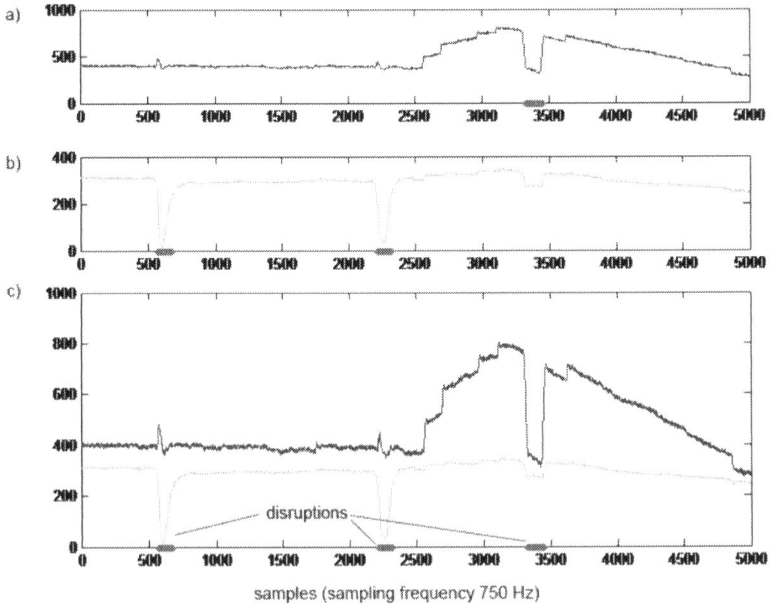

Fig. 2. The results of filtration of the oculomotor signal by examination of the average: a) horizontal component of the oculomotor signal with the detected disturbance, b) vertical component of the oculomotor signal with the detected disturbance, c) both components of the oculomotor signal with marked interference points

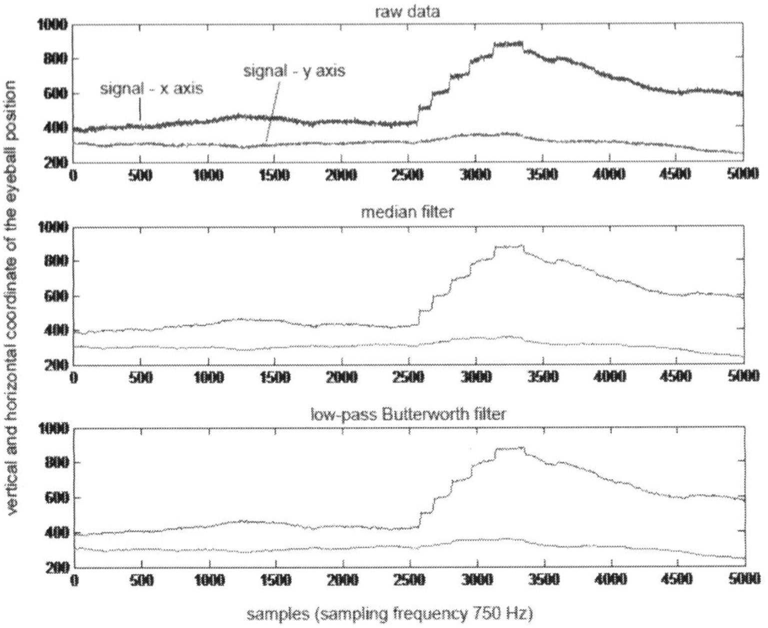

Fig. 3. The oculomotor signal after applying the median filter and the Butterworth filter

3.2 Detection of saccades and fixations

Assuming that the output of the ophthalmograph is a series of pairs (x_i, y_i), i=1..n, corresponding to the ocular position at the i-th moment of measurement, to determine saccades in the oculomotor signal, an algorithm was designed to detect a sudden change in the average value of the signal by comparing the Euclidean distance d measured for two adjacent samples up to the set threshold h. If, however, the saccadic movement includes several samples and $d>h$ for every comparison, then the algorithm would return the information about several saccades. In order to eliminate this limitation, the average value of d may be calculated for every sample (1) [16,19]. The right choice of the r-factor influences the right marking of all saccades in the signal.

$$d_i = \sqrt{(spx_i - swx_i)^2 + (spy_i - swy_i)^2} \tag{1}$$

where:

$$spx_i = \frac{1}{r}\sum_{k=1}^{r} x_{i+k}\,,\, swx_i = \frac{1}{r}\sum_{k=1}^{r} x_{i-k}$$

$$spy_i = \frac{1}{r}\sum_{k=1}^{r} y_{i+k}\,,\, swy_i = \frac{1}{r}\sum_{k=1}^{r} y_{i-k}$$

While determining the value of the r-factor, it should be taken into account that the average length of a saccade is 30-120 ms, while the average length of a fixation is 150-600 ms [15]. Therefore, with the measuring frequency of 750 Hz, the analysis was conducted with the r-factor=15, taking into account the possibility of faster saccades.

When the averaged value d is calculated (Fig. 4), p_i peaks can be easily selected (2).

$$p_i = \begin{cases} d_i, for\ d_i > d_{i-1} \wedge d_i > d_{i+1} \\ 0, for\ d_i \le d_{i-1} \vee d_i \le d_{i+1} \end{cases} \tag{2}$$

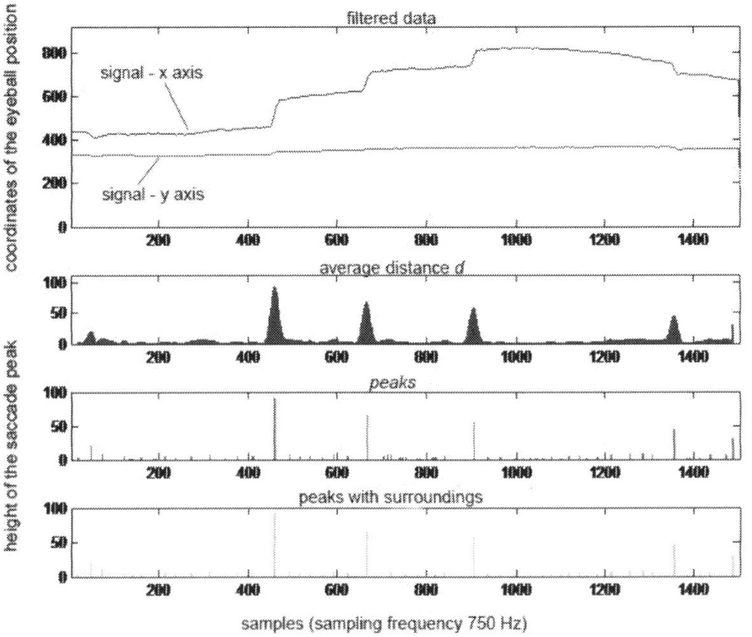

Fig. 4. Stages of peak detection in the oculomotor signal

The saccades are hence marked in the input signal (Fig. 5).

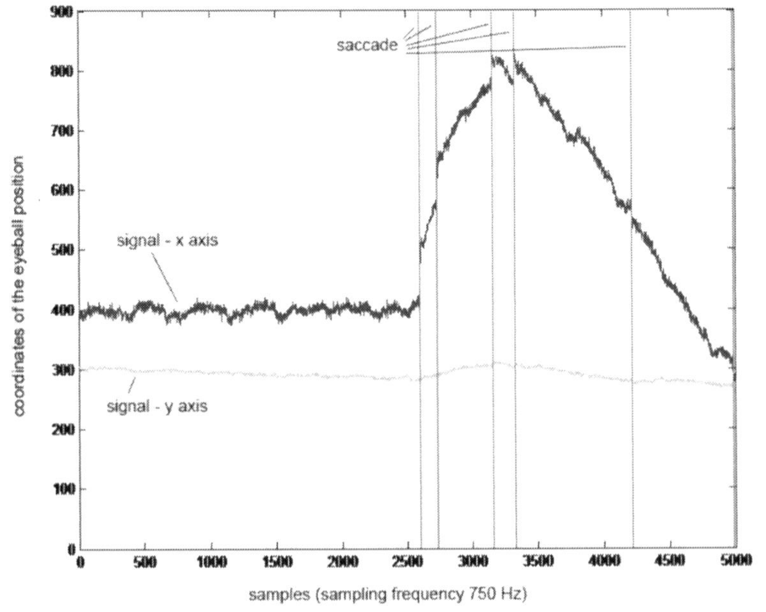

Fig. 5. The oculomotor signal with marked places of saccade occurrence

The next step of the algorithm is the estimation of points of attention focus. This can be achieved by calculating the median of all samples in the ranges determined by the vector p indices, for which values are greater than 0 [19]. This results in a sequence of pairs (f_x, f_y) that constitute the coordinates of points of attention focus (fixations). These points provide important information about places where the eye movement of the examined person has been stopped, and in combination with the knowledge of content of the presentation they can be a starting point for considerations regarding the classification and assessment of oculomotor disorders (Fig. 6).

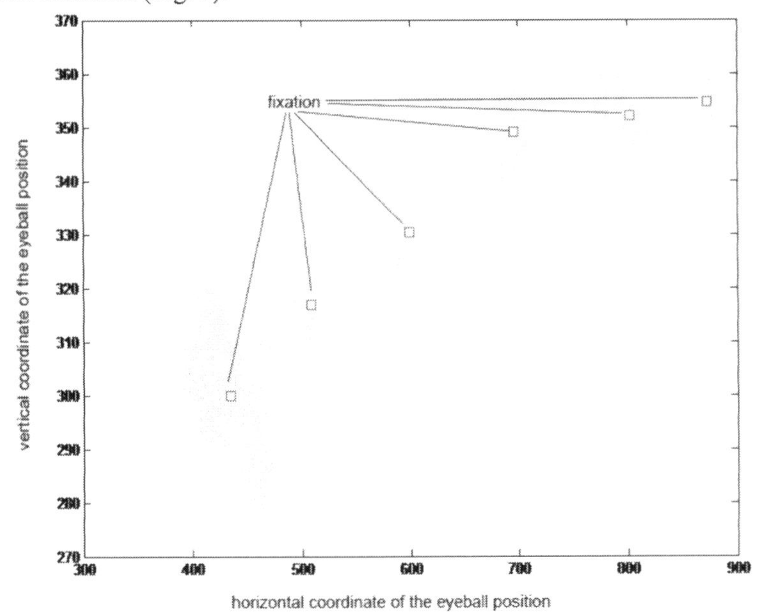

Fig. 6. Trajectory of eye movement during a visual experiment with marked points of attention focus (fixations)

3.3 Determination of characteristic oculomotor parameters

Having designated places for the occurrence of saccades and fixations, it is possible to proceed with the determination of oculomotor parameters. In order to perform further calculations, it is necessary to register coordinates of the eye in degrees of viewing angle [15], taking into account the resolution and physical measurements of the measurement monitor.

To determine the duration of the saccade, it is possible to use a method based on the information about the previous eye condition (fixation or saccade), the average absolute value of the signal for previous samples and appropriately selected threshold values [15,20], whose task is to estimate if the current values of the signal can be assigned to the current state, or whether the state should be changed (Fig. 7). The selection of appropriate threshold values in this case is particularly important, as it directly affects the accuracy and precision of the estimation. Thanks to the knowledge of the frequency of measurement and the number of samples belonging successively to states of fixation and saccades, the time of the duration of each and every saccade can be calculated as the sum of samples belonging to the state of the saccade divided by the measurement frequency.

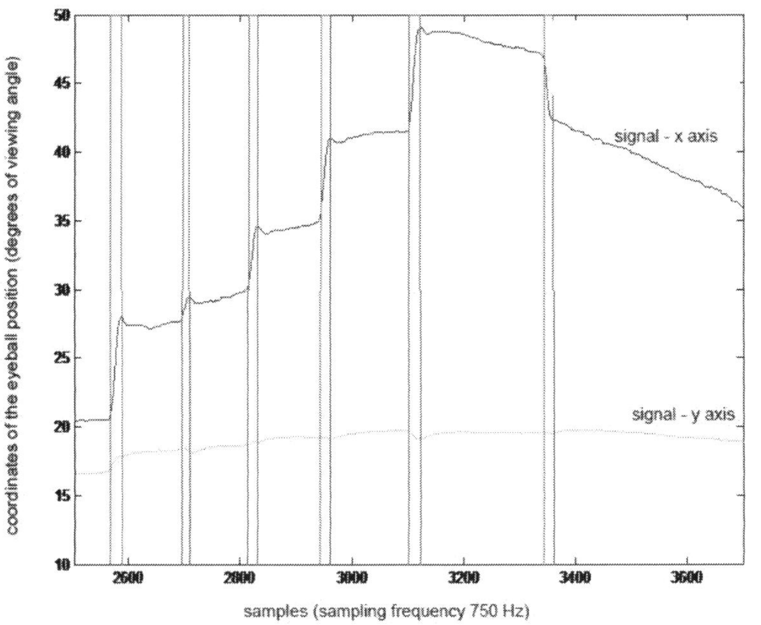

Fig. 7. The oculomotor signal with marked places of beginning and end of every saccade

Knowing the duration and coordinates of individual samples that make up the saccade, it is possible to calculate average (3) and maximum (4) speeds of saccades as the average value of Euclidean distances of individual samples multiplied by the sampling frequency.

$$v_{śr} = \frac{1}{k}\sum_k \frac{\sqrt{\left(x_k^e - x_k^b\right)^2 + \left(y_k^e - y_k^b\right)^2}}{n_k} f_p \tag{3}$$

$$v_{max} = \max_k \frac{\sqrt{\left(x_k^e - x_k^b\right)^2 + \left(y_k^e - y_k^b\right)^2}}{n_k} f_p \tag{4}$$

where:

k – number of the saccade; n – quantity of samples; x^e, y^e – coordinates of the end of the saccade; x^b, y^b – coordinates of the beginning of the saccade; f_p – sampling frequency.

3.4 Analysis using neural networks

Taking into consideration the dynamic development of artificial intelligence methods together with enormous possibilities of their application, automatic classification of the oculomotor signal has been achieved by means of neural networks. Their ability to learn, generalise knowledge and tolerate faults, give an opportunity to estimate the input data in a manner similar to the natural one [21,22]. On the basis of scientific experience [22-26], considering the specificity of the input data for the purpose of classification, two models of neural networks were selected.

The first solution was based on a unidirectional, two-layer neural network, and the network learning process was carried out in the form of supervised learning (backpropagation method) [21,22], using the unipolar sigmoid function as a function of activating neurons. The mean square error was used as the function of the target [25,27,28], setting an error threshold value at 0.001. In order to increase the speed of the neural network learning process, the method of adaptive selection of the learning speed factor was used [25]. Parameters were selected by means of a heuristic method, so that the process dynamics would be as high as possible.

The second solution was based on the Kohonen's self-organising network. Networks of this type, having only the input patterns, during the learning process (competitive learning) create the output patterns themselves, at the same time creating a structure that would be mapping dependencies in the space of input vectors in the best possible way [24,29]. In the presented model, the Manhattan metric was adopted. It determines the distance between two points as a sum of absolute values of their coordinate differences [30].

The task of neural networks was to classify unknown oculomotor signals in terms of belonging to one of three groups: healthy young people, healthy elderly people, sick people.

In each of the solutions the matrix of input vectors consisting of selected fragments of the eye movement path was determined. Both the location of the fragment and its length can be determined arbitrarily. An important aspect of the success of the learning and testing process is appropriate selection of the trajectory fragment on the basis of which classification is to take place. It can be, for example, a moment at which the following movement begins or when the subject observes a stationary object. In order to adjust the value, this matrix was subjected to a min-max standardization process.

The learning was carried out for three variants of data forming a matrix of input vectors: Network 1 – the matrix of input vectors is created by selected parts of the eyeball movement path, Network 2 – the matrix of input vectors is created by differences between the reference and the actual value in selected parts of the eyeball movement path, Network 3 – the matrix of input vectors is created by differences between consecutive measurements in selected parts of the eyeball movement path.

For the neural network architecture adopted in the task, with the input vectors defined above, the learning processes were carried out and the training of the network, with the assumed criteria, was successful.

As a result of testing the first solution for particular networks, the following results were obtained: Network 1: a sick person is correctly diagnosed in 60% of cases, in 30% as an elderly person and in 10% as a young person; a young person is diagnosed correctly in 80% of cases, in 20% as an elderly person, an elderly person is correctly diagnosed in 60% of cases, in 20% as a young person or a sick person. Network 2: a sick person is correctly diagnosed in 60% of cases, a young person in 70%, and an elderly person – in 50%.

Network 3: a sick person is correctly diagnosed in 50% of cases, a young person in 70% and an elderly person – in 30%.

While testing the second solution, for every network highly satisfactory results were obtained in the form of unambiguous classification of signals to specific groups: the closest to the neuron representing patterns are data representing young people, in the immediate vicinity of both neurons there are also data representing healthy elderly people. The results obtained from sick people stimulate the neuron located at a distinct distance from the remaining neurons on the Kohonen map.

3.5 Application supporting the analysis process

In order to improve the process of visual path analysis of people subjected to visual experiments described above, an application was prepared using Graphical User Interface, working in the MATLAB computing environment (Fig. 8).

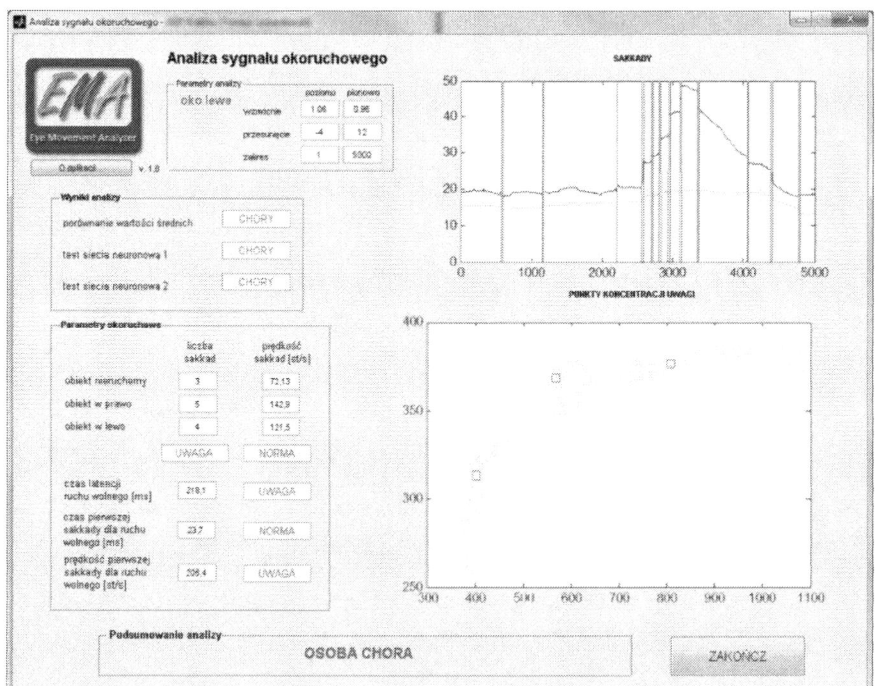

Fig. 8. The window of the application supporting the process of analysis of oculomotor data presenting the result of analysis of the selected visual path (polish translation)

The presented application is of a demonstration nature only. As far as its diagnostic use is concerned, it is necessary to consult with specialists the selection and presentation of parameters and the possibility of regulation of selected threshold values.

4 Conclusions

As a result of the measurements taken, analysis of the data obtained, and design and testing of proper processing algorithms, the following conclusions can be made:

- it is possible to effectively classify a visual path to one of the three groups defined by the study (sick, healthy young and healthy elderly) on the basis of a discrimination analysis by median differences between successive measurement points and on the basis of discrepancies between the measurement data and the standard,

- the use of neural networks in order to classify oculomotor signals into one of the three groups gives satisfactory results (about 80% of the recognition efficiency),
- correct process of filtering the measurement data has a direct impact on the results of further analyses, while the development of filtration methods that take into account the specificity of the data under consideration and knowledge of their model shape brings good results,
- selection of the right parameters enabling the automatic processing of oculomotor data is carried out experimentally and is a time-consuming process,
- combined use of the classification methods presented in the article allows obtaining reliable results.

To sum up, it should be stated that the proposed test method allows registration of a view path followed by its automatic analysis to obtain objective parameters characterising the movement of the eyeball. The motor apparatus of the eyeball, due to its high sensitivity to changes in the body, can serve as a measure of general health.

References

1. P. Augustyniak, *Determination of diagnostic parameters of time-frequency scanners with characteristics adapted adaptively - PhD dissertation* (AGH Univ.of Sci&Tech, Kraków, 1995)
2. S. Chu, N. Paul, L. Ruel, Inf. Des. J. **17**, 31–43 (2009)
3. Z. Guan, E. Cutrell, SIGCHI Conf. Hum. Fact. in Inform. Syst. 417–420 (2007)
4. Y. Yesilada, C. Jay, R. Stevens, S. Harper, 17th Int. Conf. WWW, 11–20 (2008)
5. H.S.S.L. Joseph, S.P. Liversedge, H.I. Blythe, S.J. White, S.E. Gathercole, K. Rayner, T.Q J.Exp.Psych. **61**, 708–723 (2007)
6. B.J. Juhasz, Lang.&Cogn. Proc. **23**, 1057–1088 (2008)
7. S.J. White, J.Exp.Psych.: HP&P **34**, 205–223 (2008)
8. M.H. Yen, J.L. Tsai, O.J.L. Tzeng, D.L. Hung, Mem.&Cogn., **36**, 1033–1045 (2008)
9. S. Devuyst, T. Dutoit, T. Ravet, P. Stenuit, M. Kerkhofs, E. Stanus, 13th IFMBE **23**, 146–150 (2008)
10. B. Jammes, H. Sharabty, D. Esteve, Somn.S&S **12**, 227–232 (2008)
11. N. Khasawneha, M.A.K. Jaradatb; L. Fraiwanc, M. Al–Fandib, Appl.AI Int.J. **25**, 163–179 (2011)
12. M. Klemensowicz, *System for performing visual psychophysiological experiments using the Jazz multisensor - master thesis* (Poznan Univ.of Tech, Poznan, 2003)
13. J. Winiarska, *Examination of the information stream acquired by the human eye system - master thesis (*AGH Univ. of Sci&Tech, Kraków, 2005)
14. D. Salvucci, J. Goldberg, Eye Track. Res.&App.Symp (2000)
15. A. T. Duchowski, *Eye tracking methodology* (Springer, London, 2007)
16. M. Nyström, K. Holmqvist, Beh.Res.Meth. **42**, 188–204 (2010)
17. R. Krupiński, P. Mazurek, 14th IEEE/IFAC Int. Conf.Meth&Mod.Aut&Rob MMAR (2009)
18. P. Larsson, *Automatic visual behavior analysis - master thesis* (Linköping Univ., Sweden, 2002)

19. P. Olsson, *Real–time and offline filters for eye tracking - master thesis* (KTH Royal IofT, Sweden, 2007)
20. P.M.J. Van Diepen, L. Ruelens, G. d'Ydewalle, Act.Psych. **101**, 91–103 (1999)
21. J. Herz, A. Krogh, R.G. Palmer, *Introduction to the theory of neural calculations* (WNT, Warszawa, 1995)
22. D. Witkowska, *Artificial neural networks and statistical method* (C.H. Beck, Warszawa, 2002)
23. W. Kwiatkowski, *Methods of automatic pattern recognition* (Bel Std., Warszawa, 2007)
24. M. Nałęcz, *Biocybernetics and biomedical engineering Vol. 6. Neural networks* (EXIT, Warszawa, 2000)
25. S. Osowski, *Neural networks in the algorithmic perspective* (WNT, Warszawa, 1996)
26. R. Tadeusiewicz, *Neural networks* (RM, Warszawa, 1993)
27. T. Lewandowski, Z. Gomółka, M. Pieszko, AI Met. 115–130 (2010)
28. T. Lewandowski, M. Piróg, Polish J. Env.Stud. **17**, 219–223 (2008)
29. T. Kohonen, *Self–Organizing Maps* (Springer, Heidelberg, 1997)
30. Z. Gomółka, T. Lewandowski, Tech-Comp-Edu. 51–56 (2006)

Performance comparison of parallel fastICA algorithm in the PLGrid structures

Anna Gajos-Balinska[1*], *Grzegorz M.* Wojcik[1], *Przemyslaw* Stpiczynski[2]

[1]Department of Neuroinformatics, Institute of Computer Science, Maria Curie-Sklodowska University, ul. Akademicka 9, 20-033 Lublin, Poland
[2]Institute of Mathematics, Maria Curie-Sklodowska University, Plac Marii Curie-Sklodowskiej 1, 20-031 Lublin, Poland

Abstract. During processing the EEG signal, the methods of cleaning it from artifacts play an important role. One of the most commonly used methods is ICA (independent component analysis) [1-3]. However, algorithms of this type are computationally expensive. Known implementations of ICA type algorithms rarely include the possibility of parallel computing and do not use the capabilities provided by the architecture itself. This paper presents a parallel implementation of the fastICA algorithm using the available libraries and extensions of the Intel processors (such as BLAS, MKL, Cilk Plus) and compares the execution time for two selected architectures in the PLGrid structure (Zeus and Prometheus).

1 Introduction

Electroencephalography as a non-invasive diagnostic method has been used for many years both in medicine and in experimental psychology. For this purpose, various methods of signal analysis and processing are applicable [4-5]. The recorded signal of brain activity is easily disturbed by external events, therefore an important element of working with the EEG signal is to clean it from artifacts [6].

Another important element of signal analysis is the extraction of features for specific stimuli in ERP experiments (event-related potentials). A very often used method that accomplishes both tasks is the so-called blind source separation, while independent component analysis (ICA) is one of these methods [7].

While working with various types of EEG machines, it could be noted that the EEG system manufacturer does not always provide the right tools for effcient and desired processing. It is common that one should use external software to take advantage of the aforementioned method. This prompted the authors of the research to write an application with its own implementation of ICA, integrated with the software used in the Department of Neuroinformatics at Maria Curie-Sklodowska University in Lublin (NetStation) [8–11].

However, the algorithm itself is computationally expensive (as an iterative algorithm that uses the Newton approximation method) [12]. It can take many hours to process one data

* Corresponding author: agajos@hektor.umcs.lublin.pl

recording, which is bothersome for both the researcher and the patient who is waiting for results. Therefore, the next step was to develop a method of time optimization of the selected ICA algorithm by using the capabilities of modern parallel architectures. The fastICA algorithm [13] was adopted as a model in studies. In this paper, a comparison of the time efficiency of the algorithm for two selected machines made available by PLGrid (Zeus and Prometheus) will be presented. The main purpose of this research is to develop a faster method of preprocessing EEG data.

2 Independent Component Analysis and fastICA implementation

2.1 The ICA method

The recorded EEG signal is, in fact, a mixture of many signals coming from different sources. If on the basis of these mixtures one can separate the source signals from each other, this is called blind source separation (BSS) [12, 14].

We can illustrate this problem using the equation:

$$\mathbf{S} = \mathbf{W}\mathbf{X}, \tag{1}$$

where $\mathbf{S} \in \mathbf{R}^{C\mathrm{x}M}$ is the matrix of C components for M samples, $\mathbf{W} \in \mathbf{R}^{C\mathrm{x}N}$ is the transition matrix with the weight vectors between each signal and electrode and $\mathbf{X} \in \mathbf{R}^{N\mathrm{x}M}$ is the data from N electrodes.

The problem is to find a separating matrix **W** that satisfies this equation. However, it should be noted that no more sources can be found than the number of signal mixtures (N) and that the found sources will have a similar shape, but it is not possible to find the original amplitude.

The ICA discussed, in this case, is one of the approaches to blind source separation. Unlike other BSS methods, ICA is based on higher-order statistical methods. It should be noted that the use of statistical methods results in one more disadvantage: if the primary signals have a distribution close to normal, the result is ambiguous. ICA is based on the assumption created on the central limit theorem, that the signal sources are independent components, and the mix of these signals has a normal distribution. Therefore the task of the algorithm is to separate the independent components [12].

For this purpose, the data is preprocessed, i.e. centering (the mean of each signal is zero) and whitening (the variance of each signal is equal to 1, this is done by decomposition into eigenvectors and eigenvalues of the matrix). As a result, uncorrelated signals are received, but they are not yet independent of each other.

Finally, one needs to find such weights (**W** matrix) so that the received signals have the least normal distribution. Different measures of normality (negentropy and kurtosis) are used, and weights are modified using Newton approximations using non-quadratic functions [14]. In our case, the hyperbolic tangent function was used.

As previously mentioned in the work, the fastICA algorithm was used, as a very common implementation of ICA algorithm. It is relatively stable, it is characterized by quick convergence, and the source code is available. In addition, its design allows using parallel computations. It differs from other algorithms by way of weight modification [12].

2.2 Implementation and data representation

The implementation of the fastICA algorithm presented in this paper is based on the version that can be found in the open library it++ and in MATLAB. In contrast, the implementation discussed in this work does not use the reduction of the matrix dimensions, which increases the accuracy of calculations. During subsequent modifications of weights, the tanh function (hyperbolic tangent) from the standard mathematical library is used. To prevent the so-called cache misses, the data is properly arranged and the Intel mm malloc compiler function is used.

In the parts of the code where the entire signal is used, parallel blocks are applied. With the most time-consuming parts of the algorithm, i.e. matrix multiplication or eigenvectors calculation, functions from the BLAS and MKL libraries are used.

Thanks to the Intel Cilk Plus extensions for C and C++, it is possible to use array notation and built-in reduction functions (such us searching maximum in the array) that not only make the code more transparent but most of all force the effective vectorization [15].

3 Results

All tests were performed on two architectures:

1. Zeus: Intel Xeon X5650 2.67GHz – 12 cores (+12 virtual)
2. Prometheus: Intel Xeon E5-2680 2.5GHz – 24 cores (+ 24 virtual)

Prometheus and Zeus are superfast computers providing computing servers as part of the ACK Cyfronet AGH platform. In the latest release of TOP500 list, Prometheus was classified on 77th position. It has over 53 000 computing cores. Zeus was listed on the TOP500 list twelfth in a row and for many years was the fastest supercomputer in Poland. It provides over 25 000 computing cores.

A test comparing the speed of fastICA implementation for 1 second, 10 seconds, 100 seconds and 1000 seconds of the signal recording was performed. For both architectures, the time performance was compared depending on the number of threads for which the program was run.

In Table 1 and Table 2 there is the program execution time for all data in seconds. The Figure 1 and Figure 2 show the speed-up performance of multithreaded launching of application for both architectures compared to single-threading launching. The application of the aforementioned methods (parallel blocks, vectorization, functions from BLAS and MKL libraries) has increased the speed of calculation compared to the single-threaded version. It can be seen in Figure 3 that parallel implementation is scalable and the increase in data size generates more profits. However, the physical number of threads matters. Using more threads than their physical amount (24 threads for Zeus and 48 for Prometheus) does not generate more and more profit. It can also be seen that the efficiency in Zeus decreases after exceeding the physical number of threads. At Prometheus, it is kept at the same level. This may mean that newer architectures cope better with hyperthreading.

Table 1. Zeus.

Number of threads	1 second	10 seconds	100 seconds	1000 seconds
1	7.853036	24.3698	249.89457	2654.8714
2	5.59254	15.7137	152.722401	1658.469306
4	2.653978	11.044857	97.381287	714.447443
6	2.311765	8.702663	67.243015	616.629619
8	2.379572	5.509977	49.668591	476.512014
10	2.931615	5.529254	44.437239	460.055876
12	2.132589	5.374643	46.453258	419.557943
14	3.816939	9.196031	53.868611	449.6515
16	4.867699	8.662239	56.572302	440.946023
18	4.902744	8.41807	50.672497	684.304196
20	5.509669	9.079854	76.22381	495.427938
22	5.153895	9.94856	78.739455	634.250165
24	5.3544	10.513036	64.507768	669.666002

Table 2. Prometheus.

Number of threads	1 second	10 seconds	100 seconds	1000 seconds
1	2.712171	10.101657	122.676974	1229.070627
2	2.382829	7.668297	96.769035	947.622293
4	1.941356	5.153685	61.690553	639.179694
6	1.930588	4.479713	44.180151	437.537964
8	1.876067	3.467063	38.85796	372.240371
10	1.841483	3.101005	34.147887	386.33065
12	1.388474	2.916747	30.698477	268.486074
14	1.416901	2.871293	26.730792	274.935783
16	1.304905	2.20292	27.630703	242.159316
18	1.525153	2.215691	27.36333	249.796984
20	1.459399	2.804208	24.865453	193.747517
22	1.629841	2.787488	25.010329	229.511152
24	1.853309	3.124078	24.873183	170.942183
26	2.167185	3.659332	27.361812	204.138773
28	2.935814	3.502416	26.860298	239.987754
30	2.556604	3.5886	28.249686	226.862231
32	3.357873	4.52818	28.521366	217.752913
34	3.56577	5.151289	30.850415	240.55447
36	4.140595	4.335072	34.031625	212.100187
38	3.13482	4.85156	28.672792	237.856584
40	4.259223	5.806984	29.720013	292.608695
42	4.067353	5.023907	36.669899	235.577985
44	4.78252	5.347281	36.054015	302.960874
46	4.877022	5.014137	33.573492	308.539336
48	4.414425	6.715821	41.665372	272.523367

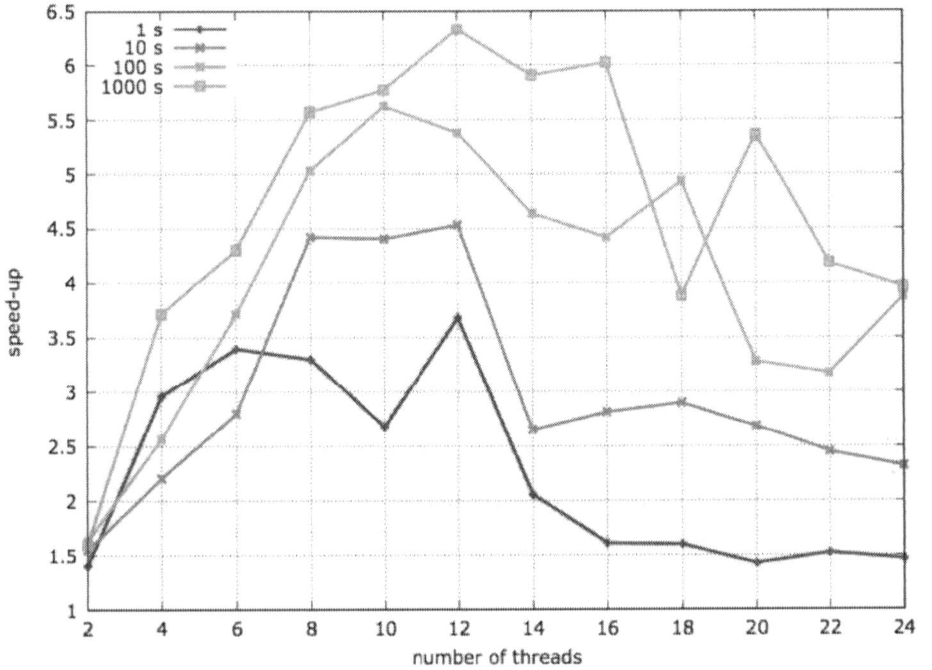

Fig. 1. Speed-up of multithreaded launching – Zeus

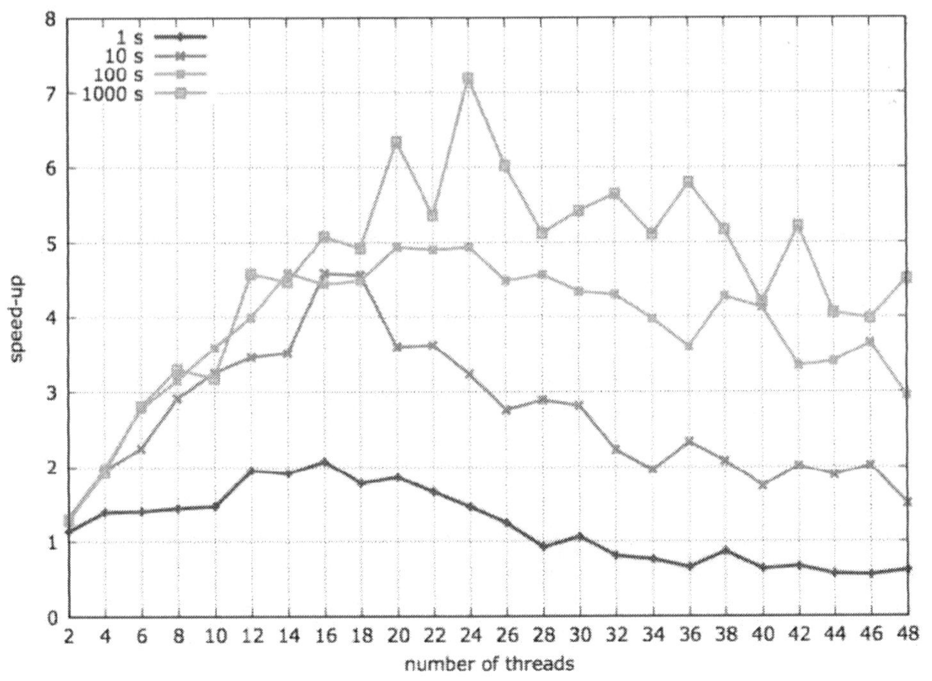

Fig. 2. Speed-up of multithreaded launching – Prometheus

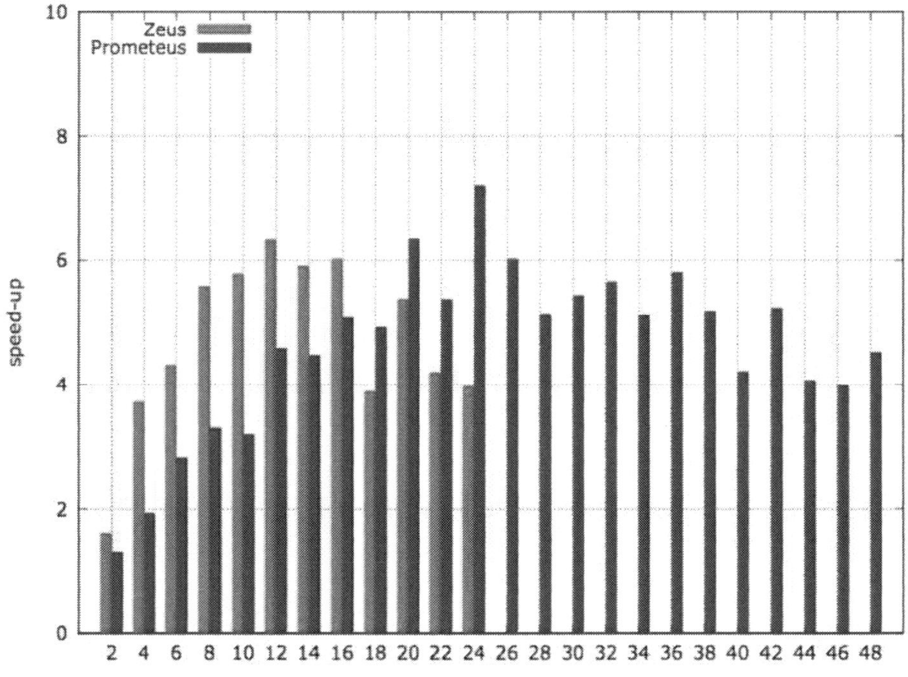

Fig. 3. Speed-up comparison for Zeus and Prometheus architecture

4 Conclusions

The obtained results showed that the execution time scales with the increase of the problem. It can also be seen that on Prometheus (a machine with a newer architecture) the optimal number of threads increases with the size of the problem, while in Zeus it is constant (12 threads).

The studies have shown that architecture and the physical number of cores have a fundamental impact on the speed of calculation in the parallel version of fastICA. The newer generation machine performs better with hyperthreading and it is cost-effective to use the capabilities of the latest generation processors and parallelism.

5 Summary

This paper presents a parallel version of the fastICA algorithm. It includes the capabilities of multicore Intel architecture and processor. The algorithm has been applied to real EEG data. It was launched on two machines (Zeus and Prometheus in the PLGrid structure).

In addition, the number of physical cores is important, because efficiency decreases (in the case of Zeus) or does not grow (in the case of Prometheus) if we run the program for the number of threads exceeding the number of physical cores.

The future plan is to integrate our solution with tools for EEG signal processing such us NetStation [8-11]. It is also worth considering the adjustment of the existing solution to the capabilities of a particular architecture to achieve even better results.

We have an experience in parallel computing when we modelled some cognitive processes occurring in the simulated cortex of mammalian brains [16–19]. From our point of view, it is interesting if it is possible to find such methodology for algorithm optimization so that the given architecture could achieve maximum performance.

This research was supported in part by PLGrid Infrastructure. Computations have been performed at ACC Cyfronet AGH.

References

1. G.D. Brown, S. Yamada, T.J Sejnowski. Trends in neur., **24**, 54 (2001)
2. A. Delorme, T. Sejnowski, S. Makeig. Neuroimage, **34**, 1443 (2007)
3. M. Ungureanu, C. Bigan, R. Strungaru, V Lazarescu. Measur. Science Review, **4**, 18 (2004)
4. R. Tadeusiewicz. *Computers in psychology and psychology in computer science.* (2010)
5. R. Tadeusiewicz. *Using neural networks for simplified discovery of some psychological phenomena* (2010)
6. C.L. Dickter, P.D. Kie□aber. *EEG Methods for the Psychological Sciences* (2014)
7. A. Albajes-Eizagirre, L. Dubreuil Vall, I. David, A. Riera, A. Soria-Frisch, S. Dunne, G. Ru□ni. *EEG/ERP Analysis: Methods and Applications* (2014)
8. A. Gajos, G.M. Wojcik. Bio-Alg. and Med-Sys., **12**, 67 (2016).
9. A. Gajos-Balinska, G.M. Wojcik, P. Stpiczynski. CGW'15 (2015)
10. A. Gajos-Balinska, G.M. Wojcik, P. Stpiczynski. CGW'17 (2017)
11. A. Gajos-Balinska, G.M. Wojcik, and P. Stpiczynski. Lect. N. in Comp. Sci. **10777**, 495 (2018)
12. A. Hyvarinen, E. Oja. Neural networks, **13**, 411 (2000)
13. G. Sahonero-Alvarez, H. Calderon. IMCIC'17 (2017)
14. A. Hyvarinen, IEEE Transactions on Neural Networks, **10**, 626 (1999)
15. R. Rahman. *Intel Xeon Phi Coprocessor Architecture and Tools: The Guide for Application Developers*. (2013)
16. M.Wazny, G.M. Wojcik. Neurocomputing, **135C**, 139 (2014)
17. G.M. Wojcik, J.A. Garcia-Lazaro. Procedia Computer Science, **1**, 845 (2010)
18. G.M. Wojcik, W.A. Kaminski. Neurocomputing, **70**, 2593 (2007)
19. G.M. Wojcik, W.A. Kaminski, P. Matejanka. In Lect. N. in Comp. Sci. Springer **4671**, 468 (2007)

ITM Web of Conferences **21**, 00027 (2018) https://doi.org/10.1051/itmconf/20182100027
CST 2018

Searching for optimal machine learning algorithm for network traffic classification in intrusion detection system

Alicja Gerka[1,*]

[1]Rzeszow University of Technology, The Faculty of Electrical and Computer Engineering, ul. Wincentego Pola 2 35-959 Rzeszów, Poland

Abstract. The main problem associated with the development of an effective network behaviour anomaly detection-based IDS model is the selection of the optimal network traffic classification method. This article presents the results of simulation research on the effectiveness of the use of machine learning algorithms in the network attacks detection. The research part of the work concerned finding the optimal method of network packets classification possible to implement in the intrusion detection system's attack detection module. During the research, the performance of three machine learning algorithms (Artificial Neural Network, Support Vector Machine and Naïve Bayes Classifier) has been compared using a dataset from the KDD Cup competition. Attention was also paid to the relationship between the values of algorithm parameters and their effectiveness. The work also contains an short analysis of the state of cybersecurity in Poland.

1 Introduction

Technological progress and increasing computerization of the society means that along with the development of technologies commonly used in computer networks and information systems, cyber attack and data breach techniques are also developed. Cybercriminals find new vulnerabilities and develop new techniques for their exploitation. According to a report published in 2017 by Panda Security, on average, about 280,000 new malware samples are produced every day [1].

Therefore, the protection of communication and information systems is becoming a growing challenge and generates ever-growing costs. According to estimates by Cybersecurity Ventures, the global IT security services and products spending will exceed $1 trillion over the next 5 years, from 2017, and the amount of losses related to the cybercriminal activities will increase from $ 3 trillion in 2015 to $ 6 trillion in 2021 [2].

In view of these facts, it is necessary to search for new, computationally efficient methods of detection of attacks in intrusion detection systems. One of the solutions to this problem is the use of unconventional methods such as machine learning algorithms.

* Corresponding author: alicja.gerka@op.pl

2 The state of cyber security in Poland

According to cybersecurity reports published by the Republic of Poland Governmental Computer Security Incident Response Team CERT.GOV.PL over the years 2014-2018, the number of reports of breach of security is constantly increasing as shown in Figure 1 [3-7].

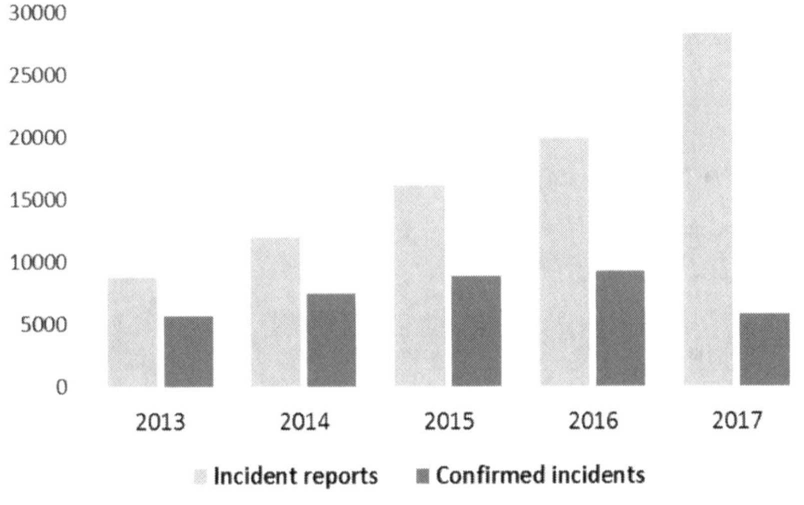

Fig. 1. The number of reports of potential security incidents and actual security incidents in 2013-2017 [3-7].

In 2017, an overall decrease in the number of cases of actual IT security breaches could be observed, including a significant decrease in the number of security incidents caused by incorrect configuration of devices. That tendency may be associated with an increase of public cyber security awareness. It is important that despite the use of newer methods of electronic systems protection and the increase of cyber threats awareness - the number of incidents caused by malware, as can be seen in Figure 2, increases each year, and in 2017 increased by over 70% in comparison to the previous year [3].

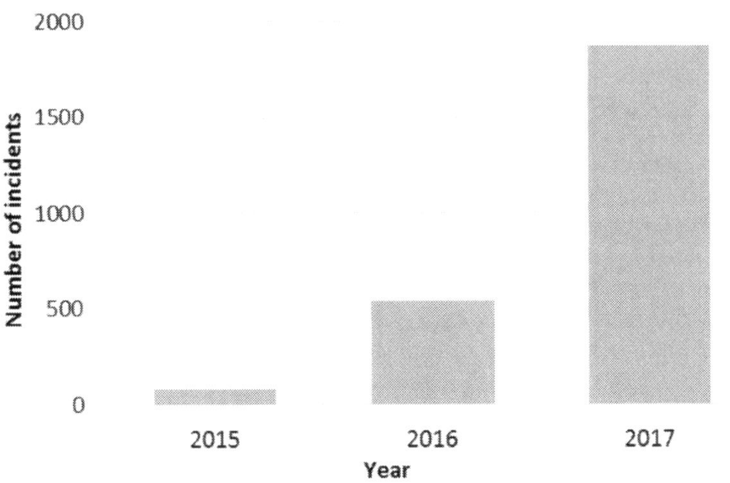

Fig. 2. Increase of number of security incidents caused by malware [3].

In turn, in 2018, cryptojacking became one of the most important global security challenges. This is a relatively new form of attack consisting of the installation of coin miner malware on the victim's device without his consent and awareness [8].

According to the McAfee Labs report, in the first quarter of 2018, the amount of coin miner malware increased by 629% (as shown in Figure 3) to more than 2.9 million known samples from nearly 400,000 samples in the fourth quarter of 2017. This suggests that cybercriminals have changed their tactics in relation to last year, when during global attacks using ransomware, they forced victims to make payments and are now more likely to choose less risky and simpler solutions that allow them to earn through the proliferation of malware. In this case, attackers can avoid brokers and the situations in which the victim refuses to transfer the ransom, as well as hide behind some of the misuse detection systems [8].

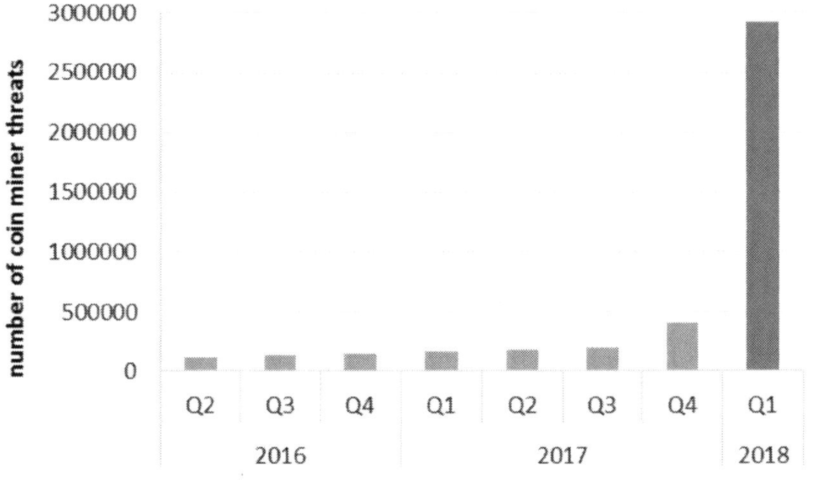

Fig. 3. Increase of samples of coin mining malware over the past two years [8].

3 Methods of Defense

The growing number of cyber threats and the development of techniques used by cybercriminals entail the necessity to develop new methods of information systems protection.

In accordance with the technical recommendations included in the report on the state of cybersecurity in Poland in 2017, in order to ensure the security of IT systems, it has to be implemented, inter alia, an intrusion detection and prevention system that will enable the detection of attacks using them network behavior anomaly detection [3].

Currently, the device protection strategy based on signatures is not sufficient to provide a basic level of security. Researchers and enterprises from the IT industry have long been aware of this, that's why they have been looking for new, more effective detection methods that will be able to detect attacks not only on the basis of system behavior, but also of the entire network. Therefore, anomaly detection methods based on the analysis of network behavior are increasingly used in Intrusion Detection Systems [9].

Systems that use network behavior anomaly detection techniques are particularly useful in situations where the analyzed network traffic is encrypted, and also enable the detection of zero-day attacks that are not detectable by signature-based detection systems. That is why enterprises and institutions are increasingly investing in such solutions [9].

Currently, machine learning methods are increasingly used in behavioral anomaly detection. Within this paper there has been examined the effectiveness of three o the most used supervised learning algorithms - ANN - artificial neural network, NBC - naive Bayes classifier and SVM - support vector machine. The chosen methods operate in different ways and they are characterized by a different computational complexity [10].

4 Research

The main goal of the research was to find the optimal method of attacks detection for IDS dedicated to small networks, which can work on host device. The research compares the effectiveness of attack detection using three different methods of network packets classification. The implementation of the goal consisted of several steps. First, three machine learning algorithms were implemented in Python language, then the algorithms' parameters were selected based on the conducted simulations, and finally, the accuracy and training time of the implemented algorithms were compared.

The work uses commonly used measures of evaluation of network traffic classifiers: length of training time, accuracy, F-measure, false negatives and false positives [11].

The study used a well-known dataset KDD Cup 1999 developed by MIT Lincoln Labs. According to a study conducted in 2015, KDD Cup 1999 is the most commonly used dataset in research related to the use of machine learning methods in intrusion detection systems. This dataset contains a standard set of audit data, which covers a wide range of intrusions simulated in the network environment. This set contains 22 types of attacks, whereby in this study, the classification model was binarized and all types of attacks were assigned to one "attack" class [12,13].

4.1 Stage I – searching for optimal values of algorithms' parameters

Before conducting a comparative analysis of the operation of the created classification models, it was necessary to select the optimal values of classifiers parameters. This is about: a regularization parameter C and the Gaussian function parameter gamma for the SVM based classifier and number of learning epochs and the batch size of neural network classifier.

During the test, the accuracy of the attack detection and the classifier learning time were chosen as quality criteria. The study consisted in teaching the classifier on a subset of 70% of the loaded dataset and then predicting class membership of samples from the rest of the set (constituting a classifier's test set).

For each configuration of parameters, 50 trials were performed, which in total gives over 5,000 simulations for both algorithms.

Classifier learning time results were rounded to two decimal places, and the results on the accuracy of the classification to five decimal places. The classifier's time of teaching was expressed in seconds, while the unit of accuracy of classification was a number between <0,1>, where 1 means 100% correctness of classification.

4.1.1 SVM

In order to maintain or increase the level of accuracy of classification, increasing the value of parameter C, the value of the gamma parameter should be simultaneously reduced, in example: increasing the fit of the classification model, is important to simultaneously increase the flexibility of the decision boundaries of the SVM model. In turn, Figure 4 presents the relationship between the classifier's training length and the value of parameter C.

For the discussed set, the classifier training time was the shortest for gamma value equal to 0.001 and C parameter value equal to 10,000.

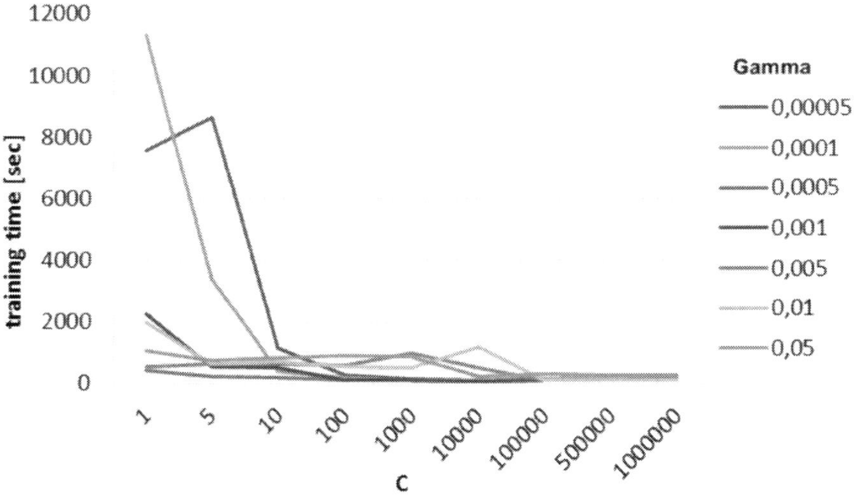

Fig. 4. The relationship between SVM classifier training time and value of C parameter for different gamma values.

As can be seen in the figure above, the change in the value of the gamma parameter has an increasingly lower influence on the length of training of the classifier along with the increase in the value of parameter C. The next figure (Figure 5) presents a graph of the relationship between the accuracy of classification and the value of parameter C.

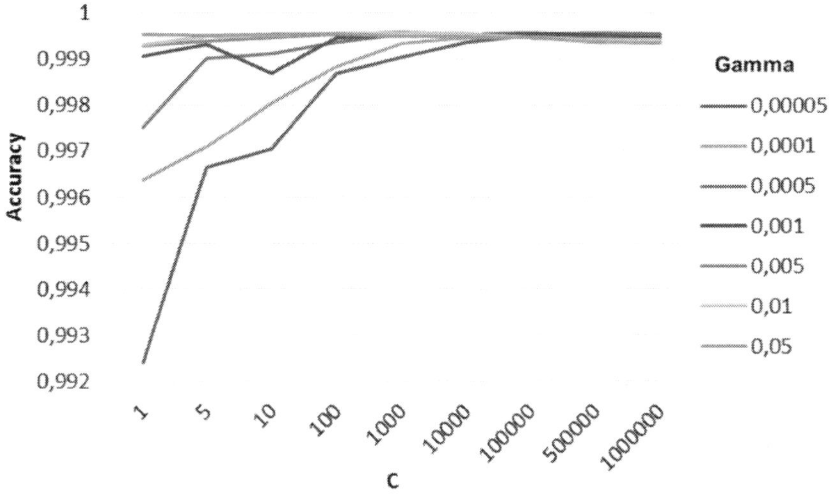

Fig. 5. The relationship between classification accuracy and C parameter value for different SVM classifier's gamma values.

At first glance, it may seem that the level of accuracy stabilizes after taking the appropriately high value of parameter C, but by zooming the graph (as shown in Figure 6), it can be observed that after reaching a certain maximum level, the accuracy of classification begins to decrease as the value of parameter C increases for each of the selected values of the gamma parameter.

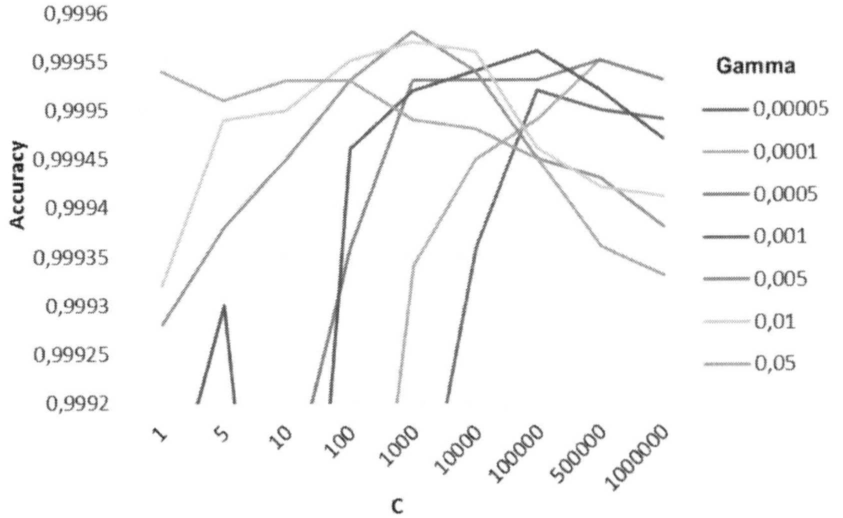

Fig. 6. The zoom of relationship between classification accuracy and C parameter value for different SVM classifier's gamma values.

Considering the dependences presented in Figures 4-6, it can be assumed that the selection of appropriate, optimal values of gamma and C coefficients consists in finding such values of these parameters for which the accuracy is as high as possible with the classifier training as short as possible.

In this case among the configurations with the shortest learning time, the highest accuracy value was obtained for the parameter gamma equal to 0.001 and C parameter equal to 100,000, therefore these parameter values were considered optimal.

4.1.2 ANN

Figure 7 presents a graph of relationship between training time and batch size of neural network for four different numbers of learning epochs. In turn, Figure 8 presents a graph of the relationship between the neural network batch size and the level of accuracy of classification.

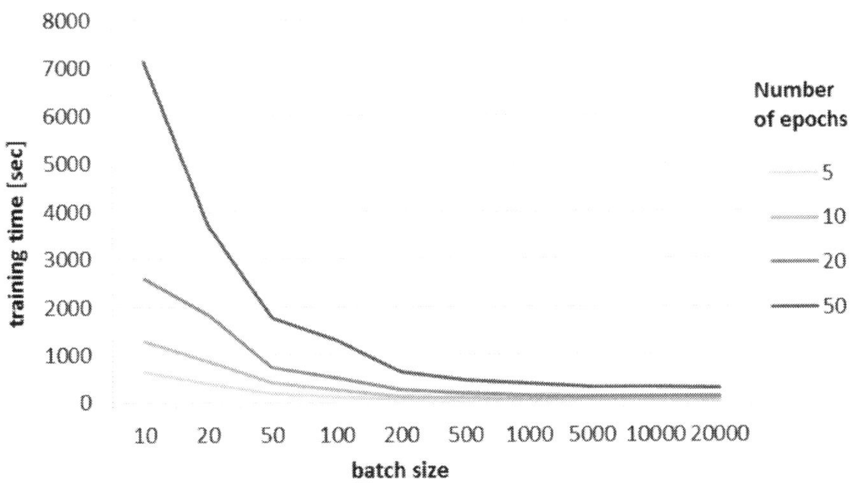

Fig. 7. The relationship between classifier's training time and neural network's batch size for different number of neural network lerning epochs.

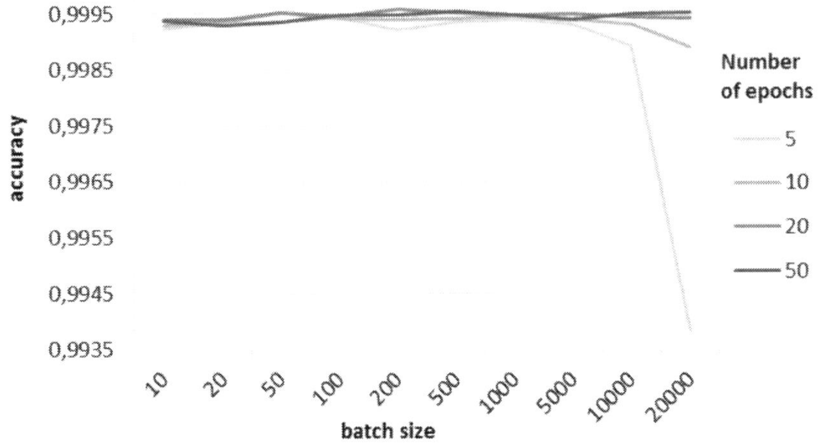

Fig. 8. The relationship between classification accuracy and artificial neural network's batch size for different numbers of learning epochs.

The worst results, both for learning time and accuracy, were obtained in the case when the network was taught only for several epochs with a large batch size. Unsatisfactory results were also obtained in the case when the network was taught for many epochs with a small batch size. In the first situation the classification model is underfitted, in turn in the second case, the classification model is overfitted.

This stage of research shows the relationship between the accuracy and the training time of the classification and the values of the parameters of both implemented algorithms.

Based on the results of the experiment, the following parameter values were adopted for further research:

a) for the neural network: number of epochs = 20 and batch size = 5,000,

b) for a classifier operating on the basis of SVM: C parameter = 100,000 and gamma parameter = 0.001.

4.2 Stage II – comparison

The second stage of the study was to compare the operation of three network attacks detecting methods. Each of them was based on a different network traffic classification algorithm and used another machine learning method.

100 trials were conducted for each algorithm. The average simulation results are shown in Table 1. The results were rounded to five decimal places.

The evaluation criteria while comparing the selected methods were: classification accuracy, classifier training time, F-measure and the error rates (false positives and false negatives).

Table 1. Comparison of three network attacks detection algorithms.

	ANN	NBC	SVM
Training time [sec]	125,72235	0,94814	95,59625
Accuracy	0,99947	0,94708	0,99956
False Positives [%]	0,0336%	6,5709%	0,0227%
False Negatives [%]	0,0318%	0,0228%	0,0319%
F-measure	0,998664	0,881651	0,998885

The obtained results confirm that the naive Bayesian classifier, due to the low computational complexity and simple structure, is characterized by a much shorter (more than hundred times) training time compared to other methods. Training the classifier based on the Bayes' theorem is very short but this is being done at the expense of the accuracy of the prediction and the increase in the number of false positive errors.

An interesting phenomenon is the fact that despite the general low accuracy of classification, this method achieved the lowest false negatives error rate in the study.

The study shows that the most accurate of the selected methods of attacks detection is the network traffic classification based on SVM. The advantage of detecting attacks using SVM over the use of ANN for this purpose has already been described in various articles, so the obtained results are in line with the results of other authors [14].

In addition, SVM-based detection method guarantees the best balance between the accuracy and sensitivity of the classification, as evidenced by the highest value of measure F. Although the SVM-based classifier achieved the worst result in terms of the false negatives rate, the result was only 0.0001% worse than in the case of classification using an artificial neural network, while the neural network being characterized by the longest training time of all discussed classification methods.

The presented results prove that even with a small computational effort, using machine learning methods, you can detect attacks in data collected as a result of network traffic sniffing. The low computational complexity of the presented classification methods (achieved by optimizing the values of parameters of the algorithms), means that they can be successfully used on the host devices.

5 Conclusion

A key element of each IDS is the threat detection subsystem. Finding an effective method of classifying network traffic is not a simple task. The analyzes show that attack detection modules based on binary classification using machine learning methods ensure effective detection of attacks with a small percentage of false alarms.

Considering the results of the conducted research, the author proposes to use the SVM algorithm as a method of classifying network packets, because this algorithm allows the most accurate detection of attacks with relatively low class time of the classifier. The solution gives optimal results in terms of the classifier's learning time as well as the accuracy of the detection. The advantages of using SVM in intrusion detection systems have also been presented in many other articles [15,16].

Due to the assumption that the system should work on the host device and be dedicated to small networks, this solution seems to be sufficient. However, for larger networks and networks with high security requirements, it is worth considering using several independently operating classifiers.

The conducted research is a contribution to the understanding of the relationship between the implementation of machine learning algorithms and the effectiveness of network attacks detection in behavioral based intrusion detection and intrusion prevention systems.

When analyzing the results of the conducted research, one should take into account the fact that the dataset used to test the implemented prediction models are not the perfect representation of network traffic. However, due to the lack of publicly available IDS learning data sets, these sets can be still good help in comparing different intrusion detection methods.

References

1. Panda Security, *PandaLabs' Annual Report 2017* (2017)
2. S. Morgan, Cybersecurity Ventures, *2017 Cybercrime Report* (2017)
3. Republic of Poland Governmental Computer Security Incident Response Team CERT.GOV.PL, *Report on the security status of the cyberspace of the Republic of Poland in 2017* (2018)
4. Republic of Poland Governmental Computer Security Incident Response Team CERT.GOV.PL, *Report on the security status of the cyberspace of the Republic of Poland in 2016* (2017)
5. Republic of Poland Governmental Computer Security Incident Response Team CERT.GOV.PL, *Report on the security status of the cyberspace of the Republic of Poland in 2015* (2016)
6. Republic of Poland Governmental Computer Security Incident Response Team CERT.GOV.PL, *Report on the security status of the cyberspace of the Republic of Poland in 2014* (2015)
7. Republic of Poland Governmental Computer Security Incident Response Team CERT.GOV.PL, *Report on the security status of the cyberspace of the Republic of Poland in 2013* (2014)
8. C. Beek, T. Dunton et al., McAfee, *McAfee Labs Threats Report June 2018* (2018)
9. A. Szmit, M. Szmit, *On the use of econometric models for forecasting network traffic.*, Scientific Notebooks Organization and Management of the Lodz University of Technology **55**, 1154, p.193-201 (2013)
10. J. Rusnacko, *Self-optimizing traffic classification framework*, Faculty of Informatics Masaryk University (2013)
11. D. M. S. Zekrifa, *Hybrid Intrusion Detection System*. Theses, School of Information Technology & Mathematical Sciences (2014)
12. N.F. Haq, M. Rafni, A.R. Onik et al., *Application of Machine Learning Approaches in Intrusion Detection System: A Survey*. International Journal of Advanced Research in Artificial Intelligence, **4**, 3, p. 9-18 (2015)
13. KDD Cup 1999, Available on: http://kdd.ics.uci.edu/databases/kddcup99/kddcup99.html
14. S. Mukkamala, G. Janoski, A.H. Sung, *Intrusion Detection Using Neural Networks and Support Vector Machines*. IEEE International Joint Conference on Neural Networks 2002, IEEE Computer Society Press, p. 1702-1707 (2002)
15. J. Hussain, S. Lalmuanawma, L. Chhakchhuak, *A two-stage hybrid classification technique for network intrusion detection system*, International Journal of Computational Intelligence Systems, **9**, 5, p. 863-875 (2016)
16. Chen, W. H., S. H. Hsu, H. P. Shen, *Application of SVM and ANN for intrusion detection*, Computers & Operations Research, **32**, 10, p. 2617–2634 (2005)

Clustering qualitative data based on the flow networks

Arkadiusz Lewicki[1,*], *Krzysztof Pancerz*[2]

[1]Department of Applied Informatics, University of Information Technology and Management, Sucharskiego str. 2, 35-225 Rzeszow, Poland
[2]Department of Computer Science, University of Rzeszow, Rejtana str. 16c, 35-225 Rzeszow, Poland

Abstract. The paper presents research results referring to the use of flow networks and ant colony algorithm in the problem of generating decision rules for the cluster analysis process. The experiments showed that proposed approach may prove particularly important, when we are dealing with data sets represented by categorical variables associated with the same number of objects for each variance. There are many cases when we have no knowledge about the allocation group of individual data received and in addition defining any metric to measure the distance between observations, does not give any satisfactory results. Meanwhile, the selection of features and the choice of the performance metric is the basic condition for the use of most known classifiers. The article presents a new approach to solve this problem and obtain satisfactory results. It is based on mapping the set of analyzed data into the flow network, calculating the maximum flow and determining the validity of nodes in the network to use the Ant Colony Algorithm to structuring information and determine significant relationships between data.

1 Introduction

In the process of obtaining important information from available data sets, we can apply supervised learning [1] or unsupervised learning [2] approaches. In the first case, we have to use the training data. We have a set of samples in which the desired output signals (labels) are known. If we use discrete class labels, it is a classification. Those discrete class labels are unordered values that determine the affiliation of specific objects to designated groups. That process allows prediction of class labels in new occurrences based on previous observations. In this case, we know the right answer before training the predictive model. However, when we have the unidentified data or datasets about an unknown structure and we have no knowledge about the group assignment, then it is much more difficult to organize the available sets of information into significant subsets. In that case, we can use a multidimensional statistical analysis to extract homogeneous subsets of the studied objects. This process is called cluster analysis or clustering.

The cluster analysis requires: selection of objects and variables, selection of a normalization formula for variable values, selection of distance measure, selection of a

* Corresponding author: alewicki@wsiz.rzeszow.pl

classification method, the determination of the number of classes, evaluation of the classification results and their interpretation. That approach allows to detect whether the received aggregations indicate some regularity, reduction of large data sets, and also to carry out further multidimensional analysis. The available solutions for the problem of cluster analysis allow the use of partitioning algorithms, hierarchical algorithms or density-based algorithms.

The partitioning algorithms concern the attempt to find the optimal division of a set of objects, in such a way that the objects within the cluster are more similar to each other than to objects from other clusters. This method requires defining a clustering criterion. This type of algorithm includes the k-means algorithm [3, 4] and the k-medoids algorithm [5, 6]. The first of these divides n objects into k-clusters, in which each object belongs to the cluster with the nearest average. The target function used in k-means algorithm is usually a squared error. The main disadvantage of this algorithm is that we have to determine the number of clusters in advance. Unfortunately, there is no universal method to find the optimal number of clusters. Another disadvantage is that the algorithm fails for categorical data. Also, if there are two very overlapping data, the k-funds will not be able to determine that there are two clusters. The k-medoids algorithm, in contrast to the k-means algorithm, assumes the median as the center of the cluster. However, the resulting clustering depends on the units of measurement.

The hierarchical algorithms [7, 8] rely on a hierarchical attempt to discover the structure of the set by decomposing the cluster. These algorithms build a cluster tree (a dendrogram) showing relationships between selected elements. The hierarchical clustering algorithms are monotonic, because they either increase or decrease. There are two types of hierarchical clustering: bottom up (agglomerative method) or top down (divisive method). In top-down clustering method we assign all objects to a single cluster and next partition this cluster to two least similar clusters. This step is repeated until each object is in a separate cluster or interrupt condition will be fulfilled. In bottom-up clustering method we assign each object to its own cluster. Then, these clusters are successively combined until all are in a single, hierarchical group. Clusters are combined according to a specific measure, e.g. the distance between their centers.

The last group of cluster analysis algorithms are the density-based algorithms, which divide sets of object using the probabilistic model for base clusters. This algorithm group includes, for example, the DBSCAN (Density-Based Spatial Clustering of Applications with Noise) algorithm [9] and OPTICS (Ordering Points To Identify Clustering Structure) algorithm [10]. These algorithms connect objects to form clusters based on regions with high data density and separated from other clusters by regions with low data content. This means that until the number of objects around the cluster is large (with a given parameter), the cluster will grow. However, the quality of the DBSCAN and OPTICS algorithm depends to parameters, such: neighborhood radius and the number of minimum points required to form a cluster. The parameter selection process is tricky.

The characteristics of cluster analysis methods show that we need to define a metric for the space representing objects [11]. The metric d (1) can be a mapping of the X x X Cartesian product to a set of non-negative numbers R.

$$d: X \, x \, X \rightarrow [0, +\infty) \tag{1}$$

The defined assumptions for all vector pairs $x^a, x^b \in X(a,b=1,2,\ldots)$ are related to rules 2, 3 and 4:

$$d(x^a, x^b) = 0 \leftrightarrow x^a \equiv x^b \tag{2}$$

$$d(x^a, x^b) = d(x^b, x^a) \tag{3}$$

$$d(x^a, x^b) \leq d(x^a, x^c) + d(x^c, x^b) \quad (4)$$

One of the most commonly used metrics in cluster analysis is the Euclidean metric. However, a generalized measure of the distance between the points of the Euclidean space is the Minkowski metric (5):

$$d(x, y) = (\sum_{i=1}^{N} |x_i - y_i|^{\alpha})^{1/\alpha} \quad (5)$$

If we use $\alpha = 2$, then we will get the Euclidean metric. For $\alpha = 2$ we will get the get a Manhattan metric. Other popular distance measures for measurable features are: the Mahalanobis measure (6) and Canberry (7).

$$d_{Ma}(x, y) = \sum_{ij}(x_i - y_i) \sum (x_i - y_i)^{-1} \quad (6)$$

$$d_{Ca}(x, y) = \sum_{i=1}^{N} \frac{|x_i - y_i|}{|x_i + y_i|} \quad (7)$$

where x, y are vectors, $\sum$ is the covariance matrix of the x and y, and N is the number of vector features.

The cluster analysis algorithms often use also Hamming metric and the Jaccard similarity coefficient. Hamming metric (8) is used for data vectors that have attributes represented by binary values. The Jaccard similarity coefficient (9) measures similarity between finite sample sets, and is defined as the size of the intersection divided by the size of the union of the sample sets.

$$d_H(x, y) = \sum_{i=1}^{N} \overline{(x_i \oplus y_i)} \quad (8)$$

where $\oplus$ means the sum of modulo two.

$$J(x, y) = \frac{|x \cap y|}{|x \cup y|} \quad (9)$$

The values assumed by the Jaccard coefficient are contained in a subset of a set of real numbers <0.1>. If the Jaccard coefficient assumes values close to zero, then the sets are different from each other. If the Jaccard coefficient assumes values close to 1, then the sets are similar to each other. This is particularly important for objects represented by vectors of binary data. For example, we can consider two objects (O_1 and O_2) represented by vectors of binary data, where there are 4 dichotomic variables (Table 1).

Table 1. The example objects represented by vectors of binary variables

Items of variables	x_1	x_2	x_3	x_4
O_1	1	0	1	0
O_2	1	1	0	1

In order to measure similarity of asymmetric categorical data, we can calculate: number of attributes where O_1 is 1 and O_2 is 0 – formula (10), number of attributes where O_1 and O_2 are 1 - formula (11), number of attributes where O_1 and O_2 are 0 - formula (12), number of attributes where O_1 is 0 and O_2 is 1 – formula (13).

$$D = \sum_i x_{O_1}(1 - x_{O_2}) \quad (10)$$

$$E = \sum_i x_{O_1} x_{O_2} \tag{11}$$

$$F = \sum_i (1 - x_{O_1})(1 - x_{O_2}) \tag{12}$$

$$G = \sum_i (1 - x_{O_1})\, x_{O_2} \tag{13}$$

where x_{O1} is value of observation O_1 in the variable i-th, and x_{O2} is value of observation O_2 in the variable i-th.
The Jaccard coefficient for similarity of asymmetric binary attributes of object O_1 and object O_2 is defined by formula (14):

$$J(O_1, O_2) = \frac{E}{E+G+D} \tag{14}$$

Which algorithm and metric are therefore the most effective for the problem of cluster analysis? The research and analysis conducted by the authors this article have shown that there is no such classifier that would work effectively (or even satisfactorily) in all possible situations. There are also such cases in the field of problem analysis of categorical data sets that without a priori knowledge, even the density-based algorithms will return erroneous results. The solution presented in the further part of the article deals with this type of problem.

2 Problem definition

The categorical data are variables representing one of the finite number of categories. Examples of such data are ID numbers, nationality, purchased product, interests, etc. We can use the Jaccard coefficient (14) as a measure of dissimilarity (or similarity) for many collections of categorical variables. This coefficient is defined as the ratio of the number of variables for which the objects differ to the total number of all variables describing the objects. However, what if this measure for many case objects returns the same values, but these objects should be assigned to different groups?

Let's consider a set of only 24 objects represented by 4 categorical variables. For example, contact lenses dataset. Each of the 24 objects of this set (Table 2) is described by the vector of the following attributes: age {young, pre-presbyopic, presbyopic}, spectacle prescription {myope, hypermetrope}, astigmatism {no, yes}, tear-prod-rate {reduced, normal}.

Table 2. The characteristics of the variable objects from the lenses dataset

Object/ attributes	Age	Spectacle prescription	Astigmatis m	Tear-prod rate
O_1	young	myope	no	reduced
O_2	young	myope	no	normal
O_3	young	myope	yes	reduced
O_4	young	hypermetrope	no	reduced
O_5	young	hypermetrope	no	normal
…	…	…	…	…
O_{10}	pre-presbyopic	myope	no	normal
…	…	…	…	…
O_{24}	presbyopic	hypermetrope	yes	normal

The set presented in table 2 is available from the UCI Machine Learning Repository. this object collection is very interesting, because contains all possible combinations of values of categorical data. Therefore, we have the same number of young (8) patients, pre-presbyopic (8) and presbyopic (8). The same number of patients having myope (12) and hypermetrope (12). The same number of patients who have astigmatism (12) and don't have astigmatism (12). The same number of patients who have a reduced tear production rate (12) and the same number who have normal (12). We could apply the algorithm of rule induction or one of the density-based algorithms. However, we need to know the number of clusters for the correct division of objects and the decision attribute. We know from the repository that each of the 24 objects can belong to one of three groups: hard contact lenses (class1), soft contact lenses (class2) or none contact lenses (class3). Then we could point out the classification rules. We could use the proposed by Cendrowska an algorithm for inducing modular rules. These rules are:

1) If astigmatism = no
   and tear-prod-rate = normal
   and spectacle-prescrip = hypermetrope then soft contact lenses
2) If astigmatism = no
   and tear-prod-rate = normal
   and age = young then soft contact lenses
3) If age = pre-presbyopic and astigmatism = no and tear-prod-rate = normal then soft
4) If astigmatism = yes
   and tear-prod-rate = normal
   and spectacle-prescrip = myope then hard contact lenses
5) If age = young
   and astigmatism = yes
   and tear-prod-rate = normal then hard contact lenses
6) If tear-prod-rate = reduced then none
7) If age = presbyopic and tear-prod-rate = normal
   and spectacle-prescrip = myope
   and astigmatism = no then none contact lenses
8) If spectacle-prescrip = hypermetrope
   and astigmatism = yes
   and age = pre-presbyopic then none contact lenses
9) If age = presbyopic
   and spectacle-prescrip = hypermetrope
   and astigmatism = yes then none contact lenses

However, let's consider the case, that we have this set of data without the knowledge about the decision attribute and without the knowledge about the correct number of classification groups. The experiments carried out by the authors showed that both the k-means algorithm and k-medoids algorithm, proved to be ineffective. The density-based algorithms also required knowledge on the expected parameters. The cluster analysis using similarity metrics for such a dataset is difficult, because even Jaccard's coefficient does not give correct results. If we consider an objects: O_3 [young, myope, yes, reduced] and object O_8 [young, hypermetrope, yes, reduced], and next O_8 [young, hypermetrope, yes, reduced] and object O_{24} [presbyopic, hypermetrope, yes, normal], we will see that they differ in one argument (first or last) and they belong to 3 different classes. However, the difference and the rule is the same in case O_7 [young, hypermetrope, yes, normal] and object O_8 [young, hypermetrope, yes, reduced], and next O_{16} [pre-presbyopic, hypermetrope, yes, reduced] and object O_{24} [presbyopic, hypermetrope, no, normal], but the objects belong to the same class. Therefore, we propose using the flow network and Ant Colony Classification Algorithm, as a possibility to solve the described above problem.

3 The proposed solution, experiments and results

We do not know the criterion of division for the objects of described above dataset. Let's assume that we also do not know how many object groups should be. If we considering this type of problem, we can map the dataset of qualitative data as a bipartite graph, where vertices will represent possible values of categorical variables. The edges between the vertices in the bipartite graph should be related to the number of occurrences of the categorical data values (represented by given nodes). The bipartite graph may represent a flow network, but at the beginning with zero flows. This is illustrated in Figure 1.

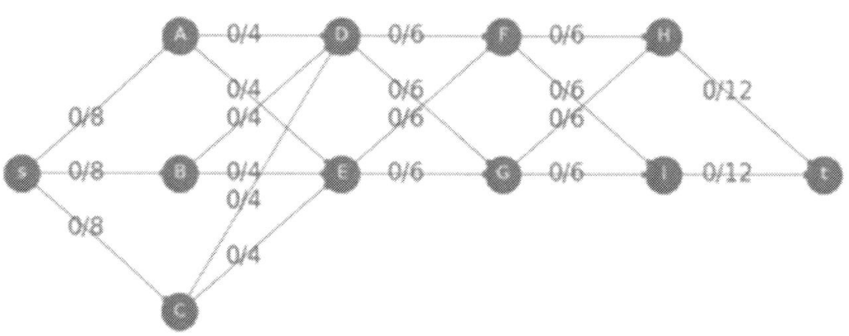

Fig. 1. The mapping of lenses dataset structure as a bipartite graph.

The nodes A, B and C represent the values of the 'age' attribute - {young, pre-presbyopic, presbyopic}, i.e. A corresponds to young, B corresponds to pre-presbyopic and C corresponds to presbyopic. The nodes D and E represent the values of the 'spectacle prescription' attribute - {myope, hypermetrope}. The nodes F and G represent the values of the 'astigmatism' attribute - {no, yes}. The nodes H and J represent the values of the ' tear-prod-rate' attribute - {reduced, normal}, s in the flow network represents the source, and t - outlet. If we next apply the Ford-Fulkerson algorithm or its modified version, we will begin the process of saturating the edges of the transition from the source to the outlet. This is shown in Figures 2 and Figure 3.

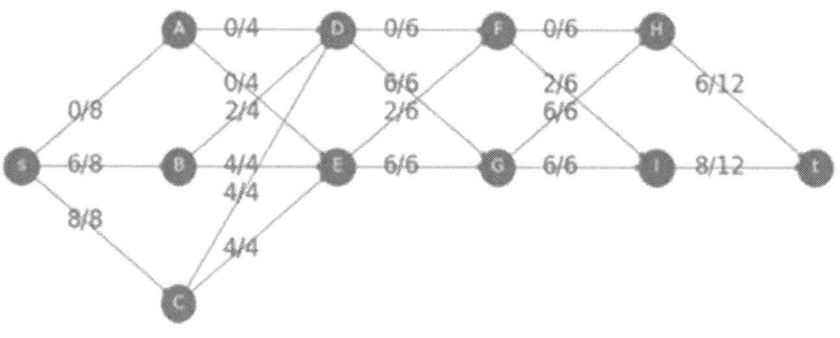

Fig. 2. The process of saturating the edges for a flow network (representing the lenses dataset).

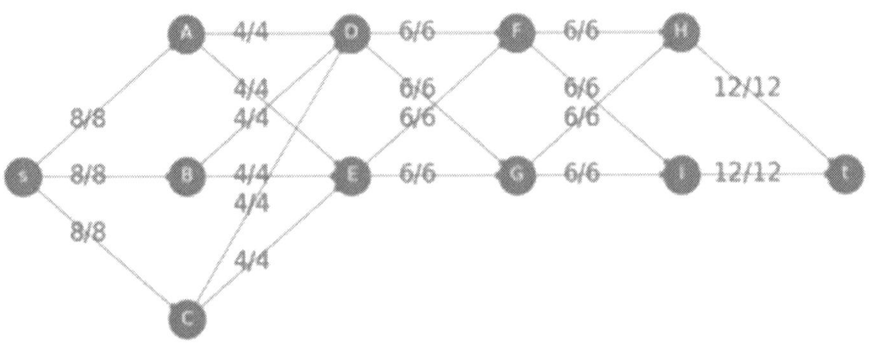

Fig. 3. The maximum flow in the flow network.

The maximum flow in our network is 24. However, the process of saturating individual transitions in the our flow network is important here. It is associated with transitions: s – C-E – G – I – t, s – D – E – G – I – t, s – D – E – G – H – t, s – B – E – G – H – t, s – B – E – F – I – t, s – B – D – G – I – t, s – B – D – F – I – t, s – A – E – F – I – t, s – A – D – F – H – t. The order in which the attributes are mapped is irrelevant because the weights of the A, B and C attributes are the same. The same situation is for the attributes D and E, F and G and H and I. The indicated paths are associated with the set of objects: {O_{24}, O_{20}, O_{19}, O_{15}, O_{14}, O_{12}, O_{10}, O_6, O_1}. This subset will be indicated as a decision collection.

Let's denote by Φ(N) the maximum flow associated with the node (where N represents A or B or C, etc.). Let's denote by maxΦ(G) the maximum flow network. It will allow us to define the validity of a particular node N as (15):

$$valid(N) = \frac{\Phi(N)}{max\Phi(G)} \tag{15}$$

where vaild(N) is the validity of the rule attribute represented by N node. We have: valid(A) =0.33, valid(B) =0.33, valid(C) =0.33, valid(D) =0.5, valid(E) =0.5, valid(F) =0.5, valid(G) =0.5, valid(H) =0.5 and valid(I) =0.5. So, we can see that our vector consists of the attributes [A | B | C, D | E, F | G, H | I], but the most important for the decision process are pairs {H | I, F | G}, {H | I, D | E} and {F| G, D | E}. We will have three different groups of objects for each pair considered in the set of objects: {O_{24}, O_{20}, O_{19}, O_{15}, O_{14}, O_{12}, O_{10}, O_6, O_1}. For the pair of attributes {H | I, F | G} it will be: class1=[G-I], class2 = [G-H] and class3=[F-H]. In addition, the saturation of the last possible transition is associated only with one pair of values [F-H].

Let's examine how the proposed approach will work for another case and other types of objects, for example for the problem of grouping quantitative data. For this purpose, let's choose the most popular dataset – iris dataset. This collection has 150 objects with 4 elements (sepal length, sepal width, petal length, petal width). The three expected classes are: Iris Setosa, Iris Versicolor and Iris Virginica. The sample dataset of Iris Setosa is shown in Table 3, Iris Versicolor - in Table 4 and Iris Virginica - in Table 5. However, let's assume also for this set, that we do not know how to group objects and what is the expected number of classes. All attributes of the iris dataset have real values. Therefore, they should be rounded to integers, according to the laws of mathematics. It will be a set of vertices of the bipartite graph. This is illustrated in Figure 4.

Table 3. The sample dataset of Iris Setosa

Sepal length	Sepal width	Petal length	Petal width
5.0	3.5	1.6	0.5
5.1	3.5	1.5	0.5
5.4	3.9	1.7	0.4
5.7	4.4	1.3	0.4

Table 3. The sample dataset of Iris Versicolor

Sepal length	Sepal width	Petal length	Petal width
7.0	3.2	4.7	1.4
6.4	3.2	4.5	1.5
5.5	2.3	4.9	1.5
6.5	2.8	4.0	1.3

Table 3. The sample dataset of Iris Virginica

Sepal length	Sepal width	Petal length	Petal width
6.3	3.3	6.0	2.5
5.8	2,7	5.1	2.9
7.1	3.0	5.9	2.1
6.3	2.9	5.6	1.8

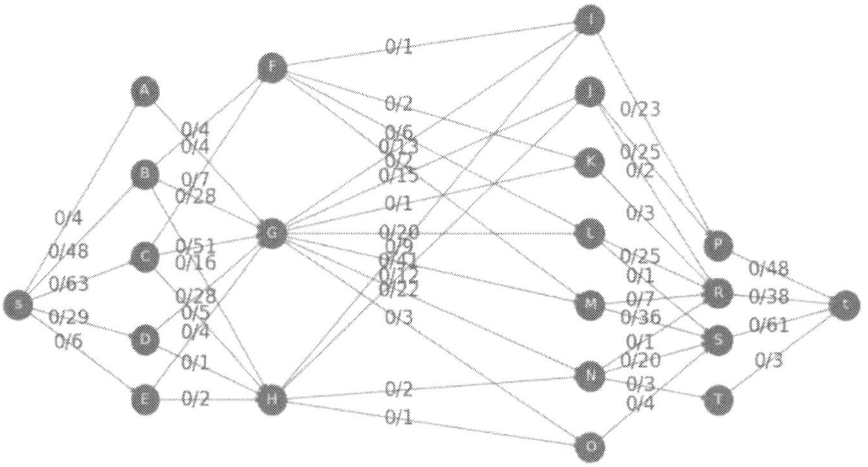

Fig. 4. The labelled iris dataset for flow network.

For the examined set of objects (where A represents 4, B–5, C6, D–7, E–8, F-1, G-1, H-4, I-1, J-2, K-3, L-4, M5, N-6, O-7, P-0, R-1, S-2 and T-3), we have: valid(T)=0.02, valid(S)=0.406, valid(R)=0.25, valid(P)=0.32, etc. As we can see, the value of valid(T) is very small and differs significantly from other output nodes. Besides, valid(P) + valid(R) + valid(S)= 0.976. Therefore, we will consider a maximum of only three classes. The edge saturation process in this flow network returned a set of decision, in the form of nodes with the highest decision-making importance. These pairs are: {I, P}, {J, P}, {N, S}, {M, S}, {L, R}. Earlier attributes (A, B, C, D, etc.) are less important due to the significant weight P, R, S, I, M, N nodes. We have indicated decision rules and the knowledge about the number of classes. Then we can use any classification algorithm that uses the Euclidean distance (Figure 5). The carried out experiments showed that the proposed method returns the result which is 84.6% of the expected accuracy.

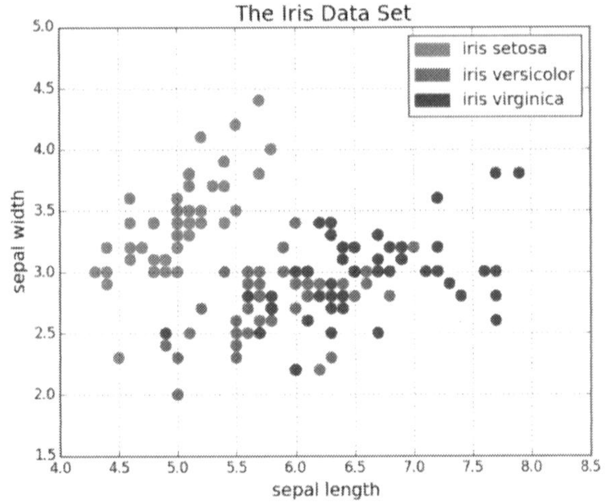

Fig. 5. The classified iris dataset objects

We have checked the proposed method of returning the decision-making collection also on the following datasets: car evaluation dataset, nursery dataset and dermatology dataset. We have achieved a result confirming the correctness of selecting the number of groups and a set of decision attributes, for each of these datasets.

Thanks to the construction of a flow network for categorical data sets such as the lenses dataset, car evaluation dataset, nursery dataset and dermatology dataset, we have received data on the number of classes. Moreover, we have received the data set, from which a specific number of reference groups should be created (according to the validity of attributes). We next used the Ant Colony algorithm as a classifier. The ant based clustering algorithm used in our experiments is mainly based on the versions proposed by Lumer and Faieta [12]. The difference is the calculation of similarity to the reference objects. It is calculated based on the formula (16):

$$d(x, y) = \frac{k-w}{k} \tag{16}$$

where k is the total number of variables but not related to the decision attribute pairs, and w is the number of variables whose value is the same for both objects (for attributes other than decision pairs),

The proposed approach allowed to obtain for the lenses dataset an accuracy of 94.7%, 87.3% - for car evaluation dataset, 87.9 – for nursery dataset and 95.2% - for dermatology dataset. These results are fully acceptable.

3 Conclusions

In the paper, we have examined the problem of clustering data categorical, for which there was no a priori knowledge about the expected number of groups. The decisive attribute was also unknown. The proposed use of flow networks and method is an option to solve this problem. The carried out experiments allowed to achieve satisfactory results. However, proposed approach requires further research for other data sets.

References

1. T. G. Dietterich, Approximate Statistical Tests for Comparing Supervised Classification Learning Algorithms. Neural Computation, (1998).
2. N. Grira, M. Crucianu, N. Boujemaa, Unsupervised and semi-supervised clustering: a brief survey, A review of machine learning techniques for processing multimedia content, (2004).
3. A. K. Jain, Data clustering: 50 years beyond K-means, Pattern Recognition Letters, (2010).
4. P. S. Bradley, K. P. Bennett, A. Demiriz, Constrained K-Means Clustering, Machine Learning, (2000).
5. S. K. Popad, Review and Comparative Study of Clustering Techniques, International Journal of Computer Science and Information Technologies, (2014).
6. T. Velmurugan and T. Santhanam, Computational Complexity between K-Means and K-Medoids Clustering Algorithms for Normal and Uniform Distributions of Data Points, Journal of Computer Science (2010).
7. Y. Zhao, G. Karypis, U. Fayyad, Hierarchical Clustering Algorithms for Document Datasets, Data Mining and Knowledge Discovery, (2005).
8. R. Lior, M. Oded, Clustering methods, Data mining and knowledge discovery handbook. Springer US, (2005).
9. R. Campello, D. Moulavi, A. Zimek, J. Sander, Hierarchical Density Estimates for Data Clustering, Visualization, and Outlier Detection. ACM Transactions on Knowledge Discovery from Data, (2015).
10. M. Ankerst, M. M. Breunig, H. P. Kriegel, J. Sander, OPTICS: Ordering Points To Identify the Clustering Structure. ACM SIGMOD international conference on Management of data. ACM Press, (1999).
11. P. M. B. Vitanyi, Information Distance in Multiples, IEEE Transactions on Information Theory, (2011).
12. E. Lumer, B. Faieta, Diversity and adaptation in populations of clustering ants, Proceedings of the Third International Conference on Simulation of Adaptive Behaviour: From Animals to Animats, MIT Press, Cambridge, (1994).

AUTHOR INDEX

EDP Sciences – Web of Conferences
17, Avenue du Hoggar
Parc d'Activité de Courtabouf
BP 112
F-91944 Les Ulis Cedex A
France

ISBN 978-1-5108-7314-8

CURRAN ASSOCIATES INC.
proceedings.com

Connecting The Dots/Intelligent Trackers 2017 (CTD/WIT 2017)

EPJ Web of Conferences Volume 150 (2017)

Orsay, France
6 - 9 March 2017

edp sciences